Praise for *Thomas Mann in English*

'Horton (Saarland Univ., Germany) p[...]
English translations of Thomas Mann [...] [...]
unearthed much little-known information about the remarkable triangle of Mann, Lowe-Porter, and Knopf [...] Summing Up: Highly Recommended. All students, researchers/faculty, general audiences.'
—*Choice*

'David Horton's *Thomas Mann in English* is a sophisticated and well-researched attempt to pierce the film of ignorance and commonplaces surrounding the field of literary translation, in the context of a specific author whose works became classics thanks largely to the popularity of their translations into English. The most admirable aspect of Horton's work is forensic: with recourse to the correspondence of Thomas Mann, his translator Helen Lowe-Porter, and his publisher Alfred Knopf, he shows the specific factors that went into such decisions as cutting or modifying large blocks of text, changing titles, presenting potentially controversial aspects of the author's work, or discouraging interference from competing translators. [...] Taken together, Horton's book provides an excellent introduction for the uninitiated to the field of practical translation studies [...] For translators, Horton points out many potential minefields, and illustrates a number of approaches translators have taken to sidestepping them; and students of Thomas Mann will enjoy the discussion of Mann's years in America, and his partnership with his American publisher in a very deliberate and ultimately successful quest to become one of the signal voices of his time.'
—*Asymptote*, Adrian West

'Horton's clearly written, well-researched study is an important contribution both to the fields of literary translation studies and Thomas Mann scholarship. Especially those interested in the intersection of linguistic and literary analysis and in the psychology of literary reception will find this in-depth study of Mann's English translations thought-provoking. The volume is well-edited with an extensive index and scholarly bibliography and will attract experienced scholars and those new to translation studies equally.'
—*Monatshefte*, Esther K. Bauer

'Horton is a great scholarly stylist, and his erudite and deeply theoretically grounded book is a pleasure to read. It is also enormously informative, adding to our knowledge of Mann's manifestations in English as well as to our acquaintance with the latest thinking within the field of contemporary translation studies.'
—*Pacific Coast Philology*, Friederike von Schwerin-High

'Horton's study shows the merits of descriptive translation studies. The sustained close readings make it a valuable resource for anyone interested in the specific stylistic qualities of Mann's work. […] Deliver[s] some superb close readings. It is to be hoped that these close readings will assist readers in articulating their own responses to Mann's work.'
—*Orbis Litterarum*, Ernest Schonfield

'This volume will not only be of considerable interest to anyone involved with Mann and his reception, but also to all those engaged in the translation of German literature.'
—*The Year's Work in Modern Language Studies*, Michael White

'Thomas Mann is regarded as the most erudite author of German literature in the first part of the twentieth century as well as the most eloquent explicator of its cultural traditions and political trials and tribulations. His relatively early rise to international recognition became only possible through the timely translations and consecutive re-translations of his work into English. David Horton's study is the first comprehensive account and assessment of this complex history of translation and subsequent transculturation of Thomas Mann's work into the English language. By interrogating a variety of theoretical models, Horton provides pertinent frames and focal perspectives to illuminate the multifaceted aspects of this elaborate process.'
—Frederick Lubich, Professor of German, Old Dominion University, USA

'Mann's worldwide reputation as one of the preeminent figures in twentieth-century literature rests on the dissemination of his works through the medium of translation. Horton's subject is thus an important one. He approaches it with great expertise in the fields of translation studies and cross-linguistic and intercultural transfer. His analysis is grounded not only theoretically, but also in a thorough knowledge of Mann's works. Anyone interested in Mann and the literary and linguistic aspects of the transformation a text undergoes in the process of translation will profit from this meticulously argued study.'
—Jens Rieckmann, Emeritus Professor of German, University of California, Irvine, USA

NEW DIRECTIONS IN GERMAN STUDIES
Vol. 8

Series Editor:
Imke Meyer

Editorial Board:
Katherine Arens, Roswitha Burwick, Richard Eldridge,
Erika Fischer-Lichte, Catriona MacLeod, Stephan Schindler,
Heidi Schlipphacke, Ulrich Schönherr, James A. Schultz,
Silke-Maria Weineck, David Wellbery, Sabine Wilke,
John Zilcosky.

New Directions in German Studies

Volumes in the series:

Vol. 1. *Improvisation as Art: Conceptual Challenges, Historical Perspectives*
by Edgar Landgraf

Vol. 2. *The German Pícaro and Modernity: Between Underdog and Shape-Shifter*
by Bernhard Malkmus

Vol. 3. *Citation and Precedent: Conjunctions and Disjunctions of German Law and Literature*
by Thomas O. Beebee

Vol. 4. *Beyond Discontent: 'Sublimation' from Goethe to Lacan*
by Eckart Goebel

Vol. 5. *From Kafka to Sebald: Modernism and Narrative Form*
edited by Sabine Wilke

Vol. 6. *Image in Outline: Reading Lou Andreas-Salomé*
by Gisela Brinker-Gabler

Vol. 7. *Out of Place: German Realism, Displacement, and Modernity*
by John B. Lyon

Vol. 8. *Thomas Mann in English: A Study in Literary Translation*
by David Horton

Vol. 9. *The Tragedy of Fatherhood: King Laius and the Politics of Paternity in the West*
by Silke-Maria Weineck

Vol. 10. *The Poet as Phenomenologist: Rilke and the New Poems*
by Luke Fischer

Vol. 11. *The Laughter of the Thracian Woman: A Protohistory of Theory*
by Hans Blumenberg, translated by Spencer Hawkins

Vol. 12. *Roma Voices in the German-Speaking World*
by Lorely French

Vol. 13. *Vienna's Dreams of Europe: Culture and Identity beyond the Nation-State*
by Katherine Arens

Vol. 14. *Thomas Mann and Shakespeare: Something Rich and Strange*
edited by Tobias Döring and Ewan Fernie

Vol. 15. *Goethe's Families of the Heart*
by Susan Gustafson

Thomas Mann in English

A Study in Literary Translation

David Horton

Bloomsbury Academic
An imprint of Bloomsbury Publishing Inc

B L O O M S B U R Y
NEW YORK • LONDON • OXFORD • NEW DELHI • SYDNEY

Bloomsbury Academic
An imprint of Bloomsbury Publishing Inc

1385 Broadway	50 Bedford Square
New York	London
NY 10018	WC1B 3DP
USA	UK

www.bloomsbury.com

BLOOMSBURY and the Diana logo are trademarks of Bloomsbury Publishing Plc

First published 2013
Paperback edition published 2016

© David Horton, 2013, 2016

All rights reserved. No part of this publication may be reproduced or transmitted in any form or by any means, electronic or mechanical, including photocopying, recording, or any information storage or retrieval system, without prior permission in writing from the publishers.

No responsibility for loss caused to any individual or organization acting on or refraining from action as a result of the material in this publication can be accepted by Bloomsbury or the author.

Library of Congress Cataloging-in-Publication Data
A catalog record for this book is available from the Library of Congress.

ISBN: HB: 978-1-4411-6798-9
       PB: 978-1-5013-1870-2
       ePDF: 978-1-4411-6680-7
       ePub: 978-1-4411-8277-7

Series: New Directions in German Studies

Typeset by Fakenham Prepress Solutions, Fakenham, Norfolk NR21 8NN
Printed and bound in the United States of America

For Oliver

Contents

	Acknowledgements	xi
1	Introduction: Thomas Mann in English	1
2	Translation and retranslation: The history of Thomas Mann's works in English	24
3	Helen Tracy Lowe-Porter, Thomas Mann and the practice of translation	52
4	An exercise in translation comparison: *Der Zauberberg*	83
5	Transferring the paratextual: The translation of Thomas Mann's titles	122
6	The translation of discourse forms: Speech and thought presentation in *Buddenbrooks*	147
7	Translating modes of address as an index of interpersonal dynamics	176
8	Syntactic form and literary meaning in translation	199
9	Conclusion	220
	Bibliography	224
	Index	239

Acknowledgements

I would like to thank all those who have generously found time to provide support during my work on this book. Among them, I am especially grateful to Jörn Albrecht, Jean Boase-Beier, Osman Durrani, Jeremy Munday and Ritchie Robertson, all of whom commented on parts of the study at various stages of its genesis, and to John E. Woods, who patiently answered questions concerning his (re)translations of Thomas Mann's novels.

I am further indebted to staff at the Beinecke Rare Book and Manuscript Library, Yale University, who arranged access to unpublished documents relating to the genesis of the Lowe-Porter translations of Mann's works; to Marc Kupietz at the Institut für deutsche Sprache, Mannheim, who provided me with statistical data from the electronic Thomas-Mann-Korpus held at the institute; and to Sarah Materna, Saarland University, who painstakingly carried out a large number of analyses on the texts which form the basis of the present study.

Finally, I would like to thank the editors at Edinburgh University Press for permission to reprint in Chapter 8 of the present study parts of my article 'Linguistic structure, stylistic value and translation strategy: Introducing Thomas Mann's Aschenbach in English', first published in the journal *Translation and Literature* 19 (2010), 42–71.

Universität des Saarlandes, Saarbrücken
September 2012

1 Introduction: Thomas Mann in English

Introductory remarks

Thomas Mann's elevation to the highest ranks of the international literary canon was the direct result of the dissemination of his works through the medium of translation. In the German-speaking world, Mann's reputation was established early in his career by the resounding success of his first novel, *Buddenbrooks* (published in 1901). Over the following two decades, he produced no major novels. Instead, he devoted his literary energies mainly to short prose fiction, much of it highly regarded in Germany but at that stage virtually unknown elsewhere, and he spent the years 1915–18 formulating his monumental political treatise, *Betrachtungen eines Unpolitischen* (not translated into English until 1983). His only novel of that period, *Königliche Hoheit* (1909), met with a modest reception in the German-speaking world, where it was widely regarded as a somewhat trivial distraction after the weightier concerns and broader sweep of his debut work. It was also the first of his novels to appear in an English translation (*Royal Highness* in 1916, by A. Cecil Curtis), which was virtually ignored (Wagener 2001: 927).

Mann had to wait until 1924 for his next large-scale success. The publication of *Der Zauberberg* in that year cemented his reputation as a novelist in Germany, and it was Helen Tracy Lowe-Porter's English translation of that work (1927) that brought him international fame, achieving something her translation of *Buddenbrooks* in 1924 had failed to do. The reception of *The Magic Mountain* was 'grudging' in England, as Lowe-Porter herself commented, but the novel was highly successful in America (Lowe-Porter 1966: 185; Wagener 2001: 929–30). Mann himself was delighted at the reception of *'des in Amerika außerordentlich angesehenen und bewunderten Magic Mountain'* (diary entry of 27 June 1934; see also *GW* 11: 610). The international success of *Der Zauberberg* secured the attention of the Nobel Prize committee, which bestowed the award upon Mann in 1929 (the citation referred explicitly to *Buddenbrooks*). As Mandel writes in his essay on Lowe-Porter: 'The rest is literary history' (Mandel 1982: 31).

It is hardly surprising, given Mann's status as an exile from 1933 onwards, that he took a great interest in the translation of his works. This interest is well documented in scores of letters and diary entries relating to versions in a variety of languages. It is, however, the English renditions that feature most centrally in the extensive records: Mann spent the years 1938–52 in the United States, and enjoyed a particularly long and fruitful partnership with his New York publisher Alfred A. Knopf and his 'authorized' American-English translator Helen Lowe-Porter. Throughout his lifetime, Mann's intense interest in the English versions of his work was driven by his desire to establish and cultivate an international literary reputation, something that could only be achieved with the help of high-quality translations. He devoted much energy to this endeavour, intervening frequently in the translation process and systematically nurturing his public image (Adolphs 1990). At one juncture, he became directly involved in the choice of an 'official' English translator. Once that issue had been resolved, he provided extensive assistance and detailed comment over a period of some twenty-seven years. Although his response to the work of his regular English translator was always ambivalent and at times downright contradictory, it was her efforts – as he was very well aware – that gained him the ultimate accolade of 'the greatest living man of letters' (Vaget 2001a: 70). The hundreds of documents from Mann's years of residence in the United States reveal just how hard he worked to ensure that his literary reputation could stand alongside his representative political role as the anti-fascist conscience of Germany. In this latter context, too, Lowe-Porter was instrumental, translating the vast majority of his dozens of essays and speeches on political and cultural issues.

At the same time, Mann's concern with the English versions of his texts was motivated by material considerations. He had been financially independent from a relatively early age thanks to payments made from the estate of his father, who died in 1891, and he had received a generous allowance from his wealthy father-in-law following his marriage to Katia Pringsheim in 1905. However, his financial situation deteriorated significantly during the inflation of the early 1920s. In a letter to his German publisher Samuel Fischer on 1 September 1922, he commented that foreign income was indispensable to him during the period of high inflation (*Reg* 1: 341). Long before he had any inkling that he would one day settle in the United States, i.e. in the years 1922–5, he earned additional income by writing a series of cultural essays for the American magazine *The Dial*. Later, the fact that his German assets were seized – and his works banned and burned – by the National Socialists meant that foreign-language sales constituted the major part of his income. In fact, his financial success during his years in American exile was considerable. While none of his works sold more than 10,000 copies in Britain, sales in the US were very high. Five of his books were selected by the Book-of-the-Month Club, guaranteeing significant sales: 200,000 copies of *Doctor Faustus* were printed for the launch alone, and by 1949 223,000 copies had been sold, compared with just 15,000 copies of the German original. The selection of *Joseph the Provider* in 1944 brought him 85,000 dollars in licence fees, and in 1951 he expected to earn at least 50,000 dollars from *The Holy Sinner*, a sum which was equivalent to the estimated value of the comfortable home he had had built in California in 1941. Between 1929 and 1949, thirty American first editions of his works, and (including British editions) over one hundred impressions of the English translations of his works appeared (Bürgin 1959; Waldmüller 1980; Potempa 1997). Throughout his lifetime, Mann was well aware of his dependence on the English versions of his works. In 1940, by which time his material position was relatively comfortable thanks to the income from his various sinecures, frequent speeches and not least his books, he commented: *'diese englischen Ausgaben sind ja mein ein und alles'* (letter to Lowe-Porter of 20 June 1940, *DüD* 2: 599).

As the many obituaries published in the international press following Mann's death in 1955 clearly show, his campaign to achieve global fame and fortune – primarily through the medium of his American publisher and translator – was a great success. After 1955, by which time Mann was a revered classic, the Lowe-Porter versions of his texts were regularly reprinted, appearing in countless editions and licensed reprints. It was in these versions that they entered the canon of world literature, becoming an indispensable part of publishers' catalogues, featuring widely in comparative literature courses, and inspiring musical compositions and film versions. Due to copyright restrictions, Lowe-Porter's texts were the only available English versions until the 1970s. The first new English versions following the expiry of copyright protection were those of selected short prose texts by David Luke in 1970, to which a version of *Der Tod in Venedig* was added in 1988. These have been followed by frequent retranslations ever since. The novels, by contrast, have been retranslated only once: in the 1990s, Knopf publishers commissioned John E. Woods to produce new versions. These appeared between 1993 and 2005.

Given the great importance of the English translations of Mann's work, it is surprising that they have never been subjected to thorough examination within the terms of modern translation studies. With one or two exceptions, virtually all the work undertaken to date has focused on the texts from a purely evaluative point of view, and has been primarily concerned to identify errors and omissions. It has, for the most part, been divorced from modern discourse on the parameters of literary translation, operating with an inexplicit and problematic notion of equivalence. There has been little attempt to draw on insights from literary and linguistic analysis in order to arrive at a more balanced view of translator strategies and translational phenomena. The discussion has rarely moved beyond subjective responses to isolated textual examples which show little sense of any overall functional-explicatory framework. And it has been guided by an ahistorical view of the translation process which has failed to grasp the translators (and especially the 'original' translator, Lowe-Porter) as agents operating in response to the norms and conventions of their age within a broader institutional context. This failure to achieve any significant methodological sophistication is all the more surprising in view of the fact that Lowe-Porter's translations have, to the present day, served as a common point of reference in the discipline of translation studies. They have frequently been referred to in key texts ranging from Bassnett-McGuire's pioneering study of 1980 through to Snell-Hornby's historical overview of the subject in 2006 (Bassnett-McGuire 1980; Snell-Hornby 2006; see also Snell-Hornby 1997; Newmark 1982; Hervey et al. 1995). More than this: Lowe-Porter's versions of Mann's texts were the subject of a sustained debate conducted in the pages of *The Times Literary Supplement* in the mid–1990s, a heated exchange which has been extensively reported in the literature though rarely placed in the context of translation studies in general.

The current state of the debate

As has often been pointed out, the contemporary reception of Mann's work in English translation was generally positive (France 2000: 333). Reviewing Mann's reception in the United States in the period to 1945, Walter A. Reichart wrote: 'Never has a foreign writer been acclaimed so spontaneously in America nor has any literary work in translation enjoyed such sudden popularity' (1945: 389). American and British reviewers, most of whom were not in a position to compare Lowe-Porter's renderings with Mann's originals, were impressed above all by the sheer scale of her achievement. Both the compass and complexity of Mann's works were seen to constitute a daunting task which she managed to overcome, by and large, with considerable skill and sensitivity. In the early media reception of the texts, only isolated voices questioned the quality of Mann's writing in translation. Orville Prescott described *Joseph the Provider* as 'aggressively dull, soporifically dull', and wrote of *Doctor Faustus*: 'As a novel it is clumsy, stilted, wonderfully tedious […] Members of the Book-of-the-Month Club are in for a shock when they tackle *Doctor Faustus*' (Prescott: 1944, 1948).

Even fewer commentators challenged the reliability of Lowe-Porter's versions. The Germanist Harry Levin, for example, criticized her 'archaic English, inaccuracies in choice of English equivalents' in her version of *Doktor Faustus* (1948; see also Thirlwall 1966: 114 and Schmidt-Schütz 2003: 89). But the majority of critics voiced conclusions similar to that published anonymously on *The Magic Mountain* in the *Guardian* on 1 July 1927, commenting positively on the translator's English while simultaneously expressing reservations about the novel's content: 'Mr [sic] Lowe-Porter's excellent translation, in two heavy volumes, is so convincing that the impression left on those readers who are sufficiently detached from its subject to endure Herr Mann's grim and often painful pathological study to its end is that they have done their reading in the original German and made their own mental translation as they went along.'

The first sustained (academic) discussion of the problematic nature of Lowe-Porter's work was provided by E. Koch-Emmery in 1952–3. Restrained and non-hortatory in tone ('I would find it very hard to improve on Mrs Lowe-Porter's translations'), this study draws attention to the translator's frequent reduction and recasting of Mann's complex syntax (1952/3: 284). Exploring examples drawn from a selection of Mann's works, Koch-Emmery summarizes his prime objection to Lowe-Porter's stylistic simplification in metaphorical terms: 'What was a beautifully planned park, with a castle on the horizon, is now a maze of jerry-built houses with pocket-handkerchief gardens, all neatly fenced and independent, but the reader no longer knows where to go, he has lost the guiding hand of the artist – in other words: he feels bored' (1952/3: 276). Koch-Emmery's discussion has the merit, compared with much later critical work, of a specific thematic focus: sentence structure. It avoids the mere cataloguing of errors drawn from textual samples selected at random, and resists the temptation to juxtapose Lowe-Porter's allegedly defective renderings with purportedly more accurate or equivalent solutions. It is, however, – and this is typical of earlier studies – guided by a fundamentally normative approach which fails to appreciate the inevitable textual transformations occasioned in the process of cross-linguistic transfer, and erects an ultimately insurmountable hurdle: 'Even if we assume that the translator can never be completely successful we can demand from him that he presents the work as a whole; whatever else he may have to alter, interpret, adapt – he must never dissect, he must never upset the balance between the various parts and the whole' (1952/3: 277).

Since Koch-Emmery's pioneering article, the discussion of Lowe-Porter's versions has taken three main forms. In many cases, commentators have practised a somewhat unsystematic form of textual comparison which seeks to capture distinctive features of the English versions as compared with both Mann's originals and other translated versions, but which is not guided by any visible methodology. For example, this is the case in Mandel's discussion of 1982, which sees Lowe-Porter's work as marred by 'personal preferences or slips' (Mandel: 1982: 38), in Witton's essay of 1991, which concludes that 'Lowe-Porter is now astute and inventive, now only mediocre, and now completely off the track' (Witton 1991: 255), and in Sixel's article published in 1994 (Sixel 1994). For all the interesting individual insights they provide, such discussions mix quite indiscriminately macrostylistic and microstylistic criteria, and descriptive and evaluative statements. In seeking to combat this trend, a second group of commentators has proceeded with a higher degree of methodological awareness, and has sought to lend its investigations a more systematic quality by adopting critical-descriptive schemes of varying sophistication. The first of these studies was by Hayes, who in 1974 compared the translations of *Der Tod in Venedig* by Burke and Lowe-Porter along a number of dimensions in an effort to determine the 'reliability' of the translated versions: 'The degree to which the final translation succeeds in reproducing the word-sense and in suggesting the unique literary qualities of the original work is the measure of its reliability' (Hayes 1974: vii). Hayes' conclusion is so general that it is not really helpful: '[Burke's] is the more reliable of the two translations. Lowe-Porter distorts Mann's writing by altering too many of its stylistic features' (1974: ix). Subsequent commentators, including Guess and Kinkel, have applied similar though more systematic schemes to the texts they examine (*Lotte in Weimar* and *Doktor Faustus* respectively), further refining the analytical instrumentarium as they do so (Guess 1977; Kinkel 2001). Kinkel's conclusion might be cited as representative of their approach: she finds that the multiplicity of *'einzelne Untersuchungsbereiche'* examined is not conducive to any coherent overall assessment. Lowe-Porter's version, she concludes, produces *'ein gemischtes Bild, das tendenziell durch Sinn- und Wirkungsverschiebungen im inhaltlichen und formalen Bereich sowie partielle kreative Ansätze im stilistischen Bereich gekennzeichnet ist'* (2001: 274). Her assessment of the latter is undermined by her occasional inability to judge the nuances of the English versions.

The third group of commentators – and this is the one which has had by far the loudest voice and the largest audience – has engaged in a sustained critique of the translations, and above all those of Lowe-Porter. I dwell on these contributions at greater length because they are the most widely quoted modern responses to Lowe-Porter's versions, and raise important questions about literary translation. The impetus behind this negative and wide-ranging reassessment of Lowe-Porter's work was provided in 1970 by Luke's comments in his first anthology of Thomas Mann's stories, and these were developed further in his second edition of 1988. While grudgingly (and torturously) acknowledging Lowe-Porter's achievement in the introduction to his first volume of translations ('it would be churlish to deny that her renderings are often by no means infelicitous', Luke 1970: xxxviii), his main concern is to demonstrate that her translations are 'of very poor quality'. To do so, he provides several pages of 'palpable factual mistakes, that is to say, unwitting errors of comprehension' which in sum constitute 'flagrant mistranslations' that 'have continued, unrectified and largely unnoticed, through all the reprintings of Mann's works in English for about the last sixty years' (1988: l). Lowe-Porter's translations do, indeed, contain a large number of errors, and Luke's renderings soon established themselves as the preferred – or at least as the more semantically accurate – versions. Fifteen years later, in 1995, Timothy Buck developed Luke's critique in an article in *The Times Literary Supplement* (Buck 1995). The motivation behind his essay was to draw attention to the scandalous state of affairs in which one of Europe's great writers was still being read in allegedly highly defective English versions. This discussion, which constitutes a damning critique of Lowe-Porter's work, was Buck's first contribution in what was to become a series of diatribes against English translations of Thomas Mann, later also extended to the work of John E. Woods (Buck 1996, 2002). Buck's *TLS* article prompted responses from the translation scholar Lawrence Venuti (letter to the *TLS* on 24 November 1995) and David Luke (letter of 8 December 1995). It was followed up by further replies from Venuti (22 December 1995) and Luke (29 December 1995), and even prompted an intervention from Lowe-Porter's surviving daughters (19 January 1996). This debate has gone down in the annals of modern translation studies. Indeed, Hermans introduces his standard text on descriptive translation studies with a preamble entitled 'Mann's fate', in which he reviews the often implicit assumptions underlying what became a polemic on the relative status of linguistic equivalence and historically conditioned transformation in translation: in short, between prescriptive and descriptive conceptions of literary translation (Hermans 1999). And Venuti has returned to the issue in a number of studies. He included it as one of his 'scandals of translation' in 1998, and it serves as a symptomatic reference point in the theory of retranslation he put forward in 2004 (Venuti 1998: 32–3; Venuti 2004). The debate takes us to the very heart of recent conceptions of literary translation.

In his contributions, which are summarized in the *Cambridge Companion to Thomas Mann*, Buck takes Lowe-Porter to task for her frequent (and in his view frequently unnecessary) syntactic transpositions, for her omissions, additions, 'catastrophic errors' and 'countless howlers' (Buck 2002: 238). He criticizes her 'unidiomatic, ungainly, ungrammatical, even incomprehensible' English, 'irksome archaisms' and 'failure to understand the German'. The sum total of these shortcomings is 'botching', a 'series of grossly distorted and artistically diminished versions', a 'pseudo-Mann'. Buck's discussions do indeed identify many shortcomings in Lowe-Porter's versions, at least at the level of semantic accuracy. Luke and Buck rightly rebuked Venuti for suggesting that simple cases of lexical error might be excused by changing canons of accuracy. Sometimes, even in professional translation work, the solutions offered are simply wrong. However, the critics show little understanding of the intrinsic linguistic qualities of Lowe-Porter's texts, on which Mann's reputation in the world at large rested for half a century and more. They fail to enquire in any detail into the interpretive impact of her 'distortions', and they lack any sense of historical development in translation theory and practice. Buck's catalogue of errors is just that: a sustained and unordered stream of mistranslations which is not guided by any heuristic purpose other than to log deficiencies. The list was expanded in a later full-length study by Gledhill, which appeared in 2007 under the extraordinary title *How to Translate Thomas Mann's Works* (Gledhill 2007). There, an appendix lists no fewer than 187 errors in the Lowe-Porter versions of *Der Tod in Venedig* and *Tonio Kröger*, in most cases comparing her lexical solutions with dictionary definitions. This survey of alleged mismatches abounds in comments highly reminiscent of undergraduate language classes: 'overliteral translation', 'yet another example of a typical second-language interference mistake', 'wrong use of the adjective "elder"', 'a non-English collocation', etc. Luke's translation emerges by contrast as 'a reliable translation of Thomas Mann's work with regard to the content or surface meaning' (Gledhill 2007: 4). However, Gledhill goes a step further, setting up an idealized notion of 'literariness', of which both translations (and presumably all literary translations) inevitably fall short. He regards them as instances of 'academic translation' which 'is often dull and always fails totally at the high literary level' (2007: 4). As an alternative, he proposes a rather unsubstantiated concept of 'strategic translation', according to which 'the translator should understand the semiotics of the original and then recreate a new text along the same lines', drawing on 'techniques of compensation and "creative transposition"' (2007: 196). Hardly surprisingly, Gledhill concludes: 'It is no coincidence that the successful translators of literature have also been writers; Hölderlin's translation of Sophocles, James Joyce's translation of *Finnegans Wake* and Beckett in French translating Beckett into English' (2007: 197).

Such approaches to the Thomas Mann translations are guided by a no doubt entirely legitimate concern to evaluate the translator's work. Even in the most highly descriptive and empiricist quarters of contemporary translation studies, the need to assess translation performance is regaining its place. But the contributions outlined above evaluate their objects of study in a theoretically unreflective manner, constructing universal and ahistorical standards of translational acceptability. Perceived deviation from a notional standard of accuracy (and after all, any translation of a thousand-page novel is almost certain to contain errors) is the only object of enquiry. Surely, as France insists, this cannot be the sole criterion in assessing literary translation (2000: 8). The philippics – and this is precisely Venuti's point – show no regard for the possibility of competing conceptions of translation, which might be the product either of idiosyncratic preferences or of historical conditioning, or of both. They seek to enumerate perceived divergences rather than to understand and explain their impact on the text and its potential for reception (Harman 1994: 7; Rabassa 2005: 43). Just how difficult it is to develop a systematic translation critique by applying a procedure of error identification can be seen in a paper published by Freudenberg in 2001. He claims to strive for a higher degree of systematization by establishing not a random list of errors, but rather a 'Fehlertypologie [..., *welche zunächst nach den Auswirkungen auf die* Rezeption *fragt, ehe der harte* Vorwurf einer Verfälschung des Originals *erhoben wird*' (Freudenberg 2001: 374, emphasis in the original). However, his discussion too exhausts itself in a limited number of disconnected observations, entirely divorced from the surrounding literary context. He ultimately offers, by his own admission, little more than '*einige sympomatische Beobachtungen als Kostproben von Helen Lowe-Porters Übersetzungsschwächen*' (2001: 374). This drawback is evident, too, in the otherwise valuable discussions published by Shookman (2004) and Simon (2009). Both focus almost exclusively on the mismatch and abound in apodictic judgements, such as 'is better than', 'comes closer to what Mann says in German', 'far from perfect', 'not strictly equivalent', and are highly impressionistic in character.

The major problem evident in the kind of evaluative critical response outlined above is its subjectivity. As soon as they move away from the realm of 'palpable errors', such discussions quickly descend to the level of unfounded and unfoundable judgements on felicity and acceptability of the type made by Gledhill: 'overliteral translation'. Resting as they do on empirically unsubstantiated criteria, such judgements are highly unstable. This can be read off from the many positive assessments of Lowe-Porter's achievement, compared with that of rival translators, expressed over recent years. The tenor of these responses is that accuracy does not always imply felicity. To cite just a few examples: Hatfield, reviewing Luke's 1988 anthology in 1990, writes: 'While Luke is remarkably accurate and Mrs Lowe-Porter less so, she does, it seems to me, come closer to the rhythm, the melody, indeed the style of those narratives' (Hatfield 1990: 192). Michael Wood, discussing the relative merits of Lowe-Porter and Woods, writes: 'I have to say I find the language of both Lowe-Porter and Woods lucid and serviceable' (Wood 2003: 4), a view which is echoed by Peter Craven: 'I don't think [Woods'] versions improve the original translations of Helen Lowe-Porter (although they sometimes correct her errors), and I once stopped reading his *Buddenbrooks* because it seemed inferior to hers' (Craven 2007, no page number). And in an extensive comparative essay published in 1999, the poet and translator Martin Greenberg defends Lowe-Porter, arguing that her versions are far more idiomatic than those of her successors Luke and Woods. In his view, much of her work has 'the cadence, the lyrical lift, the forward movement of the original, without stumbles or hesitations', whereas the more modern, literally accurate versions are 'sluggish', 'clumsy', 'literalism verging on the grotesque', 'deficient in literary feeling and literary style', in places 'cardboard stuff, pure contrivance'. He concludes: 'I found myself turning away from Woods, irritated and often bored, to Lowe-Porter' (Greenberg 1999: 27). Newmark speaks of 'a beautiful lyrical translation' in parts of *The Magic Mountain* (2000: 908), while Stanley Appelbaum, himself a translator of Mann, comments on her *Death in Venice*: 'Her elegant English prose makes her translation by far the most delightful and readable of the three [Burke, Luke, Koelb] I have consulted' (1995: 64).

What conclusions can be drawn from this debate? Surely, that item-by-item comparison of textual features under the banner of 'equivalence' cannot produce any form of theoretically grounded analysis. Translation, at every level, implies transformation. Even the apparently unproblematic duplication of features of the source text (e.g. syntactic patterns, metrical forms) in the target text – a seemingly straightforward method of generating 'equivalence' – cannot be guaranteed to produce the same effect across the linguistic divide, since the value of structural features can diverge interculturally (Albrecht 1998: 94). Accepting this, an alternative approach has been applied to English, French and Italian versions of *Der Tod in Venedig* in a recent study by Renée Barter. Based on the work of Patrick O'Neill, her 2007 book reads all translations as inevitably subjective manipulations of the original which do not degrade, but actually enrich each other over time, and which thus add to the meaning potentials of the source text. The age-old lament on inevitable translation loss has here been reversed, and all translation is seen to generate gain through a process of accretion and mutual interpretive modification. Here, though, there is no claim to quasi-scientific objectivity or reliability, but rather a purely subjective engagement with the original. Reading is based on a process of 'innumerable impressions, associations, inquiries and suggestions, only a fraction of which have actually made it as far as the page' (Barter 2007: 132). The emphasis on individual reader reception of the text is so pronounced that the results are entirely non-replicable. What is needed, surely, is a discussion of the English versions of Thomas Mann's works which (a) takes the hybridity of translations seriously, (b) accepts the inevitable processes of transmutation that intercultural transfer implies, and (c) seeks to relate form to function within a framework of literary interpretation. Precisely this is the focus of modern descriptive translation studies.

The present study: theoretical foundations and methodology

The present study is guided by an approach to the phenomenon of translation which is literary, descriptive, transfer-oriented and stylistically-driven. As a product-oriented analysis in the tradition of '*Übersetzungsforschung*' (Greiner 2004), it is informed by the fundamental conviction that the notion of 'equivalence' – a much-discussed concept in linguistically-oriented translation scholarship – is of little relevance in the consideration of literary translation, and proceeds instead on the assumption that all translation implies significant transformation. In considering specific translations, I am concerned to identify the manifestations of that process of metamorphosis (shifts), enquiring into their motivation, their place within the translator's overall strategy, and their impact on potential readings of texts. The thrust of the study is, then, analytical rather than evaluative, although the insights gained in the process of cross-textual comparison might, it is hoped, be able to suggest varying degrees of translational efficacy.

In theoretical terms my approach owes much to the descriptive paradigm in translation studies which was born in the 1980s out of impatience with the highly prescriptive, didactic models which had been promoted at institutes of translator and interpreter training from the 1960s onwards. The descriptivists discarded restrictive notions of interlingual correspondence and narrow definitions of translation as a specific form of text production. Instead, they chose to focus on translation as product rather than as process. Emphasizing that 'all translation implies a degree of manipulation of the source text', its early proponents became known as the 'manipulation school', after the title of their seminal work (Hermans 1985a). The scholars associated with the group viewed translations as products of the target system only, since they are triggered by, and operate only within, that system. They examined extensive corpora in an attempt to explain – rather than to judge – translational behaviour. Their ultimate goal was to identify the historically variable norms evident in literary translations as a subsystem of the superordinate system of literary production, in which the importance of translation in cultural interchange has always been understated. The fundamental assumption underlying this model is undoubtedly valid: translators do not merely opt for solutions on the basis of personal preference and linguistic competence, producing texts that can be objectively evaluated in terms of their degree of correspondence to the original without regard for the historical context. However, three other tenets of the manipulation paradigm are less uncontroversial. The conception of literature as a 'system' in anything but the most abstract and reductive sense appears questionable. So, too, does the possibility of reliably establishing 'norms' other than in the most generalized terms, and over extended historical and cultural distances. Both of these principles run the risk of simplification (for similar reservations see Gentzler 2001; Baker and Saldanha 2009; Pym 2010). Nor does it appear legitimate to assume that the only valid approach to translations is via the target text/culture, a premise which prompted scholars, logically, to include pseudo-translations and overt adaptations in their field of enquiry. In these qualifications, my approach is closer to that which was developed by the Göttingen translation research group in Germany and is documented in an extensive series of publications on extrinsic and intrinsic phenomena in literary translation in the years 1988–2004.

This latter paradigm was similarly descriptive in nature, but had a more overtly historical-hermeneutic orientation. Its proponents set out to explore systematically the history of literary translation within its diverse contexts – national, political, ideological, cultural, institutional, linguistic, literary, biographical. The goal of the twelve-year project was to discover what was translated, when, how often, why, by whom, and how. Most of these 'wh-'questions were subsumed under the rubric of *'äußere Übersetzungsgeschichte'*, the study of contextual parameters. The practitioners of the Göttingen model rejected the idea of literature as a 'system', which had been developed by polysystem theorists, and preferred to focus instead on traditions and conventions of the national literatures in question. They also opposed the exclusively target-culture orientation of the manipulation school, developing a transfer-oriented model of translation which they saw as an alternative to, and a synthesis of, one-sidedly source- or target-directed models. Inevitably, the heavily contextual thrust of the project led well beyond the analysis of individual texts. It encompassed the entire network of literary communication, comprising publishers, authors, translators, readers, critics, scholars and historians, in its endeavour to trace cultural-historical developments in translation. But individual texts were of necessity the starting point for many of the group's enquiries, and under the heading of *'innere Übersetzungsgeschichte'* the scholars posed the last of the 'wh-' questions cited above: '*Wie ist die vorliegende Übersetzung beschaffen?*'(Frank and Kittel 2004: 41). The quest to establish the kind of changes that take place in the process of translation generated an extensive descriptive apparatus designed to highlight deviations and shifts between originals and translations. The present study owes much to the impetus provided by the Göttingen researchers, but is more restricted in its historical orientation.

It is on the broader contexts of translational activity that most contemporary research in the field has focused. The widening of the discipline since the 1990s has triggered a veritable explosion in its areas of enquiry. As a more broadly conceived enterprise within the human sciences, translation studies has shifted in the wake of cultural studies and postmodernism towards the exploration of wider historical and ideological issues, and the 'turns' of the discipline have led it down new avenues. The last two decades have seen an increasing focus on sociological, cultural, philosophical and political dimensions, important inputs from gender and queer studies, and significant advances in empirical models (for an overview see Prunc 2007; Munday 2008; Baker and Saldanha 2009). But it is not only in the latter of these endeavours that the preoccupation with individual authors and their texts has remained a central object of enquiry. Since the early 1990s, an increasing number of scholars have sought to combine rigorous contrastive pragmalinguistic analysis with the procedures of comparative literary study. They have typically done so within the broader stylistic tradition. Understanding style as 'both culturally bound and universal ways of conceptualizing and expressing meaning' (Boase-Beier 2006: 2), this 'translational stylistics' (Malmkjaer 2004) recognizes the multifarious relations between source and target texts in seeking to explicate the motivation behind linguistic choices, and embraces sociocultural and historical factors through the notion of context. Detailed textual analysis has, then, remained an important component part of the discipline (Parks 2007; Boase-Beier 2011; Hewson 2011). Indeed, much of the progress towards an interdisciplinary approach to literary translation has come via the linguistic analyses conducted under the rubric of historical and descriptive models of translation research, which have relied extensively on case studies (Hermans 1985b: 10).

In the present study, I focus on the intercultural transfer of a single author, seeking to shed light on the vicissitudes of literary translation through the selective analysis of textual phenomena. In doing so, I am aware of the theoretical problems inherent in the descriptive enterprise. The first of these, referred to above, is the result of the fundamental hybridity of translations as derived texts. The fact that translation is, at one and the same time, both a creative and a recreative enterprise raises the question of orientation in translation studies in general, and in translation analysis in particular. I adopt an approach which is not primarily target-text based, but which takes account of the dual thrust of translation as a mediating activity between two discursive phenomena. In this approach, the source text remains important. First, because any concept of translation proper depends on the unidirectional transposition of material from one language into another in a manner which allows some form of alignment (however loose) between the source text (ST) and the target text (TT): if we take translation seriously as a process of text-reconstitution, the ST is the logical point of departure. And second, because I am concerned to establish the differences between a text's original meaning potential and the meaning potential that can be generated from the translation.

The latter concern links in with the second theoretical problem: the descriptive enterprise is ontologically problematical, dogged as it is by the theoretical, metalevel problem of the 'tertium comparationis'. All textual description (and comparison) is inevitably subjectively determined and historically conditioned, performed on the basis of features that have been identified as salient by the individual analyst. There can be no stable object of enquiry. The idea of an invariant core that must remain constant or 'equivalent' is an illusion in any text which is designed to serve more than the most basic goal-directed communication. However, it is impossible to jettison the notion of the object of comparison against which a translation is measured, if only as a heuristic tool which admits variability. The variability inherent in the descriptive enterprise is inevitable, given the multiplicity of the angles of perception involved: the process of translation embraces a number of sender and receiver roles. Thus, at the process level, the translator has a dual role as receiver of the ST and sender of the TT, extracting the text from one cultural context and preparing it for reception by readers in another. The translator's voice must, then, be understood as a second voice, an intervention between the original author and the reader of the translation (Hermans 1996; Koster 2000). And on the product level, the work of the translation describer must be seen as similarly subjectively coloured and culturally bound. While the translator of a text has an empirical presence as a cultural-historical subject who is inscribed into the text, the analyst seeking to extract that inscription from the text is equally conditioned by the environment in which he/she operates, which is likely to be very different from that prevailing for the translator. Translations are not produced in a vacuum; nor can they be studied in a vacuum (for a useful survey of this issue see Pym 2010, Chapter 8).

As well as such theoretical considerations, the activity of translation analysis is hampered by instabilities on the level of descriptive method. The first of these is undoubtedly the decision on the adoption of a top-down or a bottom-up approach. Is the analytical motion to proceed from macrolevel categories of textual organization, of which specific microlevel phenomena are seen as instantiations? Or should the analyst seek to capture textual characteristics at the level of microtextual detail and then integrate such phenomena into a coherent broader design? Once this procedural decision has been made (the *how?*), the question arises as to which features are to be selected for description, analysis and comparison (the *what?*). This raises the concomitant issue of representativeness. Given the sheer impossibility of analysing and comparing everything (even in the shortest of texts), the analyst must apply an operational model that will expose the degree of quantitative and qualitative similarity between original and translation. In his pioneering work on translation studies, Holmes identified two essential approaches to this task. In the first, the describer creates a 'list of distinctive features which strike him as significant and deserving of comparative analysis': the focus here is on specific phenomena that are perceived as text-constitutive or foregrounded in some way. In the second, the analyst sets up 'beforehand a required repertory of features always to be analysed, regardless of what specific text is involved' (Holmes 1988: 89), i.e. a pre-designed catalogue of replicable analytical criteria. Whichever methodology is adopted, it must be capable of fulfilling the essential requirements of translation description: explicit directionality, operationability, principled selection and explicatory power. The approaches to these core issues over the years inevitably reflect the main strands of thinking in translation studies since the 1980s. Thus celebrated distinctive feature models have been developed by Toury (Toury 1995), and the German 'Skopos' group (Ammann 1990), while sophisticated – and in some cases extremely detailed – repertory models have been suggested by Lambert and van Gorp (1985), van den Broeck (1985), Leuven-Zwart (1989/90), Chesterman (1997, Chapter 4) and Hewson (2011). The most frequently cited models are usefully outlined by Rodriguez (2007).

As mentioned above, the model which underlies the present study is closest to that proposed by the Göttingen group, which seeks a coherent '*innere Differenzierung von Ausgangs- und Zieltext*' (Frank and Schulze 1988: 107). As a self-declared 'transfer-oriented' conception, this approach does not prioritize either the source or target text, but is concerned to attend to both in equal measure, and thus to synthesize the two perspectives. The comparative method outlined by the Göttingen scholars is an extremely comprehensive 'repertory-based' approach, outlined in detail by Frank and Kittel (2004). It seeks to establish the degree of correlation between ST and TT by applying an extensive catalogue of clearly identified microlevel features (from graphemics and phonetics through lexis and syntax to suprasentential units) and attending to higher level principles of textual structure (recurrences and schemes). The features thus established 'horizontally' are then collated to produce a 'vertical diagnosis' of the relations between TT and ST, and to allow conclusions concerning the motivation and impact of the translation solutions adopted. This diagnosis seeks to identify the ways in which the literary worlds (the 'inferents') potentially constructed by readers from the two texts differ. It is this meaning potential that serves as the 'tertium comparationis', and which might provide a basis for tentative evaluation. In the words of one of the group's leading members: 'the best *evaluation* of a translation is tantamount to a complete and non-judgmental *description* of the ways in which its structure, and hence its meaning, have been affected by the act of translation. What parts of the original potential for meaning were lost in the process? [...] In what ways does the potential for understanding and response represented by the translation differ from that offered by the original?' (Frank 1984: 218, italics in original). The model has the advantage of principled selection, and avoids overrigidity. Indeed, its analytical criteria feature in other models, some of which explicitly privilege the target side (Koster 2000).

The notion of 'meaning potential' is a key component in the approach of the present study. Instability of 'meaning' is typically considered to be an essential feature of the literary text. In seeking to decode it, readers are compelled to relate directly observable textual phenomena to a more abstract level of significance via a process of interpretation. Interpretation is a search for coherence of design in the text. It involves a quest for the maximal relevance of the constituent parts, and is driven by the assumption that authorial choice in expression carries significance. In this endeavour to explicate the relations between textual form and literary function, the reader is engaged in a participatory process of reconstruction, of identifying communicative clues that suggest relevance beyond conventional semantics. In the literary text, 'second-order meanings' that require active reader engagement are as significant as 'first-order' meanings, which draw on established cultural and linguistic knowledge (Katz 1990). But the reader (and, of course, the translator-as-reader) engaged in this process is not a dislocated mind. The recipient of the literary text is embedded within a social-historical-ideological, psychological, pragmatic context, and brings various types of knowledge to the text: linguistic, genre, world, author, text world, personal knowledge. These extralinguistic factors provide the context in which texts are produced and received: they are inscribed into texts during the process of production and govern the reception of texts as products.

The openness of the literary text does not mean that the object and process of scrutiny are entirely unconstrained and unverifiable. While literary interpretation is, by virtue of the polyvalence of the text, an open-ended and empirically untestable process, its procedures can claim a certain level of intersubjective verifiability on the strength of the analytical models which underpin it. Replicable identification and exploration of the relevant linguistic and textual structures that constitute the internal system of the text (or, in the case of specific feature analysis, parts thereof) enable the reader-critic to construct an underlying significance (*Sinnentwurf*) from the semantics of the text (*Bedeutung*). Interpretation is the explicitation of implicit signals, and is thus theoretically open. But where interpretation is derived from a coherent and rational analytical model, it becomes replicable, if not stable. Interpretation, then, might be understood as the possibility of expressing subjective views on the literary text in an objective manner (Jahrhaus 2004: 360; on literary hermeneutics see Ricoeur 1981; Ray 1984; Eco 1991; MacKenzie 2002).

Recognizing the openness of the text, in all its historical, cultural and social variability, rather than seeking to reduce it to an invariant core, is the essence of the hermeneutic-descriptive tradition in translation studies. Translation analysis seeks to identify the ways in which textual features at various levels have been handled (manipulated, distorted) between languages and cultures. The nature of the relations between source and target texts, which are manifested in correspondences and shifts, serves as an indication of the manner in which the text has been transferred via a creative act on the basis of an interpretation (Venuti 2008: 13). That interpretation is only implicit in the translation (Frank 1987: xiv; Greiner 2004: 39). The notions of shift and correspondence do, of course, imply measurement against some form of stable element, which – given the inevitable variability of textual readings – is an interpretive construct (Hewson calls it the 'critical framework', 2011: 26). In other words, the translation analyst measures his/her interpretation of a TT against his/her interpretation of an ST. Given the many variables involved in the literary text itself, the goal in literary translation can only be to provide a route into the polyvalence and indeterminacy of the original text, offering a similar – but never identical – '*Potential für imaginatives Verstehen*' (Frank and Kittel 2004: 18). This, ultimately, is the object of enquiry in translation evaluation: not a misguided insistence on equivalence, but an assessment of whether a translation has opened up the paths that enable a similar receptive experience. A useful and highly succinct working definition of translation, which encapsulates the notion that a translation is always at one and the same time a reading, a reproduction and ultimately a modification of a historically embedded literary construct, is offered by Apel and Kopetzki:

> *Übersetzung ist eine zugleich verstehende und gestaltende Form der Erfahrung von Werken einer anderen Sprache. Gegenstand dieser*

Erfahrung ist die dialektische Einheit von Form und Inhalt als jeweiliges Verhältnis des einzelnen Werks zum gegebenen Rezeptionshorizont (Stand der Sprache und Poetik, literarische Tradition, geschichtliche, gesellschaftliche, soziale und individuelle Situation). Diese Konstellation wird in der Gestaltung als Abstand zum Original spezifisch erfahrbar.
(Apel and Kopetzki 2003: 9)

It is this 'distance from the original' that can be identified, on the textual level, via a consideration of correspondences and shifts.

The sum total of the correspondences and shifts between ST and TT indicates the translator's strategy. That strategy is most fundamentally present in the text as a conscious or unconscious preference for an underlying orientation towards poles which are typically described as 'adequacy' or 'acceptability' (Toury), as 'anti-illusory' or 'illusory' (Levy), 'foreignizing' or 'domesticating' (Schleiermacher, indirectly) and, viewed in more overtly ideological terms, 'resistant' or 'fluent' (Venuti) translation. The translator's strategy is an amalgam of individual preferences and idiosyncratic practices on the one hand, and of responses to prevailing conventions/norms on the other: an 'interrelationship between patterned translation behaviour and the translator's personal choices' (Crisafulli 2002: 41). The former might be largely predictable, while the latter require exploration via a hermeneutic process. The description of shifts, then, serves as an indication of the translator's voice, fingerprint or discursive presence. In comparing the meaning potentials of texts, we must be aware that it is ultimately the function of the TT element in the TT as a whole that matters. We cannot simply isolate and compare individual textual phenomena across the ST-TT divide – as has so frequently been done in Thomas Mann research – divorcing phenomena from their functional relevance in a broader context. Instead, we must look at the patterns and recurrences of shifts at the microstylistic level and consider their macrostructural implications, i.e. their relative roles in the creation of the text world of the two texts. It is the fictional worlds generated by the respective discourses that serve as the object of comparison, and it is the means by which these are constructed that are the object of description.

Despite the development of a number of models over the years, some of which are highly sophisticated, it has proved impossible to arrive at any real consensus on a universally applicable scheme for translation description. Thus Hewson, at the end of his recent detailed and highly systematic study, acknowledges that translation criticism 'can never be comprehensive or complete' (2011: 257), and he remains acutely aware of the problems of representativeness, interpretation, selection and categorization (259). These are classical conundrums in monolingual stylistics, too. As Leech and Short write in their introduction to literary stylistics: 'There is no infallible technique for selecting what is significant. We have to make ourselves newly aware, for each text, of the artistic effect of the whole, and the way linguistic details fit into this whole' (Leech and Short 2007: 60). In establishing an instrumentarium of criteria to be applied for the purposes of description, comparison and possible evaluation, linguistic models (however refined) have never been regarded by those working within the literary-analytical tradition as sufficiently powerful. For all the expansion of focus evident in modern pragmalinguistic models, literary researchers have remained convinced that the meaning potential of the literary text exists beyond the systemic level of its linguistic constitution, and cannot simply be identified by mapping features to functions. Leech and Short stress: 'The function of literature being primarily aesthetic, we must search for explanations of stylistic value [...] in terms of considerations internal to the work itself' (2007: 110; see also Halliday 1983: ix). All models will inevitably be guided by expectations and intuitions, and by a process of selection. Perhaps, ultimately, Hermans is correct to conclude: 'schemes and procedures can help and offer hints and pointers, but they remain ancillary. In the end it will be the questions to which the researcher seeks answers, on whatever grounds, which focus the attention [...] Their positive uses in providing the means to distinguish, classify and tick off checklists are best harnessed within a research project that sets out its own parameters' (1999: 71).

The structure of the present study

The present study seeks to apply modern analytical techniques in a consideration of Thomas Mann's works in English. In so doing, it is located at the interface of linguistic and literary analysis. My discussion is, as indicated above, motivated primarily by the literary-historical importance of the Lowe-Porter translations in securing Mann's place in the world-literary tradition, and by the methodological shortcomings evident in the discussion of Mann translations to date. Given the inherent complexity of literary translation in general, the sheer scale of Thomas Mann's work, and the large number of translations, any consideration of our subject implies a radical process of selection. Since Lowe-Porter's original versions were published, many retranslations of Mann's works into English have appeared, offering interesting perspectives on varying conceptions and modes of translation. Only a few of those issues can be covered within the space of a single study. But it is possible to ensure that the selection and treatment of the dimensions to be analysed are governed by a broad understanding of the parameters of literary translation analysis, and are systematic in character.

That a large part of the focus in the following chapters should be on the work of Lowe-Porter is inevitable, given her standing as Mann's 'authorized' translator and the central importance of her work in his canonization. In considering her work, and in placing her renditions alongside those of subsequent translators, I do not seek to re-evaluate her achievement, although much of the following discussion might at least ground certain evaluative conclusions. Nor do I attempt to rehabilitate her as a translator (her reputation has suffered badly in recent years). In view of my comments above on the parameters and variables of literary translation analysis, any global conclusions would be questionable. Rather, I set out to describe some of the transformations apparent in her versions, and in those of others, and to explicate the effects they have on the reception of the text.

The opening chapters of the following study derive their impetus from the need to understand literary translation as a contextualized social practice involving a number of interacting and interdependent agents. Modern translation research has demonstrated that strategies adopted by translators are shaped by factors such as systemic linguistic incompatibilities, the translator's language-historical position and cultural background – and not least by the expectations prevailing in the host culture at a given time. In broader-based historical studies, the series of 'wh-'questions cited earlier – what was translated, when, how often, why, and by whom? – assumes major importance in the exploration of translation as an intercultural exchange. This extrinsic mode of enquiry can assume a major historical dimension, examining diachronic corpora for underlying trends, and exploring such phenomena as canon formation, anthologization and adaptation. The present study, by contrast, is more restricted in scope, examining aspects of the importation of a single author into English. To that extent, the notion of context is also restricted. But it cannot be ignored. In existing studies of Thomas Mann – as of so many other authors – the sociocultural environments in which translations have been produced and received have been almost entirely neglected. The discussion has proceeded as though all the available translations of his work (I focus on texts produced between 1914 and 2010) were created simultaneously, read by readers in a static receptive context, and rendered by translators operating as free agents entirely unbound by social norms and institutional pressures. In fact, of course, the translator is but one agent in a mutually determining interaction between the wider culture, book market, publisher and original author. This power network of the publishing industry has been afforded greater attention in the wake of the cultural and ideological turns in translation studies. Since Bassnett and Lefevere directed a sharper focus towards 'the larger issues of context, history and convention' in translation studies in 1990, wider contextual studies have very much come to the foreground in the discipline (Bassnett and Lefevere 1990: 11; Munday 2007). Lefevere, for example, explored the instruments of control within the literary system in his 1992 book, whose title foregrounds the phrase 'the manipulation of literary fame' (Lefevere 1992a). He posited a correlation between the power of professionals and patrons active in the literary system, the dominant poetics of the age, the way translators operate, and the status they are accorded. In recent research, much attention has been devoted to the role of editors, reviewers, academics, the media, and public and private institutions. In some manifestations, this work provides a committed perspective on the interdependence of translation production and political and ideological agendas. In more general terms, it has triggered efforts to grasp translation as a socially regulated activity within a broad-based sociology of translation (for a summary see the extensive introduction to Wolf and Fukari 2007).

In considering the fortunes of Thomas Mann in English, two extratextual dimensions require consideration before attention can be turned to the intratextual characteristics of the works themselves. The first of these is a broader localization: an overview of the history and reception of English versions of Thomas Mann, from the publication of the first English editions of his works to the present day. It is not possible here to trace in detail the genesis or the contexts of the translation, retranslation and reception of his work over a period of some ninety-five years, but central issues are outlined to provide a historical basis for the subsequent discussion. These include a consideration of why and when his works were translated, and of why and by whom they were retranslated. Particular attention will be paid to the crucial triadic relationship between Thomas Mann, his American publisher Alfred A. Knopf, and Lowe-Porter in the years 1923–51. As is well-documented in many letters, essays and diary entries, the three enjoyed a long and very close collaboration. Put simply: Knopf had a closer relationship with Thomas Mann than with any of the other authors on his books, and promoted him with especial vigour; Mann had – with one single exception – no other commissioning publisher for the English versions of his works during his lifetime, and no other English translator of his major works in the years 1924–51; and Lowe-Porter translated almost exclusively for Mann/Knopf during the same period. Despite the appearance of new documentary material in recent years, however, little has been written about the differing interests and motivations of the three agents, or on the ways in which the dynamics of their relationship influenced the process of translation production itself. Similarly, no serious attention has previously been paid to the second contextual parameter identified by Lefevere in the work cited above: translation poetics. The second chapter of the present study, then, explores the competing conceptions of translation held by Mann and his translator, which might serve to shed light on the way the translator went about her work. In view of criticism levelled at Lowe-Porter's versions in recent years, it is important to identify and reflect on her own theoretical-methodological approach to translation, to enquire into the relationship between her views on the subject and the conceptions prevailing at the time, and to ask whether there was any fundamental incompatibility between her views on translation and those of the author.

My intrinsic studies of aspects of Mann's texts in English translation seek to pinpoint the 'something new' that has been created during the process of transfer. The subsequent chapters of the study, then, offer a contrastive analysis of selected features which enable us to see the discourse world of Thomas Mann as filtered through the translator's vision. These chapters constitute the larger part of the present book and provide case studies of salient dimensions of the cross-linguistic transfer of literary works. Those salient features have been selected (from the multitude of potential objects of enquiry) in accordance with a series of guiding principles which are located at the interface of distinctive feature and repertory-based models. Given the inevitable incompleteness of the latter, I have chosen not to apply a quasi-exhaustive catalogue of criteria to the translations, but rather to limit my analysis to a number of phenomena which are especially relevant in literary-analytical terms. In some cases, these dimensions have been included as features which typically play a constitutive role in literary texts, and which might therefore be expected to repay analysis (Chapter 6: discourse forms). In others they are features which have, more specifically, been identified in Mann scholarship as especially relevant, i.e. as characteristic of his literary 'style' (Chapter 8: syntax). In both these cases, the selection is guided by criteria of literary study: these might be held to predict areas of interest in the translational exchange, and have been neglected in previous studies of Mann in English. The third principle addresses features which are interesting for reasons of systemic asymmetry, i.e. cross-linguistic incompatibilities that are especially evident in 'integral' translations (Chapter 7: modes of address). In terms of Toury's norms, all the texts under discussion here are 'integral', i.e. do not intervene dramatically in structures of narrative organization. Rather, the major points of contrast are located on the 'textual-linguistic' level, with concomitant consequences for the literary level. It is at this 'phraseological' level, as recent work in the field has confirmed, that most transformations occur in translations in the stricter sense of the term (Munday 2007: 41). Finally, as a further dimension, features have been selected which are relevant not merely in directional terms (ST-TT), but also in terms of translation comparison (TT-TT), in an attempt to identify and explicate (i) different translation procedures and (ii) different potential impacts on meaning

(Chapter 5: titles). These have, in some cases, been suggested by the critical reception of Mann's work in English.

The phenomena selected for analysis on the basis of the above-mentioned selection criteria represent a variety of textual dimensions: the intertextual dimension of translation comparison, i.e. the attempt to characterize translations in broad terms on the basis of general and specific criteria (Chapter 4); the paratextual issue of title translation, in its importance for the activation of reader expectations and influence on text reception (Chapter 5); the macrostylistic phenomena of speech and thought representation, both of which constitute key dimensions of discourse presentation in texts (Chapter 6); the handling of modes of address as a key index of the treatment of interpersonal relations as they develop in texts (Chapter 7); and microstylistic features at the level of syntax, which are consistently identified as a key challenge in translating Mann (Chapter 8). In each case, the textual dimension in question is discussed in terms of its function within literary discourse in general and its status as a translation-relevant phenomenon, before being considered in the specific context of Thomas Mann's work. While an examination of such selected aspects cannot claim to provide an exhaustive characterization of the translations, it is hoped that it may place the discussion of Thomas Mann translation on a more systematic footing by exploring the dynamics of cross-linguistic transfer from a variety of descriptive perspectives, in all cases paying attention to the literary consequences of decisions taken at the linguistic level.

2 Translation and retranslation: The history of Thomas Mann's works in English

Introductory remarks

The translator, as much recent research has stressed, is embedded within a broader institutional context which frames the selection, production and distribution of translations, impinges centrally on the strategies adopted by translators as social agents, and impacts on the modalities of reception of translated texts in the receiving culture. In considering the case of Thomas Mann's work in English, account must be taken of the ways in which the publisher and author systematically strove to create a specific receptive context in the primary target culture, the United States. The Lowe-Porter versions inevitably stand at the centre of attention here, since they were produced more or less contemporaneously with the originals, and in direct consultation with Mann and Knopf. However, the phenomenon of retranslation – later versions produced in a different contextual environment – has also played an important part in the history of Thomas Mann's reception in English. All the author's key works have been rendered into English more than once, and a number of them have been reworked several times. Retranslation can shed light on the changing conditions that influence the production and reception of translated texts.

The history of Thomas Mann translations in English is more complex than is often suggested. So too is the process by which Lowe-Porter eventually became the author's 'official' translator. In fact, during Mann's lifetime alone some thirty different translators produced English versions of his texts. The majority of these translated various of the author's many essays, speeches and letters, and the better known names included Mann's daughter Erika and her sometime husband W. H. Auden, the writer's American benefactor Agnes E. Meyer, his personal secretary Konrad Katzenellenbogen, the Germanists H. J.

Weigand and Elizabeth M. Wilkinson, and Clifton Fadiman, an editor at *The New Yorker* and an influential judge for the Book-of-the-Month Club. Meanwhile, at least half a dozen others, quite apart from those who published texts in book form, produced versions of literary texts for journals and anthologies (in alphabetical order: Maida Darnton, Henry Hart, Winifred Katzin, Julian Leigh, Ludwig Lewisohn, Edgar Rosenberg and Harry Steinhauer). Alfred A. Knopf did not have exclusive rights to publish Mann in the USA until 1925, by which time the author was well-established in Germany and had already been translated into a large number of other languages. Nor did Knopf draw exclusively on the services of Lowe-Porter during the early years of their cooperation. The emergence (though not the final establishment) of Thomas Mann in the English-speaking world was, then, secured by various other hands.

The fortunes of Thomas Mann in English illustrate the often quite random ways in which texts are selected for translation and translators are engaged, as well as the cavalier fashion in which the latter are treated. These processes are evident in the publication history, and can be traced in some detail through the voluminous body of correspondence and diary entries which arose in connection with the genesis of the texts. As we shall see, it was a single US publisher, Alfred A. Knopf, who effectively took control of Mann's English-speaking career in the 1920s, drawing on groundwork done by others. Knopf retained that control throughout Mann's life and beyond. The British editions of Mann's work in English were secondary in every sense: from an early stage it was the New York-based Knopf who selected the translators, commissioned the translations, and sold the rights to UK publishers Secker & Warburg. The relations between Knopf, Mann and Lowe-Porter provide a fascinating insight into the vicissitudes of the interaction between publisher, author and translator.

The beginnings: Morgan, Curtis, Burke and Scheffauer (1914–25)

While it is customary in the literature to hail A. Cecil Curtis as the first English translator of Thomas Mann, the earliest translation to appear in English was actually produced by an American academic who was to play a major role in the importation of German literature into the English-speaking world. As early as 1914 – ten years before Lowe-Porter's first Mann translation appeared in print – Bayard Quincy Morgan published a version of *Tonio Kröger* in an anthology of German stories (Morgan 1914). Why that particular text was chosen for translation is not clear: after all, even at that time *Der Tod in Venedig* was well-established as the author's key short text. Born in 1883 (died 1967), Morgan was a distinguished Germanist who developed a considerable reputation as an active translator of German authors, a teacher of translation theory, and a critical bibliographer. His monumental *Critical Bibliography of German Literature in English Translation* was a highly influential guide to German letters available in English, first appearing in 1922 and later expanded in two stages to include literature to 1960 (Morgan 1965).

The 1914 Morgan translation of *Tonio Kröger* represents a milestone in three respects. Not only is it the earliest attested English translation of a text by Mann, but it also formed the focus, some thirty years later, of the first sustained critical academic discussion of Mann's work in English translation. In an article published in 1945, Marianne Zerner criticizes a number of 'obvious mistranslations' in English translations of the author's texts, setting the tone for decades of hortatory commentary by translation critics (Zerner 1945: 178). Focusing particularly on Morgan's text, Zerner identifies a number of lexical inaccuracies, which range from what she judges to be 'ludicrous misconceptions' (Zerner 1945: 179) at one end of the scale of infelicity to a 'loss of subtle nuances' (183) at the other. All of these, she claims, 'interfere harmfully with the intention of the author in matters of characterization' (181). The third sense in which Morgan played a pioneering role was that he also produced the earliest attested metatextual discussion of the difficulties of translating Mann into English. In the first published piece of self-justification by a Mann translator, Morgan responded to Zerner's charges 'with a view to justifying, against Miss Zerner's objections, my solutions' (Morgan 1946: 220). He responds in turn to each of the charges she levels at his work, outlining in the process 'important principles which must continue to guide the conscientious translator'. These, he believes, she 'overlooks'.

The first English version of a novel by Thomas Mann, and thus the first translation in book form, was produced by A. Cecil Curtis in 1916. Eight years were to elapse before a further novel appeared in English, and in the interim period a number of stories, excerpts and essays translated by various hands were published in journals. It was the publication of *Royal Highness* in Britain that first drew the attention of the aspiring American publisher Alfred A. Knopf to Thomas Mann. In a memorial essay published in 1975, Knopf reports that the growing number of translations of European works appearing in the United States prior to the First World War prompted him to seek foreign authors to add to his own list (Knopf 1975: 2). He had already signed a number of Russian authors, and was keen to add other literatures. The Cecil Curtis translation of *Königliche Hoheit* appeared first in Britain, published by Sidgwick and Jackson. No information is available on how it came to be published, on why this rather lightweight (and only modestly successful) work was given precedence over the earlier, more substantial and much more successful *Buddenbrooks*, nor on the procedure by which the translator was commissioned. Knopf recalls in his essay only that he bought the American rights from the British publisher, and that he imported unbound sheets for release in the USA. Nor is very much known about A. Cecil Curtis, who also translated works from Italian and Danish. But the novel occupies a unique position in the history of Mann's oeuvre in English, in as far as it is the only one of the author's texts that Knopf did not have subsequently retranslated by Lowe-Porter. Despite its poor sales, Knopf re-released it twice (in 1926 and 1939). In both cases, the reason for the re-issue of an existing translation seems to have been the pressure Lowe-Porter was under to keep abreast of ongoing projects. In 1926 she was struggling with *Der Zauberberg*, and in 1939 was immersed in the monumental Joseph novels. Under his agreement with Fischer, Knopf was required to publish one book per year (Berlin 1992: 284), and he appears not to have considered *Königliche Hoheit* worth retranslating. The Cecil Curtis text remains to this day the only English version of this novel, though it was 'fully revised' by Constance McNab for publication in the United Kingdom in 1962 by the New English Library.

Developments between the publication of *Royal Highness* in 1916 and the final establishment of Lowe-Porter as Mann's sole authorized translator, which Knopf finally declared to her in a letter dated 11 January 1928 (Berlin 1992: 311), are rather confusing. There has been much discussion of the emerging competition between Lowe-Porter, who produced *Buddenbrooks* in 1924, and Hermann Georg (known in America as Herman George) Scheffauer, whose translation of *Herr und Hund* appeared a year earlier under the title *Bashan and I* with W. Collins in London and Henry Holt in New York. In fact, though, the 1920s saw a protracted series of English publications of Mann's work in leading American journals, produced by various translators. The significance of these periodical publications in Mann's early English-speaking career should not be underestimated. Literary journals played a key role in the rehabilitation of German culture in the USA after the First World War, and contributed significantly to the lifting of the 'cultural blockade' that had been imposed on all things German. They prompted the 'American discovery of a New German Literature' (Koepke 1992, title). Largely due to the concerted efforts of committed editors, contributors and reviewers, German literature gradually attracted growing numbers of publishers and readers, especially from 1925 onwards. The names Gerhart Hauptmann, Erich Maria Remarque, Lion Feuchtwanger, Franz Werfel, Stefan Zweig, Rene Schickele, Emil Ludwig, Jakob Wassermann, Alfred Neumann and Bruno Frank regularly appeared in their pages. While the journals themselves never attracted a large readership, they did provide a forum for the dissemination of translated fiction in literary circles. The influx of German imports in the mid-1920s, which they heralded and encouraged, contributed significantly to the 'consolidation of the American book market' (Koepke 1992: 96).

In the 1920s, three journals in particular championed the cause of Thomas Mann. *The Freeman*, edited by Albert Jay Nock, published six translated excerpts from *Herr und Hund* in 1922–3, all by Scheffauer. These later formed part of the 1923 book version. *The Dial*, edited by Scofield Thayer, published versions of the stories *Luischen*, *Tristan* and *Der Tod in Venedig* by the American literary theorist and philosopher Kenneth Burke (the second of these with S. Thayer). It also carried a series of eight original contributions by Mann on German culture under the title "German letter" (also translated by Kenneth Burke), as well as Scheffauer's version of *Unordnung und frühes Leid* and a number of other literary and political essays. And *The Nation* published an extract from a version of *Die Hungernden* by Ludwig Lewisohn, who was to become best known as a novelist in his own right, and as the English translator of Werfel's highly successful *Das Lied von Bernadette* in 1942. Lewisohn, who was also a friend of Knopf, played an important role in Mann's early fortunes in the English-speaking world. A Germanist and staunch champion of the cause of German literature, he had published a work on contemporary German letters in 1917 (Lewisohn 1917), and penned a long series of contributions on German culture for *The Nation*. In 1924 he published an influential review of the English *Buddenbrooks* in that journal, extolled the virtues of *Der Zauberberg* a year later ('Thomas Mann at Fifty', December 9 1925), and wrote the preface to Lowe-Porter's retranslation of *Death in Venice* (1930).

Among these journal publications, all of which played an important role in bringing Mann to the attention of the serious American reading public, *The Dial* is especially significant in terms of the author's reception in the USA. As a leading forum for the literature of early modernism, the periodical regularly published in its pages work by Valéry, Yeats, Eliot, Pound, Lawrence and Virginia Woolf, and as a '"who's who" list of the decade's literati', devoted much space to translations (Brown 1983: 4). The material which appeared in this journal broke the ground for Mann's emergence in the USA as both a creative author and a cultural-political commentator. It was, as noted above, in the pages of *The Dial* that versions of important short stories by Mann first appeared. Some of those texts were later republished in book form, making Mann accessible to a broader and more general readership. Burke's *Dial* versions of *Tristan* and *Death in Venice*, for example, were republished by Knopf in a single volume in 1925 alongside *Tonio Kröger*. And it was in the same journal that Mann first appeared as a cultural commentator: his contract to contribute a regular column, paid for in dollars, was a most welcome source of income in the wake of the inflation in Germany in the early Twenties.

The first English translator with whom Mann had direct personal contact was Hermann Georg Scheffauer (1878–1927). After translating extracts from Mann's *Herr und Hund* for *The Freeman*, Scheffauer published his rendering of the entire novel as *Bashan and I* with Collins/Holt in 1923. It was the second book by Thomas Mann to appear in English. A few years later (1928), Knopf published an anthology of nine translations of Mann's stories by Scheffauer under the title *Children and Fools*, which included *Disorder and Early Sorrow*, previously published in *The Dial* in 1926. Knopf also issued his own edition of Scheffauer's translation of *Herr und Hund* as *A Man and His Dog* in 1930, at a time when Lowe-Porter was busy translating work by Bruno Frank. The fortunes of *Herr und Hund* in English are interesting in the development of Mann's oeuvre in English. They illustrate the process of increasing concentration systematically pursued by Knopf in his efforts to secure exclusive rights to all Thomas Mann's texts produced in English. First, he acquired the rights to republish this text, retaining Scheffauer's original translation but changing its title. Then, at a later stage, he had the text newly translated by Lowe-Porter under its new title: the revised version appeared in the anthology *Stories of Three Decades* in 1936.

It is not clear from the sources when Mann and Scheffauer first established contact with each other. However, in March 1924, when consideration was being given to an English translator for *Der Zauberberg*, Mann informed Lowe-Porter that he had been approached by Scheffauer on the matter of further translations (letter of 16 March 1924, *Reg* 1: 370), and expressed his conviction that Scheffauer was the more qualified to undertake the new novel. The two remained in contact until the latter's untimely death (by suicide) in 1927, and figured as co-editors of a series of novels (*Romane der Welt*) for Verlag Th. Knaur Nachf. Mann wrote in glowing terms about Scheffauer after his death, not least *'weil er mehrere meiner Arbeiten mit außerordentlicher Kunst und Liebe ins Englische übersetzt hatte'* (GW 11: 760–1). While Scheffauer was clearly Mann's choice as translator for *Der Zauberberg*, Knopf insisted that Lowe-Porter be commissioned, having apparently heard negative comments about Scheffauer's work (Berlin 1992: 298).

The era of Helen Tracy Lowe-Porter (1924–51)

The process by which Lowe-Porter became Thomas Mann's designated translator is outlined in various sources, including Knopf's personal reminiscences (Knopf 1975) and Lowe-Porter's own 'On translating Thomas Mann' (first published in 1966). It can also be traced through Mann's letters from the period (he destroyed the diaries for 1922–32, the relevant years in this respect). In recent years, further letters have been made available by Jeffrey Berlin (1992, 1994, 1996, 2001, 2005a, 2005b) and, most recently, by Cathy Henderson and Richard W. Oram (Henderson and Oram 2010). Of interest in the present context, however, is not so much the process by which Lowe-Porter was enthroned as Thomas Mann's English translator, but rather the developing dynamics between translator, author and publisher in as far as these influenced the production and reception of Mann in the English-speaking world.

Lowe-Porter's first contact with Mann's work came about, she reports, when she was approached by the William Heinemann publishing company in London with a view to translating *Buddenbrooks*. According to Thirlwall, she first read the novel in 1922, by which time she had already translated one work from French for that house. Following Heinemann's death in 1920, the company had been bought by Doubleday, and the Heinemann imprint was the responsibility of Sydney Pawling, with whom the US publisher Alfred A. Knopf enjoyed friendly relations. When Doubleday failed to show any interest in pursuing the publication of Thomas Mann in English, Knopf secured a contract – through Pawling's mediation – with Mann's German publisher Samuel Fischer in 1921. Thus it was that the *Buddenbrooks* translation which Lowe-Porter had begun for Heinemann was first published not in London, but in New York by Knopf, who then sold the UK rights to Martin Secker.

Alfred A. Knopf (1892–1984), a graduate in literature and history from Columbia University, founded his own publishing company in 1915 with the assistance of his fiancée Blanche Wolf, whom he married in 1916. Highly ambitious and enterprising, the young Knopf adopted an unusually cosmopolitan outlook to the publication of literature, actively seeking foreign authors for his catalogue. Knopf was, according to George H. Doran, 'among the first to sense [a] new and broadening market […] He had rare courage and daring and proceeded to publish translations from the writings of many Europeans' (Doran 1952: 83). He is now widely acknowledged to have been a pioneer in the publication of texts by foreign authors (Baker and Saldanha 2009: 218). In his monumental history of US publishing, Tebbel writes: 'About the Knopf list clung the aura of great names in world literature' (Tebbel 1981: 145). While the advent of modernism had served to promote the importation of foreign literature – especially poetry – into the USA, the publication of non-English writing remained a considerable commercial risk, and only very few European novels sold well in the 1920s. Nevertheless, Knopf built his early reputation predominantly on his bold commitment to European works in translation (Turner 2003: 41), and only gradually signed up American writers. By 1917 more than half of Knopf's books had been translated from other languages, and his unfailing commitment to the finest literature of the day meant that his company ultimately had more Nobel Prize-winning authors on its list – seventeen in total – than any other. Alongside Mann (who became a personal friend), its European authors included Knut Hamsun, André Gide, Jean-Paul Sartre, Simone de Beauvoir, Albert Camus and Franz Kafka. The preoccupation with quality, even at the expense of commercial success – 'Knopf intended to publish what he considered to be the best literature whether it sold or not' (Tebbel 1981: 145) – was also evident in the physical design of the books. They featured richly textured paper and carefully designed covers, and were published under a distinctive and uniform borzoi (Russian wolfhound) logo. Knopf gave his series a true corporate identity, and Borzoi books became the most immediately identifiable on the market (Tebbel 1975: 170). They enjoyed acclaim as design objects, purchasable as furnishings or commodities irrespective of the quality of their contents. The elaborate advertising campaigns devised by Knopf served to underpin the link between good visual taste and literary discernment: 'In Knopf advertisements, books became a way of owning and displaying the sense of civilization for which consumers in the United States were searching' (Turner 2003: 89). Skilful marketing through a clear brand identity, extensive and innovative advertising, and the forceful presence of the flamboyant owner ensured that the company secured a unique and highly visible position in the trade. It became synonymous with publishing excellence, and successfully positioned itself as 'an arbiter of cultivated good taste' (Turner 2003: 41). Knopf, whose company became part of Random House in 1960 and remains a leading imprint of that house, became a publishing legend.

The relations between Mann, Knopf and Lowe-Porter have been widely documented in the larger biographies, and recent publications from the Knopf archives have provided much additional detail. However, as Berlin concedes, the new findings 'will not substantially alter the positions advanced in the currently available Mann biographies [...]' (2001: 198). In our context, we are less concerned with the developing personal relations between author, translator and publisher than with those factors which played a salient role in creating the environment for the publication and reception of Thomas Mann through the medium of translation. With respect to the publisher, there are five key areas here: Knopf's marketing strategy for Thomas Mann, his determination to establish and maintain a monopoly on Mann's work in English, his dominant role in the selection of English translators, his interventions in the translation process, and his determination to control Mann's non-literary activities (and thus the public perception of him).

From the very beginnings of his work with Thomas Mann, Knopf devoted particular energy to the creation and cultivation of an image for the author in the USA, consistently promoting him as the 'greatest living German writer', or even the 'world's living greatest author' (1936 copy for *Stories of Three Decades*). He was keen to nurture the notion that Mann's status as a classic author in Germany (and elsewhere in Europe) meant that he had to be read by all discriminating intellectuals, a notion that was underpinned by the author's receipt of the Nobel Prize in 1929. In his advertising copy, Knopf ensured that Mann was consistently mentioned in the same breath as classic writers ('Tell your customers that Thomas Mann occupies a position in Germany today similar to that of Hardy in England or Anatole France in France', Berlin 2005b: 137), and his innovative sales promotion techniques exploited all manner of marketing instruments: lengthy advertisements, flyers, publisher's circulars, information sheets, pocket reader's guides, even instructional guidelines for booksellers. Apart from his profound faith in Mann as a major writer, Knopf's confident promotion of the author was based on his faith in the attractiveness of his own Borzoi brand: 'The Borzoi imprint means a book that leaves an imprint on the mind!' (Berlin 2005b: 140). He injected into his advertising copy a strong element of personal involvement, inviting readers to rely on his literary judgement, and often signing advertisements in his own name. In his publicity activities, Knopf entered into a pseudo-dialogue with the critics, on occasion explicitly countering negative comments that had appeared in reviews. Thus, while affirming the intellectual demands of *The Magic Mountain* which had been stressed by one reviewer, who had complained of the 'incessant ruminations and discussions of a boring young German', Knopf insisted that the book also had a 'mighty undertow of sheer narrative power' (Turner 2003: 99). Nor did he refrain from protesting vociferously against what he saw as unfair press coverage of Mann, complaining personally to editors about negative reviews. Always concerned to sell his books to both the middlebrow and elite markets, he successfully positioned Mann as a highly visible, top-selling author in the USA without compromising his aesthetic integrity. Mann became, in Turner's words, a 'commercially viable highbrow artist' (Turner 2003: 109). So successful was Knopf's promotion of Mann that it became self-perpetuating: from the 1940s onwards, the publisher no longer sent out review copies to the press. His success in marketing Mann, coupled with the meteoric rise of the Knopf house in US publishing, gave Knopf the confidence to assume that his own reputation as a publisher was a major factor in Mann's success in the USA. This placed him, he believed, in a position of equality – at the very least – in his dealings with the author.

Throughout his career, Mann had only one single German publisher and, with minor exceptions, only one publisher in the United States.

There were irritations and tensions in both relationships. In fact, in 1929 Mann went as far as to seek the cancellation of his contractual arrangements with Knopf, a breach which the latter was able to avert by offering improved conditions (letter to Mann of 17 September 1929, Henderson and Oram: 318). Mann subsequently wrote to him: 'I felt I had been treated in a grievous manner in my American business interests, in comparison with other German authors' (letter to Knopf of 2 September 1929, Berlin 1992: 316). At all times, Knopf jealously protected the exclusivity of his relations with Mann, seeking to ward off approaches from other interested parties. In doing so, he did not shy away from the threat of legal action: he informed Lowe-Porter in connection with the aforementioned dispute that he would 'protect our legal rights to Dr Mann's further works to the fullest extent that the courts would allow' (letter to Lowe-Porter of 4 April 1929, Berlin and Herz 1994: 230).Thus Knopf was unwilling to allow Yale University to publish a collection of Mann's essays in 1931, which Mann himself was keen to pursue for financial reasons. When, in 1939, the author was approached by a Dutch publisher who wanted to issue a luxury edition of two essays, Knopf reacted angrily. He blocked a proposed Viking portable edition of selected works in 1947, and was most upset by the publication of a translation of *Das Gesetz* by George Marek in 1943, to which Mann had agreed without consulting him. In keeping with his usual policy, Knopf had the latter text retranslated by Lowe-Porter, and published it in 1945 after protracted negotiations with the original editor and his lawyers. And in 1951, when Beacon Press in Boston approached Mann about publishing a series of lectures, Knopf's reaction was terse and resolute: 'We are still your publishers and if you have a book in mind which you would like to see done over here, for heaven's sake tell me about it and send me the manuscript as soon as it is available' (letter of 16 February 1951, *TB* 9: 382). Knopf had, after all, committed himself in his contract with Fischer to publish books at regular intervals: on occasion, this necessitated the reissue of volumes, or the insertion of collections of occasional essays.

Knopf's dominant role in the selection of translators is most evident in his rejection of Scheffauer as Mann's appointed translator, and in his unfailing loyalty to Lowe-Porter. Despite Mann's concerted efforts between March and June 1925 to secure the services of Scheffauer to translate *Der Zauberberg*, the Knopfs insisted that Lowe-Porter be given the commission. In his determination to establish Lowe-Porter as the English voice of the author, Knopf was actively supported by his wife Blanche, by Mann's American agents Brandt & Brandt, and also by Martin Secker in London. Mann was motivated by unfavourable comment he had heard in connection with the quality of Lowe-Porter's *Buddenbrooks* as well as by his conviction that the masculine complexion of the *Der Zauberberg*, its intellectual complexity, and (it is widely assumed) its homoerotic undertones might be best handled by a male translator. Knopf, on the other hand, had apparently received negative reports on Scheffauer, and was pleased with the response to Lowe-Porter's *Buddenbrooks*. By June 1925 Mann had accepted Knopf's appointment of Lowe-Porter as a fait accompli, and the death of Scheffauer in 1927 closed the chapter completely. After that, Knopf moved quickly to 'cement relations' with Lowe-Porter (Knopf 1975: 4), and insisted that Mann should subsequently express his support for her at all times.

Throughout Mann's career, Knopf retained complete control of the choice of translators. He refused to countenance Scheffauer's widow, Ethel Talbot Scheffauer, as translator of 'Goethe and Tolstoi' and other essays, on which she had continued to work following the death of her husband in 1927. Years later, in 1953, he rejected Mann's suggestion that Lowe's daughter, Frances Fawcett, might undertake the translation of *Die Betrogene*. And the publishers simply commissioned Willard R. Trask and Denver Linley for later translation contracts without any consultation with the author. The only occasion on which Knopf was prepared to give serious consideration to a translator at Mann's suggestion was in the production of *Doctor Faustus*, where he had no objection to Agnes E. Meyer, who had already translated a number of Mann's essays and addresses. Mann spent some time trying to persuade Meyer to take on the work, insisting that she would be the *'ideale Lösung'* and assuring her: *'Dass* you could do the job, *ist mir garkeine Frage* (letter of 6 July 1943, *AEM* 495). She eventually declined in January 1944. Mann accepted her decision reluctantly, having been frustrated in his attempts to find a late replacement for Lowe-Porter, about whom he still had reservations (letter of 13 September 1944, *AEM* 588). However, Knopf retained his innate preference for Lowe-Porter. When Lowe-Porter did finally agree to take on the translation of *Doktor Faustus*, it was apparently under pressure from Knopf (Thirlwall 1966: 105). Once again, then, Knopf had effectively imposed his preference.

In the case of many writers on his books, Knopf undertook interventions in the texts themselves during the editing process. In a 2007 study, Jeremy Munday stresses the ways in which the husband-and-wife publishing team controlled the image of Latin America as presented to audiences via the medium of English translation, making abridgements and generally practising 'blatant editorial interference in the translation process' (Munday 2007: 92). They did so, Munday concludes, in order to 'impose certain genre norms in a bid to maximize the attractiveness of the TT product' (231). In the case of Thomas Mann, there were no such interventions. Indeed, Knopf and his editors appear never to have suggested or made any changes to the texts they received, over and above corrections to spelling and punctuation. The typescripts held in Yale show no more than minimal formal amendments to Lowe-Porter's submitted versions. As Berlin notes: 'a translation review process was never systematically integrated into the production schedule, at least with Thomas Mann's writings' (Berlin 2005b: 144). This is confirmed by the text of the contract Blanche Knopf sent to Denver Lindley for his work on *Felix Krull*. One clause reads: 'It is understood that no further editorial work will have to be done on the typescript which will be ready to go directly into page proofs' (Berlin 2005b: 151).

In terms of the actual constitution of the English texts, then, Lowe-Porter dealt directly with the author himself, and Knopf relied entirely on their collaboration. From the very outset, Mann took a great interest in Lowe-Porter's work, and constantly sought to guide her and improve the quality of her output. In the latter stages of her work on the texts, Lowe-Porter often submitted questions to Mann for clarification. These queries related exclusively to questions of meaning (unknown words, phrases or specialist terms) and cultural references, and were especially frequent during her work on the Joseph novels. Mann invariably obliged. As his letters indicate, he rarely saw her work in manuscript form prior to the publication of the English versions, the major exception being the drafts of *Lotte in Weimar*, which were produced while the two were neighbours in Princeton. Generally, he seemed prepared to rely on the judgment of Blanche Knopf – '*eine belesene und kritische Frau*' (letter to Lowe-Porter of 16 November 1926, Berlin 1992: 307) and her husband: '[...] if you are satisfied, there will be no reason for me to be exacting' (letter to Knopf of 28 March 1951, Winston and Winston 1990: 434). Mann's reaction to the finished product always followed the same pattern, one which was repeated in his letters to his translators into other languages. First, he would bestow copious praise on the translator's achievement, often indulging in hyperbole, before following his laudation with apologetic criticism of details '*ein paar Kleinigkeiten*' (letter to Lowe-Porter of 20 October 1942, *DüD* 2: 265). At the same time, in references to other correspondents he would typically express frustration and embarrassment, at times even seeking to distance himself from his English versions. Thus, an inaccuracy he describes in a letter to Lowe-Porter as a '*winzige Ausstellung*' (letter of 3 October 1948, *DüD* 3: 189) is presented in a message to Agnes E. Meyer a few days later as a '*sonderbare Dummheit*' (letter of 9 October 1948, *AEM* 712).

While Knopf did not seek to influence the composition of the texts, there were areas in which he did intervene to shape Mann's American identity: in the sequence and anthologization of publications, in the choice of the titles under which the works were to appear, and in various paratextual elements. When, for example, Mann wished to publish his Wagner essay as a separate volume (as had been the case in Germany and France), Knopf declined, preferring instead to use it as a key text in the volume *Past Masters* (1933). With Mann's support, Knopf also intervened in Lowe-Porter's proposed foreword to *Doctor Faustus* (Thirlwall 1966: 102–3). The publisher and author were both concerned that Lowe-Porter had overstressed the intellectualism of this novel, which they feared might prove detrimental to sales. More substantively, Mann felt that Lowe-Porter had understated the book's universal relevance as *'ein durchaus internationales, für die Lage der abendländischen Kultur allgemein gültiges Werk'* (letter to Lowe-Porter of 1 April 1948, *DüD* 3: 156). Mann sent her a series of suggestions, and Lowe-Porter amended her essay accordingly. Furthermore, as will be explored in more detail in Chapter 5, Knopf imposed his own ideas in terms of the titles of the works in English. To cite just one example here: in advance of the publication of the omnibus edition of stories in 1936, Mann was keen to have a title which indicated the autobiographical dimension of his works: *'Mir wäre [...] ein Titel am liebsten, der das "Lebensgeschichtliche" der Sammlung betont, also etwas im Sinn vom "Ernte" oder "Lebensernte", aber auch ein Titel, der mit "Füllhorn" oder dergleichen zu tun hätte'* (letter to Knopf of 19 February 1936, Berlin 2001: 203). He proposed a number of titles, including 'A life in stories', or 'A life in fiction' or 'A life in tales'. A correspondence ensued. Knopf, writing on 25 January 1936, was dismissive: 'won't do – please believe me, it isn't possible in English'. In that letter Knopf clearly defines his expectations of titles: 'The most desirable title for a book of this kind is one that is attractive, striking, easy to remember and that doesn't do the contents any violence. Stefan Zweig called his KALEIDOSCOPE. If you can't hit on that kind of a title, the next best, but much less desirable, is a prosaic, descriptive one, as for example, THE SHORTER PROSE FICTION OF THOMAS MANN' (Berlin 2001: 202). In subsequent letters to Lowe-Porter, Thomas Mann and (on one occasion) his wife Katia pursued the matter further. Knopf, under pressure of time, grew impatient and informed Mann on 13 February 1936: 'We have decided to call the Omnibus volume STORIES OF THREE DECADES, which I think is about as good a title as any of us seem able to think up. So that's that' (Berlin 2001: 203). Mann had little choice but to accept.

Knopf's desire to control Mann's public image was further evident in the role he adopted in the author's public activities. The importance of Mann's highly visible persona in US intellectual circles can hardly be underestimated in its impact on the reception of his work. For Wagener, the author's political engagement was one of the fundamental planks of his reputation, alongside the publication of *The Magic Mountain* and the award of the Nobel Prize: these three factors constituted, in Wagener's view, *'die wichtigsten Faktoren für seine Beachtung durch die*

Kritik und, um es gleich hinzuzufügen, auch für die positive Bewertung seiner Werke' (2001: 926). Mann benefited from a wave of political sympathy following his final commitment to the anti-fascist cause in 1936/7, and Knopf carefully exploited and controlled the author's capital as a political commentator. Long before Mann settled in the USA in 1938, Knopf promoted him with the utmost vigour and professionalism, arranging three high-profile visits to the country. He skilfully drew on Mann's growing reputation as the voice of a civilized, anti-fascist Germany, encouraging him to take on interviews, addresses, functions, radio broadcasts and sponsorships, and arranging birthday events and receptions. It was, effectively, Knopf who 'selected' the causes which the author supported. Mann's success as a 'homo politicus' was unprecedented for a foreign intellectual in the United States: he spoke in front of audiences as large as 6,000 (Hayman 1995: 440), and the essay 'The Coming Victory of Democracy' sold more copies in the United States than *Joseph in Egypt* (Heilbut 1995: 568).

Mann, too, was very keen to control the image that was created of him in the mind of the American public, carefully nurturing his democratic credentials and seeking to deflect attention from his pre-1922 nationalist reactionary phase. Thus he refused to allow his treatise *'Betrachtungen eines Unpolitischen'* to be translated into English when Lowe-Porter suggested this in 1932, saying that it contained parts *'die auf das englische Publikum befremdlich wirken müssten'* (letter to Lowe-Porter of 7 June 1932, *DüD* 1: 715). He was equally careful to have his *'Gedanken im Kriege'* (German version 1914) omitted from English anthologies, and did not want *'Friedrich und die große Koalition'* (1914/15) included in *Order of the Day* (1942). Furthermore, he gave extensive consideration, expressed in his letters to Lowe-Porter in 1941/2, to the contents and sequence of essays to be included in the latter volume, and suggested *'tentative Korrekturen'* to her foreword (letter of 16 July 1942, *DüD* 2: 607). Earlier, he had been impressed and moved by Lowe-Porter's foreword to *Past Masters* (1933), since it had stressed the continuity and organic wholeness of his political thinking. At all times, Mann was keen to be seen as a visionary, as an early warning voice against emerging fascism (Thirlwall 1966: 70ff.). He wrote to the editors of the *New York Times* in 1948: 'I belonged to those few who from the beginning recognized in National Socialism the doom of Germany and of Europe' (letter of 31 October 1948, *DüD* 3: 194). In his attempt to influence his reception in the American media, Mann frequently drew Knopf's attention to favourable reviews that might be used in the USA (e.g. in the letters of 20 January 1934, *DüD* 2: 144 and 17 March 1934, Berlin and Herz 1994: 258).

Knopf, meanwhile, was happy for Mann to act as a commentator on European affairs and the voice of anti-fascism, a role he knew could underpin the author's reputation as a leading intellectual, democrat and humanist of the age. Mann had, after all, undergone a major political evolution from conservative monarchist to social-democratic republican. The shift had been signalled in the address '*Von deutscher Republik*' (1922), and was consummated in the 1936 open letter to Korrodi in the *Neue Zürcher Zeitung* (3 February 1936), about which Knopf was highly enthusiastic when he read it in translation in the *New York Times*. He wrote to Mann: 'We might be able to get a little additional publicity for you in some way in connection with this' (16 March 1936, Berlin 2001: 209). He was also delighted by the reception of Mann's letter to the University of Bonn of March 1937, a further anti-fascist statement that had also been published in the United States, and was keen for the essay 'This War' to appear in English in 1940. At the same time, though, Knopf was aware of the volatility of the political climate in the USA. He urged Mann: 'Don't have anything to do with politics – don't write political articles or political pamphlets or make political speeches, or lend your name to political committees or groups, or appear at political dinners. If you stick to this rule you will save yourself endless embarrassment and, I am convinced, sooner or later some really serious difficulty' (letter of 12 December 1939, Berlin 1996: 204). Mann promised in his reply to bear these (prophetic) words in mind, but stressed that he was no longer '*nur ein Dichter*'. He saw his '*moralisch-politisch-kulturelle Denkarbeit*' as the complement to his '*dichterisch-imaginative*' impulse, an integral part of his '*geistige Persönlichkeit und Tätigkeit*' (letter of 28 December 1939, Berlin 1996: 206). He had become a committed intellectual. But Mann's position in the United States was not helped by the fact that, while he continued to wage war against fascism in his writings, he simultaneously saw the need to decry what he regarded as America's rabid anti-communism. Thus it was that the director of the FBI, J. Edgar Hoover, formed the view that Mann had 'communistic inclinations' as early as May 1942 (Vaget 1992: 137), and had an extensive file compiled on the author's activities. Mann began to fear that he might be summoned (like Brecht and Hans Eisler) to appear before the House Committee on Un-American Activities. The cancellation of an address he was scheduled to hold at the Library of Congress in 1950 – it was called off because of the nervousness of the organizers – was a decisive event in his decision to return to Europe (Harpprecht 1995: 1800).

In early 1951 Knopf was shocked when Mann joined a group of eminent figures called 'The American Peace Crusade' in putting his name to an article published in the *New York Times* (1 February 1951). The article called for a ceasefire in Korea and negotiations with the Soviet Union, and attracted much adverse attention. Knopf's alarm was prompted by the fact that a number of notorious American communists, including the singer Paul Robeson, were (unbeknown to Mann) associated with the group. Knopf fumed: 'I cannot imagine any kind of publicity for you which could be more damaging in every single respect, personal and professional, than this – particularly in this time' (letter of 2 February 1951, TB 9: 765). The 'Affaire' and 'smear-story' as Mann called it, caused him a great deal of anxiety and involved him in extensive correspondence, as is well documented in the diaries of the period. Mann acted quickly to defuse the situation, distancing himself from the group and insisting that he would never again sponsor a political movement. He wrote an explanatory letter to the editor of the *New York Times*, and was surprised when it did not appear in print. In fact, it was Knopf – in a dramatic intervention – who had caused Mann's letter to be withdrawn, in consultation with Agnes E. Meyer and New York Times publisher Arthur Hays Sulzberger. Mann notes his '*Erbitterung*' at this blatant intervention in his diary on 14 February 1951, and commented in a letter to Knopf dated 20 February 1951 (TB 9: 386) that the affair had made him 'utterly sick'. 'Never before, to my mind, had I been so miserably treated than I seemed to be during that week,' when he felt he had been 'put under tutelage' (letter to Knopf of 14 February 1951, TB 9: 770). Knopf obviously mistrusted Mann's political judgement. He later advised him: 'Tommy, you are a Dichter and you must dicht!' (quoted in a letter to W. Emrich of 18 January 1954, Reg 4: 273). Throughout Mann's career, and well into the author's relative old age, Knopf sought to influence the environment in which the translations would appear. By promoting and protecting Mann's image as a committed and moderate democrat, he was determined to underpin the author's perceived status as lynchpin of the establishment. Only in this way, he believed, could Mann's image as a highly marketable classic writer in the liberal-humanist tradition be sustained.

Other translators during Mann's lifetime

In the years between the installation of Lowe-Porter as Mann's 'authorized' translator (1927) and her retirement (1951), there was only one exception to her monopoly on the translation of Mann's literary oeuvre. For once acting without consulting Knopf, Mann agreed in 1942 to submit a contribution to an American anthology of texts edited by Armin L. Robinson on the subject of the Ten Commandments (Horton 2010). The function of the anthology was to provide a literary forum for anti-fascist sentiment, and Mann agreed to participate in the venture as a brief distraction following his exhausting work on the Joseph novels. Since Lowe-Porter was working on the final volume of Joseph, Mann sought an alternative translator, and finally settled on George Marek. *Thou Shalt Have No Other Gods Before Me* was the only literary text by Mann that appeared in English first, published by Simon & Schuster in 1943. Knopf had it retranslated by Lowe-Porter for publication as a separate volume on Mann's 70th birthday in 1945. Marek, who was a music critic and later became general manager of RCA Victor, was not an experienced translator, and never worked for Mann again. During the production of the translation, Marek was closely advised by Mann, who commented extensively on the draft version and even proposed alternatives for some 75 specific words and phrases – something he did only very occasionally for Lowe-Porter, whose judgement he seems to have trusted more implicitly. In virtually all cases, Marek adopted Mann's suggestions.

Lowe-Porter informed Mann in the summer of 1953 that she would no longer be available to translate for him, since she wished to devote the remainder of her declining powers to literary ventures of her own (Thirlwall 1966: 131). She therefore declined the commission to take on *Die Betrogene*. She was the last English translator with whom Mann had direct contact. Knopf reports that he 'finally persuaded' Willard R. Trask to accept the assignment for the latter story: 'He had a considerable reputation as a translator – a reputation we found he fully deserved' (Knopf 1975: 8). Trask was, indeed, an established translator, having rendered into English all twelve volumes of Casanova's monumental autobiography (from French), many of Mircea Eliade's works on the history of religion (also from French), individual works by Goethe, and Erich Auerbach's classic *Mimesis*. He was chosen without any consultation with Mann (letter from Knopf to Mann of 10 October 1953, *TB* 10: 508). Mann commented in his diary on 10 October 1953: '*Kontrakt von Knopf über die "Betrogene", für die ein Übersetzer namens Willard Trask gewählt.*' The text appeared as *The Black Swan* in 1954.

Finally, in 1954, Lowe-Porter contacted Mann again in the hope of resuming her work for him, and expressed an interest in taking on what was to be the last work published in his lifetime, *Die Bekenntnisse des Hochstaplers Felix Krull*. Despite Mann's apparent relief at her decision, he soon had to inform her that she was too late: Knopf, not having heard from Lowe-Porter 'in any way whatever' (letter to Mann of 15 September 1954, *TB* 10: 674), had already made arrangements (letter from Mann to Lowe-Porter of 18 September 1954, Thirlwall 143). He confirmed that he had commissioned Denver Lindley, 'an old friend who had much experience as an editor for more than one distinguished publishing house' (Knopf 1975: 8), Lindley had translated Maurois and Remarque into English, and was, at various times, a respected editor with Henry Holt, Harcourt Brace and Viking.

Translations and retranslations since 1955

Since Mann's death in 1955, a number of his works have appeared in English for the first time. The bulk of the new material is non-fictional in character, and has been motivated by the desire to make key secondary sources available to an English-speaking readership. Thus, Richard and Clara Winston, who became Knopf's preferred Thomas Mann translators after the author's death, translated *Last Essays* in 1959 (with Tania and James Stern), *The Story of a Novel: The Genesis of Doctor Faustus* in 1961, and *Letters of Thomas Mann 1889–1955* in 1970, all of which were published by Knopf, as well as *Thomas Mann: Diaries 1918–39* (published by Harry N. Abrams/New York, 1982). As he explains in his essay 'On translating Thomas Mann' (Winston 1975: 17), Richard Winston had cherished 'dreams of glory' following his first renditions of sections of Mann's diaries in 1946–47, and had hoped to be appointed as Mann's regular English translator following Lowe-Porter's retirement. He was working on a major biography of Mann at the time of his death in 1979, and that volume was published in incomplete form, also by Knopf, as *Thomas Mann: The Making of an Artist* in 1981.

Other material which appeared for the first time in English subsequent to Mann's death includes *The Letters of Heinrich and Thomas Mann, 1900–1949*, translated by Don Reneau (University of California Press, 1998) and *Reflections of a Nonpolitical Mann*, translated, with an introduction, by Walter D. Morris (New York: Frederick Ungar Publishing, 1983). The only new literary work to appear for the first time in English since 1955 has been *Six Early Stories*, translated by Peter Constantine and published in 1997 by Sun & Moon Press, Los Angeles. According to the publisher's cover notes, this anthology, which was awarded the PEN/Book-of-the-Month Club Translation Prize in 1999, was released to fill a gap: the earlier omnibus edition *Stories of Three Decades* had 'purposely excluded several early tales of Mann'. It was also designed to offer readers the opportunity to discover a new Mann: 'Readers who enjoy the older Mann's forceful writing, his controlled style and rhythm, will find the twists and turns in the younger writer's prose a refreshing surprise' ('Translator's note', p. 25).

Even during Thomas Mann's lifetime, a number of his works were translated into English more than once. In most cases, as we have seen, the new versions were prepared by Lowe-Porter on instruction from Knopf. The process by which Knopf had works retranslated within a relatively short space of time of their original publication in English – sometimes to Mann's surprise (see his letter of 16 November 1926 on *Death in Venice*) – illustrates one of the key motivations underlying retranslation as a literary phenomenon: the impulse on the part of publishers to forge a coherent target-language identity for authors on their books through a consistent translating voice. This, coupled with an apparently unshakable faith in Lowe-Porter's abilities, prompted Knopf to have her retranslate, for example, all the texts contained in

Burke's *Death in Venice* volume and in Scheffauer's *Children and Fools*. Comparisons between the various versions of the texts are instructive, and shed an interesting light on competing conceptions of translation. Thus there are striking differences between the Lowe-Porter and Marek versions of *Das Gesetz* in terms of lexical innovativeness and literalism (Horton 2010), although the translations were separated by a period of only two years. Lindley's 1955 retranslation of the first forty pages of *Felix Krull* (which had been included as a fragment in Lowe-Porter's version in *Stories of Three Decades* in 1936) reads very differently from the first published version in terms of the modernity of the diction employed. And in the case of the only text to be translated three times during Mann's lifetime, *Tonio Kröger*, there are also interesting divergences between the Morgan, Burke and Lowe-Porter versions, which were separated by some 20 years.

By far the most ambitious project in terms of the retranslation of Thomas Mann's works was the publication of new versions of seven of the novels, including the entire Joseph tetralogy, by Alfred A. Knopf (Random House) in the years 1993 to 2005, in translations by John E. Woods. The American Woods (born 1942) is a celebrated and award-winning translator from German into English. The motivation behind the decision to have the novels reworked was, according to personal information provided by the translator, twofold. One consideration was purely commercial: the publisher was keen to exploit the remaining term of its exclusive copyright which it holds until 2025, and to stimulate demand for Mann's books by launching new versions of texts. In his 2002 essay entitled 'A Matter of Voice' (Woods 2002), Woods comments that if a new translation 'establishes itself in the marketplace, you can effectively scare off competitors once the copyright runs out in another decade or so' (86). In its promotional activities – as expressed for example in cover notes – the company thus stresses the newness of the Woods' versions. The new *Buddenbrooks* is heralded as a 'major Literary Event [capitals in the original]: a brilliant new translation of Thomas Mann's first great novel' and on the cover of the Joseph volume we read: 'This remarkable new translation of the Nobel Prize-winner's great masterpiece is a major literary event [...] a definitive new English version of *Joseph and His Brothers* that is worthy of Mann's achievement.' The other, connected, motivation was the publisher's awareness that more modern, more accurate and more faithful versions of Mann's novels were needed for a contemporary readership. Sales of the Lowe-Porter versions translations were, according to the publisher, steady but modest, and remain so to this day (they are still available). Woods is aware of the commercial motive here, too: 'There is also money to be had by ensuring that a title on your backlist gets a solid new translation to replace a questionable old one' (86). Woods was instated as the 'in-house' translator for Knopf, devoting himself full-time to the Mann novels over a number of years.

Woods provides paratextual information in the form of notes or prefaces only for the Joseph novels. But his translation strategy, as he has pointed out in personal communications and in various interviews, is to combine a higher level of accuracy than that achieved by Lowe-Porter with a greater fidelity to the structures of Mann's German, thus attaining enhanced felicity in terms of the aesthetic experience offered to the modern (American) reader. His versions avoid conscious archaisms and anachronisms, what he calls Lowe-Porter's 'purplish prose' (Woods 2002: 86), while seeking to suggest a historical flavour. As Woods points out (personal communication), his versions do enter into a dialogue with Lowe-Porter as a reference point. He consulted her texts at regular intervals, and occasionally adopted her solutions when they met his criteria. But his translations were conceived as explicit alternatives to her versions, and in his 2002 essay (written at a time when he was still working on the Joseph novels) he singles out six features of her work on which his own versions – by implication – seek to improve: prudishness, lack of humour, odd diction, turgid syntax, obfuscation of leitmotifs, and a 'tin ear' for irony. These issues will inevitably form the focus of much of the following discussion.

Since Mann's death, then, all his key works have been retranslated, in some cases more than once. This confirms the frequently voiced observation that canonical texts of all literatures are rendered anew for each generation of foreign readers. While original texts remain eternally 'young' (Berman 1990), translations age and lose their acceptability to the target culture as expectations, tastes and conventions change. But 'aging' is only one possible motivation for the re-working of texts that already exist in the target culture, and recent work on the phenomenon of retranslation has highlighted a number of other contributory factors. All of these apply in the case of Thomas Mann, whose oeuvre serves in this sense too as a highly apposite illustration of the processes of intercultural exchange.

Retranslations reveal the changing norms and ideologies in society, and in a large number of cases are implicitly triggered by those changing norms and cultural expectations as they develop diachronically. As Venuti writes: 'The retranslator's intention is to select and interpret the foreign text according to a different set of values so as to bring about a new and different reception for that text in the translating culture' (Venuti 2004: 29). Such differences are, inevitably, most substantive in the case of translations separated by a significant period of time. Historically oriented translation research has focused on shifts in literary, linguistic and translational norms in corpora of translated works as they have developed over centuries. But even over shorter historical distances, major divergences can be observed. In one central respect, the fortunes of Mann in English confirm a common (though by no means uncontested) assumption that has become known as the 'retranslation hypothesis' (Brownlie 2006). It has frequently been noted that first translations typically display a target-oriented orientation, suppressing the alterity of the source text in a concern to enhance readability for recipients in the host culture (Berman 1990; Gambier 1994). They do so by 'smoothing' the translation in a number of ways, e.g. by reducing semantic implicitness and suppressing lexical novelty and variety, transposing syntactic structures to bring them into line with target-culture norms, reducing redundancies, obscuring recurrences and loosening structurally cohesive relations, normalizing exotic features, etc. In doing so, they accommodate the text to the taste and habits of the target readership. Many of these features, as we shall see, characterize the work of Lowe-Porter in comparison with her successors. If there is one common denominator in the many retranslations of Mann's texts produced over the years, it has been increased attention to the style of the source texts. As a number of the more recent translators comment, their versions are expressly conceived as an alternative to existing translations, to which they refer in translator's notes. Here, too, a feature of retranslation as a literary phenomenon is evident: retranslations are a projection not only of the source-language original from which they are derived, but also stand in a relation of tension and even competition vis-à-vis pre-existing target-language versions. The latter dialogic relation can on occasion shine through in the new version: translators may adopt or adapt solutions from an earlier translation, or purposely amend them to a drastic degree in a search for innovativeness.

A case study in retranslation: Deaths in Venice

The clearest illustration of the modalities of retranslation in Mann's oeuvre is his classic novella, *Death in Venice*. Given the sheer scale of Mann's novels, publishers have typically opted to commission retranslations of his short prose fiction. The resulting availability of short texts from leading publishers is no doubt one reason why Mann is best known for his novellas and stories in the English-speaking world. A number of common features emerge from a consideration of the broader environment surrounding these retranslations. All the retranslators have been highly experienced mediators of texts from German and, in some cases, from other European languages. Furthermore, they share a common educational background: of the six producers of the more modern versions, all have academic qualifications in languages and literatures, and four have been university scholars working in the field of literary study. In all cases, their texts are accompanied by paratextual material in the form of translator's notes, commentaries and explanatory footnotes. While translators' (usually retrospective) remarks on the principles and methods underlying their work cannot always be considered reliable, the comments they provide in respect of Mann's short prose fiction illustrate all the typical reasons for the re-rendition of existing texts, and offer interesting information on the background to their genesis. In all cases, *Death in Venice* has been the central text, providing the title of each of the three anthologies in which it appears alongside other works. It is, indeed, true to say that the Venice story has been the most important text in the English-speaking reception of Mann since his death. Widely viewed as a masterpiece in its own right, its reception has been aided by Britten's opera and Visconti's film, and by the fact that it has featured as the key point of reference in the context of Mann's homoeroticism since the publication of the diaries.

The motivations for the retranslations are numerous, and can best be generalized with reference to the impetus from which they are derived. Thus the impulse for a new version can come from publishers who wish to include works from the classical canon in their catalogues. The motivation here is the prestige associated with the publication of texts that enjoy cultural authority, as well as the relative inexpensiveness of releasing books which are no longer in copyright. These are commercial considerations, and in such cases publishers are invariably at pains to stress the 'newness' of their versions as a key selling point: the texts considered below are thus advertised as a 'superb new translation', 'acclaimed new translation', 'excellent new translation'. As a result, retranslations of Thomas Mann's short fiction feature in the catalogues of a number of leading general publishers: Penguin, Signet, Bantam, Dover, Norton and HarperCollins. On other occasions, in response to developments in the academy, publishers can elect to release critical annotated versions which appeal to the student market. This can be assumed to have been the motivation behind the first republication of a work by Thomas Mann to appear after the author's death. In 1970, a revised edition of *Death in Venice* was released as one of the final volumes in the successful 'Modern Library' series (College Editions) 'by arrangement with Alfred A. Knopf Inc.' It appears to have been prompted by the key position Mann had gained in university comparative literature courses, and formed part of an inexpensive paperback series designed for student use. For reasons which are not clear, it offers a (substantially) 'revised edition' of the Burke translation rather than the Lowe-Porter version which was established at the time. There is no indication as to who revised the text, which is accompanied by an extensive essay by Erich Heller. In the academic market, publishers can also opt to provide full scholarly volumes. The edition prepared by Clayton Koelb in 1994 forms part of the 'Norton Critical Editions Series'. It is an academic edition of a translation prepared by Koelb himself, which is extensively 'annotated for undergraduate readers', and is accompanied by 'contextual and source materials, and a wide range of critical interpretations' (series cover notes). The materials are translated by Lynda Hoffmann-Jeep and John Jeep

The impulse behind a retranslation can also come from translators themselves, who wish to provide their own renderings of texts, and approach publishers on their own initiative. Their reasons for doing so can include material considerations, their personal appreciation of the source text, their desire to address a particular challenge, or – more fundamentally – their conviction that they can make a difference (retranslation as improvement). The latter motivation is evident in the work of David Luke (1970 and 1988). He justifies his edition of Mann's stories on the basis of transfer-oriented considerations which play a central part in retranslation, i.e. perceived deficiencies in existing translations in terms of their accuracy and felicity as representations of the source text. Luke's versions were explicitly motivated by what he saw as the 'very poor quality' of Lowe-Porter's versions (Luke 1988: xlv), and he includes in his introduction an extensive catalogue of errors designed to illustrate 'the linguistic inadequacy of the hitherto accepted sole mediator of Mann's collected works to the English-reading public' (xlv–xlvi). More discussion of Luke's work is included elsewhere in this study (Introduction, Chapter 8). His aims were, he asserts, twofold. Alongside the primary objective of correcting errors in the existing versions ('trying to be more accurate'), he also sought to bring his translations more into line stylistically within the German originals, i.e. to 'reflect, so far as is possible in English, the complexity of Mann' prose' (xlvi), which, in his view, Lowe-Porter had manifestly failed to do. These twin motivations of correction and enhanced stylistic fidelity have long been central considerations in retranslation. The latter consideration is also relevant in the case of Neugroschel's 1998 version. In view of the discrepancies between source and target languages, he claims that he has created 'a special brand of English […] stretching limits in order to convey the music and meaning of the original style' (xv). This translator goal is a response to changes in prevailing conceptions of translation: 'stretching limits' has not always been considered a legitimate translation strategy, and is associated with changes in general literary norms and values in the target culture. Developing translational norms appear to demand new versions of old texts at regular intervals. As we shall see in the next chapter, Lowe-Porter's approach to the issue of translation was very much in line with the spirit of her age, which has since changed significantly.

A further motor in the publication of new translations can be perceived deficiencies in the literary quality of existing versions. In his introduction to his 1999 version, Chase stresses the complexity of Mann's style, and draws special attention to the necessity of syntactic transpositions and lexical shifts due to 'inexact vocabulary equivalents' (xvi). His aim is to provide a more faithful and felicitous representation of the original. But his ultimate goal is ambitious: 'to allow the contemporary American reader to experience Mann much as a contemporary German reader would' (xvi). Other translators are more modest in their aims: aware that it is impossible to achieve an aesthetic substitution of the original, they seek to provide access to the text rather than to provide a target-language replacement for it. Thus, in translation-theoretical terms, Koelb's version does not seek to emulate the status of the original by striving for a similar level of literary acceptability. The translator explicitly states that his text 'does not strive to be "poetic" in the sense of offering the translator's notion of high style' (vii). Instead, it is offered as a text for use in comparative literature courses. Appelbaum makes the same point. His 1995 translation of the same text also contains metatextual material: a 'Note', 'A Word about the Translation', 'Commentary' and annotations. It enters into a specific dialogue with existing versions, from which it seeks to differentiate itself: Burke's is described as 'serviceable and neatly expressed [...] but vitiated by a large number of careless errors and hilarious misapprehensions' (63); Lowe-Porter's as 'by far the most delightful and readable' of those consulted, but 'at great cost to completeness and a true representation of the original' (64); and Luke's is hailed as 'scrupulously accurate' but 'a little stiff and stuffy' (64). Appelbaum modestly describes his own translation as an 'analytic translation' rather than a 'truly new synthesis', i.e. as an entry point for foreign readers rather than as a text of equal value. However, he does seek a level of fidelity that might 'communicate to the reader of the English the same impression of architectural stateliness or flickering nervousness that a German reader derives from threading his way through the labyrinthine sentences of the original' (64).

New versions can be prompted by impulses which emanate from the receptive context of the target culture and which are articulated by readers, critics or academics. These come in many forms. One is the relatively straightforward textual issue of the availability of a revised source text, something which does not apply in the case of Thomas Mann. Another is the desire to restore a complete and authentic text after expurgated versions have appeared in the target culture. Neugroschel's 1998 anthology of short prose texts seems motivated primarily by the intention to provide an updated version for the Penguin series. However, it also promises in its cover notes a further innovation, highlighting the somewhat exaggerated claim that it 'restores the controversial passages censored from the original English version' of *Death in Venice*. What these are is not made clear.

A further motivating factor in retranslation is a reinterpretation of the text, i.e. a divergent conception of the meaning of the source text. All literary texts, after all, have the potential for reinterpretation, and a translation encapsulates one individual reading. Processes of interpretation draw on the previous reception of the texts in question, and can also benefit from the growing scholarship surrounding the text and its author. Heim's 2004 version of *Death in Venice* appears to have been motivated not by a concern with enhanced accuracy or stylistic fidelity, but in the first instance by the publisher's desire to have a superior version of the text in literary terms: 'the editor who asked me to retranslate *Death in Venice* had only one end in mind: he had read that the original is a paragon of German prose and he had failed to find a paragon of English prose among the contending translations' (Heim 2008: 79). But Heim is motivated by a further consideration: the desire to embody a re-reading of the text, and in particular of its protagonist. In a lecture entitled 'A Life in Translation' held in 2009, Heim included among his 'principles of translation' the notion that a translation is always a new interpretation. He stressed that the literary articulation of a new view of the text, which has not come out in existing translations and which can be activated by the retranslator ('you can make it come out'), is a legitimate reason for a retranslation (Heim 2009, no page number). Heim stresses in a 2008 article that a retranslation serves a different function from an original translation due to 'the very fact that a work is deemed worthy of a new translation' (Heim 2008: 77). The cover notes to his text confirm this motivation: citing the extensive introduction to the volume by Michael Cunningham, they claim: 'By fine-tuning certain details, by reconsidering word choices, Heim's translation achieves a startling effect. It rescues Aschenbach from the realm of the cautionary and places him where he belongs, in the pantheon of fictive men and women whose impossible yearnings make them as deeply human as characters can be.' The motivation here is innovation: 'Michael Henry Heim's new translation of Death in Venice subtly but clearly extends and alters previous translations' (viii). In Cunningham's view, Aschenbach now emerges as a heroic rather than as a foolish character, a man struggling heroically against decay and degeneration. 'That may or may not be exactly what Mann had in mind. There's no way of knowing. But it is, for my purposes at least, the grander and more human book that Mann meant to give us all along' (xvii).

Finally, the new versions of Mann's texts confirm a further common impulse behind the process of retranslation: the desire to combat the aging process of texts by amending style and diction in line with changes in the linguistic expectations of the target readership. Thus, while Lowe-Porter is often castigated for cultivating an antiquated style, Chase strives for 'temporal neutrality' (xvi), and Neugroschel seeks to avoid a 'retro' translation (vii). At the same time, the language of translation can be brought into line with the norms of a regional variety: thus most of the translations discussed above are cast in a linguistic form that will be familiar to a contemporary American readership. To cite just one example: Koelb seeks 'to offer North American students a text that strives to stay as close to Mann's German as one can without straining the norms of American English' (vii). The extent to which these various versions succeed in achieving their objectives can only be revealed, of course, by close analysis.

Conclusion

Mann's work has achieved enormous success in English, and to this day the author has retained his position as a central figure in European literary history of the twentieth century. Carefully guided and promoted by Knopf, and translated by Lowe-Porter into an English that was generally well-received, Mann established an unrivalled position among foreign writers in the USA, securing his reputation as a writer of world-literary importance. Even before he moved to the USA, Turner comments, Knopf's marketing efforts had borne fruit: 'Knopf's promotions were so successful that once Mann moved to the United States in 1938, people throughout the country saw him as an American author' (Turner 2003: 97). By the mid-1940s, Mann had achieved both fame and material security. The success of *Joseph the Provider* (published in 1944) had brought him a measure of financial independence, and enabled him to relinquish the various sinecures that had been arranged for him. The regular selection of his works by the Book-of-the-Month Club guaranteed high levels of sales. In 1947 he took second place after George Bernard Shaw in an international poll among 3,000 authors, critics, editors and librarians to find the 'best writer' (proudly referred to in his diary entry of 23 October 1947). In the same year, he was the subject of a major celebratory volume featuring contributions by some sixty eminent persons from the world of arts, entitled *The Stature of Thomas Mann* and edited by the well-known scholar, novelist and essayist Charles Neider. The editor of that volume stresses the scale of Mann's impact in the USA: 'Mann has the distinction of simultaneously appealing to the person of esoteric leanings as well as to the general reader' (Neider 1947: 11). Mann had indeed succeeded in bridging the gulf between the high- and middle-brow markets, and was instrumental in rehabilitating the reputation of German literature in America. Koepke writes: 'There was one point where the interests of academics, the New York liberals, and the public at large coincided: Thomas Mann's work, specifically *The Magic Mountain*. [...] His American prestige went well beyond the usual idea of the reception of literature'

(Koepke 1992: 97). In all these achievements, as Mann himself was well aware, the work of Helen Tracy Lowe-Porter had played a key role. As he was at pains to stress in two articles published in *Time Magazine* (20 June 1944) and *PM Daily* (6 July 1945), she was the pillar of his reputation in the USA. In Britain, by contrast, his reception throughout his lifetime remained much less positive, a fact he frequently bemoaned (see, for example, his letter to his UK publisher Frederic J. Warburg of 11 October 1954, *Reg* 4: 333).

Since his death in 1955, Mann's stock in English has fared in much the same way as it has in the German-speaking world (Wagener 2001; Kurzke 2010). The author remains a central part of the literary canon, but interest in him is more widespread in educational-academic circles than it is among the general readership. Despite a resurgence in attention following the publication of the diaries from 1977 onwards, sales figures in both language communities in recent years show that he has been overtaken by writers of a more overtly modernist bent, such as Kafka. This observation is underlined by readers' blogs and the activities of reading groups. However, the Random House decision to have Mann's major novels retranslated by John E. Woods has certainly served to revive interest in the author's work in the English-speaking world, further underpinning the interest that had been sustained by a steady supply of retranslations of his shorter texts, especially *Death in Venice*, from the 1980s onwards. The near universal acclaim that has greeted Woods' more modern versions of the texts has drawn new readers to the author, whose *Magic Mountain* was recently celebrated in the pages of the British *Guardian* newspaper as an enduring classic ('a modernist classic, a traditional bildungsroman, a comedy of manners, an allegory of pre-war bourgeois Europe, and […] the ideal book to keep you company on the long winter nights'). Mann's novel is heralded, in Woods' version, as a work strikingly in touch with the spirit of the contemporary age: 'a work of sick-lit par excellence'. The reviewer discovers in the new version 'a lucid prose-style and readability' which does supreme justice to 'simply one of the greatest novels ever written' (Wooderham 2011). Thus a reputation which was most effectively established in the English-speaking world by the efforts of Helen Tracy Lowe-Porter has been sustained, and in part revived, by retranslations, which continue to this day. At the end of 2010, a new version of Mann's *Das Gesetz* was published in the United Kingdom. The motivation for the retranslation of the text, by Marion Faber and Stephen Lehmann, was one noted earlier in this chapter. The translators state their aim of being true to 'Mann's identity as a writer' via a close attention to his 'stylistic elements', which include 'wordplay and puns, archaic formulations and neologisms', and in which 'a unique tone, both erudite and arch, dignified and playful' is seen as central

(Faber and Lehmann 2010: 5). The version was greeted in the *London Review of Books* (Alter 2010: 23) as 'brisk and direct [...] a welcome replacement of the fussier and less accurate version done by Helen Lowe-Porter', while the *Boston Globe* concluded that it 'can rank with the best of Mann's writing' (cover notes). As such responses demonstrate, new translations of Mann's work continue to act as a stimulus to the renewal of interest in the author.

3 Helen Tracy Lowe-Porter, Thomas Mann and the practice of translation

Introductory remarks

Discussions of the views on translation voiced by Thomas Mann and his established translator, Helen Tracy Lowe-Porter, have typically exhausted themselves in the most cursory of overviews. Commentators have been keen to stress that neither the author nor his translator ever produced a sustained discourse on the subject, and they have generally relied on a small number of apodictic utterances to underpin what is seen as an essential discrepancy between two underdeveloped views of the translator's task (e.g. Buck 2002: 236; Gledhill 2007: 12). Thus Lowe-Porter's comment in her preface to *Buddenbrooks* that she had set herself the task of 'transferring the spirit first and the letter so far as might be' is frequently quoted as evidence of a rather unreflective commitment to a 'free' approach to translation. And Mann's statement in a letter to his translator dated 9 August 1926 that he favoured *'eine so wörtliche und genaue Wiedergabe, als es die fremde Sprache nur irgend gestattet'* is commonly cited to substantiate the notion that he inclined towards a more 'literal' form of transfer (*DüD* 1: 520). However, the isolation of these two comments as representative of competing conceptions of translation is problematic. Lowe-Porter's remark stands in the preface to her very first Thomas Mann translation, which was to be followed by dozens of further renditions over the following twenty-seven years. To draw conclusions on the basis of her first engagement with Mann's work is to suggest that her view of translation was not refined during her production of thousands of pages over the subsequent decades. Mann's comment, on the other hand, was made specifically in the context of an individual translation problem – that of Mynheer Peeperkorn's idiosyncratic diction in *The Magic Mountain* – and can hardly be regarded as his last word on more general issues of translation.

In fact the matter is more complex than such apparently conflicting statements suggest, and the real tensions lie elsewhere. Mann was highly ambivalent on the issue of translation, being torn between an idealized notion of translation as productive cross-cultural transplantation on the one hand and an acute awareness of the very real limitations faced by translators (and not just by Lowe-Porter) on the other. This was a contradiction which much preoccupied him, and which he never fully resolved. His extensive dealings with his translators, as we shall see, testify to a constant tension between highly demanding standards of textual accuracy and a surprisingly pragmatic and cavalier attitude towards the everyday activity of translation. Many of his recommendations and suggestions on the actual practice of translation contrast starkly with his loftier pronouncements on translation as an inspired re-creative exercise. Indeed, he was not averse to having large parts of his texts excised completely for the purposes of translation, a fact which has eluded many critics who have complained about unwarranted omissions and incomplete versions. Lowe-Porter, for her part, was inevitably preoccupied first and foremost with the more practical task of finding solutions to specific and often intractable translation problems, very often under considerable time pressure. It was her experience in dealing with Mann's complex texts that led her to formulate, sporadically rather than systematically, her views on the activity of translation. In order to shed a fuller light on the interaction between Mann and his translator at the level of translation poetics, it is necessary to explore their pronouncements in greater detail. While it is true that neither of them ever engaged in extensive deliberations on translation, we can arrive at a more sophisticated definition of their views by examining both explicit (metatextual) and implicit (intratextual) sources.

Lowe-Porter: 'a portrait, not a photograph'

As she points out in her essay 'On translating Thomas Mann', Lowe-Porter brought to the translation of *Buddenbrooks*, which she began in 1923, a limited amount of experience in translating. She had hitherto undertaken renditions from French, producing a version of Bulteau's *L'Âme des Anglais* for the Loeb classics series in 1912, and had translated plays by Sudermann and Hauptmann from the German. The latter had appeared in *Poet Lore*, the journal founded and edited in Boston by her aunt, the Shakespeare editor Charlotte Endymion Porter. Born into a Pennsylvanian family in 1876, Lowe-Porter had grown up in an intellectually stimulating environment and was introduced to literature and the arts at an early age. She became more widely exposed to literary affairs while assisting her aunt on her literary journal after graduating from Wells College, Aurora (NY) in 1898. During a fifteen-month stay in Germany in 1906–7, during which she learned German, she met her later husband, the palaeographer Elias Avery

Lowe. After they were married in 1911, she moved with her husband to Oxford (1913) and Princeton (1937) as his career progressed. In the latter university environment she had intensive contact with the circle of German exiles including Albert Einstein, Hermann Broch, Theodor Adorno, Erich von Kahler and, from 1938 onwards, Thomas Mann. She was known throughout her life for her passionate interest in literature and her outspoken liberal views. Apart from Thomas Mann, she later went on to translate work by other German-speaking authors, including Bruno Frank, Lion Feuchtwanger, Franz Werfel, Hermann Broch and Arthur Schnitzler.

The tenor of Lowe-Porter's approach to translation can be reconstructed from a number of sources. Virtually all of her letters are lost, but Thomas Mann's surviving correspondence with her allows us to reconstruct parts of the dialogue that took place between them during the years of their collaboration, as do entries in his diaries. Some 130 letters by Mann to Lowe-Porter are held in the Beinecke Rare Book and Manuscript Library at Yale, along with 28 others from his wife Katia. There is still no published edition of the correspondence between Mann and his translator, but many of the letters between them have been made available, in translated and abridged form, in Thirlwall's biography *In Another Language* (Thirlwall 1966). Written by a close friend of the translator, this book has often been criticized for its hagiographical stance towards its subject, and it certainly celebrates Lowe-Porter's life and achievement with an almost complete lack of critical distance. It can, it is true, hardly claim to be a fully researched or documented academic study (Lehnert 1969: 97). But it does contain pertinent reminiscences, and quotes letters which remain unpublished elsewhere to this day. In its chronological structure, it provides a somewhat fragmented view of Lowe-Porter's ideas, and fails to construct from her correspondence anything approaching a coherent view of translation. The following discussion seeks to remedy this omission, referring extensively to the sources provided by Thirlwall and others in an attempt to extract from them the principles underlying Lowe-Porter's approach to Mann's texts. Further information is contained in Lowe-Porter's letters to Knopf, a few of which are also quoted in Thirlwall (henceforth referred to as T), in the various compilations prepared by Berlin (Berlin 1992, 1994, 1996, 2001, 2005a, 2005b: henceforth quoted as B), and in Henderson and Oram (2010). Berlin's compilations are an invaluable resource, citing large numbers of hitherto unavailable letters between the three which are now held in the Alfred A. Knopf records collection at the University of Texas at Austin. However, the majority of these focus on issues relating to the publication history rather than to the textual composition of the English versions. Further comment on Lowe-Porter's aims and procedures is provided in the prefaces she appended to a number of her translations. And finally, her essay 'On translating Thomas Mann' (written in 1950 but first published in full in Thirlwall's volume) offers an overview of her activities as Mann's translator. This essay is historical-biographical rather than conceptual in design. In it, the translator traces her career as Mann's mediator, and provides comment on translational issues only as a postscript to the story of her career: 'This is probably the best place to set down a few comments on technical problems' (T: 199). All of her metatextual comments, of course, are to be treated with the caution that must be afforded to all a posteriori self-commentary by translators.

In her various references to the activity of translation, Lowe-Porter mentions the names of contemporary translators only in passing: Scott Moncrieff, the famous translator of Proust, and Constance Garnett and Aylmer Maude, celebrated translators from Russian. But her comment that 'there has been little written on the craft of translation' (T: 203), and especially 'about the translation of modern [tongues]' (T: 57), indicates that she was not familiar with the broader debate going on at the time: these were, after all, the years during which Ezra Pound, Vladimir Nabokov, Walter Benjamin, I. A. Richards, Jose Ortega y Gasset and Benedetto Croce were elaborating their ideas on translation theory (for useful overviews see Kelly 1979; Steiner 1992; Venuti 2008). It was a period which George Steiner, in his major historical survey, calls an 'age of philosophic-poetic theory and definition' in the field of translation (Steiner 1992: 249). At that time, major issues of translation poetics, such as the question of translatability, the relative capacity of languages to express ideas, the connection between language and thought, and hermeneutic avenues of enquiry were being explored within an epistemology of translation in the post-Romantic tradition. It was also an age during which the tension between foreignizing and domesticating conceptions of translation, to adapt Schleiermacher's terms, was becoming acute. On the one hand, the translator's sense of responsibility towards the foreignness of the original text, i.e. the valorization of the foreign, was growing (Ezra Pound). On the other, the primacy of the target culture was still being passionately upheld by writers such as Hilaire Belloc. As a well-read individual, Lowe-Porter was undoubtedly generally aware of the currents of thought prevalent at the time. Indeed, her comment on the relative importance of 'spirit' and 'letter' in respect of *Buddenbrooks* echoes in both sentiment and formulation Belloc's distinction, first published in the same year as Lowe-Porter's version of Mann's debut novel (1924): 'Good translation [...] must consciously attempt the spirit of the original at the expense of the letter' (quoted here from Belloc 1931: 153). In her metatexts, though, she refers only in passing to scholars who wrote on translation theory: Hilaire Belloc and George Moore 'are all I can recall just now', she wrote to Knopf on 11 November 1943 (T: 57). She appears to have undertaken her work as a translator in virtual isolation from the current discourse on the subject.

Indeed, in the aforementioned letter Lowe-Porter deliberately plays down the relevance of theoretical discourse on translation, perhaps as a defence against potential charges of theoretical naiveté or ignorance. She advances a consciously obscurantist, atheoretical view of the translation process, drawing a line between the 'real' translator and an implied over-theoretical counterpart: 'The "*Kleinkunst*" of translation is, I think, like all art, a "mystery" in the guild sense; and all real translators have their own notions about how it should be practised.' Translation is presented here as an individualistic enterprise in the pre-scientific tradition: an acquired craft ('mystery' in its archaic sense of a trade or occupation) practised by initiates and, by implication, inaccessible to those outside the guild. Where Lowe-Porter does provide comment on the issue of translation in general, she does so in the most universal terms. Indeed, she frequently approaches the central conundrum of translation as she sees it – the dichotomy of what today would be described as source-oriented versus target-oriented impulses – through the vehicle of metaphor, a device which has a long tradition in anecdotal approaches to the subject (Round 2005). She opens her 'Translator's note' to *Doctor Faustus*, for example, with a popular quotation from the tradition of *'traduttore, traditore'*: *'Les traductions sont comme les femmes: lorsqu'elles sont belles, elles ne sont pas fidèles, et lorsqu'elles sont fidèles, elles ne sont pas belles.'* In the foreword to her *Magic Mountain* she echoes Shelley's famous words in the *Defense of Poetry* on 'the curse of Babel', with its metaphor of the violet and the crucible: 'It were as wise to cast a violet into a crucible that you might discover the formal principle of its colour and odour, as seek to transfuse from one language into another the creations of a poet.' In all her utterances (as in her comments on *Buddenbrooks* above), she places her work within the ancient polarity of spirit and letter, aligning herself with the Jeromian tradition of sense-for-sense translation rather than word-for-word rendition. She thus subscribes to the tenet of 'non verbum e verbo, sed sensum exprimere de sensu', which can be traced back to Cicero and has completely dominated the history of translation theory (Steiner 1992: 290; see also Kelly 1979, Chapter 8). In this, she reveals herself to be rooted in a fundamentally dualistic view of translation. However, her deliberations on the issue do reach considerably further than has been recognized to date.

From the various comments made by Lowe-Porter in her metatexts it is possible to piece together something which amounts, if not to an underlying theory, then at least to a guiding conception of translation. Her ideas are intuitive rather than explicitly rationalized, deductive rather than analytically founded. Her conception is wholly target-oriented. In her translations, her ultimate aim was to produce a text that read as naturally as possible in English, adapting the original work to the expectations of the foreign readership. Conformity with the norms of the receptor culture was her overriding principle: the English to which she aspired, she often stressed, was one that met the requirements of 'acceptable literary usage'. The idiom of her versions was to be neither American nor British, but was intended to be a hybrid that would find favour 'on both sides of the ocean' (T: 191). This 'international impasse', as she called it, was an important consideration, given that her translations invariably appeared more or less simultaneously in New York and London. She claimed that this linguistic balancing act inevitably led her to 'emasculate the style, in some degree' (T: 191), but she felt that she was generally successful on this score.

The target-oriented thrust of Lowe-Porter's thinking on translation is evident in her insistence that a translation must, above all other things, read naturally in the host culture. The post-Romantic notion that a translation should foreground the otherness of the original, alienate its readers through the adoption of source-language structures, and retain exotic elements in an attempt to grant access to the workings of the parent text and culture, was far from her mind. At all times, she argued for the primacy of fluency over replication. Her fundamental tenet was that translation into another tongue was a subordinate activity that must not betray – at least on the level of linguistic structure – its derived status. Her concern was to ensure that 'the work of art [...] should, in English, at least not come like a translation – which is "God bless us, a thing of naught"' (*Buddenbrooks* note). In this respect, she subscribed to the age-old view that translation must be transparent, 'given the appearance that it reflects the foreign writer's personality or intention or the essential meaning of the foreign text – the appearance, in other words, that the translation is not in fact a translation' (Venuti 2008: 1). She sums up her views in a letter to Knopf dated 30 March 1934 (T: 31):

> [...] there are these two schools of translation: the one which believes that the right method is to reproduce the atmosphere of the foreign style by preserving very exactly the wave length, so to speak, the etymological significance of words, etc.; and the one which feels that it is insulting to an author who is worth translating to render his style into a sort of bastard English. I belong [...] to the second school.

That she was perceived as generally successful in this aim is attested by the many laudatory reviews of her work at the time. Read as products in the target language, rather than measured against the pre-existent parameters of the parent text, they elicited a positive critical reaction. The contemporary reception of Thomas Mann in the English-speaking world shows the enthusiasm with which her versions of his texts were welcomed into the canon of world literature (Wagener 2001). The assessments of the Book-of-the-Month Club judges, who selected five of Mann's titles for inclusion in the prestigious series between 1936 and 1951, attest to the degree of assimilation. In the view of Dorothy Thompson, the political journalist who was herself an occasional translator, Lowe-Porter achieved what was considered by the majority of commentators at the time to be the highest honour a translator could possibly claim: invisibility: 'as I read the English text I wasn't conscious of you at all, and this sort of self-effacement is the finest thing a translator can perform' (T: 20).

In her concern to attain a high degree of target-language acceptability, Lowe-Porter was well aware of obstacles she faced. However, once again underlining her view that translation was an acquired skill akin to a form of manual dexterity, she defined such features as 'technical problems'. In 'On translating Thomas Mann' she draws up a somewhat unsystematic catalogue of translation problems. She mentions the relative degrees of explicitness and logical elaboration in German and English and dwells on issues of lexical equivalence, citing words like '*Geist*' and '*Erkenntnis*' as notorious examples (1966: 200). She discusses the impossibility of transferring regional dialect and the difficulties of rendering idioms. Of particular significance in her work on Mann, she claims, is the frequent need for syntactic rearrangement and simplification ('sentences, in order not to produce a clumsy English, must be broken up', T: 55). Here, once again, she emphasizes her desire to conform to target-language norms and, referring to her procedures in *Death in Venice* and *The Beloved Returns*, she stresses the central importance of smoothness in translation: 'I thought I would eliminate the recurrent German "which", clumsy to an English ear; I would seek to make the clauses glide smoothly into each other' (T: 58). She talks of the need to shift words across word classes (transposition) in order 'to make English out of it' (T: 26), and of her conscious and consistent adoption of an English historical idiom in handling dated or archaic linguistic features in *Lotte in Weimar* and *Doktor Faustus*. At all levels, her endeavour is to obscure, as far as possible, the mediated quality of the discourse.

Lowe-Porter's favourite analogy in circumscribing her approach to the task of mediating Mann's dense and complex texts is that of prestidigitation. Defining translation as a 'craft' and a 'mystery' – i.e. an activity honed through actual occupational practice – rather than as a theorizable intercultural and interlingual transfer procedure, she stresses on a number of occasions the importance of 'sleight-of-hand', or, in one instance, 'sleight-of-mind' (T: 53, 59). By this she appears to mean the exploitation of compensation procedures which seek to make good inevitable deficiencies occasioned by instances of untranslatability (she again cites dialect as an example) through the adoption of alternative techniques elsewhere:

> After all, every translator knows that translating is a sort of trick, a device like the sleight-of-hand operator's to attract attention to something in order to distract it from something else. There is a sense in which all art fits such a definition – witness the double sense in which the word itself can be used. So also word-craft. When we speak of the little art of translating I am content to have the word used in this double sense. On the other hand I please myself, privately, by thinking of it as a "mystery" in the archaic and now very modern literary sense. (T: 53)

On a number of occasions, Lowe-Porter describes such a technique in terms of 'distraction', and appears to imply that translation is tantamount to an act of deception: an attempt to hoodwink the reader into accepting inevitable shortcomings in some translation solutions by offering recompense elsewhere. In fact, though, she also defines it – more in line with modern thinking on translation procedures – as a process of 'substitution'. Only in this way, she claims, can a piece of creative work written in one language be rendered as a work approaching equivalent status in another: '[…] to do this, the principle of substitution must be freely employed: i.e. getting the special effect of the original in one place if the resources of the language fail to produce it in another' (letter to Knopf of 30 March 1934, T: 31). The use of compensation techniques, then, is an important instrument in her attainment of what in the 1960s became known as 'dynamic equivalence' and 'equivalent effect'. It is a key strategy in an approach to translation which subordinates semantic correspondence to functional efficacy, as part of an overriding concern to capture something of the quality of the original text. Key concepts here are 'effect' on the reader and 'literary virtue': 'I may come on a fine idiomatic or allusive phrase in German and find that the English just does not lend itself to the same effect. But perhaps another sentence elsewhere in the text can display the same kind of literary virtue in English, where it did not happen in German (T: 60; on compensation in translation see Harvey 1995, Thome 2002).

It is this 'literary virtue' of the text in translation, the 'perfect transference from German into English' (T: 61), that drives Lowe-Porter's conception of translation as a relatively free cross-linguistic reformulation of the essence of the literary work. In her view, the translator's licence is restrained only by what she perceives as the integrity of the original. She sees that original as the 'organic work of art to be remoulded in another tongue' (preface to *The Magic Mountain*), a Platonic fusion of 'matter and style', 'word and thought' that are as inseparable as body and mind. In her writings, Lowe-Porter frequently advances this conception of literature. In her foreword to *Past Masters and Other Papers* she speaks in connection with Mann's oeuvre of the 'organic nature of creation', of 'organic unity', of 'inward harmony' (Lowe-Porter 1933: 6–7). The translator's task is to emulate the 'literary performance of the original'. In her letter to Knopf of 11 November 1943, she encapsulates her view of the dilemma facing the translator in the classic metaphor of Scylla and Charybdis: the need to reconcile fidelity to the meaning and style of the original (again seen as a dualism) with literary quality:

> I cannot think a creative artist would be glad to see his delicate balance quite upset, his true marriage of word and thought turned into something which, however word-accurate, had ceased to be literature at all [...] And herein lies the Scylla of translators: the Charybdis would be the failure to give a faithful rendering of the sense. (T: 59)

It is no wonder, in view of such a mystical conception of the translator's art, that she insists on the principle of congeniality in literary translation. The process of successful literary translation presupposes, she believes, a degree of intellectual affinity and empathetic creative engagement with the text, an ability to grasp and ultimately mirror its organic artistic wholeness. In this, she is rooted in the tradition of hermeneutic translation theory popular in the nineteenth and early twentieth centuries. It is therefore only logical that she concludes: 'I cannot enter into the work of other writers unless their themes and techniques and general *"Lebensauffassung"* appeal to me as what I should have been employing as original work' (T: 188). Here we are at the very interface of creativity and re-creativity in the translation process, for which she uses the phrase 'creative authorship' (T: 180). The logical final move is her reference, pilloried in many modern discussions of her work, to her promise 'of never sending a translation to the publisher unless I felt as though I had written the book myself' (T: 182). This was the faithfulness she sought when she claimed – as in the foreword to *The Magic Mountain* – that her versions were 'in every intent deeply faithful'. By faithfulness she means not the slavish atomistic reproduction of features of the original text in the target language, but a far higher responsibility incumbent upon the translator: fidelity to the author's artistic intentions. This, she considered, resulted in a transfer that was 'a portrait, not a photograph' (T: 56). She adumbrates this principle in her reaction to Harry Levin's criticism of her Faustus translation in 1948 (Thirlwall 114; see also Mann's letter to Lowe-Porter of 8 January 1949, *DüD* 3: 213). In her view, the application of 'scholarly principles' by the translator will inevitably produce 'a wooden piece of work, boring to read and unfaithful to the creative imagination of the author'. She defends herself against Levin's criticisms of inaccuracy by seeking recourse to her guiding principle: 'I conceive that the author might prefer his translator to be faithful to his creative imagination.' In this conception of translation, with its belief in the retrievability and replicability of authorial intentions, she was well in tune with the mainstream of thinking at the time. As Kelly notes, referring specifically to the competing views of Belloc and Pound:

> Fidelity [...] was the obligation of deciding what was important, and the choice of how this was to be reproduced or represented in the target text. Much depends on the insight the translator brings to his text, on the balance perceived between meaning, sound and form [...] Operatively, the problem here is that considerable linguistic freedom has been claimed in the interests of preserving the expressive priorities of the source text. The reasoning is one based on personal responsibility.
>
> (Kelly 1979: 211)

It was on precisely this conception of translational excellence that Knopf drew in framing cover notes for his editions of Mann. Thus the note for *Essays of Three Decades* (published in 1947) tells us: 'Again, as always, H. T. Lowe-Porter's versions are not so much mere translations as re-creations in fine English of the very spirit of the German originals.' This notion of fidelity was, of course, based on the assumption that the translator, as the receiver of the original, has access to the author's deeper concerns. On this score, Lowe-Porter had no doubts: 'I was arrogantly sure that I was nearly always well aware of the author's larger creative purposes' (T: 181). Empathizing with what she held to be the essence of the writer's purpose, she recast his texts into a form which she herself considered to meet the standards of the 'literary performance' of 'original work' in English, thus echoing Belloc's claim that 'the translator must be of original talent; he must himself create; he must have power of his own' (quoted in Kelly 1979: 211). The understanding of the translator's task outlined here illustrates the fundamental hybridity of all literary translation: the challenge of serving two cultures simultaneously. While the translated text has to find a place in the target culture (gaining acceptability), it also points back to a text in the source culture, which it claims to re-enunciate (principle of adequacy). Thus the translator is inevitably caught between the competing claims of reflection (transparency) and active construction (visible presence). As a mediator between languages and cultures, Lowe-Porter felt empowered to intervene in the originals as long as the aesthetic qualities she perceived in the source-language work were reconstituted in the target-language text. The line between empathetic identification, idiosyncratic assimilation and problematic appropriation has become a truly thin one at this point.

The extent to which Lowe-Porter was in fact aware of Mann's 'larger creative purposes' is open to question. She always insisted that the major challenge she faced as Mann's translator was not intellectual-interpretive understanding, but rather practical execution (the 'technical problems' referred to above). She believed that she was successful in her endeavours, although she does appear to have been prone to moments of self-doubt. Many of the attempts at self-assessment contained in her metatexts are humble and self-deprecating. In her note to *The Magic Mountain*, for example, she comments self-effacingly: 'It seems better that an English version should be done ill than not done at all'; referring to her work on *Lotte in Weimar* she exclaims that she is 'committing murder' (quoted in Mann's letter to Gömöri of 15 November 1951, *DüD* 2: 538), and on various occasions she stressed her own inadequacy as a linguist (T: 204), as a speaker of German (T: 183), and as a poet (T: 198). At the same time, however, she was fundamentally convinced of her qualifications and qualities as the mediator of Thomas Mann – a position she had fought hard to secure – and responded sensitively to criticism.

In a letter to Knopf dated 11 November 1943, Lowe-Porter outlines the procedures she adopted in her work on Mann's voluminous and complex texts. Her comments are borne out by the testimony of others who were familiar with her work pattern (e.g. Judith Heller, T: 62, and her daughters). The starting point, she writes, was a process of assimilation.

> When I receive one of Dr Mann's works to translate, what I try to do is to read it, not merely to get the sense but the flavor, the mood and tempo, the atmosphere […] Well, then I try to decide whether the book has its peculiar characteristics of style and atmosphere which it would be my duty to try to represent […] And when I got this well into my ear and feeling, I would use it to clothe as meticulous, supple, and intuitive a rendering of the original as I possibly could […] It is clear that the author of *Buddenbrooks, Der Zauberberg*, the Joseph series, and *Lotte* would and did fuse his matter and style into an organic whole. The

translations ought to show an effort on the part of the translator to do the same. (T: 57–9)

In this statement, she reiterates the six essential principles of her conception of translation: the onus incumbent on the translator to find an appropriate stylistic voice, the importance of empathetic understanding ('ear and feeling'), attention to detail ('meticulous'), elasticity and flexibility in rendition ('supple'), a pre-rational grasp of the work's import ('intuitive'), and the determination to reconstitute the 'organic wholeness of the original'. The third of these ideals – meticulousness – was especially labour-intensive. In preparing her versions of the texts, Lowe-Porter was inevitably required to undertake a significant amount of research, what she called 'collateral reading' (T: 26). Usually guided by the author himself, she would consult large amounts of specialist literature (e.g. on music for *Doktor Faustus*, on medieval legend for *Der Erwählte*) to familiarize herself with the context, as well as with the references and allusions which abound in Mann's often extensive excurses. As the correspondence shows, she would frequently consult the author on specific problems, and he invariably responded promptly, patiently and in detail. In dealing with passages of archaic language (she specifically mentions *Doktor Faustus*), she would seek and study equivalent or similarly obsolete registers, on occasions adopting the style of a different historical period in order to suggest broadly similar atmospheric qualities. In her version of *Lotte in Weimar*, for example, she employed a somewhat anachronistic Victorian idiom, and in places drew on the diction of Coleridge. Once again, her procedure highlights the primacy of artistic effect over strict (historical) accuracy.

Judith Heller, who often assisted Lowe-Porter in her work and herself translated some of Mann's short essays, explains that Lowe-Porter would follow up her preparatory studies by completing 'a rough draft in manuscript, translating more or less literally from German' (T: 62). This procedure has a long tradition in the history of translation, later becoming known as 'minimal transfer'. The production of a source-oriented draft which remains close to the structures of the original has long been regarded as a key initial stage prior to the preparation of a later, target-oriented version marked by a higher degree of idiomaticity and naturalness in the receptor language. She would then leave the manuscript for some time before taking it up again 'to English it' (T: 62). The final result, Judith Heller claims, is not 'a literal translation', but a textual fabric in English that 'is so well-woven that one does not feel the German through it, which is, after all, what Helen wanted it to be' (66). Once again, the ultimate goal is the translator's invisibility. The extant typescripts of Lowe-Porter's versions of Mann's texts held in Yale show just how extensive her revisions to the 'rough drafts' were: even the first typed version of her translation of *Doctor Faustus* (prepared presumably after the handwritten version Heller mentions), for example, contains dozens of emendations in Lowe-Porter's hand on each of its sheets. The opening sentence of that text provides a brief illustration of the processes of recasting – lexical and syntactic – which she undertook, changing sections, inserting new material in stages, and shortening sentences:

Original	*First typed version*	*Changes (and published version)*
Mit aller Bestimmtheit will ich versichern, daß es keineswegs aus dem Wunsche geschieht, meine Person in den Vordergrund zu schieben, wenn ich diesen Mitteilungen über das Leben des verewigten Adrian Leverkühn, dieser ersten und gewiß sehr vorläufigen Biographie des teuren, vom Schicksal so furchtbar heimgesuchten, erhobenen und gestürzten Mannes und genialen Musikers einige Worte über mich selbst und meine Bewandtnisse vorausschicke. (GW 9: 493)	I want to state quite definitely that it is by no means out of any wish to bring my own personality into the foreground that I preface to these communications on the life of the departed Adrian Leverkühn, to this first and surely very premature biography of the beloved being and musician of genius, so afflicted by fate, lifted up and cast down, a few words about myself and my situation.	I wish to state quite definitely that it is by no means out of any wish to bring my own personality into the foreground that I preface with a few words about myself and my own affairs this report on the life of the departed Adrian Leverkühn. What I here set down is the first and assuredly very premature biography of that beloved fellow creature and musician of genius, so afflicted by fate, lifted up so high, only to be so frightfully cast down.

In her essay 'On translating Thomas Mann' Lowe-Porter provides an instructive example of her method from her work on *Joseph in Egypt*: 'first, a literal translation, and second, the same paragraph "tidied up", as it were, into what one fondly hopes is literary English' (1966: 201). It is worth considering this extract in more detail, since the translator herself sees it as a salient (and presumably successful) example of her transformational procedures. I quote the opening of the above-mentioned passage here:

Original	Literal	Literary
In Schlangennot	In the toils	In the toils
Wie geringfügig ist, verglichen mit der Zeitentiefe der Welt, der Vergangenheitsdurchblick unseres eigenen Lebens! Und doch verliert sich unser auf das Einzelpersönliche und Intime eingestelltes Auge ebenso träumerisch-schwimmend in seinen Frühen und Fernen wie das großartiger gerichtete in denen des Menschheitslebens – gerührt von der Wahrnehmung einer Einheit, die sich in diesem wiederholt. So wenig wie der Mensch selbst vermögen wir bis zum Beginn unserer Tage, zu unserer Geburt, oder gar noch weiter zurückzudringen; sie liegt im Dunkel vorm ersten Morgengrauen des Bewußtseins und der Erinnerung – im kleinen Durchblick so wie im großen. (GW 5: 1085)	How insignificant, compared with the depth of time of the universe, is the vista through the past of our own life! And yet our eye, fixed on the individual and intimate, loses itself as dreamily, floating in his own early and distant life, as the eye grandly directed upon the life of humanity, moved by the perception of a unity which repeats itself therein. As little as man himself can we dive down to the beginning of our days, to our birth, or further still; it all lies in the first dawn of consciousness and memory, in the small view as in the large.	How narrow is the span when we look back upon our own lives; how vast when we contemplate the world's abysmal past! And yet we lose ourselves as easily, as dreamily, in the one as in the other; by virtue of our perception of a unity between the two. As little in the small sphere as in the large can we go back to the time of our birth and the beginning of our days, to say nothing of further back. It lies in the darkness before the beginnings of the dawn of consciousness or memory.

It would, of course, be unreasonable to claim wholly representative status for such a limited passage, and subsequent chapters of the present study will explore the nature and the impact of Lowe-Porter's translation strategy in greater detail on the basis of more extensive examples. However, this short extract may serve to indicate the kind of transformations Lowe-Porter has in mind when she speaks of 'tidying up' a 'literal' translation in order to produce 'literary English'.

Lowe-Porter has chosen this particular illustration well. Mann's text, which opens the fifth chapter of the sixth '*Hauptstück*' of *Joseph in*

Ägypten' has a rhetorical structure which is typical of the narrative onsets in the Joseph novels, with its introductory exclamation in the form of an inclusive first-person appeal to the reader (sentence 1), following qualification (sentence 2), and further comparative expansion (sentence 3). In the passage, the narrator exploits and develops the image of vision (*'Vergangenheitsdurchblick'* – *'Auge'* – *'Durchblick'*) in reflecting on two different modes of conceptualizing the past: the universal (mankind in general) and the specific (individual), and the ultimate unity of the two. Thus the chapter picks up two of the key themes of the Joseph tetralogy as a whole: the fusion of the 'principium individuationis' with the mythic collective, and the notion of the *'Brunnentiefe der Zeiten'* (Dirks 2003). The cohesion of the text derives from referential chains which sustain this polar view: *'Welt'*– *'Menschheitsleben'* – *'Mensch'* – *'großer (Durchblick)'* versus *'unser eigenes Leben'* – *'das Einzelpersönliche/ Intime'* – *'wir'* – *'im kleinen Durchblick'*. The narratorial *'wir'* appears initially to be a universal voice. However, it soon emerges as (or merges with) a specific authorial perspective in the truest sense of the word. Over the following sentences, reference is made to Mann's own past as a writer – his birth, as it were, as a creative artist – and to the fundamental theme of his early works (*'die Idee der Heimsuchung'*), which he is to resume now, in the story of Mut-em-enet: a link which Mann himself explicitly confirmed (GW 13: 135). The title draws on the image of the coiled snake as a metaphor of entrapment, and evokes mythological associations (Fischer 2002: 629ff.). Mut-em-enet is trapped in a passionate erotic attraction to Joseph, as the narrator tells us towards the end of the chapter: '[…] *in der Umstrickung ihrer Begierde gleichwie in den Leibesschlingen einer gottgesandten Schlange'* (GW 5: 1090).

The passage contains a number of potential translation problems which are typical of Mann's texts. It has two unlexicalized compound abstract nouns: the first, *'Zeitentiefe'*, occurs on only two other occasions in Mann's entire work (both in the Joseph novels), while the second, *'Vergangenheitsdurchblick'*, is a unique usage; de-adjectival nouns (*'Frühe und Ferne'*); a compound adverb (*'träumerisch-schwimmend'*); a heavily premodified nominal group containing two adjectival nouns (*'unser auf das Einzelpersönliche und Intime eingestelltes Auge'*); and an example of nominal ellipsis (*'das großartiger gerichtete [Auge]'*). From a syntactic point of view it shows the techniques of accumulation and expansion which characterize Mann's writing in general. The introductory proposition is refined and reformulated as the paragraph progresses. Thus the first sentence is short; the second, qualifying, sentence presents a comparison (*'ebenso … wie'*) followed by a participial structure, itself modified by a relative clause; and the third draws a syncretic conclusion from the first two in another comparison, in which constituents are further specified. The closing prepositional phrase picks up on the lexeme *'Durchblick'* (which appears on only one other occasion in this temporal-visual sense in Mann's work), and marks the three sentences as a thematic and textual unit, underpinning the cohesion via a bracketing function.

Lowe-Porter's versions are distinctly different from one another. A superficial quantitative analysis alone suffices to demonstrate that her literary version is eminently more readable than her literal rendition. It has fewer words (96 v. 104: Mann's original has 92), and introduces an additional sentence break, bringing the average number of words per sentence down from 34.67 to 24.00. It uses a smaller number of different words (59 v. 68), contains shorter words (fewer average number of characters syllables per word), and has a lower degree of lexical density (61.46 per cent v. 65.38 per cent). The application of two established automated readability measures (Textalyser and the Text Content Analysis Tool, both of which are available online at http://textalyser.net and http://www.usingenglish.com respectively) confirms this:

	Original	*Literal*	*Literary*
Automated readability index	26.87	21.13	14.32
LIX readability index	57.84	52.94	36.50

Both of the English versions, the statistical measures suggest, are significantly easier to process than Mann's own version: this is in large part due to the number of long words in his version (which is itself the result of extensive compounding in the first sentence). However, by undertaking extensive transformations in her second version, Lowe-Porter has ensured that this 'literary' version is much less complex than her first, 'literal' rendition. The latter follows the German very closely, tracking the syntax and seeking to render the lexis at the level of word-for-word substitution. This mirrors the structures of the German, and also secures the retention of the lexical chains. But it creates a fragmentary syntax, since both the heavily premodified noun phrase *'unser auf das Einzelpersönliche und Intime eingestellte Auge'* and the complex adverbial structure *'(sich) träumerisch-schwimmend (verlieren)'* are exploded into non-finite structures. Furthermore, in its proximity to the original it generates idiomatically problematic combinations: 'the depth of time of the universe', 'the vista through the past of our own life', 'the eye grandly directed upon the life of humanity'. The literary version, on the other hand, is certainly 'tidied up'. Indeed, it is so extensively tidied up that it is difficult to align with Mann's original at first glance. It displays several features which are characteristic of Lowe-Porter's translation procedures. Firstly, she transposes the syntax of the first sentence, adding a layer of rhetorical parallelism through the anaphoric 'how narrow' – 'how vast', which has been created by separating out what in German is an interposed participial clause (*'verglichen mit ...'*): here, the second contrastive adjective ('vast') has been supplied by the translator herself for reasons of symmetry, and a further verb has been added ('contemplate') to sustain the parallelism. In the same sentence, the translator has resolved the two problematic abstract nouns by altering their morphological form: the noun *'Zeitentiefe'* becomes the noun phrase 'abysmal past', while *'Vergangenheitsdurchblick'* becomes the clausal 'when we look back upon', creating idiomatic solutions at the expense of abstraction and lexical innovation. Secondly, the literary version omits a large portion of the second sentence, deleting everything from *'in seinen Frühen'* all the way through to *'des Menschheitslebens'*: here, a complex structure containing a series of variations on the central theme of the text is reduced to the summary 'in the one as in the other': a clear example, perhaps, of the way in which 'sense' is adapted to 'spirit'. Thirdly, she reconstructs the penultimate sentence of her literal version, moving the last constituent forward to the front, deleting the cohesive visual reference (*'Durchblick'*, just as she has deleted *'Auge'* in the preceding sentence), and also omitting the reference to the *'Mensch selbst'*, which constitutes a link in the referential chain of the individual versus the generic. Overall, then, the text has been trimmed. Its lexical variation, which in the original constructs networks of considerable inter-referential tautness, has been reduced. Its high level of integration has been dissolved by the creation of fewer and shorter phrases and clauses. All told, it has been transformed into a more easily digestible text whose fluency is enhanced by the introduction of connecting elements ('by virtue of ...', 'to say nothing of ...'). Whether the latter version is a 'literary performance' in Lowe-Porter's sense is a matter of individual judgement. But certainly, her text has a clear rhetorical structure, and it conveys the 'message' of the original, though in a simplified and much distilled form.

Translation norms in the inter-war years: 'a first class native thing'

In an essay on literary translation, Lew Zybatow reports on the outburst of general mirth (*'ein lautes, lang anhaltendes Lachen'*) that erupted when the Norwegian translation scholar Per Qvale quoted to a translation conference in Vancouver (2002) Lowe-Porter's words on never dispatching a translation unless she had the feeling she had done it herself (Zybatow 2008: 10). Lowe-Porter has often been criticized for the licence she allowed herself in her extensive reformulations and transpositions, omissions and additions. Invariably, however, commentators have failed to see her conception of translation in its historical context. They have, in most cases quite unconsciously and inexplicitly, applied late twentieth-century standards of accepted translational practice. In other words, they have been oblivious to the influence of a dominant poetics of translation alongside other conditioning norms to which translators are subject, such as the pressures exerted from within the institutional system, i.e. by publishers and editors, and patronage by the political and economic elite. As exponents of descriptive translation studies stress, the conception of translation prevailing at a given time plays a major role in delineating the framework within which translators operate: their decisions at the level of individual textual selections are guided not merely by personal predilections, but also by their view of the expectations of the target culture. Like all poetic systems, the poetics of translation comprises two levels: 'one is an inventory of devices, genres, motifs, prototypical characters and situations, and symbols; the other a concept of what the role of literature is, or should be, in the social system as a whole' (Lefevere 1992b: 26). The exploration of such norms has been a central issue in historical translation research. Hermans is surely right to ask, then, referring specifically to Lowe-Porter in his prefatory 'Mann's Fate': 'Should we not, before passing judgement on the translator, compare her position and her performance with that of some of her contemporaries? [...] Considering that the Lowe-Porter translations were generally well received by the critics and proved commercially successful, could it be that the translator was correctly anticipating reader expectations?' (Hermans 1999: 4). A glance at the principles of translation operative in the first half of the twentieth century confirms that Hermans' question is justified: Lowe-Porter did indeed work in line with the conceptions prevailing at the time.

It would, of course, be an unjustifiable simplification to reduce translational practice at a given historical juncture to a binary opposition of strategies, e.g. fluent versus literalist. Norms and conventions in translation are more complex than this, and it is rarely possible to encapsulate the practices in operation at any particular time in a single governing principle (Hermans 2000: 12). Generally speaking, however, English-speaking cultures have tended to favour conceptions of translation that obscure cultural difference (Venuti 2008). The trend towards free, heavily target-oriented translation was, in fact, especially strong in the 1920s and 1930s as translators sought to make the texts of nineteenth-century and modernist European writers accessible to an English audience by bringing them into line with contemporary (receptor-culture) aesthetic criteria such as elegance and textual smoothness, exploiting various techniques of normalization (lexical, syntactic and cultural). A translation should, according to Belloc, be 'a first-class native thing' (Belloc 1931: 22). The ultimate aim of such translation strategies was to ensure the fluency or natural readability of the target text at the expense of the foreign: Belloc's 'the resurrection of an alien thing in a native body'. The active role of the translator in the process of literary communication was to be obscured to the greatest degree possible. Thus what Venuti in his history of translation calls the 'regime of fluency' (from which there were, of course, dissenters, notably Nabokov) went hand in hand with the doctrine of 'the translator's invisibility' (Venuti 2008, Chapter 1). There is no contradiction between the translator as invisible presence on the one hand and the translator as quasi-original author on the other. As we saw above, Lowe-Porter espoused both these principles. While the source-language text is the sacred original (original authorship), the ideal translation obscures its second-order status, 'producing the illusion of authorial presence whereby the translated text can be taken as the original' (translator authorship: Venuti 2008: 6). The prolific American translator Willard Trask – who took on the translation of Mann's *Die Betrogene* after Lowe-Porter's retirement – expressed this ambivalence by defining the translator as an actor performing the role of the original author (Venuti 2008: 7). The work of the translator becomes a subordinated yet nevertheless creative activity, and the relationship between translator and original author is one of collaboration rather than subjection.

The very translators whose 'monumental and classic labors' (1966: 203) Lowe-Porter mentions in her essay on translating Thomas Mann may serve as appropriate illustrations of the conceptions of literary translation operative at around that time. They were, after all, mediators who produced versions that were exceptionally successful during their own lifetime, and which have since acquired the status of classics. The prolific Constance Garnett, who produced some seventy volumes of translations from Russian between 1894 and 1926, today enjoys a certain notoriety for the graceful late-Victorian prose of her renditions. Commentators note that she tended to smooth over passages in the source texts in order to enhance 'readability', simplifying and normalizing the Russian originals to create fluent English versions. She omitted entire passages which she found impossible to understand or to reformulate in the target language. Her translations 'read well but are unreliable because of numerous omissions and abridgements', recent commentators note with reference to her versions of Chekhov (Pavlovskis-Petit and Rappaport 2000: 273). As Burnett concludes in connection with Garnett's Dostoevsky translations, her work has recently been re-assessed in the wake of 'the shift in focus from the novelty of Dostoevskii's thought to the literary qualities and stylistic range of the translator', which is a 'mark of an altered emphasis on the role that translation plays in the acculturation of "strange" literary works' (Burnett 2000: 369). For many readers at the time, including

D. H. Lawrence, Joseph Conrad and Virginia Woolf, Garnett *was* Russian literature, and her versions dominated the scene for 40 years or more.

The Tolstoy translations produced a decade or two earlier by Aylmer and Louise Maude have similarly been criticized for the refinement of their English prose, and have been defined as even more strongly domesticating than Garnett's versions, bringing Tolstoy's voice more into line with the tastes and sensibilities of the receiving culture of their age (McLean 2008: 53 ff.). 'In all the classic versions,' Catriona Kelly notes, 'Tolstoy emerges as what many British readers have wished he was: a more intellectually demanding, if less pleasing, version of Turgenev', a Tolstoy rewritten in texts designed to facilitate 'the more or less effortless recovery of a "message"' (Kelly 2000: 594). The discussion surrounding the translator Scott Moncrieff, most famous for his translation of Proust, has taken a similar direction. His translation of *A la récherche du temps perdu*, long considered masterful and definitive, has been increasingly viewed by commentators as an 'adulteration', full of embellishments, additions, omissions, lexical distortions, euphemisms and simple errors arising from textual misunderstandings. From today's perspective, the target text appears to be written largely in 'period purple' and has been superseded by revisions and more modern versions (Prendergast 1993: 21). In an extended catalogue of the deficiencies of Moncrieff's version (under the headings of omissions, solecisms, diction and syntax), Grieve concludes that his version is 'high-class translationese', combining Georgian diction with 'Frenglish' syntax (Grieve 1982: 55). Grieve savages Moncrieff's 'usurped reputation for impeccability and definitiveness' (65). The translators to whom Lowe-Porter refers, then, all share the same fundamental conception of translation: mediation is viewed as an assimilative activity, which legitimately reduces the linguistic and cultural difference of the foreign text in order to create an acceptable target text. In the perennial struggle between the opposing poles of re-creative fidelity and philological accuracy, they clearly lean towards the former. It is precisely here that the paradigm change in translation practice has taken place over the past fifty years.

It is particularly instructive in this context to consider the debate surrounding the English versions of texts often cited as a contemporary comparative corpus for Mann's stylistic propensities. As Glass points out, the inter-war period saw an 'influx' of translations of German literature into the English-speaking world, ably promoted by publishers such as Knopf in the USA and Secker & Warburg in Britain (Glass 2000: 517; see also Morgan 1965 and Keenon 1997). Apart from 'the enduring monuments' that constitute today's canon, large numbers of lesser-known war novels, topical social novels and works of historical fiction crossed the linguistic divide, accompanied by innovative dramas (generally only in 'little-theatre' stagings) and poetry (expressionism, Rilke). Inevitably, however, it is the works of the 'major writers' of prose fiction that have been studied most intensively from a comparative stylistic point of view (for example in Grimm 1991), just as it is the translations of those works that have been most closely scrutinized. Kafka, Hesse and Heinrich Mann typically feature in such studies. Significantly, the parameters of the debate on their work in translation, and many of the conclusions drawn from it, are highly reminiscent of the recent discussion surrounding Lowe-Porter. They show conclusively that her treatment of Mann's texts was by no means as eccentric or idiosyncratic as it might seem at first glance.

The reception of the English versions of Kafka's works is a good case in point. The celebrated original translations by Willa and Edwin Muir have acquired broadly the same cultural-historical status as Lowe-Porter's versions of Mann. Indeed, they enjoy an even greater reputation as literary texts 'in their own right', and played a decisive role in shaping early interpretations of Kafka's works in the English-speaking world (Jacob 1988; Durrani 2002; Reitter 2006). Despite the appearance of more modern and accurate translations based on revised textual editions of Kafka, they remain the classic translations, and are still frequently reprinted. Mathews writes in connection with the Muirs' rendering of *Der Prozess* that 'it is still the classic version [...] read throughout the world in popular editions. [...] No one could deny the quality of the writing – its ability to render Kafka's words so "easily and fluently"' (Mathews 2000: 747). The Muirs have been consistently praised above all for the naturalness of their English style, despite the rather cultivated, dignified tone of their texts. However, their translations have also been roundly criticized on precisely the same counts as Lowe-Porter's versions of Mann, above all for their degree of interpretive licence. Mathews identifies 'glaring eccentricities' in their texts (Mathews 2000: 748), while Harman complains that they 'whittle away at the interpretive choices open to the reader' and 'transform the cryptic language of the original into an unambiguous sermon' (Harman 1996: 300). Further, their versions have been criticized for their lack of accuracy, a criterion that is clearly a fundamental one in modern reader expectations vis-à-vis translations (Gray 1977).

The discussion of Kafka translations, then, confirms that accuracy alone is not the ultimate yardstick in literary translation. More recent and denotatively faithful versions, like those by Harman, have been criticized in exactly the same terms as the more recent Mann translations by John E. Woods. After all, as Ormsby argues, 'literal accuracy isn't always felicity', 'more is required than the plugging in of studiously correct equivalents', and 'the correct tone or register of a phrase or sentence' can be just as important as its 'meanings' (Ormsby 1998:

36). Furthermore, their versions have been subject to criticism which is clearly derived from a more modern, foreignizing conception of translation. While the Muirs smoothe and normalize Kafka's often complex syntax, more recent translators seek to mirror the structures of the original more closely. This approach is certainly in keeping with the marked trend in modern translation practice towards source-oriented adequacy and away from target-oriented acceptability. B. Mitchell, who himself retranslated *Der Prozess*, sums up the Muirs' procedure and its possible effects: 'in attempting to create a readable and stylistically refined version of Kafka's *Trial*, they consistently overlooked or deliberately varied the repetitions and inter-connections that echo so meaningfully in the ear of every attentive reader of the German text' (Mitchell 1998, no page number). Confirming the change in conceptions of the translator's task, a recent translator of Kafka's stories, Joyce Crick, writes in the notes to her 2009 translation: 'But I made one decision very early: to try to render Kafka's exceedingly complex syntax as closely as possible. This often meant going further than English syntax can accommodate' (Kafka 2009: xxxv). This overstretching of the norms of English sentence structure, a procedure from which Luke shied away in his retranslations of Mann's stories as late as in the 1970s and 1980s, has become an instrument of enhanced fidelity to the linguistic structure of the original. It was a translation method which was utterly unthinkable to Lowe-Porter, writing in the 1920s and 1930s. That it is not uncontroversial today is evidenced by Ormsby's conclusion on the relative merits of the Muir and Harman translations. He concludes that the former are 'less literal than Harman but, I would argue, closer to the sense of the original' (Ormsby 1998: 38).

Similar considerations are evident in the discussion of Hesse's work in English. Here, too, standards of literal accuracy and textual integrity are played off against less rigidly defined notions of fidelity to the spirit of the original. Horrocks points out that the writer's enormous popularity in the English-speaking world has had little to do with the 'quality of the available translations, which [...] was not high' (Horrocks 2000: 639). He lists omissions, inaccurate tenses, errors in vocabulary, and numerous misreadings in Creighton's 1929 version of *Der Steppenwolf*, which combine to produce a text that is 'seriously flawed' and 'hopelessly garbled'. But more fundamental and systemic reservations have also been voiced about the early Hesse translations. In a chapter entitled 'Translation and Mis-Translation' in his 1991 collection of essays on translation, Newmark examines sections of the same *Steppenwolf* translation (as revised by Sorrell in 1963) and focuses, again from a late twentieth-century perspective, on precisely the kind of syntactical transpositions which characterize

Lowe-Porter's work: 'The SLT consists of three sentences, two in the first, one in the second paragraph. The translation has fifteen sentences in the first paragraph, two in the second. Even granting that German has longer and more complex sentences than English, it is hard to justify these divergences' (Newmark 1991: 103). He notes further that the procedure of sentence reduction necessitates the introduction of cohesive devices which 'make rather more decisive breaks than in the SLT, and add redundant shades of meaning' (103). We shall see in Chapter 8 that even celebrated modern translators of syntactically complex texts face intractable problems here. In an earlier discussion of Mervyn Savill's 1943 version of *Das Glasperlenspiel*, Riley criticizes the translation as 'often ludicrously and heartbreakingly incompetent' quoting an analysis which 'meticulously compares the original with the translation and shows beyond doubt, on the basis of approximately 2,000 examples, that the translator's knowledge of German is so poor that he should never have been entrusted with the task' (Riley 1967: 344). Here, as so often, translation evaluation is essentially an exercise in error identification.

The early English translations of Heinrich Mann's texts are characterized by essentially the same features. Boyd's translation of *Der Untertan*, as *The Patrioteer*, in 1921 has been criticized as 'dated', and marred by an entire series of 'inadequacies'. Not least of these is omission. Roche speaks of an 'expurgated text', noting the deletion of at least twelve passages consisting of one paragraph or more (Roche 1986: 492). Peitsch confirms that the sex scenes and much of the more controversial 'political business' were excised to bring the text into line with the conception of 'good taste' that prevailed at the time, and also notes the deletion of chains of leitmotifs occasioned by the quest for lexical variation (Mann, H. 1998: xvi). In his critical bibliography, Morgan questions the accuracy of this translation, noting laconically that the translator is 'apparently not completely master of the German' (Morgan 1965: 320). As Morgan makes clear in his introduction, he applies in his brief evaluative notes the very criteria outlined above as generally typical of the inter-war years. Thus his assessment of Thomas Mann's *Buddenbrooks* begins: 'The English is smooth and the general sense is well caught' (320).

Thomas Mann: 'Wie beneide ich die Musik, daß sie keine Übersetzung braucht!'

In *Doktor Faustus*, the narrator Serenus Zeitblom paints an interesting portrait of the translator Rüdiger Schildknapp, a character for whom the author drew on his friend Hans Reisiger, the Whitman translator. Schildknapp is no mere wordsmith, but rather an assiduous mediator between languages and cultures. In his devotion to the translator's task he resembles his real-life model, Hans Reisiger, whose '*Gewissenhaftigkeit und Sprachgefühl*' Mann singles out for praise in a comment on German translation work in the first decades of the twentieth century (*GW* 10: 720). Zeitblom uses virtually the same words to describe Schildknapp. Passionate about language, he lives and breathes the foreign culture, devoting himself entirely to an obsessive quest for the perfect equivalent: '*[er] betreute die Übertragung mit viel Gewissenhaftigkeit, Stilgefühl und Geschmack, bis zur Versessenheit bemüht um die Genauigkeit der Wiedergabe, das Sichdecken des sprachlichen Ausdrucks und mehr und mehr den intrigierenden Reizen und Mühen der Reproduktion verfallend*' (*GW* 6: 224). But Schildknapp is a problematic figure. He translates partly out of financial necessity, and partly because he is unable to attain true literary merit in his own right: a failure as a '*Dichter*', he becomes a '*vermittelnder Literat*'. Translation is a poor substitute for genuine production, a second-order activity. Schildknapp is ultimately an instrument, in the same way as Mann was to refer to Lowe-Porter as his '*schweigendes Instrument*' (letter to Erich von Kahler of 1 May 1945, *DüD* 3: 52). She, too, failed to achieve real success in her own literary ventures. But even for obsessive devotees like Schildknapp, genuine literary equivalence is an impossible task: the narrator Zeitblom is well aware that true correspondence – something his creator rarely found realized in the renditions of his own works – is illusory, and involves the translator in an ultimately fruitless search. Four years after we first meet Schildknapp, we find him still trapped between bitterness and devotion in his work: '*halb haßerfüllt und halb in leidenschaftlicher Verfallenheit*' (*GW* 6: 267), and during his stay in Palestrina with Leverkühn some years later he is still battling with the '*verzehrenden Schwierigkeit der Übersetzungskunst*' (*GW* 6: 292). The work of the translator is essentially frustrating, since there can be no fully or finally satisfactory rendition. In the postscript to his narration, Zeitblom tells us that he has toyed with the idea of having his lengthy manuscript on Leverkühn's life translated into English, so that it might find an audience abroad. But – like the author himself – he is painfully conscious of the cultural barriers that stand between Germany and America and, looking back at his account, is haunted by '*die sorgende Voraussicht, daß seine Übersetzung ins Englische sich, wenigstens in gewissen, allzu wurzelhaft deutschen Partien, als ein Ding der Unmöglichkeit erweisen würde*' (*GW* 6: 668; see also Mann's letter to Lowe Porter of 4 August 1946, *DüD* 3: 68). The only way to make the desired impact in the English-speaking world, Mann himself concluded, would be to write in English: '*Wäre ich nur in die angelsächsische Kultur hineingeboren*' (letter to Agnes E. Meyer, 23 December 1948, *AEM* 717) he exclaims in a letter on the same text.

The figure of Schildknapp embodies Thomas Mann's ambivalence towards the activity of translation. Like his fictional translator, he was well aware that the notion of the perfect translation was a chimera. Mann did not formulate an extended pronouncement on the issue, but his letters, diaries and essays contain frequent references to the subject, most often in the form of exclamations of complaint concerning his treatment at the hands of his many translators. The ultimate ideal, he frequently stressed, was the seamless intercultural transplantation of the literary work that retains the underlying qualities and aesthetic integrity of the original. Instances of such felicitous transfer are, he admits, extremely rare. In his essay '*Kleists Amphitryon: Eine Wiedereroberung*' (1927), he defines truly successful translation as a poetic discourse created in another language, a magical reincarnation of an artefact across cultural and historical boundaries. He writes of Kleist's version: '*Denn es ist eine Übersetzung im allerkühnsten Sinn dieses Wortes: die wirkliche und unerhörte Übertragung, Entführung und Verzauberung eines Werkes aus seiner Sphäre in eine ihm ursprünglich völlig fremde, aus einem Jahrhundert ins andere, aus einer Nationalität in die andere*' (GW 9: 191). But this is the work of a poet rather than a mere translator, and Kleist's text is an adaptation rather than a translation in the strict sense. Among his own mediators, it seems that Mann was prepared to grant a comparable status – without reservation – only to his early French translator Maurice Betz, whose version of *Der Zauberberg* (1931) he described as '*ein Glücksfall von Einverleibung*' (letter to J. T. Gömöri of 15 November 1951, *DüD* 1: 582; see also the letter to Maria Bradt of 8 November 1953, *DüD* 1: 589). Betz had established a reputation as a great translator of Rilke in the 1920s, and Mann felt privileged to be able to draw on his services. Upon learning of his death in 1946, Mann wrote a letter in which he paid tribute to a translator who was also a '*Dichter und schöpferischer Geist*' (Frères 1949: 88). The definition of translation at issue here is not one of slavish textual transfer, but rather an idealized conception of recreation. It is what Mann describes as '*Nachgestaltung*' (GW 10: 533), the product of genuine '*nachfühlende Kraft*', a congenial reconstitution casting empathetic engagement into truly beautiful linguistic form (GW 9: 783). It is the quality he saw in the work of Tieck and Schlegel (letter to Gömöri of 15 November 1951).

But such fortuitous cases are rare. To those of lesser poetic talent (including, in his view, Lowe-Porter?) he recommends a literal rendition, reiterating his ideas on close correspondence in a letter dated 18 June 1943 (*DüD* 2: 276) on the verse passages in *Joseph der Ernährer*: '*Persönlich wäre es mir das liebste, wenn sich die Übersetzung möglichst genau nach Rhythmus, Reim und Vokabular dem Original anschmiegen könnte.*' Mann was painfully aware that the reality of translation work – that which is practically attainable rather than a vain ideal – is very different indeed. Adopting a metaphor from Cervantes, he compares a translation with the reverse of a woven tapestry: '*denn ob sie gleich die Figuren zeigen, so sind sie doch voller Fäden, die sie entstellen, und sie zeigen sich nicht in der Schönheit und Vollkommenheit wie auf der rechten Seite'* (*GW* 9: 451). This inevitable impoverishment of the original was something he learned to accept. It is the essence of two widely quoted pronouncements by the author on the subject. In his letter to the American teacher Kenneth Oliver of 4 May 1951 (*DüD* 2: 533) he complains that his works in translation are but 'a shadow, a reflection [...] The translation communicates my ideas, more or less, but what is an idea deprived of its native form? In art, content and form are too much one and the same to permit the content to remain entirely unchanged when lifted from its primary form and poured into another', and he goes on to complain that his works give a distorted impression in English. In the above-mentioned letter to his Hungarian translator Gömöri on 15 November 1951 (*DüD* 2: 538) he speaks of the '*Unmöglichkeit* [...], *irgend eine Dichtung aus der Sprache, in der sie gezeugt, aus der sie geboren worden, in eine andere zu übertragen*', insisting that prose works, too, are '*denaturiert*' in translation, that '*ihr Rhythmus gebrochen wird, alle ihre feineren Nuancen unter den Tisch fallen, ja oft ihre innersten Absichten, ihre seelische Haltung und geistige Gesinnung bis zur Unkenntlichkeit, bis zum vollkommenen Mißverständnis entstellt werden, auch beim besten Willen zu getreuer Wiedergabe.*' These sentiments echo a lament expressed some years earlier in a letter to Agnes E. Meyer with regard to the Faustus novel: '*Wie soll denn ein übersetztes Buch, das aller Überredungsmittel entbehrt, die es im Original besitzt, seine natürliche und volle Wirkung tun!*' (23 December 1948, *AEM* 717).

Thus it was, then, that Mann so frequently distanced himself in his letters from the translated versions of his texts, apologetically pointing out to his correspondents that his work was inevitably debased in translation. He did so, for example, to Agnes E. Meyer on *Das Gesetz* (8 March 1944, *AEM* 542), to Jan Lustig on *Joseph der Ernährer* (22 June 1944, *Reg* 3: 48), and to Knopf on *Doktor Faustus* (8 January 1948, *Reg* 3: 420). He commented to Käte Hamburger on *Joseph der Ernährer* in a letter dated 3 October 1944: '*Nur im Original ist das Buch, was es ist. Wie beneide ich die Musik, daß sie keine Übersetzung braucht!*' (*Reg* 3: 83). The word he often used in this context was, as in the letter to Gömöri above, '*denaturiert*'. On Lowe-Porter's version of *Lotte in Weimar*, for example, he commented that it is '*bei allen Verdiensten* [...] *traurig denaturiert*' (*GW* 11: 650). It is an epithet that appears in a number of contexts in Mann's writings, used alongside often drastic synonyms such as '*beraubt*' '*kastriert*', '*verschandelt*' (*GW* 9: 890) or '*entstellt*', '*herabgesetzt*' (*GW* 12: 908). In other words, Mann focused in his comments very much on the loss occasioned in the process of translation. That this loss was an inevitable consequence of intercultural and interlingual transfer was, for him, a simple fact that had to be accepted. Speaking at an event organized by 'Writers in Exile' in 1943 he stressed: '[...] *jeder Schriftsteller wird uns nachfühlen, was es bedeutet, nur als literarischer Schatten, übertragener und denaturierter Weise am Leben zu sein*' (GW 13: 195).

Mann was torn in his dealings with his translators between a fatalistic acceptance of the limitations of literary translation on the one hand and a characteristic perfectionism and attention to detail on the other. His correspondence with Lowe-Porter clearly demonstrates the importance he attached to semantic nuance, cultural-historical accuracy and precision of detail. He encouraged her to consult him on such matters, and patiently answered questions on matters about which she was unsure. The most frequent of these – hardly surprisingly – relate to biblical, geographical and cultural references in the Joseph novels, to archaisms, foreign words and intertextual references in *Doktor Faustus*, and to medieval theological and legendary elements in *Der Erwählte*. He provided the same service for his translators into other languages, most notably Louise Servicen, who later became his established French translator. Although he often conceded that his English was not good, he felt able from the early 1940s onwards to make concrete suggestions regarding translation solutions, and never shied away from correcting what he considered to be inaccuracies in the translations. In view of his imperfect grasp of English, it was perhaps inevitable that such criticisms refer to isolated instances of error or infelicity, rather than to more general issues of style.

On the other hand, though, Mann was prepared to sanction – and even recommended – abridgements and omissions where he felt that the detrimental impact of a strained translation might outweigh the advantages to be gained by overall textual integrity. In *Doktor Faustus* he was concerned that some of the extensive passages on music and theology might overburden the translated texts, and prepared a list of 'cuts and corrections' which he sent to a number of his translators (letter to Knopf of 13 December 1947, *DüD* 3: 117). In a rare letter penned in English, he comments to Lowe-Porter with regard to the same novel (16 August 1946, *DüD* 3: 69): 'Furthermore, I keep asking myself whether or not certain abridgments of passages which are hardly accessible to a non-German public, are indicated in the English edition of the book', and he granted her free rein to excise passages of archaic German as she saw fit (to Lowe-Porter on 29 August 1946, *DüD* 3: 70–1). The same was true of the many allusions contained in *Lotte in Weimar*, especially in Chapter VII : '*Ich sehe vollkommen ein, daß für die Übersetzung manches weggelassen werden muß, und ich glaube, daß ich diese Kürzungen am besten dem Urteil und Gefühl der respektiven Übersetzer anheimgeben werde*' (to Lowe-Porter on 2 August 1939, *DüD* 2: 473). That Mann himself proposed and sanctioned such interventions has often been overlooked in the discussion of his translations. To Lowe-Porter's horror, the omission of passages in her *Doctor Faustus* – precisely those instructed by Mann – was picked up by an attentive critic, Harry Levin, and used as part of an extended diatribe against her version of the novel. And in one especially glaring misapprehension, critics have constructed an entire argument on the mistaken assumption that Lowe-Porter chose to omit homoerotic references from one of Mann's political texts, '*Von deutscher Republik*', in a conscious manipulation and bowdlerization of the text (Lubich 1994; Schmidgall 2001). In fact the omissions were ordered by Mann himself after consultation with Agnes E. Meyer, for fear of confusing the American readership (letter to Agnes E. Meyer, 26 May 1942, *AEM* 402). Mann was ever aware of the expectations and limitations of his target audience, and was not averse to making amendments to his texts in order to enhance their marketability. This can be seen both in his desire to reduce the intercultural difficulties posed by his texts and in his acceptance of commercial arguments advanced by Knopf, e.g. in respect of titles: '*Es wäre ja lächerlich, so zu tun, als ob das Geschäftliche keine Rolle spielte*' (letter to Knopf of 15 June 1940, *DüD* 2: 493).

As he so frequently stressed, Mann was acutely aware of the considerable translation problems his works presented, but was nevertheless at all times concerned to ensure the highest possible quality of their foreign-language versions. However, both these principles were increasingly compromised by a somewhat dubious grasp of the demands of literary translation. His preoccupation with the aesthetic quality of the translations was often challenged by more pecuniary considerations of rapid publication. Mann was, simply, impatient that the English versions of his texts – on which, after all, both his reputation and financial well-being depended – should appear quickly, and if possible simultaneously with the German. This concern is well-documented in his correspondence with Knopf and Lowe-Porter. With little apparent regard for notions of textual integrity and coherence, for underlying structural principles or recurrent motifs, he went so far as to urge (indeed, insist) that his translator start work on her translations before he had even completed the original text. For Lowe-Porter this was a serious problem, as she commented in a letter to Blanche Knopf dated 19 March 1926, referring to *Der Zauberberg*. Having just been informed that the publisher wished to set up her translation of the first volume before she had completed work on the second, she stressed the 'risk of endangering the continuity of the text: by which I mean, that the phrasal repetition has to undergo a gradual and *very* careful modification as Dr. Mann reintroduces his motifs with variations; and some phrases in the first volume might have to be slightly altered to harmonize with later forms' (Henderson and Oram

2010: 317). Mann also suggested piecemeal translation for *Joseph der Ernährer*, sending Lowe-Porter isolated parts to translate: '*es wäre schön, wenn die Uebersetzung neben der Arbeit daran herzulaufen begönne, sodaß wir ungefähr gleichzeitig fertig würden und Original und Uebersetzung gleichzeitig erscheinungsbereit wären*' (18 July 1941, *DüD* 2: 238). He urged the same procedure with regard to other texts, e.g *Die Geschichten Jaakobs* and *Der Erwählte*. He wrote to Knopf on 17 October 1950 in connection with the latter: 'I am busily occupied completing the strange legendary novel whose translation Mrs Lowe is already working on. Only a few more weeks, and I will be able to send her the transcript of the last chapters' (*DüD* 3: 372). He appreciated, he claimed, that Lowe-Porter had profound reservations concerning such a procedure, but his concern with speedy publication prevailed (letter of 27 January 1932, *DüD* 2: 119). On frequent occasions he asked her to interrupt her work and bring parts of the texts forward for pre-publication.

The problematic nature of this procedure is most clear in connection with *Doktor Faustus*. Here, too, Lowe-Porter was already busy with the translation while Mann continued working on the original: '*Während Sie den Kampf schon aufnehmen, bemühe ich mich redlich und nicht ohne Erfolg, mit den letzten Teilen des Romans vorwärts zu kommen*' (29 August 1946, *DüD* 3: 71). This startling procedure clearly came as something of a surprise to Knopf, to whom Lowe-Porter had obviously complained (see Knopf's letter to Mann of 5 August 1946, quoted in *TB* 1946–8: 28). Its full implications become apparent when one bears in mind that Lowe-Porter had considerable difficulty with this text. Even after reading the first large batch of manuscript material Mann had sent her – the first 261 pages of the novel – she commented that she had not yet been able to identify its underlying concerns: 'I do not yet know what he is driving at' (T: 97). Nowhere is Mann's ambivalence more evident than in the pre-publication history of the English version of this novel. Lowe-Porter, fearing that she had not produced a work which met her own standards, asked for more time to complete her translation. Mann was initially highly supportive, arguing to Knopf that all parties concerned, surely, wanted 'the most perfect translation possible' (letter of 13 December 1947, *DüD* 3: 118). When Knopf rejected this suggestion, Mann claimed to be relieved. He was sure, he wrote on 8 January 1948 (*DüD* 3: 125), that even under her current pressure Lowe-Porter would produce a 'satisfactory' version, which was all that was 'humanly possible' given the sheer impossibility of a 'truly ideal translation'.

Conclusion

Mann, like many exiles, was profoundly frustrated by the fact that he was so utterly dependent on the dissemination of his works through other languages following their prohibition in Germany. Among his favourite images was that of the writer who has disappeared behind his foreign-language versions: *'Unsere Bücher sind verbannt, wie wir selbst, sie existieren nur noch in Übersetzungen'* (GW 13: 195). He saw himself as an author who has lost his authentic voice: *'wo wird mein ursprüngliches deutsches Wort noch gehört?'* (letter to Agnes Meyer 6 October 1838, *AEM* 133). As we have seen, he was convinced that his translated voice could never fully echo his native German: his scepticism concerning the translatability of his works was profound. His frustration was, though, generally tempered by gratitude for the immensity of the work undertaken by his mediators, most notably by Lowe-Porter in the English-speaking world, acting through the professional and competent agency of Knopf.

Mann was well aware of Lowe-Porter's limitations. From both their personal meetings and their extensive collaboration he was familiar with the weaknesses of her German, which he saw as the root cause of many of the *'Mißverständnisse und Inadaequatheiten'* in her versions of his work (letter to Frau Hans Meisel 28 November 1939, *DüD* 2: 477). But her linguistic inadequacies did not, in keeping with the translational practices of the time, necessarily disqualify her as a translator. As we have seen, a number of the 'classic translators' of the first half of the twentieth century did not have the degree of competence in their translating language that one would expect today: the Muirs had no formal training in German, but acquired the language during stays in Germany and Austria, and began translating (Hauptmann) when their command of the language was still far from perfect (Mellown 1964: 311); Garnett failed to understand parts of the Russian texts she translated; and Scott Moncrieff's texts have been widely criticized for their numerous errors. It may well be the case that the frequency of errors in Lowe-Porter's versions is especially high, but this is not the only yardstick to be applied in the assessment of her achievement. In a translation poetics which champions fluency and acceptability over accuracy and adequacy, semantic equivalence was not the paramount criterion. Certainly, Mann learned to accept Lowe-Porter's undoubted shortcomings largely because he was convinced – both by his own readings and by the praise of others, above all the Knopfs – of the quality of her writing in English: *'sie beherrscht ihre eigene Sprache, das Englische, vortrefflich, das Deutsche nicht ebenso gut'* (letter to Frau Hans Meisel quoted above). He was also, of course, profoundly grateful that she had proved so effective in securing his claim to literary greatness. On more than one occasion he consoled himself with the conviction that great work will shine through even in a poor translation: *'Hat ein Buch Substanz, so bleibt viel übrig, auch in einer schlechten Übersetzung'* (letter to Gömöri 15 November 1951; see also Heilbut 1995: 459).

Overall, he stressed, he felt that fate had treated him kindly in the allocation of a translator. While he granted himself the privilege of carping at her translations, he was always ready to defend her efforts against criticism from others, and to insist that no replacement would ever be able to improve on her achievement. Thus, he was highly assertive in his defence of her against challenges from Werner G. Jensh on errors in *Die vertauschten Köpfe* (18 June 1941, *Reg* 2: 526), against Julian Leigh on *Joseph in Ägypten* (21 August 1945, *Reg* 3: 175) and against Adele Katz on *Lotte in Weimar* on 28 December 1940, *Reg* 2: 483). In a letter to Lowe-Porter of 19 April 1948 on *Doktor Faustus*, Mann – once again pursuing his customary policy of diplomacy and flattery – picked up the metaphor of beauty versus fidelity that she had used in her *Buddenbrooks* preface 24 years earlier, calling her version 'not only beautiful but faithful as well' (T 103). Perhaps a more honest summary of his feelings, though, is to be found in a letter to Agnes Meyer in which the accumulation of four modal expressions signals the genuine ambivalence which he felt at heart. – '*After all ist sie doch wohl die beste Interpretin, die Knopf für mich finden konnte*' (15 October 1942, *AEM* 434).

4 An exercise in translation comparison: *Der Zauberberg*

Introductory remarks

Some two years after the polemical debate in *The Times Literary Supplement* on the quality of Lowe-Porter's versions of Mann's texts, Timothy Buck published what he called a 'supplement' to the discussion (Buck 1997). The renewed intervention was prompted by the appearance of a new translation of Mann's *Der Zauberberg*, commissioned by Alfred A. Knopf publishers at Random House and produced by John E. Woods (Woods 1995). While Buck welcomed Woods' text as a 'considerable improvement on his predecessor's' due to its 'generally greater precision' and 'polished, fluent' style, he maintained the hortatory tenor of his previous contributions. The new version appears to be free of 'howlers', he noted, but 'the new American translator does misunderstand the German on quite a few occasions' (1997: 658). Buck illustrated his argument by listing some 17 mismatches between the German original and the new English translation, and concluded that 'reliable versions' of Mann's texts remain unavailable in English. But how much can really be said about the translation of such a voluminous novel in the space of just over three pages? And can conclusions drawn on the basis of a handful of isolated examples claim any representative status in the case of a novel which, in Woods' version, is 706 pages long? Clearly, it is difficult to arrive at a global assessment (or description) of a translation of such a long text. Newmark's entry on the novel in the *Encyclopaedia of Literary Translation into English* is representative of the approach typically taken in attempts to characterize a translator's work: he, too, isolates just a few (three) passages for comment. Like Buck, he is aware of the many errors in the original translations, but argues for a less judgmental form of critique, and is sensitive to the qualities of Lowe-Porter's work (Newmark 2000: 909).

In their combination of description and evaluation, discussions of literary translations frequently fail to provide either to any satisfying degree. Contributions are typically either too selective and anecdotally evaluative to claim any real descriptive value, or they fail to offer the kind of descriptive substance that could justify any serious evaluative conclusions. Traditional stylistics has dealt with the problems of selection and representativeness by insisting on the *qualitative* dimension of detailed textual study. Its aim is to underpin, refine and perhaps revise guiding notions about the text with the aid of supporting references and data, in an attempt to demonstrate relations between form and function with a high degree of granularity and replicability. Here, the superordinate role of literary analysis and interpretation in determining those objects of analysis is accepted as inevitable, and the analytical procedure is fundamentally example-based. In *quantitative* linguistic analyses of texts, on the other hand, modern computational resources are used to retrieve statistically relevant data from digitized versions of texts. As a specific application of corpus linguistics, 'corpus stylistics' seeks to harness the advantages of computational techniques for the purposes of literary analysis, identifying patterns and recurrences that might establish a reliable and empirically based textual foundation for a definition of the distinctiveness of the individual text, and thus for the interpretation of literary meaning. In most cases, work with electronic texts is computer-assisted rather than truly corpus-driven, and the definition of the type of data to be retrieved ultimately remains 'intuition-based' (Mahlberg 2007: 220). As Munday stresses, such work generally shows how useful computer searches can be, but also reveals 'the crucial need for qualitative analysis of individual examples to assess their relevance and importance' (Munday 2007: 33, see also Kenny 2001: 69ff.). Ultimately, no doubt, the quantitative and qualitative approaches to analysis are complementary: interpretation requires data if it is to be in any way empirically testable, and data requires interpretation if it is to be in any way useful (Stubbs 2005).

The following comparative discussion of two translations of Mann's *Zauberberg* draws on both qualitative and quantitative approaches in seeking to arrive at an overall characterization and differentiation of the texts at issue. As outlined in Chapter 1, the methodology adopted here is grounded on – and adapted from – the models developed within the framework of monolingual stylistics (Leech/Short 2007; Eroms 2008; Fix et al. 2010) and descriptive translation studies, above all within the transfer-oriented enterprise practised by the Göttingen researchers (especially Frank and Kittel 2004). The discussion thus proceeds from the metalevel (the contextual localization and preliminary characterization of the translations analyzed) via a definition and exploration of microstylistic features at the level of lexis and syntax to the broader text-constitutive dimensions of macrostylistic analysis; on the distinction between these two levels see Hoffmann 2009. In the central stage, a comparative survey of syntactic and lexical phenomena is offered in an attempt to characterize fundamental differences between translator strategies, primarily at the sentential level. The higher-order organizational principles focused on in the latter part of the discussion (what Leech/Short call 'context') have been selected in response to salient dimensions of Mann's narrative technique as identified in the scholarship. They are, then, key dimensions of the text in terms of their impact on the potential generation of literary meaning. These are the issues of cross-textual lexical cohesion (recurrences as a structuring device), discourse forms (in this case the extensive use of characterizing direct speech), and narrative stance (the celebrated ironic tone of the text.). This bottom-up approach to the textual dimension is based on the assumption that textual meanings at the macrolevel accrue from the interaction of features on the microlevel, which is more easily susceptible to detailed comparative analysis (Hewson 2011: 18). And it is further underpinned by the insight that the majority of shifts and divergences apparent in modern translations (strictu sensu) occur at the lexico-grammatical level, affecting the meaning potential of the text in subtle ways (Munday 2007: 41).

Preliminary characterization

The two versions of Mann's *Der Zauberberg* which form the basis of the present chapter (and they are the only two English versions) are separated by almost seventy years. As was noted in Chapter 2, Lowe-Porter took on the commission of translating the work in 1925 against Mann's wishes. It was the second novel she translated for Mann/Knopf. With his customary courtesy and commitment, Mann supported his translator in her work once she had been appointed, advising her on a number of points of difficulty. However, he does not seem to have had access to any drafts of the translation in progress. Upon the publication of the translation in 1927 he voiced praise for her efforts, but complained about a number of 'slight errors' (letter to Lowe-Porter of 22 May 1927, Thirlwall 1966: 15). The retranslation by John E. Woods, published in 1995, forms part of a series of Mann novels (the second, after *Buddenbrooks*) for which he was commissioned by Random House/Knopf. The express purpose of the retranslation was to provide a more modern version of the text designed specifically for an American readership. To this extent, the temporal gap separating the two versions generates a divergence in functions: the first is a contemporaneous version designed to fulfil the receptive expectations of a global English-speaking audience broadly unaware of the author, while the second is a conscious reworking of a text that has become, in the intervening period, a classic work by a canonical author.

Der Zauberberg is a massive work. The German original comprises 994 pages, over 300,000 words (tokens) and some 38,000 different words (types). The novel provides a useful test bed for a comparison of translation strategies and translator preferences, largely on account of its enormous linguistic diversity and complexity. Linguistic sophistication has always been recognized as a hallmark of Mann's style. It is, to a large degree, due to the author's lexical range. His works abound in rare, archaic, regional and foreign words, are marked by a large number of hapax legomena (words which occur only once), a high level of lexical variety (ratio of different words to the total number of words), a high degree of lexical density (ratio of content words to function words), and a large number of neologisms. They mix registers with great dexterity. This joy in lexical experimentation is evident, too, at the morphological level. Mann has a predilection for extensive compounding: nouns are fused together in unusual, even unique, combinations, adjectives are accumulated in (sometimes oxymoronic) groups of two, three, and even four, and are in many instances hyphenated to create semantically complex units. In this additive style, long attributive sequences are widespread, and adjectives – many of them abstract – are frequently nominalized. Grammatically, his texts cultivate obsolete forms, reviving classical genitive patterns, extensive absolute constructions, gerunds, anastrophes and participial forms. They exploit the full range of rhetorical schemes and tropes. Syntactically, Mann's language shows a marked tendency towards concatenation, generating complex hypotactic sentences in which entire series of clause elements are stacked in a process of retardation and anticipation. His sentence structure, which has often been described as cumulative and additive, goes far beyond the merely sequential and linear: it is, at its best, highly integrative and periodic in structure, holding large numbers of parenthetically inserted elements – sequences of nouns, attributes, adverbials, modifying and subordinating structures, conjunctive clause relations – in a carefully constructed balance between the auxiliary and main verb. His sentence-building technique has always invited description in metaphorical terms, frequently being described through analogies with architecture, music and topography. Yet Mann's syntactic structures are not as untypically complex as has often been suggested: a number of quantitative studies of Mann's texts have in the meantime demonstrated that the scale and intricacy of his sentences are by no means exceptional compared with those of some of his contemporaries: Kafka, Musil, Hofmannsthal, Hesse and Heinrich Mann have typically been used for purposes of comparison (Arens 1964; Hassan 1967; Grimm 1991).

The density and sophistication of Mann's style is now typically seen as a modernist rather than anachronistic device (Frizen 2001; Erben 2006). Classical though it may seem, it does not articulate a balanced and stable view of the world. Rather, its processes of accumulation and expansion, qualification and re-qualification are a reflex of the dislocated subject's search for clarity and stability of meaning in an unstable object world. Phenomena and mental processes can no longer be adequately described with a few well-chosen words, and packed into an economical syntactic unit. Instead, the problematic disjunction between external reality, cognition and expression necessitates multiple definitions, complementary and apparently contradictory formulations, often from an ironic distance. What on the surface may seem pleonastic and labyrinthine is seen, in modern readings of Mann, as a process of exploration and illumination from various angles. The intricate (but never convoluted) syntax of Mann's texts is interpreted as an index of a complex vision of reality: the linguistic structure itself has become iconic, mimetically reflecting the multiple perspectives brought to bear on the modern perception of experience. Lubich's definition of the thematic ambivalences in Mann's oeuvre might serve equally well as a characterization of his syntactic forms: 'The frequent illumination of both sides of an issue, and the negotiating of its various contradictions and underlying similarities, became Mann's characteristic trademarks, establishing him as his country's unchallenged literary master of ambivalences' (Lubich 1999: xxiv). The linguistic complexity and differentiation in Mann's texts constitute a challenge for any translator. Indeed, *Der Zauberberg* is a true rhetorical tour de force in which language is frequently thematized on a metalinguistic level. It is, therefore, hardly surprising that it has been called '*ein linguistischer Roman*' (Gauger 1975): language and consciousness, articulation and definition play a central role. The development of Hans Castorp's ability to give verbal expression to his views – from his initially unreflective and often confused speech patterns to more abstract and sustained quasi-intellectual discourse – is an integral part of the education he undergoes. They are an index of the '*Emanzipation der Handlungsfigur als Sprachfindung*' (Vogt 2008: 163).

Both translations under examination here are integral in Toury's sense, making no amendments to the macrostructural organization. They contain no additional paratextual material in the form of translator's prefaces or notes, and retain the device of listing all the chapters in an introductory index. They do not redistribute textual material, but replicate all the chapters and divisions in an identical sequence. The typological arrangement of the major (numbered) chapter headings and (unnumbered) subsections is retained. Only one feature of the textual layout is modified by the translators: both frequently amend the position of reporting structures which introduce passages of direct discourse, placing them directly in front of the quoted speech. This amendment to the layout of the text appears to be an adaptation to the norms of English textual organization, where passages of direct speech are commonly separated out, especially in longer dialogic exchanges. Less frequently, Lowe-Porter also changes the paragraphing of the text, extending paragraphs by fusing material from the following passage.

Both translations are full and unexpurgated versions of Mann's novel. Extensive sampling indicates that Woods' version is truly integral, with an average of no more than five omitted lexical elements per page. These are counterbalanced by an approximately equal number of additions. His modifications occur in connection with the syntactic flow of the text: closed class items such as conjunctions, modal adverbs and interjections are the most frequent word types affected, while lexical words are only rarely omitted or amended. Lowe-Porter's version, on the other hand, is marked by approximately twice the number of omissions and virtually the same number of additions as Woods. As a general tendency, then, her version is a less complete representation of the original, something which is evident in the total number of words (see below). She frequently deletes larger units: entire phrases, clause elements, and – on occasion – even complete clauses. Sampling further indicates that neither version contains extensive additions.

Two general issues of translation strategy should be mentioned before an overview of microstylistic phenomena is offered. As a preliminary norm, the question of the orientation of the translations requires consideration. *Der Zauberberg* is a novel addressed to a German-speaking readership, and is set in a sanatorium in German-speaking Switzerland. Thus, the degree of cultural adaptation (in terms of domesticization or foreignization) is a relevant overall factor. Neither of the two versions shows evidence of a markedly source-oriented thrust, i.e. consistent alienation of the reader through the retention of source-culture features, nor of widespread assimilation to the knowledge systems and presuppositions of the target readership. Both versions are neutral in this sense. In its broad range of historical, philosophical, literary, musical and scientific reference, Mann's text is highly demanding for German readers, and neither translator seeks to dilute significantly this challenge for the target readership. There are no indications of the deletion of passages that might strain the knowledge of the English-speaking reader, no annotations, nor extensive explanatory insertions into the text. In terms of their cultural orientation, as reflected in the treatment of culturally specific items, there is no significant difference between the versions. Both translators retain the German titles '*Herr*', '*Frau*' and '*Fräulein*'. Lowe-Porter retains '*Hofrat*', which Woods generally renders as 'Director' (Behrens). All other titular epithets ('*Staatsanwalt*', '*Oberin*', '*Assistenzarzt*') are translated. With regard to the conversion of systems of unit and measurement, both versions have 'francs', as well as 'marks' and 'pfennigs', but Woods converts 'grammes' into 'ounces'. Where institutional terminology (e.g.

from the education system) is translated via the adoption of cultural equivalents, Lowe-Porter uses British forms ('lower third form', the lower second', 'schoolmaster', 'holiday') while Woods favours explicitly US norms ('seventh-grader', 'sophomore year', 'educator', 'vacation'). In general, Woods remains closer to the German text, transforming fewer references: he has '*Graubünden*' for Lowe-Porter's 'Grisons', the 'Swabian Sea' for her 'Lake Constance', but uses 'Transylvania' for '*Siebenbürgen*'; he has 'luster' for her 'mohair', '*Plattdeutsch*' where she has 'dialect'. On the other hand, he prefers 'fraternity' to Lowe-Porter's '*Burschenschaft*', and provides intratextual explanations of two of the more obscure references to Goethe's *Faust* in the 'Walpurgisnacht' scene. Both translators leave the titles of quoted 'Lieder' (they use the German generic form of the noun) in the original form, and provide their own translation of textual quotations. None of the translated versions appears to draw extensively on attested English translations, with one exception: Lowe-Porter's 'But mind, the mountain's magic-mad tonight' quotes, at least in its first line, an 1886 translation of *Faust* by Theodore Martin (Goethe 1886).

In terms of the historical (linguistic) orientation of the texts, the versions must be seen in the context of both the time depicted (1907–14) and of the date of their genesis (mid-1920s versus mid-1990s). Lowe-Porter's version has frequently been criticized for its archaism (e.g. Harmann 1995: 5). This is, indeed, a characteristic of her text that spans various levels of linguistic organization, lexical and syntactic, and it is strikingly evident at the paratextual level. The contents lists (sub-chapter headings) of the two versions give an initial indication of the contrasting treatment of Mann's idiom in this regard: Lowe-Porter is at pains to capture the classical-traditional flavour of Mann's text, replicating his use of the preposition 'von' in four of the 51 title headings (e.g. 'Of the christening basin, and of grandfather in his twofold guise'). In lexical terms, too, Lowe-Porter favours older formulations in her chapter headings: 'Mental gymnastic' for '*Gedankenschärfe*' (Woods has 'Clarity of Mind'), 'Choler, and worse' for '*Jähzorn. Und noch etwas ganz Peinliches*' where Woods has 'An Outburst of Temper/Something very Embarrassing', the expansive and reader-inclusive 'Satana makes proposals that touch our honour' for '*Satana macht ehrrührige Vorschläge*' (Woods: 'Satana Makes Shameful Suggestions'), and the postmodified and quasi-religious 'Soup-everlasting' ('*Ewigkeitssuppe*') where Woods has 'Eternal Soup'. In the text itself, the differences between the temporal-historical flavour of the two versions are striking. Throughout, Lowe-Porter favours archaizing devices. On the level of individual lexemes (closed classes), she has a penchant for poetic-archaic adverbs ('hither', 'thither', 'whither', and even 'nowhither'); 'yonder' as both an adjective and adverb; 'yon' (on one occasion as 'hither and yon'), 'betimes', 'awhile'. She also uses formal/obsolete compound prepositions ('whereof', 'therein') and favours archaic prepositional phrases ('in the idea of', 'on a sudden', 'on the theory that', 'of set purpose to'). At the level of lexical words we find archaisms such as 'bedizened', 'hark', 'forsooth', 'lodgment', 'coif', 'pettifoggery', 'forenoon', 'middle-day', 'forth-putting', 'four-and-twenty', as well as dated verbal constructions such as 'make head against', 'put plainer name to', 'habituate oneself'. She adopts entire phraseological structures which are marked by an archaic flavour: 'feeling his own withers unwrung', 'white-haired and exceeding wroth', 'betook him to his balcony', 'favoured her with converse', 'her breast was wrung with a sigh', and interjections: 'Pray'. Lowe-Porter also frequently adopts an archaic-poetic sentence structure, fronting the direct object: 'Creatures like that one has to love, whether one will or no' or complement: 'Other furniture there was none', 'warm he must have it in his little room'. The dated quality of such renderings, even from the perspective of Lowe-Porter's time of writing (the mid-1920s), is confirmed by historical sources and corpora. Lowe-Porter's text is at its most archaizing, perhaps, in its treatment of pronominal forms of address in direct speech, where she uses both 'thou' and 'ye' (see Chapter 7), which she combines with obsolete verb morphologies ('thou livest').

In all these cases, Woods has significantly more modern renditions. He, too, occasionally adopts a pseudo-archaic diction to suggest something of the early twentieth-century context and to attain a level of elevation ('don apparel', 'take the notion of something', 'with utmost dispatch', 'inaugurate a new regimen', 'confabulator'). Thus, one commentator wonders whether the 'ineluctable petersham coat' attributed by Woods to Settembrini is any more transparent for the modern reader than Lowe-Porter's 'inevitable pilot-coat' (Bruckner 1995). In general, however, Woods' version is an extensive modernization which in places is anachronistic in its choice of formulations. Forms which were not fully lexicalized in American English in the 1920s include: 'play hooky', 'gay blade', 'cross-dressed', 'lamebrain', 'dimwit', 'twiddle-twaddle'. His word order conforms to contemporary English-speaking norms throughout.

Microstylistic features
Syntax
An initial overall comparison of the two versions at the microstylistic level can be derived from the use of quantitative data. For this purpose, I have analyzed the translations with the aid of the Wordsmith suite of tools, which offer global data and statistics on frequencies and distributions. For data on Mann's text, I have compared the Wordsmith output with data derived from the Thomas-Mann-Korpus in Mannheim. In

An exercise in translation comparison: *Der Zauberberg* 91

the area of syntax, the use of the statistical function of Wordsmith reveals a number of parallels and divergences between the two English versions of the text. The Woods version of the novel is longer than Lowe-Porter's, having a higher total number of words (341,803 versus 329,455). Since both versions have virtually the same number of sentences (15,613 for Woods versus 15,687 for Lowe-Porter), Woods also has a slightly longer mean sentence length (21.8 versus 21.00). However, this difference is hardly as marked as is commonly suggested in comments on Lowe-Porter's work (e.g. Luke 1988: 1). Perhaps surprisingly, Lowe-Porter's average sentence length is very close to that of Mann's original, which stands at 21.5 The mean sentence length of over 20 wps indicates that both translations follow the expansive syntactic structure of Mann's novel. This figure is in the upper range for the sentence length of literary novels in English, but is still well within the bounds of easy readability, which is commonly placed at between 19–25 words. Lowe-Porter's overall reduction in the length of the text is due to a number of features. These are illustrated below primarily on the basis of examples drawn from Chapter 4 of the novel, the section discussed by Buck: the divergence in the number of words and sentences between the two versions in this section corresponds to that which can be observed for the text as a whole.

Lowe-Porter frequently omits individual words, phrases, clause elements and clauses. In some cases she appears to do so in the interest of compression, while on other occasions there is no apparent motivation. All word classes are affected, and no pattern emerges in the exclusions she undertakes. Thus, she often transfers long and complex structures in their entirety, rendering each component part, while on other occasions she deletes elements from shorter structures. By the same token, she adds elements which are not present in the original. A very brief example of the procedure she adopts may be cited here, indicating one process of omission (the relative clause) and two instances of non-obligatory addition (the amplification of the subject, the insertion of 'at least'):

Es waren doch schließlich einund-zwanzig Tage gewesen, die sie hatten miteinander verleben sollen, eine lange Reihe, nicht leicht zu übersehen am Anfang. (GW 3: 228)	'For, after all, three weeks, twenty-one days, is a considerable stretch of time, too long, at least, for one to see the end at the beginning'. (Lowe-Porter 1960: 162)

The following general observations concerning omissions are made on the basis of sampling from Chapter 4 of the novel.

In many cases, Lowe-Porter's omissions relate to adverbs and interjections in passages of both narratorial text and direct speech (*'schon'*, '*ja*', '*kurz*', '*kurzum*', '*übrigens*'), which serve as markers of a conversational, informal form of discourse as it is frequently set off against the often ironically pompous and incongruous tone of other narratorial passages. Characteristic repeated discourse markers in direct speech ('*Prägen Sie es sich ein*', '*Hören Sie dieses*', '*in Gottes Namen*', '*meine Herren*', '*das muss ich sagen*', '*Was glauben die Herren*') are often deleted. So, too, are the many series of ellipsis marks (three dots) which Mann inserts to denote pauses and omissions, and many of the exclamation marks which appear in the text (while Woods takes these over in virtually all cases from Mann's text, Lowe-Porter omits some 70 per cent of them). These modifications at the lexical and graphemic level clearly influence the characteristic quality of the discourse representation. Other adverbial elements are omitted for no apparent reason other than they might be considered extraneous detail ('*gegen Dank und Quittung*').

Lowe-Porter frequently omits lexical items in cumulative sequences of semantically similar words. Thus, she abridges series of verbs into shorter sequences: her 'contemplated with such inward gratification' (164) renders '*blickte wohlgefällig*' and '*empfand so inniges Vergnügen*' (231). She deletes nouns in combinations: '*Joachim als der Eingesessene und Kundige*' (185) becomes 'in his character as inmate' (132), and reduces sequences of adjectives ('*forsch und fidel und gemütlich*' (209) is rendered as 'very jovial and lively', 148) or participles: '*verronnen, verflogen, enteilt*' (228) becomes 'It had rushed past, it had flown' (162). She reduces heavy abstract phrases to single nouns ('*eine heilig-selbstverständliche Unverbrüchlichkeit*' (208) is rendered as 'sanctity' (148), '*mit Religiosität und Unterwürfigkeit*' (135) becomes 'with bated breath' (95). All such cases illustrate the process of simplification which has often been considered to be a translation universal. Her treatment of extensive nominal groups – alongside concatenative sentence structure, a further hallmark of Mann's style – shows changes to the weight of the phrases. This weight is due to the number of head nouns placed in sequence, and to the scope of pre- and postmodification. Lowe-Porter often redistributes elements of Mann's text, thus simplifying processes of qualification and modification in the German text not merely via omission, but also via the redistribution and transposition of elements. As the example below illustrates, this can on occasion lead to greater density:

Er überschritt den Steg und setzte sich, um sich vom Anblick des Wassersturzes, des treibenden Schaums unterhalten zu lassen, dem idyllisch gesprächigen, einförmigen und doch innerlich abwechslungsvollen Geräusch zu lauschen […] (168)	He crossed the foot-bridge and sat down to regale himself with the sight of the foaming, rushing waterfall and the idyllic sound of its monotonous yet modulated prattle. (119)

Trailing postmodifiers become shorter participial or adjectival elements (*'des treibenden Schaums'* = 'foaming'), while adjectives are nominalized (*'gesprächig'* = 'prattle') and constituents are shifted into positions where they qualify different referents (in Mann the foam is *'treibend'*, while in Lowe-Porter's version it is the waterfall). This latter technique enables the translator to dissolve the final attributive structure (*'dem ... Geräusch'*). Mann's two-verb structure (*'sich unterhalten lassen'*, *'lauschen'*) is compressed into one single predicate, reducing the complexity of the sentence structure and diluting the additive, qualifying character of the arguments.

The fact that the discrepancy between the total number of words in the two versions is not larger despite the frequency of omissions evident in Lowe-Porter's text is due to the relatively large number of additions she undertakes relative to Woods' version. Most of these additions are undertaken in the interest of clarification or explicitation. This can take place on the level of lexis, where constituents are expanded and more fully lexicalized: the adverbial *'alles in allem'* (227) becomes the non-finite clause 'to cover the sum total of his expenses' (162), or where a specific reference is provided to clarify the meaning *'die beiden periodischen Abwandlungen des Normaltages'* (228) becomes 'the lecture and the concert, those two recurrent variations in the weekly programme' (162); the *'Rund der Taufschale, des stehend-wandernden Erbstückes'* (217) becomes 'of the old christening basin, that symbol of the passing and the abiding, of continuity through change' (154). At the level of syntax, additions are commonly undertaken to clarify reference. Thus the conjunction *'damit'* can be replaced by an entire sentence-initial phrase: 'As the result of some simple figuring' (162); simple pronouns (*'dies'*) are expanded by additional cohesive referents ('this vicarious suffering', 163); explicit subjects and additional verbs are inserted to make the context clear: *'Aber während dieser drei Wochen hätten sie der Zeit etwas besser aufpassen sollen, so, wie es während des Messens geschah'* (229: 20 words) becomes 'But Hans Castorp felt that during these three weeks they ought to have paid more attention, to have kept better watch, as Joachim did in his daily measurings' (162: 28 words).

Lowe-Porter has often been criticized for distorting the structures of Mann's syntax by introducing unnecessary sentence breaks, thus obfuscating a fundamental quality of Mann's writing. In fact, however, both translators break the German sentences down, on occasions redistributing information units. The relatively slight deviation in the total number of sentences in the translations as a whole, and in the average sentence length, indicates that Lowe-Porter does not undertake an unusually large number of reductions in her syntax. In both English versions, the vast majority (over 80 per cent) of the changes to sentence boundaries which serve to increase the number of sentences vis-à-vis

Mann's original are due to changes to punctuation. In most cases where there are divergences between sentence boundaries, the translator closes a sentence where Mann continues after a semicolon, colon or dash, or where he introduces material in brackets. In Lowe-Porter's version in particular, conjunctive relations (*'und'*, *'aber'*, *'während'*) are frequently deleted when a new sentence is opened. In the case of the omission of the latter two conjunctions, of course, an explicit logical contrastive relationship (or a temporal linkage) is reduced by the introduction of a main clause. Only relatively rarely does Lowe-Porter separate relative clauses into independent structures. Where she does this, she is forced (if she wishes to retain the linkage at all) either to move the antecedent noun into the new independent clause ('Joachim did not at once see anything funny', 102), to repeat the antecedent in the new clause ('the perception of time', 104), to add further additional material, e.g by adding explicitating elements (the latter two techniques, of course, expand the text), or to insert some form of connector.

While Woods is at pains to mirror the sequential structure of Mann's original and to account for each clause element in turn, Lowe-Porter uses a variety of techniques which result in a higher degree of syntactic compression within clauses. She does this most notably by reducing finite clauses to participial constructions (*'und dabei ist ja die ärztliche Behandlung schon einbegriffen'*, 227) becomes 'treatment included' (161)) and by reducing entire subordinate clauses to simple, and simplifying, adjectives: thus, *'trotz des naßkalten Wetters, das sich vor seiner Abreise nicht mehr bessern zu wollen schien'* (230) is rendered as 'despite the long spell of cold, wet weather' (163); *'deren ich mich gar nicht von Ihnen versehen hätte'* (138) appears simply as 'unexpected' (97); and *'ohne dass sie sich miteinander verständigt hätten'* (137) becomes 'silent agreement' (96).

In general, however, there is no significant modification of sentence complexity in Lowe-Porter's version. From the initial monumentally hypotactic structure of Mann's foreword (the *'Vorsatz'*) onwards, her syntax mirrors Mann's structures more closely than is often assumed. Nevertheless, automated readability analysis of sections of the Lowe-Porter and Woods translations using systems such as Textalyser and the Text Content Analysis Tool (see previous chapter) does show a discrepancy in the comprehensibility indices of the two versions. This is due primarily to the latter's slightly greater sentence length: in all sections analysed for the purpose of the present discussion, the Woods versions have a higher readability score, and are thus more difficult to process. This is particularly the case in the longest section of Chapter 4, *'Aufsteigende Angst …'*. There, Lowe-Porter has fewer words (9,285 v. 9,510), more sentences (364 v 331), a similar ratio of total words to different words (a type-token ratio of 25.56 v 24.7) and a lower sentence

An exercise in translation comparison: *Der Zauberberg* 95

length (25.21 v. 28.73). Her version thus has a significantly lower LIX score than Woods' (46.7 v. 50.69) – a rough indicator of the readability of the texts. These rather crude measures would appear to confirm that Woods' version approximates more closely to the greater complexity and sophistication of Mann's original formulations.

The above-mentioned procedures of modification – omission of words and phrases, removal of repetitions and parallelisms, sentence shortening with concomitant implications for cohesion, syntactic compression, redistribution of elements – can be illustrated by referring to Lowe-Porter's treatment of one typical construction in Mann's text, which contains frequent insertions and parentheses, and closes with an asyndetic coordination.

Hans Castorps Woche lief hier von Dienstag bis Dienstag, denn an einem Dienstag war er ja angekommen. Daß er im Bureau seine zweite Wochenrechnung beglichen hatte, lag schon ein paar Tage zurück, – die bescheidene Wochenrechnung von rund 160 Franken, bescheiden und billig nach seinem Urteil, selbst wenn man die Unbezahlbarkeiten des hiesigen Aufenthalts, eben ihrer Unbezahlbarkeit wegen, überhaupt nicht in Anschlag brachte, auch nicht gewisse Darbietungen, die wohl berechenbar gewesen wären, wenn man gewollt hätte, wie zum Exempel die vierzehntägige Kurmusik und	HANS CASTORP'S week here ran from Tuesday to Tuesday, for on a Tuesday he had arrived. Two or three days before, he had gone down to the office and paid his second weekly bill, a modest account of a round one hundred and sixty francs, modest and cheap enough, even without taking into consideration the nature of some of the advantages of a stay up here -- advantages priceless in themselves, though for that very reason they could not be included in the bill -- and even without counting extras like the fortnightly concert and Dr. Krokowski's lectures, which might conceivably	HANS CASTORP'S WEEK here ran from Tuesday to Tuesday, because it was on a Tuesday that he had arrived. A few days had passed since he had gone down to the office and paid his bill for the second week – the modest weekly sum of 160 francs. And it was modest and fair to his mind, even if you disregarded the priceless benefits of his stay which were not on the bill because they were priceless; but then neither were certain other entertainments, which could very well have been calculated, the band concerts every two weeks, for example, or Dr. Krokowski's lectures. The bill was solely for room

die Vorträge Dr. Krokowski's, sondern allein und ausschließlich die eigentliche Bewirtung und gasthausmäßige Leistung, das bequeme Logis, die fünf übergewaltigen Mahlzeiten. (226)	have been included. The sum of one hundred and sixty francs represented simply and solely the actual hospitality extended by the Berghof to Hans Castorp: his comfortable lodgment and his five stupendous meals. (Lowe-Porter, 161)	and board, for the basic services of the hotel – comfortable lodging and five prodigious meals. (Woods 1995: 158)

None of the changes here seems, in itself, to affect the semantics of the passage at the surface level, and Lowe-Porter's opening section retains the cumulative features of Mann's sentence. However, the voice of the writing has been changed appreciably. In Mann's text, the narrative perspective is moved close to the character's thought processes by the use of modal particles (*'ja', 'schon', 'eben', 'überhaupt nicht', 'wohl'*) and the inexplicit modifiers *'gewisse'* and *'ein paar'*. Lowe-Porter's omissions create a more detached account which only hints deictically at the mental processes of the character: the retention of 'here' in the first part, the addition of 'down' (to the office) and the translation of *'hiesig'* by 'up here', which maintains a leitmotivic chain. The passage contains three other features which are characteristic of Lowe-Porter's work: the extensive reformulation/explicitation of Mann's play on the notion of *'Unbezahlbarkeit'*, the use of a historical lexeme 'lodgment' (which appears on three other occasions in her version), and the apparent mistranslation of *'rund'*. The passage also illustrates one of the ways in which she often expands her version through the process of addition/repetition in the interest of explicitation. Like Woods, she casts the final part of Mann's extensive sentence (*'sondern ...'*) into a separate structure, necessitating the insertion of a subject. While Woods simply inserts the substitute subject 'the bill' she repeats the entire subject from the previous sentence. A glance at Woods' version shows broadly similar omissions. Although his version is closer to the original in sequential structure, he, too, omits adverbial elements and introduces additional sentence breaks.

Lexis
Turning to broad lexical descriptors, Wordsmith calculates the following for the novel as a whole:

An exercise in translation comparison: *Der Zauberberg* 97

	Mann	Lowe-Porter	Woods
Total words (tokens)	314,422	329,455	341,803
Types	37,594	19,707	19,577
Type-token ratio (TTR)	11.95	5.98	5.72
Hapax legomena	23,353	8,366	8,044

The figures show an enormous variation in lexical variety between Mann's original and the two translations, as measured by the TTR, which itself reflects the far higher number of types in Mann's text. This discrepancy is due principally to the considerably higher number of morphologically inflected forms in German, which exaggerates the number of types in Mann's original in relative terms. As these global statistics indicate, Lowe-Porter achieves a higher degree of lexical variety than Woods. Despite using fewer words (tokens) overall than Woods, she has a higher number of types (different words) in her text. Even when the French passages of the '*Walpurgisnacht*' episode (which Woods leaves in English) are removed from the calculations, she has a slightly higher ratio of different words to total words. Her TTR is then 5.84 versus Woods' 5.72, despite a lower number of overall types (Lowe-Porter's version contains 727 French types). This general observation is reflected in Chapter 4: Lowe-Porter's version of that section contains 42,020 individual tokens, while Woods' version is some 5 per cent longer, at 43,966. However, Woods does not use a significantly higher number of different words than Lowe-Porter in his chapter (6,038 compared to Lowe-Porter's 5,931): the TTR here is, then, some 3 per cent higher in Lowe-Porter's version (14.11 vs 13.73), i.e. slightly lower than the 5 per cent divergence indicated for the text as a whole. The lexical variety of Lowe-Porter's text is heightened by the fact that even when the French section is excluded she has a broadly similar number of words used only once (hapax legomena): 7,917 versus Woods' 8,029, despite a lower word count.

In terms of word frequencies, the word lists generated by Wordsmith show a broad degree of similarity between the two translations, which both mirror the frequencies in Mann's German original. Discounting grammatical words and proper nouns, the lists of the 150 most frequent words in each translation are very similar. Inevitably, the lexical words relate to thematically central fields in the novel: 'time', parts of the human body such as 'eyes' and 'head' feature prominently near the top of each list. The word frequency lists are not particularly helpful, since they are highly predictable. Nor is the statistical measure of key words – the so-called 'keyness' indicator – which also demonstrates a broad degree of correspondence (keyness is a composite of frequency in the text measured against a reference corpus). More helpful than such crude qualitative indications is a consideration of the way in which specific lexical items behave in context: in other words, the recurrence and distribution of statistically less widely represented – though textually highly salient – lexical items as they appear in collocations, as leitmotifs, in metaphorical functions, etc. Purely statistical analysis will not be able to account for these, but is useful in locating the items in their respective textual environments and facilitating comparison.

At the lexical level, there is a significant divergence between the two English translations in terms of their 'closeness' to the original, i.e. in the domain which is commonly considered to be that of lexical 'equivalence'. Woods' version, to put it simply, displays a much higher level of local correspondence, consistently seeking to account for a larger number of semantic components in terms of both denotative and connotative meaning. It is precisely in this area that most of the previous discussion of the translations has taken place (Luke 1988; Buck 1996; Simon 2009), and lexical analysis has long stood at the centre of translation analysis generally (Albrecht 2005: 130ff.). It is in this respect above all that Lowe-Porter's versions have been found wanting, and it is indeed the case that Woods' version of *Der Zauberberg* grants access to more of the meaning potential generated by Mann's novel at the level of lexical semantics: he translates more of the words in Mann's version, and does so with a greater attention to dictionary meaning.

But the issue of the equivalence of individual lexical items is highly problematic, as a glance at lists of infelicitous solutions compiled by commentators shows (Gledhill 2007; Simon 2009). Judgments on the efficacy of individual renderings are notoriously unstable, conditioned as they are by interpretive assumptions, individual readings of the text, co-text and context, and subjective perceptions of acceptability. To cite just one example: in her important early work on translation studies, Bassnett-McGuire singles out Lowe-Porter's version of the opening chapter of this novel for criticism on a number of grounds, including her choice of lexemes. She takes the translator to task for her failure to find equivalents for 'classical' and 'stylized terms' (*'das Schwäbische Meer'*, *'Gestade'*) and for her rendering of the first adjective Mann uses to describe his protagonist, *'einfach'*, as 'unassuming' (Bassnett-McGuire 1980: 112). She proposes 'ordinary'. In Bassnett-McGuire's view, 'the English translator introduces a powerful element of characterization and alters the reader's perspective' (112) at this point. This analysis has been quoted approvingly by other scholars as 'an excellent example' of Lowe-Porter's shortcomings (Snell-Hornby 2006: 104). But is the matter really so clear? Ultimately, all translations of abstract adjectives necessarily impose a perspective on the text by modifying their semantic import, given inevitable interlingual asymmetries. Can Hans Castorp really be considered 'ordinary'? Mundt is not alone in stressing his extraordinary qualities (2004: 118; see also Gloystein 2001). Indeed, a variety of other words have been suggested in the literature as renderings of the *'einfacher Hans Castorp'*, including 'simple', 'simple-minded', 'straightforward', 'ingenuous', 'mediocre', 'unremarkable'. Simon writes: '*Einfach* equals *simple*, in all the connotations of that word, i.e. plain, uncomplicated, naive, foolish, guileless, innocent, etc.' (2009: 6). She opts, in her 'model translation', for the highly interpretive rendering 'without guile'. The word *'einfach'* (in this sense) appears on a number of occasions in Mann's text, as part of a lexical network which also embraces *'mittelmäßig'*, *'simpel'* and *'schlicht'*. It occurs once in connection with the insurance agent Anton Karlowitsch Ferge, and on four occasions with reference to Castorp's blue eyes. In the latter cases in particular, the adjective takes on an almost leitmotivic function. And the same conceptual field is re-activated at the very end of the novel (in a clear echo of the opening section) as *'simpel'*, which is then amplified by the noun *'Einfachheit'*. Woods is consistent in his version, using 'ordinary' for all occurrences. Lowe-Porter, on the other hand, adopts a different approach: she not only uses different words ('simple-minded' and 'unassuming') to render the German adjective *'einfach'* at the beginning of Mann's text, where it occurs twice in close proximity (in the chapters *'Vorsatz'* and *'Ankunft'*), but also uses four other words – 'confiding', 'innocent', 'honest' and 'simple' – in connection with Castorp's eyes. She opts for 'simple' in the Ferge context. How is this apparent inconsistency to be interpreted? Is one to criticize Lowe-Porter for loosening a network of lexical recurrences in the text, or is she to be praised for seeking to cover as many meanings as possible at different points in her version? Judgements on the most appropriate renderings of individual lexical forms are far from reliable.

Quite apart from such semantic questions of lexical equivalence, Woods' version of the novel is undoubtedly closer to the original in respect of its fuller rendition of lexemes on both the quantitative and qualitative levels. As the following (randomly selected) passage shows, Lowe-Porter is prone to reduction, simplification and reformulation even where these do not appear to be prompted by systemic incompatibilities or semantic complications. Woods' version tracks the original more closely, but also raises questions of lexical correspondence: 'half-hearted' for *'unbestimmt'*; 'corrective forces' for *'Widerstände'*.

Hans Castorps Mund verzog sich, aber seine Augen blieben haften an Madame Chauchats Hand, und eine halbe und unbestimmte Erinnerung ging ihm durch den Sinn an das, was Dr. Krokowski über die bürgerlichen Widerstände, die sich der Liebe entgegenstellten, gesagt hatte ... Der Arm war schöner, dieser weich hinter den Kopf gebogene Arm, der kaum bekleidet war, denn der Stoff der Ärmel war dünner als der der Bluse, – die leichteste Gaze, so daß der Arm nur eine gewisse duftige Verklärung dadurch erfuhr und ganz ohne Umhüllung wahrscheinlich weniger anmutig gewesen wäre. (182)	Hans Castorp made a face; but his eyes remained fixed on Madame Chauchat's back, as he vaguely recalled what Dr Krokowski had been saying, about counteracting influences of a bourgeois kind, which set themselves up against the power of love. ... The arm, in its gentle upward curve, was better than the hand; it was scarcely clothed, for the material of the sleeve was thinner than that of the blouse, being the lightest gauze, which had the effect of lending the arm a sort of shadowed radiance, making it prettier than it might otherwise have been. (Lowe-Porter, 129)	Hans Castorp grimaced, but his eyes remained fixed on Madame Chauchat's hand, and a vague, halfhearted recollection passed through his mind of something Dr Krokowski had said about corrective bourgeois forces that counteracted love ... But this arm was more beautiful, this arm bent gently behind the head – and was barely clad, because the fabric of the sleeve was thinner than that of the blouse, the flimsiest gossamer, which lent the arm just a hint of delicate illusion, making it even prettier than it probably would have been without any covering. (Woods, 126)

As Buck has so forcefully pointed out in his various contributions, Lowe-Porter also has a higher error frequency. One of the most blatant lexical errors in the fourth chapter is her rendition of *'Baisers'* as 'kisses' (150) in the dialogue between Settembrini and Frau Stöhr in the section *'Auftseigende Angst'*, where the context makes it very clear that the reference must be to foodstuffs (meringues). As in the case of the 'hand' – 'back' confusion in the example cited above, many of the overt errors visible in Lowe-Porter's version are denotational. Perhaps the most drastic example of mistranslation is evident at the very end of the novel, where she translates Mann's *'überleben'* in the sentence *'Abenteuer im Fleische und Geist, die deine Einfachheit steigerten, ließen dich im Geist überleben, was du im Fleische wohl kaum überleben sollst* (GW 3, 994) as 'know' (Woods has 'survive') and amends the modal verb (to 'could'), significantly toning down the narrator's expectation that Castorp will die on the battlefield. Has she perhaps misread *'überleben'* as *'erleben'*? Although error identification should not be seen as the sole concern of translation analysis, the frequency of errors in Lowe-Porter's versions seriously undermines their ability to reflect Mann accurately.

In terms of a consideration of translator strategy (i.e. aside from lost nuances and inadvertent mistranslations), higher-level lexical phenomena are perhaps more important than individual lexemes. At the phraseological level, as we saw above, Lowe-Porter does not typically calque the sentence structures of Mann's text, but undertakes a relatively high degree of recasting. Her rearrangement of clauses displays a higher level of freedom than Woods' version in this regard. However, Lowe-Porter does frequently calque clause constituents within clauses, rendering component units with an at times surprising degree of syntactic replication and semantic literalism. This results in an English style that might be perceived as a mixture of highly literal renditions, which can generate unidiomatic formulations, and frequently creative and elegant translation solutions.

This literalistic translation strategy – which runs counter to her views on the legitimacy of textual smoothing in translation – is most visible in cases where Lowe-Porter undertakes genuine 'phraseological calquing', i.e. the through-translation of fully idiomatized expressions from German into English, rather than adopting English equivalent idioms. Thus, in terms of full idioms she has 'to give one's finger to the devil' (5), where Woods has: 'give an inch [...] take a mile' (5); 'I wouldn't trust her across the street' (32): Woods 'would not trust her out of my sight' (34); and 'to break one's head' (185): Woods 'to get into such a stew' (182). Woods' preference for established target-language syntagmatic combinations seen here is evident throughout the text, while Lowe-Porter also calques established phraseological combinations: 'to take the word in one's mouth' (7), 'with sack and pack' (7), 'to find something cheap rather than dear' (28), 'you are putting everything off on him' (32), 'not closed an eye all night' (52). On frequent occasions, she creates English constructions which are at best of doubtful idiomaticity and appear to be the product of interlingual interference. Examples such as the following are not attested in English corpora of any period: 'she is by no means a light case' (97), 'we won't lay it up against anybody' (63), 'No one troubled about Hans Castorp' (60). Often, the doubtful idiomaticity of words and expressions is due not to interlingual resonances, but rather to simple intralingual anomaly: 'the porcelain shield' (on the door) (60), 'garderobe' (131), 'that puts out all one's calculations' (94), 'you are coming to hear it' (52); 'Make yourself quite easy, madame' (52). And it applies equally to entire clauses: 'Not as though he had to look forward to some interest or effort, which would not have been so easy to overleap in spirit' (139). In some cases these renderings can be so obscure as to be difficult to understand: 'Had the swift flight of time up here anything to do with the uniformly accelerated rate of organic combustion?' (162), where Woods has the more replicatory and readily comprehensible: 'He wondered if the increase in one's general metabolism here made three weeks seem no more than a moment or two' (159). Meanwhile, other formulations which strike the modern reader as awkward or odd are attested in corpora, but are identified in databases such as the 'Corpus of Historical American English' as characteristic of older forms of English: 'looking with frequent head-shakings' (94); 'make head against' (23); 'man with parts' (100); 'Joachim answered consideringly' (102).

Lowe-Porter's preference for rather archaic words and structures has already been noted. In terms of the treatment of other registers, by contrast, there are broad similarities between the versions. The use of creative lexis in *Der Zauberberg* is limited almost entirely to the direct speech of Dr Behrens, and will be considered in that context. Most of the other words typically listed as 'neologisms' in the novel are, in fact, attested elsewhere in the German language before Mann, and are rare or creatively exploited existent lexemes (Hilscher 1955; Hardt 1957). Both translators render them with more frequent lexemes or lexical combinations in the target language, amending their translation solutions in accordance with the needs of the surrounding context. Thus the item *'Sittigung'*, which occurs three times in the novel, appears in Lowe-Porter as 'civilized state' (128), 'moral discipline' (159), 'civilizing' (525); and in Woods as 'civilized' (125, 514) and 'moral conduct' (156). The word *'Durchgängerei'*, apparently derived from the more common *'durchgängerisch'*, is rendered by Lowe-Porter twice as 'recklessness' (497), and once as 'immensity' (496), while Woods consistently adopts the metaphorical 'kicking over traces' (486 twice, 487). The adjective *'überäugig'* (which is used three times in the novel and is found nowhere else in Mann's oeuvre) is given two semantically different translations by Lowe-Porter – 'large-eyed' (132) and 'big-eyed' (532), versus 'to look both ways at once' (668) – while Woods has greater consistency here, too: 'cross-eyed' (129, 659) and 'eyes looked crossed' (522). Most of the neologisms in *Der Zauberberg*, as has long been recognized, are created through a process of creative compounding, which challenges the interpretive powers of the translators (Mater 1962). Thus, for the item *'krähenschreihart'* (the reference is to *'Nebelfrühe'*) Lowe-Porter has 'penetrating' (572), while Woods opts for a more literal phrasal rendition 'a morning harsh with the cries of crows' (562). Other compounds are resolved through dissolution into longer phrases: *'nebeldurchsponnene Mondnacht'* is rendered by Lowe-Porter as 'the mist and moonbeams that wrapped the [...] heavens' (160), and by Woods as 'the moonlit night draped in a web of mist' (157); *'Kurzluftigkeit'* appears as 'out of wind' in Lowe-Porter (118) and as 'out of breath' in Woods (116). The compound adjective *'wurmstichig'*, which Mann uses on four occasions with reference to respiratory diseases, is rendered as 'tainted within' in Lowe-Porter and more graphically as 'worm-eaten' in Woods. The above examples illustrate a trend that is widespread in the two versions: Woods adopts a more literal approach to the translation of neologisms, and appears less prepared to normalize. Other rare or novel forms are created by processes of prefixation (*'entraten'*, *'entschlagen'*, *'beglüht'*, *'ur-fürchterlich'*), which are resolved by both translators by the use of morphologically simple verbs: e.g. *'entraten'* as 'avoid' in Lowe-Porter (98) and 'eschew' in Woods (96).

With regard to the other registers evident in the text – the most central are medical, technical and scientific (Castorp's research interests), military, philosophical, historical and cultural/institutional – the procedures adopted by the translators are similar, and predictable. Both translators are concerned to retain the juxtaposition of non-specialized and specialized language which accounts for much of the linguistic character of the text and informs its extensive excursi. The solutions adopted in the two versions indicate thorough research. Much of the terminology which appears in the text is Latinate in origin and thus poses few problems in terms of equivalence in English. Indeed, the same applies generally to the extensive use of foreign lexis in Mann's text. The majority of foreign lexemes are French, and are simply taken over by the translators (*'Konfusion'*, *'Distinktion'*, *'Deduktion'*, *'kapital'*, etc.): however, they are entirely transparent in English and thus lose the exotic, frequently ironic quality which characterizes their use in the German text. Where the translators fear lack of transparency, they translate: Mann's *'larmoyant'* (208) appears as 'carping' in Lowe-Porter and as 'sentimental' in Woods (146), *'Krapüle'* (215) as 'scoundrels' in Lowe-Porter and as 'the rabble' in Woods (151), *'Konduite'* (246) as 'report card' in both versions (177, 174). The foreign phrases that are widespread in the text – Settembrini's Italian (*'idioma gentile'*, *'uomo letterato'*), Behrens' Latin (*'sine pecunia'*, *'ad penates'*, *'homo humanis'*) are retained.

One major difference between the two translations is apparent in the rendering of the extensive French dialogue between Hans Castorp and Clawdia Chauchat, which begins in the *'Walpurgisnacht'* section and is resumed subsequently. The whole of the protagonist's confession of love, on which the original first volume of the novel closes, is conducted in French, a tongue which is foreign to both interlocutors. In later editions of Mann's novel, German translations of these passages are provided in an appendix. Lowe-Porter takes over the French discourse in its entirety (it is marked by italics, like all other foreign passages in her text), and editions of her version contain no translation of the French into English. Indeed, as we shall see in Chapter 7, Lowe-Porter even expands the amount of French in her text. Woods, by contrast, translates the French into English, where it also appears in italics. In Woods' version, all passages of foreign discourse are placed in italics: in other words, the non-English status of the Castorp-Chauchat exchange is thus identified by graphological means alone. In Woods' version, the fact that the couple are speaking French is otherwise signalled only by Castorp's metalinguistic references to the language he is speaking, e.g. Mann's '*Je te le dirai en français*' (467). However, the linguistic constitution of these passages is somewhat confusing in Woods' version, culminating in the passage:

> "*Please, sir, speak German!*" [italics indicate use of French]
> "Oh, but I am speaking German, even if I am speaking French." [non-italics underline the fact that this sentence is in German]
> (Woods, 330).

According to a personal communication from John E. Woods, the decision to translate the French into English was made by the publishers, and was the solution least favoured by the translator. His preferred option – to leave the French as French, as in Lowe-Porter's version – was rejected by the Random House editors on the grounds that a late twentieth-century American audience would not have the same familiarity with that language as Lowe-Porter's 1920s global English target readership. This modification of the text has a dramatic thematic impact at this point, significantly altering the interpretive potential. The characters' use of French, which is hardly visible in Woods' version, indicates a shift to a plane beyond the real and rational, the entry into a dreamlike state in which social and personal barriers are suspended. The foreign language is, as Castorp points out, a mask which bestows freedom. Only through the idiom of a foreign language does the inhibited, supremely bourgeois protagonist feel able to express his feelings. He can 'speak without speaking'. French is also, of course, the language of eroticism. Significantly, Castorp reverts to German the moment he hears that Chauchat is to leave the next day. The dream is over.

In terms of the general lexis of the text, it is apparent that Lowe-Porter generally aspires to a more elevated linguistic register, i.e. she displays a tendency towards less frequent lexemes. This is a further reason for the somewhat antiquated quality of her writing. The following lexical contrasts may serve as an indication of the divergence between the translations in this respect (in each case, Lowe-Porter's solution is placed first): 'luncheon'/ 'lunch'; 'asininity'/'stupidity'; 'esprit'/'intellect'; 'befits' / 'is characteristic of'; 'sojourn' / 'trip'; 'to avail oneself of' / 'to put to use'; 'con' / 'take a closer look at' ; 'purple of cheek' /'purple-cheeked'; 'jurist' / 'lawyer'; 'vouchsafed' / 'granted'; 'beck' / 'with sidelong glances'; 'comfits' / 'candies'; 'restorative' / 'medicine'. The list could be extended at will. The same applies to the construction of phrases, which in Lowe-Porter's version often take on a somewhat precious quality (Woods' rendition is again quoted second): 'by that conflict daily steeled anew' (5) / 'steeled by each new day in battle' (5); 'When, his nerves being tolerably restored' (19) /'Once his nerves had settled a bit again' (19); 'such is not my office' (100) / 'that is not my calling' (98). On occasions, this striving for erudite formulations creates text which might be seen as elegant indeed, characterized by metaphorical collocations: 'the rules most honoured in the observance were precisely those which chimed with the financial interest of the proprietors' (95); 'in tones replete with filial piety' (95); 'Two principles, according to the Settembrinian cosmogony, were in perpetual conflict for possession of the world' (157). However, in other instances Lowe-Porter's preference for calquing the structures of the original German creates passages that have a distinctly unidiomatic feel. The following example, which also illustrates the processes of simplification, reduction and transposition in Lowe-Porter's version, shows the difference between her strained syntax, generated in part by her desire to retain the single-sentence structure, and the more naturally fluent version of Woods.

| *Benommen vom Biere und von der Musik, die wie immer bewirkte, daß sein Mund sich öffnete und sein Kopf sich auf die Seite legte, betrachtete er mit geröteten Augen das sorglose Badeleben ringsumher, wobei das Bewußtsein ihn durchaus nicht störte, sondern im Gegenteil dem* | Rendered torpid, as often, by the beer and the music, he sat with his head on one side and his mouth slightly open, watching the gay, resortish scene, feeling, not as a disturbing influence, but rather as heightening the general singularity, and lending | Dazed from the beer and the music, which as always made him lay his head a little to one side with his mouth hanging open, he looked with bloodshot eyes out at the resort life around him. It came to him that all these people were subject to an inner |

Ganzen eine erhöhte Merkwürdigkeit, einen gewissen geistigen Reiz verlieh, daß alle diese Leute in ihrem Inneren von einem schwer aufzuhaltenden Zerfall ergriffen waren und daß die meisten von ihnen in leichtem Fieber standen. (158)	it one mental fillip the more, the fact that all these people were inwardly attacked by well-nigh resistless decay, and that most of them were feverish. (Lowe-Porter, 111–112)	decay that would be halted only with great difficulty and that most of them were slightly feverish, but the realization did not bother him at all – on the contrary, there was a certain special intensity and intellectual charm to the whole scene. (Woods, 109)

Macrostylistic features
Leitmotifs

At the higher – macrostylistic – level of lexical composition, the phenomenon of lexical recurrence and patterning assumes major significance in Mann's novel. The author's use of the celebrated 'leitmotif' technique plays a key role in establishing associative thematic connections in *Der Zauberberg*, which is vast in scope and, from Chapter 5 onwards, increasingly episodic in structure. Large numbers of *'additive Assoziationsketten'* (Gloystein 2001: 20) have been identified in the scholarship, establishing networks of concepts, images, objects, situations, incidents or character traits. Such parallelisms take on a special salience through repetition or subtle modification, transferring semantic features across disparate contexts (Bulhof 1966). For precisely this reason, Mann himself recommended that the book be read twice, stressing the hermeneutic interplay (prospective and retrospective) generated by his technique (*GW* 11: 611). As Kurzke stresses, the repetition of elements is not a formal embellishment, but is indispensable to the interpretive processes triggered by the text: '*Die Leitmotivstruktur erst macht die Handlung verständlich*' (Kurzke 2010: 203). The '*Beziehungskomplexe*' that Mann establishes draw on a scheme of ultimately antithetical concepts which pervade and structure the novel, resting essentially on the dichotomy of mountain and flatlands, with its extended symbolic systems of form and formlessness, duty and decadence, health and disease, life and death. The major metaphorical systems of the novel identified by Weiss (1987) draw on the very same networks. The automated searching and counting functions offered by computerized analytical tools make the identification and tracking of such patterns much easier and more reliable.

The cohesive function of leitmotivic elements is central in a novel in which the unifying factors of time and plot development have been suspended. In the context of translation, therefore, the consistency with which they are rendered is important. The sheer number of intratextual links in Mann's text constitutes a challenge to the retentive powers of any reader; without the support of the search tools offered by digitized texts, a translator would have little chance of attaining a high level of consistency. Nevertheless, despite criticism that Lowe-Porter obscures chains of leitmotifs in the text (e.g. Newmark 2000: 908), there is actually a great deal of consistency in her treatment of recurrent elements. She was well aware of the significance of 'phrasal repetition' which undergoes 'a gradual and very careful modification' in Mann's text (letter to Blanche Knopf dated 19 March 1926, Henderson and Oram 2010: 317). Thus, for example, she maintains – even without the aid of a computer – the extensive lexical chain of *'Regieren'*, a 'symbolic code word' (Weigand 1965: 49) which occurs at 20 different points in the novel, with 450 pages separating the first and last instances. After consulting Mann on the subject, she uses 'taking stock' throughout. Woods is equally systematic, rendering the noun as 'playing king'. Both translators approach the rendition of leitmotivic elements with care: automated analyses of the distribution of motifs (such as Mann's *'Zeit'*, *'Augen'*/*'Hippe'*, *'Bleistift'*, *'Zigarre'*, *'Taufschale'*, *'Halskrause'*) show that the translators track them closely, generating lexical networks via conventional processes of integral translation. The same is true of recurrent epithets applied to the characters as distinctive markers.

The most frequently activated of the many leitmotivic contrasts in the novel is that between the alpine world of the Davos clinic (*'Sanatorium'*) and the sphere of the flatlands (*'Flachland'*), consistently encapsulated as *'hier oben'* and *'dort unten'*. Simple quantitative analysis is able to suggest the divergent strategies adopted by the translators here. For example, while Mann uses the pair *'hier oben'* on 190 occasions in the novel, both translators increase its frequency: Woods has 230 occurrences of 'up here', and Lowe-Porter significantly tightens the density of this network by using the phrase no fewer than 309 times. The same is true of the treatment of the contrastive *'dort unten'*/*'da unten'*, which occurs 22 times in Mann's novel: Lowe-Porter has 57 instances of 'down below'/'down there', while Woods has 43. An examination of the relative distribution of the 'hier oben' motif in the three texts shows that Lowe-Porter consistently uses the pair 'up here' to render Mann's simple preposition 'hier' (accounting for some 95 per cent of the additional occurrences in her text), regularly substitutes it for Mann's prepositional phrases *'bei uns'*, *'bei euch'* (3 per cent), and also inserts it where Mann has no corresponding deictic marker (2 per cent). Woods, by contrast, remains much closer to Mann's text, only occasionally intensifying Mann's 'hier' through the addition of 'up', and on a similar number of occasions deleting the adverb altogether.

The polarity of the 'worlds above and below', with all of its symbolic overtones, is introduced very early on in the novel. As Castorp travels south, we are told: *'Heimat und Ordnung lagen nicht nur weit zurück, sie lagen hauptsächlich klaftertief unter ihm, und noch immer stieg er darüber hinaus'* (13). As von Gronicka pointed out in an early study of the novel (1948), the patterns of pronominal use with which the adverbial phrase is combined (*'ihr'* – *'die'* – *'wir hier oben'*) function as a key indicator of Castorp's developing relationship with the world of the sanatorium. Ziemssen greets Castorp in Davos with detailed explanations of the specificities of life *'hier oben'*, at a stage when Castorp – struck by the frequency with which his cousin uses the phrase – refers to the inhabitants of the Berghof with the exclusive pronoun *'ihr/euch/Sie/Ihnen hier oben'* (seven instances in the first 122 pages of the novel). Castorp's increasing loss of distance from the ways and values of the sanatorium is signalled by the narrator's adoption of the neutral phrase *'die/denen/derer hier oben'* (often in capitalized form, 28 examples from page 208 onwards) in references to Castorp's perception of the inhabitants. In the next stage, Castorp identifies himself with the mountain world by using the inclusive formulation in direct speech *'wir/uns hier oben'* (five instances between pages 313 and 574). Furthermore, in a display of (often ironic) locational identification with the characters in the text, the narrator himself frequently uses the same combination of inclusive pronoun and proxemic deictic marker – just one of several poses he adopts in the novel. In the wake of the increased insight Castorp gains during the *'Schneetraum'*, finally, the exclusive *'die/derer/denen'* is resumed in reference to his perception (eight occasions after page 654), signalling his ultimate rejection of the values of the hermetic sphere.

In Lowe-Porter's version in particular, the subtlety of second-person pronominal use (*'ihr/euch'*) in connection with the *'hier oben'* motif is obscured. While Woods retains Mann's original structures on six out of seven occasions, Lowe-Porter deletes the pronoun in virtually all cases (six of the seven). In their renderings of the demonstrative pronominal variants (*'die/derer/deren'*) the two translators adopt different solutions: while Lowe-Porter prefers a pronominal solution ('those up here' on 16 occasions; 'them up here' twice) and on two occasions inserts a support noun ('people'), accounting for 20 instances of Mann's phrase, Woods consistently inserts support nouns 'people up here' (23 occasions), 'folks up here' (1) and also uses 'those up here' (3) and 'these people up here' (1), accounting for 28 of the 29 instances in Mann's text. With regard to the subtle *'wir/uns hier oben'* combination – which signals the increasing identification of Castorp with the alpine sphere – Lowe-Porter deletes the inclusive first-person (plural) pronoun in three of the four cases, while Woods does so in two of the four cases. In referring to the opposite sphere, the everyday world, Mann uses adverbial formulations ('*dort unten/da unten*') only on 22 occasions, preferring instead nominal realizations such as '*Flachland*', with 32 occurrences (and the adjectival '*flachländisch*', which occurs four times), '*Tiefland*' (9) ('*tiefländisch*' once), '*Ebene*' (25). Both translators increase the frequency of adverbial formulations here (see above: Woods 43, Lowe-Porter 57). Woods, however, more consistently captures the nominal realizations of this motif: 'flatlands' on 72 occasions, versus 47 instances in Lowe-Porter (as 'flat-land'), 'plains' 25 times, 'plain' twice in this meaning (twice in Lowe-Porter), 'lowlands' five times (versus one occurrence in Lowe-Porter, and one of 'lowland'). In many of the cases, Lowe-Porter replaces the nominal references with adverbial formulations, which accounts in part for the high frequency of such formulations in her text. In summary, then, Lowe-Porter is clearly attentive to lexical recurrences in the text, but diverges from the explicit instantiations used by Mann on more occasions than does Woods. The result of her procedure is a loosening of the carefully controlled intratextual relations evident in Mann's novel.

A further example of structuring lexical recurrence is provided by the concept of '*Zeit*' in the novel. The theme of time is, of course, absolutely essential to the novel's concerns (Miltenberger 2000: 101–26). Mann himself drew attention to the fact that his text is not merely a '*Zeitroman*' in the conventional sense, but also deals with '*die reine Zeit*', which it suspends through artistic means to create '*ein magisches "nunc stans"*' (GW 11: 612), in the text referred to as '*ein stehendes Jetzt*' (GW 13: 757). The narrator refers to the '*Fragwürdigkeit und eigentliche Zwienatur dieses geheimnisvollen Elementes*' as early as in the '*Vorsatz*'. The simple (uncompounded) noun '*Zeit*' occurs 353 times in Mann's novel, while it occurs on hundreds of further occasions in compounds. This semantic dimension of the text assumes further significance via Mann's frequent exploitation of an antonymic pair which presents a significant lexical challenge in the process of translation: the '*langweilig*'/'*kurzweilig*' dichotomy. This lexical contrast illustrates a central issue in equivalence-based translation scholarship: that of abstract nominal concepts which might be held to have no one-to-one correspondent between languages (lexical gaps). The subjective perception of the passing of time in terms of '*Lang-*' and '*Kurzweiligkeit*' is an important projection of the theme of time in Mann's novel: the narrator announces in the '*Vorsatz*' that the story is to be told slowly and in detail – '*denn wann wäre ja die Kurz- oder Langweiligkeit einer Geschichte abhängig gewesen von dem Raum und der Zeit, die sie in Anspruch nahm?*' (GW 3: 10), and returns to the motif at the very end, some nine hundred pages later: '*sie war weder kurzweilig noch langweilig*' (GW 3: 994). Castorp himself muses on the issue at various points in the text, seeking to conceptualize his gradual drift into the timeless state of the hermetic world of the sanatorium.

But the notion of *'Lang-'/'Kurzweiligkeit'* is used ambiguously in the novel: Mann plays with the semantics of the words, obfuscating the apparently clear distinction between the antonyms. In a number of instances, he uses the concepts in their literal, objective meaning (*'langweilig'* = of long duration) and plays that meaning off against their modern, subjective meaning (= appearing long, because uninteresting), stressing the unstable quality of the human perception of time: *'Was man Langeweile nennt ist also eigentlich vielmehr eine krankhafte Kurzweiligkeit der Zeit infolge von Monotonie'* (148). The semantic components of the two words are reversed here, before being resumed at a later stage in their surface meaning (Wirtz 1962: 162). The problem translators face here is that of finding renderings that can function across the different contexts in which the terms appear. Mann uses the lexeme *'Langeweile'* seven times in the novel (including two occurrences as *'Langenweile'* and *'Langerweile'* respectively), has *'Langweiligkeit'* twice, and uses the adjectival form *'langweilig'* 15 times. Woods is careful to maintain this lexical chain, using the noun 'boredom' on all occasions on which the nominal *'Lang-'* compounds appear in Mann's text, and using the adjective 'boring' 12 times in his translation; he also has 'tedious' on four occasions, and 'tiresome' once. Lowe-Porter, on the other hand, seeks a higher level of lexical variety here: she has 'boredom' twice, 'tedium' three times, 'ennui' once, and on the remaining occasions undertakes clausal transpositions: 'time did not hang heavy on his hands' (141); 'time passing slowly' (184). To render the adjectival form she prefers 'tedious' (six times, and twice for 'langwierig'), 'tiresome' (five occurrences), 'long' (four instances), 'dull' (once) and also uses transpositions: 'hang too heavy' (189), 'makes time seem too long' (488). Both translators, perhaps inevitably, have a problem with *'Kurzweiligkeit'*, which Mann uses twice in nominal form and thirteen times as an adjective. Again, Lowe-Porter uses a variety of terms: most frequently simply 'short' (seven occasions), but also 'fleeting', 'amusing', 'brief', 'passing too fast', 'the swift passage of time'. Woods consistently uses the concept of 'diversion'. Thus the central wordplay in this thematic context (*'auf eine langweilige Weise kurzweilig oder auf eine kurzweilige Weise langweilig'*, GW 3: 752) is rendered by Lowe-Porter as 'tediously brief, or briefly tedious' (544), and by Woods as: 'diverting in a boring sort of way, or boring in a diverting sort of way' (534). Woods achieves a higher degree of interconnectedness between the occurrences and thus also ensures a clear parallelism between the beginning and end of the novel, where he has 'neither short on diversion nor long on boredom' (706). In Lowe-Porter's version, on the other hand, the contrasting pair at the end of the novel is reduced simply to 'it [your tale] was neither short nor long' (715). This semantic reduction from subjective perception to factual statement obscures one of the central themes in Mann's novel, which reflects the underlying leitmotivic chain: time (world below) versus enchanted timelessness (world above) – the notion that time cannot be measured objectively, but can only be experienced subjectively.

Irony

In terms of the narrative voice of the novel, Mann's *Zauberberg* has often been described as a highly ironic novel in which the narrative tone shifts from one of detached, arrogant, at times almost supercilious mockery to one of profound seriousness towards the end (Kurzke 2010: 209). Indeed, its narrative ductus is characterized by constant qualification, deflation and even open contradiction of the characters' perspectives, and by a tongue-in-cheek portrayal of their idiosyncrasies and physical appearance. But what is the function of this narrative relativism, this ironic distancing which is regarded by many as the hallmark of Mann's literary art (Heller 1958)? Clearly, it forms a central part of the humour of the novel, and lends it its unmistakable timbre. But the ubiquitous, all-debunking cynicism of the 'winking narrator' has a serious root. The apparent playfulness is actually *'ein ernstes Spiel'*, as Mann told Princeton students, and the novel as a whole is characterized by a high degree of *'Hintergründigkeit'* (*GW* 11: 513). As Mann defines it in *Betrachtungen eines Unpolitischen*, irony is not simply a mode of all-encompassing scepticism, but functions as a mediating instance between rigid intellectual and ideological standpoints which, in their absoluteness, have no sustainable claim to precedence. It is an intellectual position which acknowledges the fragility of all intellectual positions. Born out of a modernist sense that long-held certainties are disintegrating, it is an attempt to hold disorder at bay (Dowden 2001: 19). It is ambiguity understood as a positive value (Koopmann 2001: 850). In literary-historical terms, it shows Mann's rootedness in the 'traditional novel' of nineteenth century realism, but also his concern 'to detach himself critically from that tradition' through 'parody [...] and an ironically, often comically heightened' version of realism (Dowden 2001: xviii).

Dilution of Mann's irony has often been singled out as one of the major defects of Lowe-Porter's renditions, while Woods' versions have commonly been seen as doing greater justice to Mann's style (Newmark 2000: 908). It is not possible to reduce the discussion of irony in translation to the identification of linguistic clues alone, since it is a complex cognitive phenomenon which is potentially generated by extratextual factors: the wider evaluative and interpretive processes which can, in turn, be determined by cultural knowledge and conventions (Pugliese 2010). Nevertheless, repertory-based intrinsic methodologies are an indispensable tool for textual comparison (Chakhachiro 2009; de Wilde 2010). The application of such methods to the Lowe-Porter translations demonstrates that there is no consistent obfuscation of Mann's tongue-in-cheek stance at the level of the translation unit, such as has been established (for example) in the Spanish translation of the same novel. In a detailed examination of the opening and closing chapters of Mann's novel, Fehlauer-Lenz (2008) tests a catalogue of 133 '*ironische Textstellen*' identified in the source text against the Spanish version, establishing that some 30 per cent of them are lost in translation. Applying Fehlauer-Lenz's criteria to the Lowe-Porter and Woods versions of Mann's novel, one discovers that – at least in terms of the formal signals of irony – both translators transfer the vast majority of the devices employed by Mann, exploiting the wide repertoire of stylistic features evident in the original German text. Woods accounts for all but five of the 'signals of irony' in the 120-page section analysed by Fehlauer-Lenz, while Lowe-Porter's version transfers all but eight of them (and some of those she omits are relatively minor graphemic elements). The repertoire of signals spans all the classical formal manifestations of verbal irony: euphemism, cliché, ambiguity, oxymoron, paradox, stylistic contamination, hyperbole, litotes, rhetorical questions, repetition and echo, parenthesis, paranomasia, free indirect speech, authorial asides (parabasis) (Baumgart 1966; Müller 1995). In *Der Zauberberg*, the ironic tone is largely the product of the narrator's use of such devices in his presentation of characters and his stance vis-à-vis the reader on unfolding events. It is underpinned by widespread narratorial comment, appeals to the reader and feigned uncertainty, which combine to undermine the essential omniscience of the point of view.

While it certainly appears that Lowe-Porter does not consistently reduce the ironic tone of Mann's novel as a consequence of a conscious translation strategy, and is at pains to mirror the stylistic incongruities of Mann's style, her generally reductive approach to translation – noted above in the techniques of deletion and syncopation – does dilute the ironic effects which Mann achieves through carefully differentiated distributions and combinations. Her frequent omissions tend to obscure the highly differentiated style of Mann's text. The deletion of speech markers, modal particles, adjectives in extended premodifying sequences and series of nouns serves to dilute the quality of the original. The following example demonstrates a variety of ways in which her version reduces the carefully controlled structure of the discourse steered by – on this occasion – an omniscient narrator (the very length of the two translated versions underlines the process of reduction: Lowe-Porter has 138 words, Woods 165):

An exercise in translation comparison: *Der Zauberberg*

Eins aber bereitete ihm Genugtuung, wenn er lag und auf sein Herz, sein körperliches Herz achtete, das rasch und vernehmlich in der Stille pochte – der vorschriftsmäßigen Hausordnungsstille, die während der Haupt- und Schlafliegekur über dem ganzen 'Berghof' waltete. Es pochte hartnäckig und vordringlich, sein Herz, wie es das fast beständig tat, seitdem er hier oben war; doch nahm Hans Castorp neuerdings weniger Anstoß daran als in den ersten Tagen. Man konnte jetzt nicht mehr sagen, daß es auf eigene Hand, grundlos und ohne Zusammenhang mit der Seele klopfte. Ein solcher Zusammenhang war vorhanden oder doch unschwer herzustellen; eine rechtfertigende Gemütsbewegung ließ sich der exaltierten Körpertätigkeit zwanglos unterlegen. Hans Castorp brauchte nur an Frau Chauchat zu denken – und er dachte an sie – so besaß er zum Herzklopfen das zugehörige Gefühl. (198)	One thing there was which pleased him: when he lay listening to the beating of his heart – his corporeal organ – so plainly audible in the ordered silence of the rest period, throbbing loud and peremptorily, as it had done almost ever since he came, the sound no longer annoyed him. For now he need not feel that it so beat of its own accord, without sense or reason or any reference to his non-corporeal part. He could say, without stretching the truth, that such a connexion now existed, or was easily induced: he was aware that he felt an emotion to correspond with the action of his heart. He needed only to think of Madame Chauchat – and he did think of her – and lo, he felt within himself the emotion proper to the heart-beats. (Lowe-Porter, 140–1)	He did take satisfaction in one thing, however, as he lay there listening to his heart, his physical heart, pounding rapidly and audibly in the stillness – the stillness that was prescribed by house rules and reigned over the entire Berghof during the main rest cure of the day. His heart was pounding insistently, urgently, the way it had done almost constantly ever since he had arrived here: and yet of late that did not upset Hans Castorp as it had the first few days. One could no longer say that it thudded on its own accord, for no reason, and without any connection to his soul. There was a connection now, or at least it would not have been difficult to establish one – a justifiable emotion could easily be assigned to his body's overwrought activity. Hans Castorp needed only to think of Frau Chauchat – and he did think of her – and his heart had a suitable emotion to make it pound. (Woods, 138)

A variety of modificatory, non-obligatory shifts can be noted here: the removal of recurrences and contrasts ('*Herz*', '*pochen*', '*Zusammenhang*'); the simplification of anaphoric modifying elements ('*in der Stille ... Stille*'), of ironic combinations and compounds ('*vorschriftsmäßigen Hausordnungsstille*', '*Haupt- und Schlafliegekur*') and lexical selections ('*hartnäckig*', '*waltete*', '*exaltierte Körpertätigkeit*'); the deletion of the second mention of the protagonist's full name, which Mann uses instead of pronominal substitution; the obfuscation of the change in the focus of the narrative from the impersonal '*man*', through the existential '*war vorhanden*' and the use of the impersonal '*ließ sich*' to '*er*', which Lowe-Porter replaces with a consistently subject-dominated form of narrative focus ('he need not feel' – 'he could say' – 'he was aware'): the insertion of the antiquated 'lo'. While the Woods version is much closer to the German original in its lexical and syntactical composition, it too shows simplification: the omission of the '*Schlafliegekur*', the dissolution of the cataphoric pronominal reference ('*es*' – '*sein Herz*'), and – like Lowe-Porter's version – the loss of the deixis of proximity in the leitmotivic '*hier oben*'.

A further passage may serve as an illustration of Lowe-Porter's modification of the degree of intimate pseudo-complicity between narrator and reader: the removal of interjections, particles, adverbs and the inclusive perspective ('*das sah man ihm an*') all serve to weaken the ironic instability of the mimetic, engaged perspective. Once again, Woods' rendition is a more accurate representation of the German in this instance:

| *Und welches sei denn nun die Gestalt und Maske, worin die nicht zugelassen und unterdrückte Liebe wiedererscheine? So fragte Dr Krokowski und blickte die Reihen entlang, als erwarte er die Antwort ernstlich von seinen Zuhörern. Ja, das mußte er nun auch noch selber sagen, nachdem er schon so manches gesagt hatte. Niemand außer ihm wußte es, aber er würde bestimmt auch dies noch wissen, das sah man ihm an.* (180) | But what then was this form, this mask, in which suppressed, unchartered love would reappear? Dr Krokowski asked the question, and looked along the listening rows as though in all seriousness expecting an answer. But he had to say it himself, who had said so much else already. No one knew save him, but it was plain that he did. (Lowe-Porter, 128) | And in what form or mask did suppressed and unsanctioned love reappear? Dr Krokowski looked up and down the rows as he asked this question, as if seriously expecting an answer from his listeners. But no, he would have to provide the answer himself, though he had already provided so many. No one else knew the answer, but he would be sure to know this, too – you could see it just by looking at him. (Woods, 125) |

An exercise in translation comparison: *Der Zauberberg* 115

On occasions the narratorial intimacy can be reduced to such an extent that the mode of narration seems to change from one of conversational relaxedness to one of neutral omniscience:

So drängte denn Joachim abends schon nach einer Viertelstunde aus der Geselligkeit fort in die Liegekur, und das war gut, denn seine militärische Genauigkeit kam dem zivilen Sinn Hans Castorps gewissermaßen zu Hilfe, der sich sonst wohl, sinn- und aussichtsloserweise, gern noch des längeren an der Geselligkeit beteiligt hätte, mit Aussicht auf den kleinen Russensalon. (207)	Joachim invariably went upstairs after only a quarter-hour in the drawing-rooms; and this military precision of his was a prop to the civilian laxity of his cousin, who would otherwise be likely to loiter unprofitably below, with his eye on the company in the small salon. (Lowe-Porter, 147)	And so each evening, after perhaps fifteen minutes, Joachim would propose that they leave the social gathering for their rest cure; which was fine, since his military scruples made up somewhat for Hans Castorp's civilian attitudes, for he would probably have preferred to linger there, for no good reason and with no prospects, except a view to the little Russian salon. (Woods, 144)

The ironic tone of Mann's text is diluted in the Lowe-Porter version not merely by omissions, recastings and changes to the narrative focus, i.e. by active interventions in the discourse structure. It is also a consequence of her lexical selections. Her predilection for a generally elevated and archaic diction throughout her text – noted above and elsewhere in discussions of her work – makes it difficult for her to replicate the stylistic incongruity which arises from Mann's ironic juxtaposition of trivial reference and hyperbolic formulation. The following extract is a typical example of the manner in which apparently banal objects – here the reclining chair used for the rest periods in the sanatorium – are described in incongruously bombastic terms. In the Lowe-Porter version, elevated formulations such as 'reasserted themselves [...] whenever he resorted to it anew' and 'comfortable provision for relaxed limbs [...] purveyed by this excellent chair' are hardly marked off in terms of their precious and antiquated tone from the remainder of her text, in which she cultivates a polished and elevated tone:

Die unangenehmen Empfindungen jedoch wurden aufgewogen durch die große Bequemlichkeit seiner Lage, die schwer zu zergliedernden und fast geheimnisvollen Eigenschaften des Liegestuhles, die Hans Castorp beim ersten Versuche schon mit höchstem Beifall empfunden hatte und die sich wieder aufs glücklichste bewährten. Lag es an der Beschaffenheit der Polster, der richtigen Neigung der Rückenlehne, der passenden Höhe und Breite der Armstützen oder auch nur der zweckmäßigen Konsistenz der Nackenrolle, genug, es konnte für das Wohlsein ruhender Glieder überhaupt nicht humaner gesorgt sein als durch diesen vorzüglichen Liegestuhl. (146)	But such unpleasing sensations were outweighed by the great comfort of his position, the unanalyzable, the almost mysterious properties of his reclining-chair, which he had applauded even on his first experience of it, and which reasserted themselves in the happiest way whenever he resorted to it anew. Whether due to the character of the upholstering, the inclination of the chair-back, the exactly proper width and height of the arms, or only to the appropriate consistency of the neck roll, the result was that no more comfortable provision for relaxed limbs could be conceived than that purveyed by this excellent chair. (Lowe-Porter, 103)	These unpleasant sensations, however, were counterbalanced by the comfortable position furnished by the lounge chair and its almost mysterious properties, which Hans Castorp found difficult to analyze but which had found his highest approval from the very first and had stood the test again and again. Whether it was the texture of the cushions, the perfect slant of the back support, the proper height and width of the armrests, or simply the practical consistency of the neck roll – whatever it was, nothing could possibly have offered more humane benefits for a body at rest than this splendid lounge chair. (Woods, 101)

Direct speech

A particularly important dimension of the narrative technique in Mann's novel at the macrotextual level is the use of direct speech, which serves as a medium of characterization and is also a key source of humour in the text. In quantitative terms, a major proportion of the novel is cast in direct discourse, in which the author uses a high degree of linguistic differentiation – regional and idiolectal – in creating distinctive speech patterns. Frau Stöhr's malapropisms, Peeperkorn's *'Abgerissenheit'*, Settembrini's eloquence and rhetorical posturing (*'reine und wohlgeformte Worte'*, GW 3: 135), Joachim's sobriety of tone, not least Castorp's development towards linguistic reflection and sophistication, which is reflected in an increasing lexical and syntactical complexity – all these testify to the centrality of the theme of verbal articulation in the novel. On the metalinguistic level, attention is frequently drawn to the phonetic features of the characters' speech: the elision of syllables, the omission of consonants, the quality of vowels. To consider just one example: Hofrat Behrens (who hails from Lower Saxony) is almost exclusively characterized by his diction, which Castorp defines as eine *'flotte Redeweise'*, *'Schwadronieren'*, *'unmäßig forsch'*. The prime characteristics of Behrens' unmistakable speech patterns are lexical innovation (*'Befindität' 'Kupidität'*, *'Fußbretter'*, *'Krautwickel'*,) and the use of colloquialisms (*'die Kerls'*, *'in die Klappe gehen'*, *'auf der Walze'*, *'nicht von schlechten Eltern'*), ironic-humorous forms of address (*'Vergnügungsreisender'*, *'unbeteiligter Zuschauer'*, *'Eure Hochwohlgeborenen*), insertion of Latinisms (*'ad penates gehen'*, *'praeter propter'*) and the euphemistic use of foreign terms (*'moribundus'*, *'mortis causi'*), a predilection for foreign forms (*'poussieren'*, *'illuminiert'*, *'kujonieren'*), drastic expressions and interjections (*'zum Kugeln'*, *'herrje'*), the mispronunciation of foreign words (*'Hotevoleh'*), ironic combinations (*'gesegnete Nahrungsaufnahme'*), and the contamination of registers (*'Fiaskos den Hals brechen'*). In syntactic terms his speech is characterized by the extensive use of clipped, elliptical structures (*'Ehrt uns!'*)

Both translators seek to capture the speech patterns of the characters. It is, after all, in Behrens' case an important aspect of his character – an attempt to camouflage his fundamental cynicism and melancholy with a display of linguistic bravado (as Settembrini observes). And it is an important theme of the novel, in which Behrens is cast in the role (again by Settembrini) of Rhadamanthys and acts as the ultimate magician on the magic mountain – a magic which is mirrored in verbal dexterity (Gauger 1975: 236). Generally speaking, Woods is more concerned to mirror the properties of Behrens' discourse: he uses a more extensively elliptical style (including compensatory ellipsis when the English text makes direct rendition difficult), and seeks to capture something of the linguistic humour generated by lexical creativity: for *'Fußbretter'* he has 'planks tied to their feet,' where Lowe-Porter has 'skis', and for *'Tagesaugen'*, where Lowe-Porter has 'everyday eyesight', he has 'daytime eyes'. He also makes an effort to suggest the humorous distortion of foreign phonetics: for *'Hotevoleh'* he has 'crème de la crème', which enables him to retain the metalinguistic comment ('he made a joke of his outrageous pronunciation'), where

Lowe-Porter has 'nobs' ('he said comically'). He renders more of the interjections ('*zum Kugeln*') and strives for a broader similarity in register where Lowe-Porter opts for more extensive normalization: for '*Schlauberger*' he has 'sly old dog' where Lowe-Porter prefers 'old fellow', and for '*Jüngling*' the more chummy 'my lad' where Lowe-Porter has the slightly more formal 'young man'. Woods seeks more modern correspondents for the colloquialisms so favoured by Behrens: for Mann's '*Form ist ete-pe-tete*' he has 'Form is namby-pamby nonsense', where Lowe-Porter has 'Form is folderol' – and in describing his cigar (something he does in quasi-erotic terms): '*Ein rechter Sorgenbrecher, brennt wie Schnaps, und namentlich gegen das Ende hat sie was Fulminantes*'(353), Woods has 'Soothes one's cares away, catches fire like brandy, but, all the same, she packs something of a wallop towards the end' (249) where Lowe-Porter writes: 'Regular "begone, dull care," burns like brandy, has something fulminating towards the end' (253). This latter example, with its reference to a well-known anonymous poem, heightens and archaizes the register. This tendency is evident throughout Lowe-Porter's version:

'*Ja, ja, Gentlemen, die verfluchte libido!*' sagte er. '*Sie haben natürlich noch Ihr Vergnügen an der Chose, Ihnen kann's recht sein. – Vesikulär. – Aber so ein Anstaltschef, der hat davon die Neese plein, das können Sie mir – Dämpfung – das können Sie mir glauben. Kann ich dafür, daß die Phthise nun mal mit besonderer Konkupiszenz verbunden ist –*' (576)	"Ah, yes, gentlemen," he said, "this cursed *libido*! You can get some fun out of the thing, it's all right for you. – Vesicular. – But a man in my position, verily I say unto you – dullness here – he hath his belly full. Is it my fault that phthisis and concupiscence go together –" (Lowe-Porter, 417)	"Yes, yes, gentlemen, the damn libido," he said. "The whole affair is great sport for you, of course – it doesn't matter to you. Vesicular. But the director of a sanatorium gets a noseful, believe you – muffled – believe you me. Can I help it if phthisis is accompanied by increased concupiscence? " (Woods, 409)

Lowe-Porter's generous adoption of obsolete morphological forms is certainly not out of place in a rendition of Behrens' speech patterns: he is, after all, prone to strew his utterances with classical references and quotations, and revels in stylistic incongruity. Woods' version, in this respect too, is more modern. Overall, he strives for a more complete rendering of idiosyncratic speech patterns: an analysis of the 42 markers of idiosyncratic speech in Behrens' utterances during his first extended exchange with Castorp (the 'Thermometer' chapter) indicates that both translators transfer the same number of elliptical structures, but that Woods mirrors a higher number of characteristic speech markers overall (40 versus Lowe-Porter's 35).

Conclusion

A global comparison of the two English versions of *Der Zauberberg* demonstrates that both translators have produced versions of Mann's text which are essentially neutral in their cultural orientation (no wide-ranging adaptation of foreign references and features), and are fundamentally target-oriented in terms of their linguistic composition (tendency towards the reduction of complexity). Regarding the historical-regional quality of the language in the two versions, Woods' text is characterized by extensive modernization in line with the norms of modern American English, while Lowe-Porter's text displays a high level of both lexical and syntactic archaism which borders on the anachronistic, even for a 1920s text. Thus the timbre of her version is reminiscent of Galsworthy, the Edwardian novelist who was notoriously described by Virginia Woolf as a 'stuffed shirt', and who in turn owed much to Victorian writers such as Thackeray. Lowe-Porter's diction is marked by a clear tendency towards stylistic elevation (selection at the level of both lexemes and phraseological combinations), which accounts for the 'pomposity' identified by some commentators and bemoaned by Mann himself (letter to Irita van Doren of 28 August 1951, *Br* 3: 220). Woods' version is not only more modern: it also shows a higher degree of integrity, accounting for a considerably larger number of stylistic features of Mann's original. Marked by a lower number of omissions, as well as by fewer optional shifts and redistributions, his version achieves a higher level of local correspondence, and might thus be considered to be a more accurate representation of Mann's style. While judgements on renderings of individual lexical forms will always be subject to debate, Woods' version certainly contains fewer overt denotative errors and is consequently more accurate at the level of dictionary meaning. However, his translation of the French exchanges between Castorp and Mme Chauchat into English constitutes a truly dramatic intervention in the meaning potential of the text, obscuring the key thematic signals conveyed by the heteroglossic interplay in Mann's original.

Lowe-Porter engages in frequent reformulations, often simplifying Mann's structures even where this does not appear to be prompted by systemic incompatibilities or semantic asymmetries. Her version is freer, and thus often changes the discourse perspective of the text in subtle rather than dramatic ways, amending the meaning potential of the translation vis-à-vis the original. The procedures of modification evident in her version – the deletion of words and phrases, the removal of repetitions and parallelisms, the redistribution of sentence elements with concomitant implications for cohesion, and overall syntactic compression – generate a text which shows a high level of linguistic normalization, a tendency identified in Chapter 3 as especially prevalent in the 1920s. In terms of the much-discussed 'translation universals' (Malmkjaer 2011), Lowe-Porter's text thus shows clear signs of simplification at the level of internal sentence structure. Toury identifies such modifications as evidence of the 'law of growing standardization' in line with the repertoires of the target pole, whereby 'textual relations obtaining in the original are often modified [...] in favour of (more) habitual options offered by a target culture' (Toury 1995: 268; for a discussion see Pym 2008). Such tendencies have, furthermore, been identified as especially typical of first translations as compared with later retranslations (Gambier 1994).

With regard to Lowe-Porter's treatment of Mann's complex syntax, however, our discussion has served to dispel one of the most commonly held preconceptions: Lowe-Porter's techniques of clause combination – as reflected in sentence length and techniques of compounding – are, in fact, no less sophisticated than those of Woods, who dissolves approximately the same number of complex structures. It is in Lowe-Porter's treatment of internal clause structures that her version diverges most markedly. Simplification is not seen to the same degree in the lexical composition of her text, which shows greater diversity than that of Woods. Lowe-Porter certainly tends to omit and reduce, but her version displays a relatively high level of lexical variation. In this respect, her text does not confirm the established hypothesis of translational normalization ('flattening') through lexical generalization and levelling (Kenny 2001). While her text is characterized by a generally liberal approach to the 'word' (as opposed to what she considers the 'sense') of the novel, it displays a clear trend towards literalism at the level of phraseology. She frequently adopts calquing procedures which at times produce formulations of questionable idiomaticity. This tendency towards literalism, i.e. the 'shining through' of source-language features in target-language formulations, is an instance of the other 'law' identified by Toury, that of 'interference': 'phenomena pertaining to the make-up of the source text tend to be transferred to the target text' (1995: 275).

The effects of Lowe-Porter's transformations in terms of the generation of literary meaning are most evident in their cumulative impact. In an anthology of critical essays on the novel, Dowden insists that none of her distortions is in itself 'of major significance' (1999: xvii). This assessment might well be questioned in the light of mistranslations such as that of *'überleben'* at the end of the novel, which is problematic indeed. On the whole, however, it is the general lack of subtle differentiation in Lowe-Porter's rendition – occasioned by the modificatory techniques identified above, which she appears to have applied in the interests of improved 'readability' – that affects its quality as a representation of the aesthetic qualities of Mann's text. In terms of the 'distance' of her version from Mann's original, her text can be defined as displaying a higher level of 'dissimilarity' to Mann's original than that of Woods (on notions of similarity in translation see Chesterman 1997). Woods' version, with its higher level of accuracy and correspondence, might qualify for the status of 'divergent similarity', which allows what Hewson (following Lecercle 1999) calls a 'just interpretation' of the text despite the inevitable shifts occasioned by translation (Hewson 2011, Chapter 6). Lowe-Porter's version, on the other hand, would appear to display what Hewson terms 'relative divergence': it modifies and diminishes potential readings without proving disruptive, without eliciting 'false interpretations' or moving as far as the kind of 'radical divergence' that entirely obscures the original potential for meaning (Hewson 2011: 233). The rich intricacy and integration of the original is frequently reduced in Lowe-Porter's version, toning down precisely the multiple qualifications and ambivalences which are considered so central to Mann's style. This underdifferentiation is, perhaps, most evident in her treatment of Mann's irony. An examination of her version shows that she does 'account for' the vast majority of ironic devices in Mann's text, maintaining a certain degree of stylistic incongruity and a distancing narratorial stance. But her consistent omissions and simplifications, combined with a penchant for dated lexis and syntax, tend to obscure the tongue-in-cheek quality of Mann's writing, diluting many of the discourse markers which guide the reader's response to the text.

5 Transferring the paratextual: The translation of Thomas Mann's titles

Preliminary remarks

In Thomas Mann's novella *Der Tod in Venedig*, a number of works are attributed to the protagonist Gustav von Aschenbach which, the narrator claims, have played a key role in cementing the celebrated writer's literary reputation. The texts are listed in the long and syntactically striking sentence which opens the second chapter of the story. Indicating a wide range of artistic accomplishment that has gained in maturity and depth over the years, these works – a prose epic, a social novel, a short story and an aesthetic-philosophical disposition – bear the names of projects which Mann himself had abandoned in the years prior to the composition of the Venice story (*'Blütenträume, die nicht reiften'*: Letter to Jonas Lesser, 1 January 1943, *Reg* 2, 698). He thus 'bequeathed' them to his fictional character (Wysling 1965). In the nine English translations of Mann's story published to date, the titles of two of these works in particular show a wide degree of variation: the story *Ein Elender* and the essay *Geist und Kunst*. Indeed, in the former case each of the translators comes up with a different solution. The translated titles are listed below (for details, see the bibliography):

	Ein Elender	*Geist und Kunst*
Burke 1925	The Wretch	Art and the Spirit
Lowe-Porter 1928	The Abject	Mind and Art
Luke 1988	A Study in Abjection	Intellect and Art
Koelb 1994	A Man of Misery	Art and Intellect
Appelbaum 1995	A Miserable Man	Intellect and Art
Neugroschel 1998	A Wretched Man	Mind and Art
Chase 1999	A True Wretch	Mind and Art

| Heim 2004 | A Wretched Figure | Art and the Intellect |
| Doege 2010 | A Miserable One | Art and the Intellect |

Even a cursory glance at the English titles selected by the translators indicates the range of translation-relevant factors that are at play here. Issues of lexical correspondence arise in connection with the adjective *'elend'* in the first case and with the noun *'Geist'* in the second. In the former instance, relatively straightforward questions of semantic differentiation are at stake: in what sense is the individual referred to in the title *'elend'*, and what might be an appropriate English equivalent in this context? The latter example, by contrast, contains an abstract German term, *'Geist'*, which (as a cultural core concept) has a long and venerable tradition and has often been considered untranslatable (Pinkard 2001: 700; Apter 2008). In morphosyntactic terms, meanwhile, the title *Ein Elender* raises the question of the translation of German human adjectival nouns. These are employed frequently in Mann's works, feature as a key stylistic device in *Der Tod in Venedig*, and are generally held to constitute a near-incompatibility between the grammatical repertoires of German and English (Hawkins 1986; König and Gast 2007). This first example also demonstrates a variation in the use of determiners (definite vs indefinite article). In the second German title it is the sequence of the nouns that is interesting: in four of the English versions, the order of the two elements is reversed. These intrinsically problematic issues of interlingual transfer exist quite apart from the intratextual and intertextual references that the titles may draw upon, whereby the latter may in turn generate cultural resonances.

The categorization and translation of titles

A more detailed consideration of the translation solutions adopted above raises interesting questions about the procedures of title translation. The subject of literary titles has been much discussed since the 1980s under the rubric of paratext theory, and has spawned a sub-discipline of its own (*'titrologie'*, *'Titelforschung'*: useful overviews of the field are provided in Kreimeier et al. 2004 and Jürgensen 2007). Scholars working in this area of enquiry have essentially sought to develop and refine the three prototypical functions of titles identified by Hoek, who defines the title as an *'ensemble de signes linguistiques [...] qui peuvent figurer en tête d'un texte pour le désigner, pour en indiquer le contenu global et pour allécher le public visé'* (Hoek 1982: 17). Most scholars now regard the first of the criteria (variously called the designatory, distinctive or naming function) as obligatory: a title must, after all (and notwithstanding the existence of homonymous titles), identify the text to which it refers. The third function, too, is uncontroversial: many titles have an overtly phatic function. But the second criterion indicated by Hoek – the indication of content – is more problematic. As Genette points out: 'the relation between a title and a "global content" is eminently variable, ranging from the most direct factual designation (*Madame Bovary*) to the most uncertain symbolic relations (*Le rouge et le noir*)', and will always depend on 'the hermeneutic complaisance of the receiver' (Genette 1988: 708). This informative or descriptive function of the title is, clearly, highly elastic: a title can stand in an associative, opaque or even completely misleading relationship to its co-text. It is this dimension of the title, furthermore, that seriously restricts the value of cross-linguistic comparisons of titles in terms of their surface-level features alone.

It is common, in discussing the phenomenon of the title, to refer to the language functions developed by Jakobson on the basis of Bühler's organon model of language (Bouchehri 2008, Chapter 2). Thus the authors of the two major full-length studies in the field adapt and apply the referential, conative, emotive, poetic, phatic and metalinguistic functions in their typologies. Rothe's 1986 book remains the standard study of the subject. In the context of translation studies, where the field remains 'a rather neglected area' (Viezzi 2011: 193), the most extensive discussion to date was provided by Nord in 1993. The taxonomies proposed by Rothe and Nord diverge at some points, and the application of Jakobson's categories to the phenomenon of titles is not entirely unproblematic (Weinrich 2000). Fundamentally, however, they cover the same ground as Genette, seeking to structure the relational properties that obtain between titles and their texts. In his less rigid model, Genette calls the content-related features of the title 'thematic' ('this book is about …'). He adds a second optional functional category, the 'rhematic' ('this book is a …'), which is text-related rather than content-based in as far as it makes a statement about the genre, the time and place of production, the source, or perhaps the contextual environment of the text. In the Rothe/Nord schemes, this latter function is subsumed under the referential function, called the '*Referenzfunktion*' and '*Darstellungsfunktion*' respectively. Both the thematic and rhematic aspects of titles are, of course, descriptive functions. Furthermore, as Genette points out, the descriptive dimension of titles can also have secondary functions, which he calls 'connotations', of various kinds: intertextual allusions, stylistic marking, historical references or registers, etc. Hoek's third function – to appeal to the target audience – is defined by Genette as 'seduction'. He sees this aspect of valorization as especially, and inevitably, subjective. In the Rothe/Nord taxonomies this function is much expanded, and is covered by two functional categories: the '*phatische Funktion*', which secures the initial contact between reader and text, and can serve a mnemonic purpose, and the '*Appellfunktion*', which arouses reader expectations and guides the process of interpretation in a certain direction. All the dimensions identified and classified by Genette and others play a crucial role in the constitution of the meaning potential generated by texts: paratextual information provides the reader with clues that are pursued in the process of textual understanding.

However its 'content' function is defined, a title stands in a complex semantic relation to the text, and its actual propositional relevance is highly flexible: for this reason, the more general term '*prädizierend*' has been proposed for this dimension (Moenninghoff 2000: 19f.). Indeed, titles stand in a binary relationship to the text they designate. On the one hand, they enable a cataphoric view of the text, in their role as the preliminary contact with the as yet uninformed reader (perhaps in tandem with cover notes and other paratextual elements). But they also have an anaphoric thrust which draws on information gleaned as textual knowledge is accumulated, and a full appreciation of their implications may become possible only after the entire text has been read, through a process of hermeneutic inferencing. Titles are never decontextualized instances of language, even where they are simply mentioned in passing, without their accompanying text. As can be seen in the two examples cited at the beginning of this discussion, they are always embedded within a signifying system, be it textual, metatextual or extratextual.

At first sight, it is Nord's 1993 study that appears to have the greatest bearing on the discussion which follows. In her examination of a corpus of some 12,500 translated titles in four languages (of which some 5,000 belong to literary texts), she establishes and compares cross-cultural conventions, noting the many modifications that titles undergo in translation. Despite its solid quantitative foundations, however, Nord's study is not primarily descriptive in nature. Quite the opposite: it is explicitly designed to illustrate the functional approach to translation developed in Germany in the 1970s and 1980s, and is essentially didactic in intention (Nord 1997). But the heuristic value of the cross-linguistic cataloguing of thousands of titles viewed in isolation from the texts to which they are attached is ultimately questionable (Greiner 2004: 10). The corpus-based methods adopted by Nord can indeed identify patterns, norms and strategies, highlighting interesting phenomena in translation. However, as Nord herself readily concedes, a quantitative approach is unable to illuminate the potentially significant interpretive relationship between the title and its co-text (Nord 1993: 7). This is especially true in the case of literary texts. In a later and shorter study, Nord applies her ideas more specifically to the translation of literary titles, stressing the importance of the '*Verhältnis von Titel und*

Text' in this context (Nord 2004: 912). In doing so, she again focuses on the dual pillars of her functionalist approach to translation: functional adequacy and loyalty to the assumed authorial intention. The latter, she recognizes, can only be reconstructed, if at all, by means of a detailed analysis of the text itself. However, her study remains firmly focused on decontextualized examples, and on the normative question of the acceptability of translation solutions. She lists and classifies, but does not give consideration to the consequences of the modifications made by translators of titles in terms of literary meaning. Furthermore, a purely empirical, detextualized approach is entirely unable to account for the frequently wide degree of formal and semantic divergence between original titles and their translations where such divergence cannot be explained by linguistic or cultural incompatibilities. In extreme (but by no means rare) cases, the discrepancy between source and target language titles can completely suspend the designatory function of the title in relation to the original, making the original entirely irrecoverable. In other words, a quantitative analysis can only define what Nord calls '*die Art der unterscheidenden Merkmale*' (Nord 1993: 5): for example, it cannot evaluate the qualitative shifts evident in the translation of Mann's *Die Betrogene* as *The Black Swan*.

This reservation applies, in fact, to all titles which Levy, in the cruder typology developed in his classic text of the 1960s, classifies as '*symbolisierend*' rather than '*beschreibend*' (Levy 1969: 122–7). Where a title stands in a relationship of what Levy calls '*bildhafte Transposition*' to its parent text, knowledge of that text is a prerequisite for any serious consideration of the title's semantic value. But even familiarity with the text is not always enough to illuminate the motivation behind the choice of title translations. Very often, extra-textual questions have to be considered. For example, was there contact between the translator and the original author? Has the author or publisher exerted an influence on the formulation of the title? Have existing translations, or other target-system texts with the same or a similar title, dictated procedures? In the following discussion, I would like to comment on the translation of Thomas Mann's titles into English by adopting a broader descriptive approach, considering the translators' solutions against the background of the works themselves. Only an examination of the relations between title and text can shed light on the motivation behind, and the possible efficacy of, the solutions selected. And in many cases, the motivation behind the selection of translated titles can only be reconstructed effectively if the interventions of author and publisher are taken into account.

Thomas Mann's titles

The titles of Thomas Mann's fictional works are of great interest from the point of view of title translation. In terms of the functional descriptors outlined above, they appear to fulfil an essentially referential function, providing an initial indication of the textual context. In this sense, they are descriptive. Classically, such titles state the name of a key figure, often the protagonist (the eponymous hero). However – and this is the case with a number of Thomas Mann's texts – transparently referential titles can also point to unnamed persons via generic nouns, to persons outside the text, as well as to objects, events, spatial and temporal situations, or to abstract concepts. In the vast majority of cases, Mann's fictional titles refer explicitly to their co-text, isolating an entity or concept which appears in the text itself (the only exceptions are *Vision, Gerächt, Schwere Stunde, Wälsungenblut,* and the first noun in the composite title *Unordnung und frühes Leid*). They are 'thematic' in Genette's sense. In all such cases, of course, there is no direct or logically contiguous relationship between the named entity and its referential value in the text. As Genette stresses, even descriptive titles also have secondary functions, arousing reader expectations that can be fulfilled, undermined or indeed thwarted as the text progresses. Even in apparently referential instances, the relationship between title and text can constitute an interpretive challenge.

A number of Mann's titles also contain 'rhematic' information in the form of subtitles. These generally provide the reader with advance notification of the text genre – '*Prosa-Skizze*' (*Vision*), '*Novellistische Studie*' (*Gerächt*), '*Ein Idyll*' (*Herr und Hund*), '*Der Memoiren erster Teil*' (*Felix Krull*) – amplifying the descriptive character of the title. In two cases the subtitles assume a phatic dimension by anticipating other qualities of the text: *Der Kleiderschrank: Eine Geschichte voller Rätsel*, and *Mario und der Zauberer: Ein tragisches Reiseerlebnis*. Whereas the first of these prepares the reader for a specific type of receptive experience, the second anticipates the outcome of the story. Alone among Mann's English translators, Lowe-Porter deletes virtually all of these subtitles, thus reducing the referential/informative power of the overall title and significantly diluting this reception-oriented dimension.

The canon of Thomas Mann's prose works comprises 32 short texts and 11 novels, while the lyric output comprises an extended idyll and seven poems. There is one drama. I focus in the following discussion only on the prose oeuvre, for a number of reasons. It is these works, commonly regarded as the pinnacle of Mann's achievement, that have been translated into English almost in their entirety (the sole exception is the fragmentary *Der Knabe Henoch*). In many cases they have frequently been retranslated, providing an interesting perspective on translational variants. Moreover, in lyric poetry the relationship between title and text is often seen as governed by a different set of conventions, some of them highly ritualized. Thus Mann's lyric output testifies to the traditions of apostrophe ('*Siehst du, Kind, ich liebe dich*'), dedication (*'An Agnes Sorma'*), generic definition (*'Monolog'*, *'Gesang vom Kindchen'*), undetermined temporal reference (*'Nacht'*, *'Weihnacht'*), and rhetorical set-piece (*'Dichters Tod'*). The title of his only play, *Fiorenza*, is a proper noun, and as such belongs to a typological category more than adequately covered within the corpus of the prose works.

In morphosyntactic terms, the titles of Mann's 43 prose works are highly restricted. Like the two embedded titles indicated above, they are virtually all nominal in structure. Only four texts diverge from this pattern: the participial *Gefallen* and *Gerächt*, the prepositional *Beim Propheten*, and the clausal *Wie Jappe und Do Escobar sich prügelten*. The remaining 39 titles consist of nominal groups, in various constellations of complexity. Approximately half of them consist of common nouns in a single group, either in an undetermined (of the type *Vision*) or determined form (*Der Tod*), with premodification (*Die vertauschten Köpfe*) or without. Four of the nominal title groups contain coordinated constituents of the type *Herr und Hund*. Seventeen of the 43 titles contain proper nouns, either in the bare form (*Tobias Mindernickel*) or with various degrees of expansion (*Der kleine Herr Friedemann, Die Geschichten Jakobs*). Of this group, four contain names that do not identify characters in the text itself (e.g. *Tristan*).

In semantic terms, the common nouns may be grouped as human (*Der Bajazzo*), human adjectival (*Die Hungernden*), abstract (*Vision*), object (*Der Kleiderschrank*), genre (*Anekdote*) or event nouns (*Das Eisenbahnunglück*). However, the relative structural uniformity of Mann's titles conceals a wide spectrum of semantic values. The author exploits a number of strategies in their formulation, moving beyond the 'basic' referential and reception-oriented functions of titles (designatory, phatic, etc.). While none of them displays a high degree of syntactical complexity or poetic extra-structure, a number of Mann's titles do have a symbolic dimension. For example, among the titles built around proper nouns we find telling names (*Der kleine Herr Friedemann*), intertextual references (*Lotte in Weimar*), symbolic regional combination (*Tonio Kröger*), and intratextual references (*Luischen*), while among the common nouns there are instances of polysemy (e.g. *Der Weg zum Friedhof* (road/path or way?), *Königliche Hoheit* (form of address or abstract concept?), symbolic implication (*Die Hungernden*: physical or emotional hunger?), *Der Zauberberg* (relationship with text?), and opaque combination (*Schwere Stunde, Unordnung und frühes Leid*).

The translation of Mann's titles

The above-mentioned features raise a number of translation-relevant questions, and it is instructive to note the various solutions adopted by the translators over the years, since these illustrate competing strategies. Once again, the first title cited at the opening of the present discussion may serve as a useful starting point, because it demonstrates the importance of considering both microlevel (morphosyntactic and lexical) and macrolevel (intratextual and even metatextual) factors. The text *Ein Elender* attributed to Aschenbach is mentioned on three occasions within the Venice story itself, providing important intratextual clues to its referential status. On the first occasion, the text is characterized in a general form, described as a story which has shown (presumably *ex negativo*) an entire young generation '*die Möglichkeit sittlicher Entschlossenheit jenseits der tiefsten Erkenntnis*' (GW 8: 450). On the second occasion, further insight is provided into the intellectual impulse behind the story ('*Ausbruch des Ekels gegen den unanständigen Psychologismus der Zeit*'), and the transgression of its protagonist, who is guilty of '*Lasterhaftigkeit*' and '*ethische Velleität*', and commits a series of '*Nichtswürdigkeiten*' (all GW 8: 455). The final reference reiterates the central importance of the text in Aschenbach's oeuvre and relates it to the predominant concerns of his classical output: '*der Autor des "Elenden", der in so vorbildlich reiner Form dem Zigeunertum und der trüben Tiefe abgesagt, dem Abgrunde die Sympathie gekündigt und das Verworfene verworfen hatte*' (GW 8: 521). The information provided within Mann's text, then, serves to identify the text as a study in moral failure: the '*Elend*' referred to in the title emerges as an ethical category, the actions of the protagonist as a base and depraved display of conceit and self-indulgence which finds expression in the mistreatment of a woman. These semantic coordinates alone would seem to cast doubt on 'misery' and 'miserable' as appropriate renderings of '*elend*' (Koelb, Appelbaum, Doege), while the notions of 'wretchedness' and 'abjection' appear to correspond more closely to the semantics of the German noun in this context. Thus, Appelbaum's *A Miserable Man* implies a different text from Neugroschel's *A Wretched Man*, suggesting a state of mind rather than a mode of behaviour. Further information on Mann's plans for a text entitled *Ein Elender* is available on a metatextual level. The author's work notes and letters, which detail the biographical background to the text, reinforce the interpretation outlined above: Mann's projected novella was to be a study in moral failure (Reed 1983).

In morphosyntactic terms, too, the translators face a challenge with this title: that of finding an idiomatic rendering of the German adjectival noun. A number of procedures are used here. Five of the translators insert a support noun: 'man' (Neugroschel, Koelb, Appelbaum: these are the only versions which indicate the protagonist's gender), 'figure' (Heim), or the determined pronominal form 'one' (Doege). Two (Burke and Chase) select the full noun 'wretch', whereby the latter inserts the premodifying 'true' for the purpose of amplification. In two cases, translators select options which violate the norms of English. Lowe-Porter's nominalized adjective *The Abject* is anomalous on semantic grounds if it is intended as a human noun: nominalized forms of abstract nouns in the singular refer to abstract categories rather than to individual human instantiations of the quality referred to. If, on the other hand, Lowe-Porter intends her title to be understood as an abstract noun, it would more conventionally be rendered as the undetermined noun 'Abjection'. Doege's 'miserable one', meanwhile, is in itself an unidiomatic rendering, and in combination with the indefinite article (*A Miserable One*) even appears ungrammatical. Luke's *A Study in Abjection*, on the other hand, emerges as a highly felicitous solution in the terms outlined above: the abstract noun 'abjection' appears to capture the moral-ethical concept implied by the title, while the addition of the 'study in' obviates the need to construct a potentially awkward adjectival noun phrase. While the story is constantly referred to intratextually as an *'Erzählung'*, Luke's designation underlines its status as a psychological analysis of decadence, for which Mann had, indeed, undertaken extensive studies, as his notebooks show. The last question which merits consideration in connection with this translated title is, perhaps, the issue of nominal determination: two of the translators (Burke and Lowe-Porter) prefer a definite article. The implications of this will be considered below.

Morphosyntactic issues
On a syntactic level, procedures of nominal determination play a central role in Mann's titles. Fifteen of the author's common-noun titles contain a determining element in the form of an article, while three titles are composed of undetermined nouns. Given the fact that the systems of determination in English and German diverge, it is to be expected that the referential status of the noun phrases which constitute so many of Mann's titles will emerge as problematic. As one would expect, the translators systematically adopt the determining patterns of English wherever this appears possible. Most interesting in translational terms are those cases where there are asymmetries between the two language systems, for example in the use of abstract nouns. Here, important issues of specific and generic nominal reference arise. Thus the title of the early story *Der Tod* is rendered by its only translator, Constantine, as *Death*, favouring a generalizing interpretation of the German title. This interpretation is consistent with the text itself: while the story tells of one specific death – that of the narrator's daughter, Asuncion – it also treats the theme of mortality in general. Indeed, it is a morbid interior monologue on the subject of death (narrated through a series of 15 diary entries), which is itself personified in the tale, and also alludes to other cases: the impending death of the narrator, the possibility of

suicide, the demise of Asuncion's mother twelve years earlier, and the death of Kaiser Friedrich. In this case, the generic noun reference in the English title is clearly in keeping with the semantics of the original.

Der Tod in Venedig, meanwhile, is rendered by all nine of its translators as the undetermined noun phrase *Death in Venice*. In this example, Mann exploits the dual potential reference of the determined head noun as an artistic device, and it assumes symbolic significance. The title fuses Aschenbach's personal destiny (a death through love) with the collective destruction caused by the cholera epidemic sweeping through Venice (death through infection), suggesting an associative linkage between the two. As von Wiese points out in his classic analysis of the text, the German title has '*etwas schwebend Offenes*' (von Wiese 1964: 306). The protagonist chooses to remain in Venice, actively embracing death in the process. An analysis of the symbolic association between the individual and general would lead to the very heart of the novella's thematic concerns: the image of the beautiful but sick city ('*die schmeichlerische und verdächtige Schöne*', GW 8: 503); the seduction of death through beauty (interplay of Eros and Thanatos: Platen's '*Wer die Schönheit angeschaut mit Augen, ist dem Tode schon anheimgegeben*' alluded to in Mann's text); the tension between the Apolline and the Dionysian as it unfolds in the myth-laden city; the multiple augurs of death distributed throughout the story. All these motifs are interwoven, fusing the universal with the specific (Sprecher 2004). The English versions reduce the polysemous reference of the original title: inevitably so, since the insertion of an article in English would restrict the reference of the noun to a specific instantiation, i.e. the death of the protagonist, either anaphorically ('A') or cataphorically ('The'). The first option would appear overindividuated, while the second would seem overdetermined, perhaps claiming an excessively representative status for the fate of the protagonist. As it stands, the English version of the title does retain a certain dualism of reference through its potentially elliptical interpretation (omission of articles in title formulations). But it is unable to do so as clearly as the German, and leans heavily towards the generic interpretation. In English formulations of this title, then, the subtle interplay between the specific and generic interpretations of the head noun is obscured.

Further instances might be cited in which issues of determination play an important role. The title *Ein Glück* is problematic in as far as it consists of an uncountable German noun which is used here in an individuated sense in the singular with an indefinite article. This option is not available for the English 'happiness' as a bare noun (but might be for English modified instantiations, 'a genuine happiness', 'a happiness that knew no bounds;' see Huddlestone, Pullum et al. 2002: 339). Adopting an interesting translation strategy, Lowe-Porter renders this title as *A Gleam*, selecting a noun which is countable, if not transparent as a version of the German title. It is a title which is established through a procedure of substitution/compensation in the translation of the text itself. In Mann's story, the noun *'Glück'* appears four times in the final lines of the text, on the first three occasions in its countable form: *'ein Glück, ein süßes, heißes und heimliches Glück [...] ein Glück, ein kleiner Schauer und Rausch von Glück [...]'* (GW 8: 361). Lowe-Porter translates the first instance as 'a joy', deletes the second, postmodifying the preceding noun 'joy' with 'so warm, so sweet, so comfortable', renders the third as 'happiness' without a determiner, and translates the fourth as 'joy'. However, she translates Mann's adjectival use of the lexeme *'Du wirst [...] ein wenig glücklich sein'* (361) as 'you will have a gleam of happiness' (Lowe-Porter 1936: 282), and it is from this construction that she draws her title. This procedure has the advantage of providing a countable noun for the title, but it sacrifices both the semantic accuracy (joy-happiness) and the intratextual coherence of the original. Furthermore, the function of the title in terms of reader anticipation and orientation is changed. In Mann's text, the lemma *'Glück'* occurs on ten occasions, and in all earlier instances in the text is used to describe Baron Harry, the female protagonist's philandering husband: he is described as *'ein Glücklicher'*, and (we are told twice) is blessed with *'Glück, Rhythmus und Siegessinn'*. In his case, *'Glück'* is a condition. Only at the very end of the text does his frustrated wife, Baronin Anna, enjoy her moment of bliss: but this is a brief experience of satisfaction, when her husband is publicly humiliated by a dancing girl. Rather than a state of happiness, then, this is a specific and isolated instantiation, cast in German in the countable form. This contrast is inevitably lost in Lowe-Porter's version through the removal of recurrential cohesion. It is, perhaps, felicitously captured as 'A Moment of Happiness' in the ad hoc translation used by Ronald Hayman in his biography of Mann (1995: 16).

The case of adjectival nouns
In the instances cited above, the issue of determination is synonymous with that of the scope of nominal reference: the insertion or omission of an article serves to restrict or widen the semantic range of the head noun, implying specific or generic meanings. In the case of German adjectival nouns, on the other hand, the use of a determiner (and the concomitant changes to the morphology of the adjective) transforms the word class altogether. English is restricted in the possibilities it offers here, especially in the case of singular adjectival nouns. Indeed, even in the case of plural forms, the use of adjectives as heads of noun phrases is restricted to 'a subtype denoting categories of human being': the poor, etc. (Huddlestone, Pullum et al. 2002: 417ff.). Mann makes

full use of adjectival nouns in his works, and they have often been identified as a characteristic feature of his heavily attributive style. In view of the cross-linguistic differences involved here, the English versions of the three Thomas Mann titles which have this form show some interesting variations.

The title of the text *Die Hungernden*, as a plural human nominalized adjective (participle), is of interest predominantly in lexical terms: grammatically, English offers the same option of determiner plus plural adjectival noun, and the example 'the hungry' is actually cited as an example in dictionaries. Mann's title is ambiguous, and the selection of the dynamic participial form *'hungernd'* in preference to the stative *'hungrig'* enables him to bring out the abstract meaning alongside the physical. In the final paragraphs of the text, the artist protagonist Detlef establishes an association between the social deprivation of the malnourished vagrant he encounters outside a theatre and his own emotional deprivation. He casts both – the penniless outcast on the one hand and himself as the frustrated lover and rootless artist on the other – in the role of marginalized *'Darbende und Ausgeschlossene'*, appealing to the solidarity of the excluded: *'Wir sind ja Brüder!'* (GW 8: 269). In an extended series of adjectival nouns, Detlef develops this association: *'Daheim sind wir beide im Lande der Betrogenen, der Hungernden, Anklagenden und Verneinenden'* (GW 8: 270). Lowe-Porter translates *'die Hungernden'* in this sequence (somewhat unidiomatically?) as 'the hungering' and elsewhere uses the combination 'the hungry man'. In her title, on the other hand, she prefers *The Hungry*. This certainly has the advantage of greater naturalness and economy, but obscures the link between title and co-text, and might be held to reduce the metaphorical associations of the noun. Neugroschel, on the other hand, retains the coherence of the reference, rendering the German noun in both cases with the full noun 'starvelings'. This noun is morphologically unproblematic, and is attested in corpora in both literal and metaphorical meanings. Emptiness, a yearning for satisfaction and fulfilment, are the shared semantic components, raised here to a symbolic level. In an early translation of an excerpt from this story, Ludwig Lewisohn (1823) inserts a support noun: 'Hungry Souls'.

The two other texts with nominalized adjectives as their titles – *Der Erwählte* and *Die Betrogene* – raise particularly acute issues. As we observed in connection with *Ein Elender* above, singular human adjectival nouns in English pose serious questions of idiomaticity. In the two cases under discussion here, the translators make significant amendments, presumably for this very reason. *Der Erwählte* appeared in English in the translation by Lowe-Porter as *The Holy Sinner*, a title which is not recoverable from the original. As Mann's correspondence shows, he chose his German title at an early stage in his work on the project, although he also frequently referred to the text in passing as *'Gregorius'*. The German noun selected by Mann as his title, an epithet commonly used to denote 'religious selection', appears on thirteen occasions in the text. The message that Gregorius has been 'chosen' (*erwählt*) as Pope by the divine will is announced by the Lamb of God, and is cited nine times in its participial form. In the body of her text, Lowe-Porter translates the adjectival noun variously as 'the Chosen', and the 'Chosen One'. The latter formulation, in a historical-religious text, seems to constitute an appropriate use of the support form 'one', which is otherwise problematic in modern English. The process by which the published English title was finally arrived at will be considered in greater detail below, as it casts light on the degree of attention Mann paid to this issue. At this point, it is interesting to note that the title shows major semantic modifications vis-à-vis the original: indeed, the noun 'sinner' stands in an almost provocatively antonymic relationship to the idea of the chosen one, while the modification through the adjective 'holy' adds a new dimension, making the combination oxymoronic.

The notion of the 'holy sinner', which is by no means an unusual combination, does not itself appear in the German text. However, the two words do occur frequently in isolation from each other. The concepts of sin and selection are brought into close proximity on two occasions in the narrative: *'hier findet ihr nur, den Gott sich erwählt hat zum untersten, äußersten Sünder'* (GW 7: 226) and *'aber klug ist es freilich, im Sünder den Erwählten zu ahnen, und klug ist das auch für den Sünder selbst'* (GW 7: 260). The English title clearly contains considerably more referential information than the German original, indicating the contradiction that lies at the heart of the text, and suggests a specific interpretive direction. While the German title signals from the outset that the protagonist will emerge in some sense as 'chosen', the English title sets up a semantic tension that is typical of 'poetic' titles in Rothe's terms.

Mann's *Die Betrogene* was translated into English by William R. Trask, after Lowe-Porter had declined the commission due to pressure of work. The German title is ambiguous, and its relationship to its co-text requires a certain amount of interpretive effort. Indeed, the entire text has been subject to a large number of divergent interpretations (Vaget 2001b; Latta 1987 and 1993). The noun of the title does not refer to a woman betrayed by a man, as the reader might initially assume. In fact, Mann's title seems consciously to arouse expectations in the reader that are frustrated as the text progresses, and the text plays with the phenomenon of misconstrual on various levels. As Lorenzen-Peth writes: *'Da der Leser selbst [...] getäuscht wird, könnte man den Titel auch auf den Rezipienten ("Der Betrogene") beziehen'* (2008: 242). The protagonist Rosalie von Tümmler is not misled by her young lover Ken Keaton, and in this respect the ad hoc title 'The Betrayed Woman' used in some of the secondary literature creates an erroneous impression (Mundt 2004: 206; Lehnert 2004: 297). The *'Betrug'*, which is referred to in the closing paragraphs of the text (*'sprich nicht von Betrug'*, GW 8: 950) and which Mann defines as a *'furchtbare Vexation'* in his diary entry of 6 April 1952, is rather a 'deception' (Trask uses the verb 'deceived' in the body of his translation). The protagonist is, most ostensibly, duped not by a partner, but by the biological processes of her body: she fatefully misinterprets the haemorrhaging caused by advanced uterine cancer as a reversal of the menopause, a return to the spring of her youth, in response to feelings of love for a much younger man. It is in this sense, as Mann insists in a series of letters and diary entries, that a *'grausamer Betrug'* takes place, and the author pointed out in a letter to Loewy-Hattendorf that his title was born out of anger at the anecdote on which his novella was based, which had been provided by his wife (letter of 15 September 1954, *DüD* 3: 528). A more accurate literal rendering of the German title would, then, be 'The Deceived Woman' (as found, for example, in Robertson 2002: xxi). On a more abstract level of the text, however, the deception at issue here is tantamount to self-delusion (Luke uses the ad hoc title 'The Delusion', Luke 1988: xiii), and is related to deeper issues of truth and falsehood, to a life philosophy: the heroine is forced by events to correct her notion that the body can be governed by the soul. She accepts her fate in a spirit of confirmation, and interprets the association of Eros and Thanatos as a blessing: '[...] *wie wäre denn Frühling ohne den Tod? Ist ja doch der Tod ein großes Mittel des Lebens, und wenn er für mich die Gestalt lieh von Auferstehung und Liebeslust, so war das nicht Lug, sondern Güte und Gnade'* (GW 8: 950). Her conciliatory insight carries religious overtones.

The title of the English text, *The Black Swan* – from which the original is entirely non-recoverable – represents a considerable shift in focus in cognitive terms. The original title refers to a character in the text, and prompts the reader to anticipate from the very outset that the female protagonist is (or will become) the subject of some form of deception. The German title is, then, *'rezeptionssteuernd'*. The English title, on the other hand, isolates a central symbol in the narrative that occurs on a number of occasions in the final two sections of the story. A functional shift is undertaken from the referential to the symbolic level, and the title has marked distinctive/mnemonic features (a strong visual image). Rosalie feels the urge to visit Holterhof castle to see the black swans which she remembers from a previous visit. Together with her lover, she breaks bread at the edge of the lake, eats some stale crusts, and feeds pieces to the swans. One of the swans flaps its wings aggressively and hisses at her. A few weeks later she dies, remembering the swans as she lies on her deathbed.

The English title, too, requires analysis if it is to be linked coherently with the text. It does not have the same anticipatory, identifying impact as the German title, which arouses expectations of an individual's fate, but it does nevertheless trigger a similar process of retrospective analytical motion. Within the context of Mann's narrative, the swans have been interpreted in various ways. The protagonist associates them variously with melancholy, majesty and arrogance, and is taken aback by their aggressiveness. Most obviously, the swans function in the subtext as an augur of death (alongside a demonic-looking boatman and other symbols: Roffmann 2003: 143), while their transformation from gracefulness to aggressive desire might be seen as a parallel to the changes in Rosalie's behaviour as she confesses her love for and to Ken Keaton. The bread motif, meanwhile, evokes associations with the Last Supper, hinting at the removal of the strict border between life and death. And finally, the black swans might be seen as an ironic allusion to white swans as an Ovidian symbol of illicit love (Mundt 2004: 205). In other words, the English title is referentially very different from the original, but shows a similarly high degree of polyvalence. Thomas Mann was pleased with it: *'Ich finde auch, dass* "The Black Swan" *ein ganz guter Titel ist, da nun einmal "Die Betrogene" unmöglich ins Englische übersetzt werden konnte'* (letter to Anna Jacobson of 3 May 1954, *DüD* 3: 528).

Lexical correspondence

The second 'fictitious' text referred to at the beginning of the present discussion – *'Geist und Kunst'* - raises questions of lexical correspondence, in as far as the noun *'Geist'* denotes an abstract concept with a long intellectual tradition. The title is that of a project on which Mann worked intensively in the years preceding the composition of *Der Tod in Venedig*, 1909–10, before abandoning it. The intratextual reference to this treatise in the second chapter of the Venice story provides a broad characterization of its concerns, and the extensive notes that have survived on the project confirm that it is to be understood as an aesthetic-philosophical disposition (Reed 1983). The majority of the translators thus opt, plausibly, for 'intellect' (5), with 'mind' (3) and 'spirit' (1) less favoured renderings. The central issues in this fictitious treatise are the status of the critical intellectual in an anti-intellectual age, and the place of rationality in art generally: the preferred term therefore seems logical. In his study of Mann, T. J. Reed entitles his extensive chapter on the writer's early aesthetic conception 'Art and Intellect', and consistently uses the latter term throughout (Reed 1996: 119–43). Most other commentators have followed suit. The reversal of the word order of the German title would seem more in keeping with English sequential norms (principle of longer constituent last).

A further interesting lexical variation can be seen in the translation of *Der Bajazzo*. This title relates to a word which was much en vogue in Mann's day, being the German title of Leoncavallo's celebrated opera *Pagliacci*. Lowe-Porter selects a word with a similarly Italian root, *The Dilettante*. This choice raises questions of semantic correspondence, but fits in neatly with the notion of dilettantism which plays a central role in Mann's Bourget-inspired 'decadence' fiction in this period of his career (Vaget 1970; Bauer 1993). Lowe-Porter uses the term throughout her translation, on each of the seven occasions it occurs. Luke opts for the title *The Joker*. Clearly unhappy with a single-word translation of the difficult term, he uses extensive circumlocutions in the body of his text in an attempt to capture the meaning. Thus, Mann's '*Bajazzobegabung*' becomes 'the talent of a kind of mimicking buffoon or joker' (37), and Luke combines the two nouns 'buffoon' and 'joker' in four instances. Only on the last occasion does he translate '*Bajazzo*' with the single-word 'joker', thus ensuring that his title has intratextual resonance. In using 'joker', Luke deliberately introduces a polysemy which is not evident in the German ('I have translated it as "the joker", because this word also suggests the oddity in the pack, the outsider', Luke 1988: xv). This is an interesting target-language technique, substituting a paronomasia for an exotic term. In translation generally, there is a marked tendency to normalize wordplay, and this can be seen in the rendering of Mann's polysemous titles. The title *Königliche Hoheit*, for example, plays on the dualism of the form of royal address (titular salutation) and the abstract meaning of '*Hoheit*', a majesty which the protagonist attains in the course of events. The English noun 'highness' does not have this abstract sense.

Proper nouns
Despite Nord's insistence that issues of determination do not arise in titles containing proper nouns, pronouns or numerals (1993: 69), this question does merit attention in the context of two of Thomas Mann's texts. In keeping with the norms of English, the four translators of *Der kleine Herr Friedemann* delete the definite article: they all have *Little Herr Friedemann*, also retaining the German '*Herr*'. The translators of *Buddenbrooks*, on the other hand (Lowe-Porter and Woods), take over the German title somewhat uncritically. As Luke points out in the introduction to his first volume of Thomas Mann stories: 'the normal German way of referring to a family is without the article, but it would not be English to say "Smiths" when we mean "the Smiths"' (Luke 1970: vii), and Luke therefore uses the title 'The Buddenbrooks' in his discussion of the work. In German, Duden tells us, '*die Bezeichnung für die Mitglieder einer Familie steht meist ohne Artikel: "Meyers sind eine schreckliche Familie"*' (Drosdowski et al. 1984: 220), while in English the

definite article with plural surnames 'refers to an identifiable group of people with the surname' and the (less frequent) omission of the article refers to the totality of people with that surname (Huddleston, Pullum et al. 2002: 521). The choice of title here is also intratextually anomalous, in as far as both translators consistently use the article throughout their versions when referring collectively to the eponymous family (i.e. always 'the Buddenbrooks' where German consistently uses 'Buddenbrooks' without an article).

In a number of cases, Mann exploits names in his titles for literary effect. Indeed, only in a few cases – most notably in those of the Joseph novels – do proper nouns serve merely to identify the protagonist in a purely referential manner. In the majority of cases, the names carry extra significance. A number of his works, for example, have titles which contain telling names, none of which are translated: *Tobias Mindernickel* alludes ironically to the figure of Tobias in the apocryphal book of the Bible, who is accompanied on his travels by a dog that brings him luck; in Mann's tale, the protagonist kills his dog in a fit of rage. The character's surname, meanwhile, combines the diminutive *'minder'* with the North German *'Nickel'*, meaning a person who behaves badly. The eponymous hero's initials are those of Thomas Mann. *Little Herr Friedemann* tells of the intrusion of passion into the sheltered and peaceful (*'Frieden'*) life of the protagonist. The name of the eponymous protagonist Tonio Kröger symbolizes, in its juxtaposition of Italian and Northern German forms, the meeting of two cultures. Felix Krull's Latin Christian name, of course, requires no translation.

Several of the proper nouns used in Mann's titles are symbolic in the sense that they not only fail to designate characters in the text, but also draw on the reader's extratextual (cultural) knowledge. Two of them are Wagnerian. The title of the story *Tristan* is unproblematic, in as far as both the intertextual reference and its value in Mann's text are clear, and it can be transferred without difficulty. The second, *Wälsungenblut*, is less transparent in its significance, as a reference to the theme of incest in Wagner's *Die Walküre* (Siegmund's *'So blühe denn Wälsungenblut'*). In an ironic contrast to the heroic characters of Wagner's world, Mann's spoiled twins Siegmund and Sieglinde, who attend a performance of Wagner's opera before engaging in an act of incest, are presented as utterly decadent. While Lowe-Porter and Neugroschel use "Walsungs" as the noun, Robertson prefers "Volsungs" (Robertson 1999). Both forms are widely attested. The two other cultural references in Mann's titles are derived from, or at least via, Goethe. As a central component of the European literary canon, the title *Doktor Faustus* presents no problems in terms of referentiality: the text is Mann's twentieth-century reshaping of the Faust legend through the life of the fictitious composer

Adrian Leverkühn. But the title is also clearly symbolic in Genette's terms. The question of what is 'Faustian' about the novel's protagonist challenges the reader to identify the text's concerns, activates multiple points of intertextual comparison (especially in its relations to the sixteenth-century chapbook), and depends very much on the reader's retrospective interpretation of the novel. The subtitle, meanwhile, is rhematically descriptive: *'Das Leben des deutschen Tonkünstlers Adrian Leverkühn, erzählt von einem Freunde'* defines the text as a biography, also providing metatextual information about the protagonist and the narrator. The use of the archaic noun *'Tonkünstler'* and the old morphological form *'Freunde'*, moreover, adds a historical connotation. Mann pointed out to Agnes Meyer that he selected the former – Germanic – noun in preference to the epithet *'Komponist'* precisely because it has a particularly Teutonic quality, and stressed that *'das deutsche, das unselig dämonisch und tragisch Deutsche, zur Grund-Conception des Buches gehört und seinen tiefsten Gegenstand bildet'* (letter of 13 September 1944, AEM 586). In both translations of the novel (Lowe-Porter and Woods), the stylistic features of the subtitle are obscured: 'The Life of the German Composer Adrian Leverkühn as Told by a Friend'.

The interaction between author, translator and publisher
The second Goethe reference, the novel *Lotte in Weimar*, is a more interesting case. It may serve as a useful illustration of the extensive interaction which took place between translator, author and publisher in the process of titling. As noted earlier, Mann took a keen interest in the work of his designated translator, Lowe-Porter, frequently advising her and answering her questions, and occasionally offering corrections and suggestions. As Lowe-Porter liked to point out, Mann's English was never good enough to enable him to make entirely reliable and idiomatic suggestions (on Mann's command of English see Ferguson 1997 and Gildhoff 2001). Nevertheless, he was invariably ready to suggest what he saw as alternatives or improvements with regard to individual words and turns of phrase. It is hardly surprising, then, that he often expressed a view on the titles of the translations in his letters and diaries, though he always stressed that it was the translator – and ultimately the publisher – who must have the final word. This observation obtains for Mann's works in general. For example, he once commented that he would have preferred 'Heads and Bodies', a suggestion made by Lowe-Porter, to *The Transposed Heads* as the title of *Die vertauschten Köpfe* (letter to Harry Slochower of 24 May 1941, *DüD* 2: 517). In his first reference to the text in English, Mann calls it 'The Changed Heads' (letter to Knopf of 15 August 1940, *DüD* 2: 585). A sheet included in the typescript of Lowe-Porter's translation of this text (held in the Thomas Mann Collection at Yale) shows the extent of her

indecision with regard to this difficult title. She makes no fewer than nine suggestions, with widely varying degrees of semantic proximity to the original: 'The Wrong Heads', 'Heads and Bodies', 'The Turning of Heads', 'The Sundered Husbands', 'The Transposed Heads', 'The Transposed Husbands', 'A Matter of Heads', 'Illusion' and, added in handwriting, 'The Transferred Heads' (Box 11, Folder 199, No. 93). In this case, as in others, Knopf appears to have made the final decision. The search for an appropriate English title was, however, especially intensive in the case of two texts: *Lotte in Weimar* and *Der Erwählte*.

The latter example is relevant in the context of adjectival nouns, and was mentioned above in that context. More generally, though, the manner in which an English title was selected for this work is representative of the process of interaction and mutual consultation which typically took place between the agents involved. Mann himself once referred to this process as *'Titelfahndung'* (diary entry of 25 December 1939). A range of variants ran through his mind with regard to this text, and his statements indicate both the intensity with which he reflected on the matter and a high degree of uncertainty. In his diary entry of 10 December 1950 he reports that he has discussed the subject with his son Golo, and that 'Gregory, Son of Sin' has emerged as the most likely candidate. A letter to Lowe-Porter on the same day, however, indicates that this suggestion has been arrived at only via a circuitous route, and is by no means definitive. In this letter he quotes eight alternatives which he has been considering (Thirlwall 1966: 128ff.). His comments reveal some of the criteria which guide him in his deliberations, as well as the limitations of his own English even after 12 years in the United States. Unconvinced by the literal rendering 'The Chosen One' (*'hat mir nie recht gefallen'*: letter to Agnes E. Meyer of 15 December 1950, *AEM* 747), he writes:

> In the beginning I thought of something like 'The Story of the Great Pope Gregorius'. But I am afraid that with that too much is anticipated. Next came 'Sin and Grace' to my mind. It is not impossible, nor is 'The Holy Sinner'. What about 'The Sinner who was chosen'? But that may rather be a subtitle. One could add the names of the two and say 'Gregory, the Son of a Sinner' – 'Made of Sin' would perhaps not be bad either. Nor would 'Son of Sin', still better with the addition of the name, 'Gregory, Son of Sin'.

He reiterates some of these options in the letter to Agnes E. Meyer of 15 December 1950, asking her opinion. The range of the formulations suggested here indicates the lack of any firm preconceptions on the author's part with regard to both the form and function of titles. In particular, Mann clearly had no fixed view on the referential value of the titles proposed. Three of the suggestions he makes identify the protagonist by name, activating intertextual knowledge for readers acquainted with the Gregorius legend, while five refer to the abstract category of sin as the novel's theme. Mann seems to have been guided by considerations such as economy, distinctiveness, mnemonic impact and phonetic quality as much as by a clear preference with regard to descriptive thrust. As he himself comments, the first of the options proposed has a strong proleptic dimension, anticipating the outcome of the story by naming the protagonist and indicating his destiny. It shows clear signs of both expansiveness and explicitation. The second, 'Sin and Grace', cryptically combines two abstract religious concepts in a concise and provocatively paradoxical relationship. Other titles under consideration are clearly reader-oriented (phatic) in their suggestive compression (the unidiomatic 'Made of Sin'), and one of these –'Son of Sin' – shows a marked orthographical/phonetic parallelism in combination with a striking personification. Both of the latter examples have a sensationalistic element. The suggestion 'The Sinner Who Was Chosen', meanwhile, indicates a poor grasp of the conventions of English titling. The apparent favourite – 'Gregory, Son of Sin' – constitutes a synthesis of the options considered, combining the referential with the phatic. Interestingly, the title which was ultimately chosen ('The Holy Sinner') is mentioned here by Mann almost in passing, as 'not impossible'. The letter to Meyer cited above compounds the picture of confusion and uncertainty even further: there, a new formulation is added, 'The Good Sinner', and the favoured title now contains a plural form: 'Gregory, Son of Sins'.

However, a few weeks after writing this letter Mann still appears uncertain, and writes to his publisher that he actually prefers 'The Chosen One' after all (letter to Knopf of 4 February 1951, *Reg* 4: 13). The process of negotiation which must have followed cannot, unfortunately, be reconstructed, but on 28 March 1951 Mann informs Knopf that he finds 'The Holy Sinner', which by this stage appears to be the final title of the English version, 'Not bad'. From the surviving material it is not clear who actually made the final decision, but the editor of the diaries for the years 1949–50, Inge Jens, assumes that it was Knopf (*TB* 8: 632). In the letter cited above (10 December 1950), Mann had suggested to Lowe-Porter at the end of his list of possible titles that the choice be left to the publisher: 'You should propose all these titles to Alfred together with one or two of your own invention. He knows best what is attractive.' Marketability, saleability, reader attractiveness – the criteria Genette subsumes under 'seduction' – appear to be the ultimate priorities. The semantic value of the title has become secondary, and Mann seems quite happy here to rely on Knopf's business acumen. That the latter was well aware of the commercial importance of titles, and was prepared to assert himself, was mentioned in Chapter 2 in connection with *Stories of Three Decades*. It is further attested by Knopf's recommendations in respect of *Felix Krull*. Motivated purely by commercial interests, the publisher strongly advised against translating the subtitle 'Der Memoiren erster Teil', since he thought the suggestion of a sequel might slow sales. 'I am literally terrified' (letter of 1 June 1955, Berlin 2005b: 152). Instead, he suggested the subtitle 'The Early Years', which was used in the United States.

Mann was less happy to allow Knopf a free hand with the Goethean *Lotte in Weimar*. This latter title is clearly less transparent than that of the Faust novel, since it activates resonances on two levels, neither of which is universally accessible: the novel is a fictional treatment of the (authentic) visit of Goethe's former love Charlotte Buff – the inspiration behind his first novel *Die Leiden des jungen Werthers* – to the poet in his adopted home of Weimar 44 years after their relationship had ended. Both the personal and the place name in Mann's title are loaded with significance for the German reader. The question of finding an appropriate English title was, understandably, the subject of protracted deliberations. In fact, a number of different titles were used in early published versions of the work.

The metatextual material relating to this novel reveals the tortuous processes that took place in the search for an appropriate English title. Mann was always aware that the work would strain the patience of English-speaking readers, since it assumed *'für das breitere amerikanische Publikum wohl allzuviel kultur-deutsche Voraussetzungen'* (letter to Joseph Warner Agnell of 18 November 1939, *Reg* 2: 352). He engaged in frequent discussions with Lowe-Porter on the matter, especially with regard to the long seventh chapter. Of all his works, he claimed, 'it was the most difficult one to translate' (letter to William Hart of 1 May 1951, *DüD* 2: 532). Mann's diaries record a number of discussions on the subject of an English title, which he describes as *'schwierig'* (diary entry of 14 December 1939). Over Christmas 1939, he considered the matter with a large number of visitors to his home in California. Prior to this, in his diary entry of 15 December 1939, he mentions that Lowe-Porter has suggested the neutral 'The Beloved Returns', but he was apparently not immediately convinced by this idea. His own initial preference was for a formulation that named the female protagonist, suggested something of the plot, and contained a 'seductive' adjective: 'The Wondrous Pilgrimage of Lotte Buff'. He mentions this possibility in his diary on 25 December 1939, as well as in a letter to Kuno Fiedler on 26 December. In a letter to his German publisher in the same week, however, he distances himself from it most emphatically: *'Auf English ist schon der Titel unmöglich. Die Geschichte wird wahrscheinlich "The wondrous pilgrimage of Charlotte Buff" heißen – obwohl ich's weiß, werde ich meinen Augen nicht trauen* (letter to Bermann Fischer of 27 December 1939, *GBF* 254). In his editorial notes, Mendelssohn calls the proposed title a *'haarsträubender Kitschtitel'* (749). The fact that Mann in this letter denies and ridicules his own suggestion of a few days earlier testifies to the uncertainty of his views on the subject. The correspondence on this matter is no longer extant, but once again he must also have consulted Agnes E. Meyer. Presumably in view of the cultural implications noted above, she proposed a radically different title, 'Journey towards youth' (in a lost letter, see the diary entry of 29 February 1940). Mann responded very positively to this suggestion. In his reply to Meyer (dated 3 March 1940), he described it as 'vorzüglich', not least because the formulation has intratextual substantiation: in the second chapter of the novel, Charlotte's visit to Goethe is twice circumscribed as a *'Reise ins Jugendland'* (*GW* 2: 395). Mann felt obliged to point out, however, that the translator would have the last word, and Meyer's suggestion was never actually followed up. By 12 April 1940 Lowe-Porter's proposed 'The Beloved Returns' seems to have been accepted by Knopf, and Mann comments *'Es ist gewiss ein guter Beschluss. Ich bin mit* "The beloved returns" *ganz einverstanden'* (Berlin and Herz 1996: 211). He informed Meyer of this agreement three weeks later, apparently much less enthusiastic than his letter to Knopf had suggested. Although his own preference was now very much for the original German title (*'Das Buch heißt "Lotte in Weimar" und kann garnicht anders heißen'*), he considered Lowe-Porter's suggestion to be the least unacceptable option, *'weil er der spirituellste ist und die Idee der Wiederkehr überhaupt durchschimmern läßt'* (letter to Agnes E. Meyer dated 4 May 1940, *AEM* 204).

However, the question of the title must have continued to prey on Mann's mind even after Knopf had announced his decision, and serious doubts soon surfaced. On 9 June 1940 he wrote an urgent letter to Knopf informing him that his British publishers, Secker & Warburg, had dismissed 'The Beloved Returns', which they felt to be *'rundweg ... sentimental und unangemessen'* (Berlin and Herz 1996: 215). This view, he added, had been confirmed by other people of literary taste, who were convinced that it was completely out of place in the context of his oeuvre. He was now of the opinion that 'any title other than Lotte in Weimar would be a stylistic mistake, a deception and wanting in character', would give the 'wrong impression', and claimed the support of the translator in this. Knopf replied immediately (11 June), reluctantly accepting Mann's right to choose the title, if not his judgement: on commercial grounds, Knopf felt that the use of foreign names in a title was a mistake. Interestingly, Knopf based this conviction not on the (inter)cultural obstacles to the text's reception, but on the very practical (phonetic) difficulty customers would have in asking for the book in a bookshop. He warned of serious repercussions in terms of sales, and strongly expressed the view that the work under the suggested title would not sell the 25,000 copies budgeted for advance orders. Mann relented, apparently bowing to the commercial argument, and by way of a compromise 'Lotte in Weimar' was added in brackets as a subtitle. The English version duly appeared in the USA in 1940 with a double title, *The Beloved Returns (Lotte in Weimar)* (Alfred A. Knopf). The British edition, however, dispensed with the supplementary information, and was thus entitled simply *Lotte in Weimar* (Secker & Warburg 1940), as was the standard edition later issued by Penguin Classics. In some subsequent printings the order of the two titles was reversed (*Lotte in Weimar. The Beloved Returns*), or the supplementary part was omitted completely. In either case, of course, the English title is unable to generate the cultural associations of the original. In the version *The Beloved Returns*, the literary-historical reference is completely neutralized, and the function of the title is changed. The referential becomes expressive and reader-oriented, apparently suggesting a romantic novel (which Mann's text certainly is not). In the version *Lotte in Weimar*, the actors suggested by the juxtaposition of the two nouns remain unrecognizable to all but initiated readers. Mann was never happy with the Lowe-Porter title, which he called a 'stylistic depreciation' (letter to William Hart of 1 May 1951) and described as 'entirely unnatural to me' (to Kenneth Oliver of 4 May 1951, *DüD* 2: 533). Interestingly, in translations into other languages, the German title was taken over direct (Potempa 1997).

The extent to which titles are sometimes allocated to texts by editors and publishers entirely without the agency of the original author or the translator may be illustrated by a final brief example. In 1943, Mann wrote a story on the Moses theme expressly for inclusion in an American anti-fascist anthology (Horton 2010). This was the only case in Mann's career in which a fictional text first appeared in English. From the very outset, Mann called his German text *'Das Gesetz'*. In the volume in question (Robinson 1943), George Marek's translation (which had been given the working title 'The Law') appeared under the title *Thou Shalt Have No Other Gods Before Me*. Robinson's volume contained ten texts by ten different authors, and each was entitled with a different Commandment. In other words, the published title of Mann's text was derived not from its relation to the co-text, but rather from its position within the design of the collection as a whole. Within the anthology, coherence is thus secured by membership of a series, and intertextual resonance is assured via the quotation from the Bible. Co-textually, however, there is no coherence. As has been observed by a number of commentators, the original title of the translation fails to describe Mann's text to any meaningful degree: Mann's story deals not with an individual commandment, but rather with the promulgation of the decalogue as a whole.

For the subsequent publication of Mann's text as a separate volume, Knopf commissioned a retranslation by Lowe-Porter, apparently in order to circumvent copyright problems with the publisher of the anthology. That text duly appeared in 1945 under a new title which constitutes an expansion of Mann's German title: *The Tables of the Law* – derived intratextually in Lowe-Porter's version from the 'tables' Moses brings down from Sinai. Shortly afterwards, in 1947, Secker & Warburg republished Marek's translation as a separate volume, under the same title as Lowe-Porter's version. Thus two different translations were in circulation simultaneously on different sides of the Atlantic under the same title. In the Marek book version of the story, intratextual coherence is a problem: in the text itself, he renders the *'Tafeln des Gesetzes'* not as the 'tables', but as the 'tablets of the law'.

Conclusion

As the preceding discussion has shown, the overwhelming majority of Mann's fictional titles have been translated into English literally. This is hardly surprising, for a number of reasons. The default trend in title translation appears to be that titles are – notwithstanding cultural specificities – translated as literally as possible, in an attempt to mirror the interpretive possibilities opened up by the paratextual information contained in the source-language formulation (Nord 1993). Since the function identified for most of Mann's titles is primarily referential, interlingual transfer is less problematic than it would be in the case of titles with overtly symbolic or poetic functions. Furthermore, the referentiality of the components contained in Mann's titles is drawn in virtually all cases from within the texts themselves, virtually guaranteeing a degree of co-textual coherence. This, in turn, obviates the need for sophisticated substitutionary or compensatory translation strategies. In syntactic terms, meanwhile, the structure of the titles is dominated by relatively simple nominal groups, which pose fewer problems of interlingual compatibility than would more extensive phrases or complex clausal structures. In these nominal groups, proper nouns are frequent: some forty per cent of Mann's titles consist of, or are built around, human names. In almost all cases, such titles invite direct transfer, which can hardly be considered a translation procedure at all.

Six of the translated titles show a significant degree of manipulation. Our discussion has shown that it is impossible in many cases to grasp the motivation behind such transformations, and to consider the efficacy of the solutions adopted, without relating the linguistic form of the paratext to the body of the text itself, and without looking at the context of production. The motivation for the modifications of Mann's titles in translation is, in most cases, interlingual asymmetry, and the changes are thus systemically induced. In three cases the reasons for the changes are primarily grammatical: *Ein Glück*, *Die Betrogene* and *Der Erwählte* raise questions of the contrastive grammar of nominal groups (countability, nominalization of adjectives). The former example (translated by Lowe-Porter, as noted above, as *A Gleam*) is the most problematic in semantic terms, since its reference is initially unclear and its co-textual coherence rather forced. The English versions of the latter two examples, *The Black Swan* and *The Holy Sinner* respectively, show different processes (symbolization in the first, oxymoronic expansion in the second). They are especially interesting in the context of translational manipulation and its impact in terms of potential meaning generation, since they both amend the original functions of the titles in respect of reader orientation, amplifying the phatic dimension. In one further case the motivation for the changed title appears to be lexical (the renderings of *Der Bajazzo* as *The Dilettante* and *The Joker*), as discussed above: in both of these translation solutions the referential quality is modified. The English titles of the book versions of *Das Gesetz*, meanwhile, show signs of both expansion and explicitation: the reader's interpretation of this title is guided from the potentially abstract or generic towards a specific biblical reference. Finally, only in one case do intercultural presuppositions influence the choice of an English title, and it is hardly surprising that this was the subject of considerable metatextual debate: the referential *Lotte in Weimar* is deculturated and transformed into a phatic, indeed 'seductive' formulation (*The Beloved Returns*) which is clearly in conformity with the conventions of English titling, but which adds a marked element of sentimentality. Of all Mann's title formulations, furthermore, this is the one which is most clearly influenced by the commercial considerations of the publisher, who thus asserted his belief that an effective title is 'one that is attractive, striking, easy to remember and that doesn't do the contents any violence' (letter from Knopf to Mann of 25 January 1936, Berlin 2001: 202). The extent to which Knopf's latter claim is an accurate reflection of the relationship between title and text in the case of the Lotte novel remains open to debate.

6 The translation of discourse forms: Speech and thought presentation in *Buddenbrooks*

Preliminary remarks

The eleven parts and 97 chapters of Thomas Mann's *Buddenbrooks* cover a period of 42 years (1835–77) in the history of the titular family, and span four generations. The novel's subtitle, '*Verfall einer Familie*', promises a depiction of the gradual decline of the family's fortunes, a process which is charted via a sequence of time coordinates carefully distributed throughout the novel: some highly explicit ('*Am 15. April 1869*', GW 1: 504), others less so ('*einige Tage später*', GW 1: 101). The story unfolds in a strictly chronological and linear manner, and the narrator exploits the classic devices of temporal compression, retardation and acceleration in managing his material, bringing discourse time and story time into varying relations of anisochrony and isochrony to pace the narrative: the first part covers just seven hours, while the fourth covers a period of ten years. At first sight, we are dealing here with a chronicle in the nineteenth-century epic tradition, underpinned by a pronounced strain of social realism. This impression is reinforced by the opening scenes of the text, with their extensive and highly differentiated dialogue, detailed descriptions of the domestic setting and personae, elements of pronounced local colour, references to regional, national and even international affairs (commercial and political), and numerous character cameos. In both the handling of time and the perspective from which events are portrayed, there are signs of a strong, apparently omniscient authorial presence which controls affairs in a magisterial fashion to produce a coherent family history.

Despite the carefully researched, documentary character of the text, however, Mann's *Buddenbrooks* is a work of considerable narrative diversity. Rather than providing a seamless record of the period covered, the narrator selects episodes from the 42-year story time of the action in accordance with a strict principle of salience to the fundamental theme of his text: degeneration. Discourse continuity is clearly subordinated to the higher aim of generating a symbolic network of symptomatic episodes and motifs which plot the disintegration of the eponymous dynasty on a variety of levels: genealogical, genetic, psychological, biological, commercial, ethical-moral. And while the narrator often does withdraw into the background to chronicle events in a neutral, historicizing manner, the narrative perspective oscillates tantalizingly between a variety of modes. The diegetic authorial mode is dominant (though by no means all-pervasive) in the first half of the novel: external description, summary, narratorial intrusions and reported thought processes from a quasi-Olympian point of view are particularly evident here. Even in these sections, though, the narrator is rarely neutral, and the perspective is far from stable. It shifts between omniscience and limitation, between authorial distance from the action and personal identification with the characters. The narrator grants access to the mental processes of some characters but can only speculate about others. Many of the episodes, though mediated via the dominant narratorial voice, are viewed from a 'personal' point of view, i.e. from the standpoint of an individual character who functions, in Stanzel's terms, as a 'reflector' (Stanzel 2008: 190–239). Furthermore, the novel is characterized by an ironic (at times almost satirical) gestus which is apparent both in the characterization and in the running authorial commentary on figures, events, attitudes, personal habits and (often linguistic) idiosyncrasies. This ironization extends to the process of story-telling itself, as the narrator questions the reliability of the very fundaments of the developing fiction with frequent interventions. While the narrator is capable of promulgating apodictic universal statements (*'Jeder Mensch begreift* [...]', GW 1: 214), he also frequently feigns ignorance and raises questions, and signals a mock narratorial uncertainty through the use of modal verbs and particles.

From the seventh chapter of the novel onwards, the narrative mode shifts perceptibly towards a more consistently subjective and internalized focalization, and a pronounced psychological impetus increasingly undermines the chronological momentum: the discourse tempo is slowed significantly by expansive episodes (Thomas Buddenbrook's Schopenhauer vision, Hanno's day at school). This bifocality of external and internal perspectives has often been seen as the very hallmark of Mann's text. Vogt, for example, who entitles a chapter in his study of the novel '*Zwischen Familienchronik und psychologischem Roman*', sums up: '*Man kann die* Verschränkung von chronikalischem und psychologisierendem Erzählen *als den epischen*

Kunstgriff auffassen, der die Buddenbrooks unverwechselbar macht' (Vogt 1995: 122, emphasis in the original; see also Mathias 1967 and, for an extensive discussion of the structure of Mann's text, Moulden and von Wilpert 1988). The epic breadth and detail of narrative detachment co-exists, then, with an insight into the workings of the characters' minds. The authorial stance anchors the presence of an identifiable, mediating narrative voice which maintains a certain, often critical, distance from the action and the characters: the 'telling' mode of narration which is the prerequisite for the construction of a chronicle. The more immediate personal perspective, meanwhile, creates a proximity to the experiencing consciousness: the 'showing' mode of narration which intensifies and dramatizes the psychological dimension (Ridley 1987: 69ff.; Swales 1991: 53ff.). In view of the consistency and sophistication with which Mann combines these two narrative levels, it is hardly surprising that his first novel has frequently been quoted as an example in German studies on narratology (Lämmert 2004; Martinez/Scheffel 2007; Stanzel 2008; Vogt 2008; Fludernik 2008). There are two prime techniques by means of which the author secures a heightened (mimetic) proximity to his characters. The first is the extensive use of carefully differentiated direct speech, which provides access to the spoken voice (polyphony) and is universally regarded as the most directly dramatic of all narrative modes (in the case of *Buddenbrooks*, further direct quotation is provided in the form of nine letters). And the second is the intermittent adoption of a bifocal narrative perspective which conflates the authorial voice with the figural 'inner' voice, providing imaginative participation in the character's internal processes, i.e. free indirect discourse, internal monologue, or stream of consciousness (polyperspectivity). These devices are located at the interface of micro- and macrolevel textual structure, and thus play a key role in steering the reader's receptive processes. Since they are central in terms of the generation of literary meaning, they are of great interest in translational terms.

The issue of speech and thought presentation is well-trodden ground in the field of literary stylistics (see Semino and Short 2004). Certainly, the underlying differentiations are the same in both cases. The range of options open to authors in discourse representation is typically conceived as a cline determined by the degree of narratorial intervention in the reporting 'posterior' discourse, an intervention which is manifest in the mode of mediation and in the strength of the claim to faithfulness. The scale derived from these criteria can be used to describe both thought presentation and the rendition of speech acts in fiction (classic studies are Pascal 1977; Banfield 1982; Cohn 1978; Leech and Short 2007). Notwithstanding competing taxonomies, it is customary to distinguish as follows:

1	2	3	4	5
Narrative report of a speech/ thought act ('Bericht')	Indirect speech/ thought ('indirekt')	Free indirect speech/ thought ('erlebt')	Direct speech/ thought ('direkt')	Free direct speech/ thought ('autonom direkt')

Whereas at the least 'direct' end of the continuum (No. 1) there is merely an indication that a speech/thought act has taken place, with no claim to any reconstruction of the original ('He told her about his victory'/' 'He thought about his certain victory'), at the opposite end (No. 5) direct access is granted to the exact (fictional) 'anterior' discourse, unmediated by any introductory *verbum dicendi* or *sentiendi* ('"I won"'/'"will win"'). The mode of indirect speech/thought (No. 2), which presents only the propositional content of the discourse ('He told her he had won'/'He thought he would win'), and direct speech/ thought (No. 4), which presents the propositional content and also claims additional faithfulness ('He said "I won"'/ 'He thought "I will win"'), are located on either side of the hybrid from of free indirect discourse (No. 3: 'He had won!'/'He would win!'). This latter mode is traditionally regarded as being derived transformationally from direct discourse. Other schemes define 1) as 'narrated'/'*erzählt*', 2) and 3) as 'transposed'/'*transponiert*', and 4) and 5) as 'quoted'/'*zitiert*' forms of discourse. The free indirect form is the least clearly defined of these categories. Typically referred to in German as '*erlebte Rede*' and in French as '*style indirect libre*', it is the subject of considerable debate, since it appears to be marked by both linguistic and broader contextual criteria. The considerable difficulties linguists have experienced in framing a reliable 'grammar' of free indirect discourse for fictional texts suggest that it is frequently signalled not merely by linguistic anomalies (e.g. verb backshift, shifts in pronominal reference and deixis, use of interjections and punctuation), but also by features which relate to the ongoing conceptualization of the text world (Semino and Short 2004: 27). Transitions from authorial-diegetic presentation to figural-mimetic narration are often fluid: it can, in other words, be extremely difficult to decide whether a string of discourse is the 'voice' of the character or the narrator.

The issue of discourse representation is a highly relevant one in literary translation, since it is a central component in narrative structure (Czennia 1992, 2004b; Zuschlag 2002). Like the majority of macro-structural elements in textual organization (plot structure, discourse management, the treatment of space and time), its manifestations are not language-specific. However, the lexicogrammatical forms by means of which the various modes are realized do not always overlap cross-linguistically. To cite just one example: in reported clauses, German uses the subjunctive to signal indirect discourse, while English uses tense backshift of indicative verbs. Thus the syntactic distinction between indirect speech and free indirect speech is marked by the form of the verb in German (which uses indicative verbs for the latter), but not in English. However, in neither language is there a clear way of deciding whether an imperfect verb form in a narrative text is the result of a process of perspectivally induced shift into the mode of free indirect discourse, which places it at the intersection of two voices, or a simple continuation of the authorial narrative past tense (epic preterite). Other linguistic signals – some of them highly subtle – must be taken into account in ascertaining the origo of the discourse. Such marginal cases are naturally of greater potential interest for the translation analyst (at least in narratological terms) than are more clearly constituted discourse forms, such as direct discourse, whose status is generally unambiguous. The introduction of direct speech in fictional texts serves a number of functions: at the metalevel, it influences the time signature of the text, disrupting the generally anisochronic relation between discourse time and story time apparent in the controlling authorial perspective by introducing passages which are isochronic in nature, regulating the tempo; it imbues the text with a dramatic immediacy, adding plasticity and realism; and it is an important instrument in characterization, providing clues about the actors through the 'internal' colouring of their speech acts.

In their concern to achieve differentiation in direct speech patterns, authors commonly exploit sociolectal, dialectal and idiolectal features as an important element of characterization and verism. Phonetic, graphemic, morphological, lexical and syntactical features combine to create an illusion of genuine speech. Ultimately, of course, embedded spoken discourse in narrative texts is no more than *'fingierte Mündlichkeit'*: the verbal patterns of fictional direct discourse vary significantly from the rhythms of naturally occurring speech (Henjum 2004). Furthermore, the narrator always remains in control of the discourse: writers often introduce into direct speech elements of structuration and rhetorical stylization, which can interact with (infect) their superordinate diegetic discourse. Further salient issues arise in the narrative environment of direct discourse, i.e. in the text outside the quotation marks. Narrators frequently introduce commentary into their reporting processes through their selection of *verba dicendi*, the use of inquit formulas, and information presented in adjectival and adverbial circumstantial structures. Translational shifts in the narrative on this level affect a multiplicity of relations in the text, and can thus impinge decisively on the interpretive potential of the work as a whole.

The techniques adopted by translators in dealing with such discourse phenomena provide a useful insight into their overall strategy. Indeed, they also suggest the degree to which translators conceive the source text as a carefully integrated whole, and indicate the principles of hierarchization underlying the translation. As Czennia points out: '*Die vergleichende Analyse des übersetzerischen Umgangs mit den Erzählweisen ermöglicht Rückschlüsse auf das prinzipielle Formenverständnis literarischer Übersetzer, die einen Roman tendenziell eher als linear-additive, vornehmlich inhalts-/handlungsorientierte Langform oder aber als vielschichtiges Strukturgefüge wahrnehmen können*', 2004b: 1004). Once again, my aim is to describe the way translators handle such issues, rather than to propose '*geeignete Übersetzungsverfahren für die unterschiedlichen Fälle*' (Albrecht 2005: 232).

Polyphony in translation

The two English translations of *Buddenbrooks*, published in 1924 (Lowe-Porter) and 1993 (Woods) respectively, show interesting differences in the way discourse reporting is handled. Let us consider briefly the opening words of the novel:

'*Was ist das – Was – ist das …*' '*Je, den Düwel ook, c'est la question, ma très chère demoiselle!*' (GW 1: 9)	'And – and – what comes next?' 'Oh, yes, yes, what the dickens does come next? *C'est la question, ma très chère demoiselle!*' (Lowe-Porter 1957: 7)	'What does this mean. – What – does this mean …' 'Well, now, deuce take it, *c'est la question, ma très chère demoiselle!* (Woods 1993: 3)

In classic medias res style, the opening of Thomas Mann's *Buddenbrooks* takes the reader directly into the middle of a conversation between members of three generations of the eponymous family. The reference of the hesitantly delivered opening line – to Luther's small catechism – is not immediately clear to the reader, but is disambiguated as the conversation progresses. The voice is that of eight-year-old Antoinette (Tony). The impatient response is that of her grandfather, who replies in a mixture of Low German dialect and French. Immediately, a number of key parameters of Mann's dialogue management in the text are evident. The onset of the novel is scenic-dramatic in character, confronting the reader with an exchange of free (unmediated) direct discourse. For the moment at least, there is no sign of a narrator: we could be witnessing a theatre performance. Furthermore, the spoken discourse has a distinctly realistic – perhaps even naturalistic – quality.

Mann's presentation of Tony's introductory utterance shows an attempt to capture the patterns of spontaneous speech, with its hesitation and repetition, while the grandfather's reply contains a number of diatopic and diastratic markers: regional (Lübeck dialect), social (the use of French set phrases by the upper-middle class in their social interactions), generation-specific (the à la mode diction of the older generation), as well as diaphasic indicators (register: the use of colloquial blasphemy). It also has an idiolectal quality in as far as Johann Buddenbrook commonly expresses himself in dialect at moments of emotional intensity and spontaneity, and on occasions mixes French, Low German and High German within a single utterance. As the narrative moves forward, Mann exploits a large variety of linguistic codes, creating a truly polyphonic text.

The two English translations of the text show interesting similarities and divergences even at this early point. The first, by Lowe-Porter, does not pick up explicitly on the text of the catechism (unlike the second, by John E. Woods), but makes sense as a time-gaining move in the stalled recitation of a memorized text. Both translations retain the French discourse (as they do elsewhere in the text), presumably because it injects historical colour and might be considered consistent with the parallel sociolinguistic conventions of the English-speaking nineteenth-century bourgeoisie (it is 1831), and mark it with italics. Both adopt a historically marked euphemism ('minced oath'), retaining the satanic reference: both 'dickens' and 'deuce' are euphemisms for the Devil. Furthermore, the two English versions might be held to show signs of language-variant specificity in anticipation of their envisaged target audiences: Lowe-Porter selects an expression which has long been common in British English, but has not been fully absorbed into American English, while Woods favours 'deuce', an equally old expression which appears to be more common in American than in British English (it is attested in American corpora, but not in corpora of modern British English). Finally, and perhaps most significantly in the present context, neither of the translators seeks to capture the regiolectal flavour of the grandfather's first sentence. Instead, they both normalize its diatopic quality, adopting mildly expletive formulations to suggest at least something of the non-standard quality of his utterance.

This latter process of normalization is, as has frequently been observed, a common strategy in the translation of non-standard forms of language (Horton 1998; Czennia 2004a; Albrecht 2005). After all, the translation of dialectal forms (be they social, regional or other) presents extraordinary difficulties in translation, since such forms carry connotative values that clearly defy the attainment of 'equivalence' across language communities. It is not, of course, the constitutive phonetic, lexical and syntactic features of non-standard language use that are at stake in the process of translation, but rather the textual salience of norm deviations: either as marked forms within standard discourse (as is the case in many literary works, including *Buddenbrooks*) or as the dominant mode in entire texts. A consideration of the issue of dialect translation leads us to the very core of the long-running debate on formal versus functional approaches to translation, which has been conducted under the rubric of a multitude of polar opposites over the years. It is now widely accepted that it is the connotative values of dialectal forms which are to be observed (and, ideally, replicated) in the act of translation. Given the impossibility of formal interlingual correspondence at this level, translation becomes a quest for intertextual coherence: functional correspondence at the textual level rather than formal correspondence at the level of the individual translation unit.

Translators have at their disposal a number of competing options in their search for appropriate solutions. These options range from the complete neutralization of marked discourse forms at one end of the continuum, to conversion into a broadly 'comparable' target-language dialect at the other. In between these two extreme potential solutions there are various compromise options which indicate significant deviations from standard linguistic norms without attempting to suggest an identifiable language variety (e.g. the adoption of a hybrid and non-regionally specific 'eye dialect', humorously referred to as 'Mummersetshire', or the replacement of regiolect with sociolectal or idiolectal elements). The neutralization option constitutes – at least in literary translation – a violation of what is likely to be a key pragmatic dimension of the text, and a trend has been noted in translation generally towards a weakening of the distinctions between less elaborated (fictional) spoken discourse and more highly structured written discourse forms (Henjum 2004). The option of dialect substitution, on the other hand, runs the risk of misrepresentation or even absurdity. No two dialects can, interlingually, carry the same set of social, ethnological, cultural-stereotypical associations, and the introduction of a target-language dialect could theoretically necessitate the complete relocation of the text and all its situational coordinates. It is hardly surprising, then, that the compromise strategies around the centre of the cline have been the most favoured option throughout the modern history of translation: regional dialectal forms in original texts (diatopic) tend to appear in translations as de-regionalized but otherwise linguistically marked forms (diastratic), which seek to suggest similar connotative value (Czennia 2004a). This tendency is underpinned by the observation that extensive regional marking is often associated with social marking. In other cases, translators adopt a quite different strategy: instead of seeking to suggest a regional marking within the direct discourse itself (i.e. in the speech patterns of the characters), translators can transform direct discourse forms into indirect, or insert metalinguistic information into the surrounding reporting structures. The disadvantage thus accruing from the dilution of the mimetic dimension might, arguably, be considered to be outweighed by the advantages of avoiding often strained and even illogical discourse patterns (Berlin characters with London accents). All the issues outlined above are evident in the two English versions of *Buddenbrooks*.

The opening section of *Buddenbrooks* anticipates a phenomenon which is to prove highly significant in the text. As has frequently been noted, Mann is much concerned with patterns and habits of speech in his novel (Wandruszka 1984: 66). Their use is motivated by the classic functions, including a concern to inject an element of social realism, to heighten local colour, to activate and exploit cultural associations, to enhance the scenic-dramatic immediacy of a passage, and to utilize linguistic marking as an element of character portrayal. Throughout Mann's oeuvre, dialectal forms are also widely exploited as a form of humour and an instrument of ironic distancing. In *Buddenbrooks*, he employs a number of regional forms: West Prussian (Ida Jungmann), Swabian (Pastor Mathias) and Bavarian (Alois Permaneder), while others are not represented directly but are subject to comment by the narrator: Baltic (Pastor Sievert Tiburtius), Silesian (Hugo Weinschenk) and Franconian (Pastor Pringsheim). All of these exist alongside the local *Platt* (von Wilpert 1988). At the same time, Mann introduces levels of differentiation in the speech patterns of the native Lübeck characters, whose diction ranges between standard German, consistent Lübeck Low German (*Platt*, as spoken by Grobleben), and the hybrid form of '*Missingsch*' (spoken by the wine merchant Köppen), which inserts Low German elements into essentially standard German structures. Even within the idiom of High German, Mann uses linguistic stratification as an instrument of characterization (e.g. Grünlich's strained attempts at linguistic sophistication, the sterotyped diction of Hanno's schoolteachers, the pathos-laden style of the estate agent Gosch). In the narratorial discourse of the novel, too, Mann adopts a variety of linguistic levels and poses, which he exploits as an instrument of comment and control (von Wilpert 1988: 155).

Inevitably, much of the regional colouring of the speech in the novel can hardly be captured in translation. Neither translator, for example, seeks to suggest the quality of Pastor Mathias' sibillants ('*Liebscht den Herrn?*'), nor the extensive use of affectionate diminutives which characterize the speech of Ida Jungmann ('*Kindchen*', '*Tonychen*'). To this extent, perhaps inevitably, the English versions of the text constitute an impoverishment of the polyphony of the German original. However, both do attempt to suggest the idiosyncratic features of individual speech patterns where these are thematized by the narrator. The habitus of Sesemi Weichbrodt, which is described in some detail by the narrator, may serve as an example of the way in which the translators handle this:

| *Sie sprach mit lebhafter und stoßweiser Bewegung des Unterkiefers und einem schnellen, eindringlichen Kopfschütteln, exakt und dialektfrei, klar, bestimmt und mit sorgfältiger Betonung jedes Konsonanten. Den Klang der Vokale aber übertrieb sie sogar in einer Weise, daß sie z.B. nicht 'Butterkruke', sondern 'Botter-' oder gar 'Batterkruke' sprach und ihre eigensinnig kläffendes Hündchen nicht 'Bobby', sondern 'Babby' rief [...] und wenn Mademoiselle Popinet, die Französin, sich beim Kaffee mit allzuviel Zucker bediente, so hatte Fräulein Weichbrodt eine Art, die Zimmerdecke zu betrachten, mit einer Hand auf dem Tischtuch Klavier zu spielen und zu sagen: 'Ich wörde die ganze Zockerböchse nehmen!' (GW 1: 85–6)* | She spoke with brisk, jerky motions of the lower jaw and quick, emphatic nods. She used no dialect, but enunciated clearly and with precision, stressing the consonants. Vowel-sounds, however, she exaggerated so much that she said, for instance, 'botter' instead of 'butter' – or even 'batter'! Her little dog that was forever yelping she called Babby instead of Bobby [...] And when Mlle Popinet, the Frenchwoman, took too much sugar to her coffee, Miss Weichbrodt had a way of gazing at the ceiling and drumming on the cloth with one hand while she said: 'Why not take the who-ole sugar-basin. I would!' (Lowe-Porter, 66–7) | When she spoke, it was with spirited thrusts of her lower jaw and rapid, incessant shakes of her head, each consonant carefully stressed, each word exact, clear, definite, and free of every dialect. But she exaggerated her vowels to such an extent that, for example, she did not say 'butter', but 'botter', sometimes even 'booter', and called her obstreperous yapping dog 'Booby' instead of 'Bobby' [...] And when Popinet, the French girl, would take too much sugar for her coffee, Fräulein Weichbrodt had a way of eyeing the ceiling, playing an imaginary piano on the tablecloth, and remarking, 'Take the whool sugarbool, I soorely woold!' (Woods, 82) |

Woods' more extensively deviant rendering is typical of his approach to speech patterns as a whole in the novel, starting from the very first authorial comment on the vowel qualities of northern German: Mme Antoinette Buddenbrook's '"*Immer der Nämliche, mon vieux. Bethsy* ...?" "*Immer*" *sprach sie wie* "*ümmer*" *aus*' (GW 1: 11). Where Lowe-Porter deletes the metalinguistic comment: '"Oh, *mon vieux* – he's always the same, isn't he, Betsy?"' (9), Woods has: '"Oh, *mon vieux*, always the same, is he not, Bethsy?" She pronounced it "ollweez"' (5). This indicates the tendency in the latter English version of Mann's novel not simply to manipulate the length of the vowel, but also to amend its quality, moving it in the direction of southern US English. Similarly, Sesemi Weichbrodt's idiosyncratic ' *Sei glöcklich, du gutes Kend!*', which appears six times in the text and is rendered variously by Lowe-Porter via the vowel lengthenings 'go-od' and 'che-ild', is consistently translated by Woods as 'good chawld'.

The most consistently transcribed dialect form in *Buddenbrooks* is, naturally, that of Low German. This idiom is used throughout by lower-class characters who perform functions in the Buddenbrook household or company. Most notable among them is the worker Grobleben, who is granted extensive passages of reported speech. Mann takes great care to transcribe the phonetic and morphosyntactic features of the dialect. One example must suffice here. At the baptism of Hanno Buddenbrook, Mann draws humour from the contrast between Gorleben's formulaic expressions of elevated congratulatory sentiment and his linguistic limitations:

Ick bün man'n armen Mann, mine Herrschaften, ööwer ich hew 'n empfindend Hart, un dat Glück un de Freud von min Herrn, Kunsel Buddenbrook, welcher ümmer gaut tau mi west ist, dat geiht mi nah, und so bün ick kamen, um den Herrn Kunsel un die Fru Kunsulin un die ganze hochverehrte Fomili ut vollem Harten tau gratuleern ... (GW 1: 401)	I be a poor man, yer honour 'n' ladies 'n' gentlemen, but I've a feelin' hairt; 'n' the happiness of my master comes home to me, it do, seein's he's allus been so good t'me; 'n' so I've come, yer honour 'n' ladies 'n' gentlemen, to congratulate the Herr Consul 'n' the Frau Consul, 'n' the whole respected family, from a full hairt ... (Lowe-Porter, 309)	I'm just a poor man, ladies 'nd gents, but I got a tender heart, and the joy 'nd happiness what touches my master, Consul Buddenbrook, who's alliz been good to me, why, that touches me, too, so I'm here to heartily 'gratulate Herr Buddenbrook 'nd his good wife 'nd the whole 'spectable fam'ly (Woods, 392).

Mann's Lübeck dialect marking exploits phonetic characteristics (vowel and consonant quality, 't' for 's' substitution in final position), morphological deviations (accusative form for nominative nouns, non-standard verb forms, anomalous case markings), and grammatical deviation (accusative for the dative with *'gratulieren'*). Both English versions, on the other hand, indicate the non-standard quality of the discourse through extensive elision of syllables in initial, medial and final positions. Although they alter vowel quality ('hairt', 'allus', 'alliz') and exploit grammatical anomalies (Lowe-Porter's 'I be', 'it do' – both of which carry marked rural-historical associations in English – and Woods's relative pronoun 'what'), they do not suggest a particular regional flavour. Rather, they confirm the dialect-into-sociolect trend noted above.

The translation of consistent dialect use poses significant problems for the translators who, it must be conceded, are unable to reproduce the diatopic qualities of the original discourse. As we have noted, however, the sociolinguistic function of non-standard forms can effectively be rendered by reducing geographical markings to sociolectal features. The problem of dialect translation becomes more acute, however, when such forms are exploited as a contrastive instrument in the speech presentation of characters who have more than one idiom at their disposal. Here, the use of the Low German form by higher-class characters (in effect, the males of the Buddenbrook line) is no longer a mechanism of socio-economic definition. Instead, polyvocality becomes an important device in characterization. Again, it is Johann Buddenbrook the elder who has the greatest repertoire. Shocked by the (in this case meteorological) information imparted to his granddaughter by her tutor, Ida Jungmann, he retorts to his son Jean in the opening chapter of the work:

> *Excusez, mon cher! ... Mais c'est une folie! Du weißt, daß solche Verdunkelung der Kinderköpfe mir verdrüßlich ist! Wat, de Dunner sleit in? Da sall doch gliek de Dunner inslahn!*
>
> (*GW* 1: 14)

Johann opens with formulaic French expressions, the lingua franca commonly used in ritualized social interactions by the older characters in the novel. He then switches to standard German, though with a vowel substitution already thematized in the novel as a characteristic of local speech (*'verdrüßlich'*). Finally, at the moment of greatest agitation and emotional intensity, he slips into dialect. This is a typical feature of his speech patterns. We are told explicitly that he speaks '*fast nur französisch und plattdeutsch*' (*GW* 1: 14) during heated exchanges with members of his family, and we later witness an occasion on which

'*Er verfiel vor Verdruß in den Dialekt*' (*GW* 1: 30). Such code-switching is not generally rendered by either translator, and the distinction between the more controlled register of High German and the subsequent recourse to dialect is thus obscured. On occasions, the translators adopt a strategy of compensation, inserting narratorial comment into the reporting discourse: 'called out in dialect' (Lowe-Porter 25). Woods uses more mildly non-standard forms than Lowe-Porter in such cases (Woods 26). Thus, in the Travemünde scene, Lowe-Porter normalizes the dialectal forms '*inzückend*' and '*forchtbar*' in her version (103), while Woods has 'inchanting' and 'dradfully' (129). Such shifts are, in fact, an important element in Mann's discourse presentation. In the case of the grandfather, *Plattdeutsch* appears as the diction of spontaneity, emotional engagement, warmth, the earthiness he has retained despite his wealth and social status. In that of his descendants, by contrast, the local dialect is used only in dealings with lower-class speakers of *Platt*. In Chapter 4, 3 Jean succeeds in appeasing the (pseudo-) revolutionary fervour of the mob by adopting their idiom and thus seeking to camouflage temporarily the socio-economic gulf between the classes. In the lengthy exchange with Corl Smolt, he speaks *Platt* throughout. In both translations, he is given standard discourse, completely obfuscating his code-switching tactics: yet in both, the translators retain Mann's '*vergaß, platt zu sprechen*' (*GW* 1: 193). Lowe-Porter has: 'forgetting, in his excitement, to speak dialect' (148), while Woods has 'so indignant now that he forgot to speak in *Plattdeutsch*' (189). Indeed, in Woods' version, far from being marked by a linguistic assimilation to the patterns of the lower classes, Jean's diction is (incongruously) even more elevated than the style of the original: '*Du redest ja lauter Unsinn*' (*GW* 1: 193) becomes 'What asinine absurdity' (189), '*Tropf*' becomes 'imbecile'. Jean's son Thomas adopts the same linguistic strategy. Throughout the baptism scene mentioned above (Chapter 7, 1) he adapts his idiom to that of the lower classes in Mann's text, demonstrating an ease and fluency in his use of the local *Platt* in the exchange with the worker Grobleben. In Lowe-Porter this scene is completely normalized, while in Woods there is only one minor attempt to inject a note of colloquialism (dropping of the final 'g' at the end of verb forms, eg. 'rottin'', 393). In Chapter 8, 5, Thomas dismisses Grobleben's attempt to hold a speech at the firm's anniversary celebrations impatiently with the words '*Schön, Grobleben, is all gaut*' (*GW* 1: 486), which appears in Lowe-Porter as: 'Yes, yes, Grobleben, you're right, that's just how it is' (377) and in Woods as: 'That's fine, Gorleben, right you are' (477). In the latter generations of the family, the use of dialect is no longer a spontaneous effusion, an expression of identity, regional identification and solidarity, or a valve, but has become an instrument of condescension. As the Buddenbrooks males become more detached from the sustaining values of their family traditions, so, too, do their speech patterns become more uniform and standard (Müller 1998: 80). The translators' flattening of the multiple codes adopted by Mann's figures in response to the communicative situation detracts significantly from an element of characterization: in Mann's text, increasing linguistic standardization appears as a further indication of degeneration.

The most celebrated dialect passages in Mann's novel are those given to the man who is later to become Tony Buddenbrook's second husband, the Bavarian Alois Permaneder, who is presented as utterly incapable of speaking standard German. The Munich hop merchant's idiom stands in marked contrast to the *Platt* of the Lübeck characters, for whom it presents considerable difficulties of comprehension. Mann derives much humour from these exchanges. Inevitably, perhaps, it is at this point of the text that the most dramatic interventions by the translators are evident. In Chapter 6, 4 Madame Elisabeth Buddenbrook receives a visit from Permaneder, who has met Tony in Munich and now comes to woo her. Again, a polyphonic dialogic exchange is set up. Ida Jungmann greets the unexpected visitor with the Polish-sounding exclamation '*Meiboschekochhanne!*' (GW 1: 324). As Mann explained to one of his French translators, the word is '*korrumpiertes Polnisch*' and means '*Mein lieber Gott*' (letter to Geneviève Bianquis of 24 May 1932, *DüD* 1: 93). Lowe-Porter deletes this word (248), while Woods opts for a (rather meaningless) phonetic solution: 'It sounded like My boshy kock hanna!' (319). The servant delivering the visitor's card to Mme Buddenbrook speaks Low German ('[...] *doar wier'n Herr, ööwer hei red' nich düütsch un is ook goar tau snaksch* [...]' (GW 1: 324). Both translators once again use defective grammar, colloquialisms and elision to suggest the dialect here. Mme Buddenbrook speaks in High German throughout. Permaneder's speech, by contrast, is as consistently Bavarian as Mann can make it, marked by numerous phonetic, morphological and syntactic features, and liberally strewn with interjections ('*Geltn's*', '*O mei*', '*Is dös a Hetz!*', '*Pfüaht Ihna Gott*'), blasphemous expletives ('*Es is halt a Kreiz*', '*Himmi Sakrament*', '*Kruzi Türken nei!*') and forms of address ('*Herr Nachbohr*'). His speech is informal (he uses the familiar '*du*' form to complete strangers), and he generally adopts a tone that bemuses his interlocutors in its back-slapping joviality: '*Und vielleicht ein wenig zu viel Nonchalance im Benehmen, Tom, wie?*', comments Mme Buddenbrook: '*Ja, lieber Gott, das ist süddeutsch*', replies her son (GW 1: 333). Indeed, the narrator himself draws attention to Permaneder's '*gemütlich singende und gedehnte Betonung*' (325), stresses the fact that he speaks '*laut und mit ziemlich grober Betonung, in seinem knorrigen Dialekt voller plötzlicher Zusammenziehungen*' (326), and that he peppers his diction '*hie und da mit vollkommen unverständlichen Redewendungen*' (331). The mood in the Mengstrasse house after his departure can only be described as one of shock, exacerbated by the fact the guest uses the expression *'Guten Tag'* as a valediction rather than as a salutation. The pronounced Bavarian marking of Permaneder's speech and the concomitant coarseness and unsophistication of diction with which it is associated (from the perspective of the Lübeck characters) is an index not merely of linguistic but also of cultural difference. It thus serves an important function in the mechanics of the unfolding plot. Tony Buddenbrook's decision to divorce her south German husband seems to be motivated as much by her shock at the (for her unrepeatable) Bavarian curse he throws at her as it is by his infidelity. Never fully acclimatized in her matrimonial Munich home, Tony is a victim of cultural dislocation, as is consistently indicated by dialectal speech patterns (see her letter home, Chapter 6, 8).

Mann's translators face a dual problem here. Not only do they (ideally) have to create an English idiom that might suggest a strong regional colouring: they also have to ensure that Permaneder's diction is distinct from that of the Lübeck Platt, which the Buddenbrooks household understands very well. Woods' solution is to adopt a language that is significantly more deviant than the one he uses for his rendering of Low German. Taking his cue from what he translates as the 'lilting drawl' (320), he lends Permaneder's utterances a marking that bears a striking resemblance to southern US American. He has 'Yup, 'nuff t'floor y' (321) for *'da schauen'S'* and *'da spitzen'S'* (326); 'A pain 'n th' ol'' (322) for *'Es i halt a Kreiz'* (327), 'Hell's bells, 'm lookin' for'ard to that' (322) for *'Himmi Sakrament, werd i' a Freid' ha'm'* (327), reaching a crescendo in: 'Why, Frau Grünlich! Why, howdy do! How y' been gettin' on all this while? What 'ybeen doin' with yourself up in these parts? Jesus, m' jist plum tickled. D'you ever think back on our li'l ol' Munich and our mountains?' (323). He calls Tony 'gal', and uses 'nope' for *'ne'*. While successfully maintaining a differentiation between the various regional manifestations of non-standard speech, this version of the text runs the risk of activating cultural associations that have little in common with Bavaria. As George S. Miller notes in connection with such dialectal contortions, 'Woods goes frankly Mississippian here' (Classe 2000: 905), introducing 'inappropriate American overtones'. Reactions of American readers in online forums confirm this impression of 'American vernacular, much of which is inappropriate in a novel of nineteenth-century northern Germany. For example, characters who speak in Bavarian dialect are translated into a kind of Texan slang which reminded me more of the wild west than a Baltic trading town' (www.amazon.com/review/R4KXV4T2OONUM: [last accessed 1 January 2013]).

Lowe-Porter was well aware of this problem. She points out in a letter to Knopf, referring to the 'Hamburghese used by longshoremen', that 'to translate it into something comparable in England or this country [the USA] was to introduce a local flavor that must inevitably make the reader think of the English of American scene, and would jar' (letter of 11 November 1943, Thirlwall 1966: 59; see also Lowe-Porter 1966: 200). Perhaps it was this reservation that prompted her to undertake what can only be described as a rewrite of the text at this point. Guided by the conviction she expresses in her prefatory note to her translation ('Dialect cannot be transferred'), she opts not to imbue Permaneder's speech with any marked non-standard features. This is presumably the reason why she deletes Mann's quite specific phonological comment that the Bavarian's idiom is *'voller plötzlicher Zusammenziehungen'* (*GW* 1: 326). Instead of giving Permaneder a dialect, she relies on generalized metalinguistic comment. Some of this is provided by the narrator of the original, as noted above. In some cases, presumably in order to circumvent the problem of equivalence, she excises parts of Permaneder's dialogue altogether. On two occasions, she transforms Mann's direct discourse into indirect discourse, thus obviating the need for any faithful representation of the 'anterior' discourse. In a large number of cases, however, she makes extensive additions, inserting all told some 30 lines of her own invention into the text. Much of this extra text takes the form of paraphrase, and her translations of the '*Kreiz*' expletive are a good case in point. At its first occurrence, she circumscribes the omitted phrase as 'an exclamation in the broadest of dialect', at the second she replaces the character's direct speech with the phrase 'Herr Permaneder obliged by repeating' (250), at the third she inserts 'gave vent to his favourite outlandish phrase' (251), while she omits the fourth, translates the fifth as 'tough luck' (254), and deletes the sixth. The translator also adds further narratorial comment, for which there is no basis in the original, to compensate for the absence of dialect forms: 'He garnished his views with disjointed sighs and some perfectly unintelligible Munich phrases' (254); 'His grammar, now and then, was of the most artless and disarming quality' (253).

However, Lowe-Porter does not stop at such limited modifications to the text. In fact she adds an entirely new dimension to the narrative perspective at this point. Mann adopts an essentially external focalization in this scene, describing Mme Buddenbrook's movements, and only occasionally shifting to the personal point of view (accessing the workings of her mind through an omniscient narrator, *'verständnislos'*, *'mit erheuchelter Befriedigung'*, *'freudig'*, 326). Lowe-Porter, by contrast, constructs an entire comic drama out of the character's inability to make sense of what Permaneder is saying by adopting a variety of narrative modes. In doing so, she develops Mme Buddenbrook's incomprehension to such an extent that the focus of attention in the scene shifts away from Permaneder's appearance and speech production to Mme Buddenbrook's attempts to make some sense of his utterances, and her shock at his apparent lack of social polish. While this is a source of comedy in the original text, Lowe-Porter develops it almost beyond recognition. Mann presents Mme Buddenbrook's reactions to the rather *'laut'* and *'grob'* (326) habitus of Permaneder in a series of adverbials which highlight her insecurity and the contrast between her impeccable social manners and the Bavarian's coarseness (*'höflich, aber bestimmt'* 326, *'mit vornehmer Bewegung'* 326, *'begütigend'* 327, *'höflich'* 327, *'herzlich'* 327). Lowe-Porter, on the other hand, transforms the scene into an elaborate internal drama. Not only does she add diegetic narratorial comment in the form of reported thought processes (the insertion of 'She had not understood a single world of his remark' [250] at an early stage in the proceedings), but also constructs far more complex and creative formulations which play out the processes of her (imputed) mental processes: 'Actually, she was quite at much at sea as before, and only wondering if Antonie were really able to follow the winding of the Bavarian tongue' (250). The translator even goes so far as to invent completely unattested reactions to Permaneder's statements, shifting the discourse presentation from an authorial point of view to the more mimetic mode of free indirect speech: '[Herr Peramaneder gave a short groan] and followed it up by an exclamation in the broadest of dialect: something that shocked the Frau Consul because it sounded so like swearing, though it probably wasn't – at least, she hoped not! Should she ask him to repeat it? … Surely it was something about a crucifix? Horrors! (250). As the scene progresses, the translator adds an entire stream of additional comment, much of it in the free indirect mode (250 ff.):

[turning her eyes a little away] that he might not see the bewilderment they expressed.

[…] she had really understood him. Perhaps they could manage after all!

It might be better to talk a little oneself.

It was really touching, the efforts he made.

Again she felt as if she were almost upon firm ground.

The Frau Consul did not understand at all, but she got the general drift, and said:

The Frau Consul thought it more discreet not to inquire again into his meaning; besides, he muttered it under his breath, with a sort of groan, though his mood, otherwise, appeared to be anything but despondent.

The translator's amendments significantly alter the structure of the scene, as well as the perspective from which it is portrayed. The humour of the episode is shifted from the direct representation of Permaneder's speech patterns to the indirect presentation of Mme Buddenbrook's reactions. Inevitably, the additions also affect our reading of Mme Buddenbrook's character at this point in the text. She emerges as more prudish in her reactions to Permaneder's coarse and blasphemous exclamations, and considerably more determined to maintain the conversation in accordance with the principle of dialogic cooperation. Lowe-Porter's additions amplify in most cases the discrepancy between her inability to understand and her actual responses: she seeks desperately to conceal her confusion, even to the extent of hypocrisy, conducting a (free indirect) interior monologue with herself as she does so. She is more emotionally charged: hence she stammers 'with desperate finality', and encourages her interlocutor 'with disproportionate joy'. In the English version more than in the original, Mme Buddenbrook appears willing to compromise what she considers important principles of social propriety in the interest of securing a prosperous second husband for her daughter.

Narrative polyperspectivity in interlingual transfer

As the novel progresses, as noted above, there is a distinct shift away from dialogic to monologic forms of discourse. Prominent among the latter is Mann's consistent use of free indirect modes, which are exploited in a number of ways. As Hoffmeister demonstrates, these are used in dialogue passages in the form of 'spoken free indirect discourse' for primarily ironic purposes, or to report collectively held and expressed views. They are also widely used to intensify the dramatic quality of reflective processes by heightening internal focalization (Hoffmeister 1967: 45–72). The prime thematic significance of free indirect discourse in *Buddenbrooks*, though, is more fundamental than this: the mode is used strategically to signal the shift in the narrative voice towards a more mimetic perspective (Martinez and Scheffel 2007: 53). Mann exploits the dual perspective and overriding mimetic focus of free indirect discourse to indicate the growing introspection of the characters across the generations. The increasing alienation of the characters from the stable and sustaining values of their forefathers can be traced most clearly in the contrast between the successive heirs to the family firm – Johann, Jean, Thomas and Hanno – while the wayward Christian serves as a regular point of reference. For Johann, the pater familias of the first generation depicted in the novel, the order of the burgher world is still (relatively) unquestioned: there is no serious tension between his social persona and his sense of identity. The same is essentially true of his son Jean. However, the latter cultivates a growing religious impulse in his search for spiritual confirmation and guidance. It is in the central male figure of the novel, Thomas, that the lack of orientation reaches crisis point. In him, the gulf between social exterior and genuine selfhood assumes truly dramatic proportions. He is little more than an actor engaged in a constant process of self-representation, erecting a facade of '*Haltung*' as a defence against a profound sense of existential angst which culminates in a desperate search for philosophical truths. Finally, in his son Hanno, the rift between the pressure of social expectations and inner values is no longer presented as a conflict. Here, the other-worldly, artistic impulse is so dominant that inwardness entirely supplants any concern with the fulfilment of collective expectations or adherence to the accepted social codes, and music replaces language as a form of self-expression (Moulden and von Wilpert 1988: 305–18; Swales 1991: 82–7). The drama enacted by the series of male protagonists, then, is that of a growing tension between reflectiveness and active living. It is expressed in an instability of narrative voice, which – as Swales notes – moves from interaction through dialogue towards self-absorption in interior monologue: 'The spectrum of narrative discourse starts with the abundantly detailed catalogue of the outer world via the understated, self-effacing gesture of simply eavesdropping on the characters' linguistic patterns, and extends to the account, whether through indirect speech, free indirect speech or interior monologue, of the texture, feel, and substance of the characters' inwardness' (1991: 60). It is not surprising then, that it is the central characters of the novel – Thomas, Hanno and Tony – who are presented from a mimetic perspective most frequently in the novel (see the diagram in Lee 1994: 211). Nor is it surprising that it should be Thomas, the pivotal figure in the theme of degeneration on all levels, who is most often heard in free indirect discourse and interior monologue (Hoffmeister 1967: 59).

An examination of the two English versions of *Buddenbrooks* demonstrates that both translators are careful to reproduce the at times subtle shifts in narrative perspective by replicating Mann's modulations in pronominal reference and tense. In most cases, the translation of such shifts proceeds via the replication of the temporal, pronominal and spatial deixis of the original. For example, this is evident in their handling of Thomas' response to his mother's decision to grant her son-in-law Tiburtius a large sum of money by way of inheritance (Chapter 7, 7); in his ruminations on whether he should violate the company's long-standing business ethos by taking advantage of the financial difficulties of a farmer (the Pöppenrade harvest, Chapter 8, 4); in his thoughts on the development of his son (Chapter 8, 7); and in his musings on the best way to deal with his wife's apparent attachment to another man (Chapter 10, 5). The most sustained and significant instance of discourse modulation is, however, Thomas Buddenbrook's celebrated 'Schopenhauer vision' (also Chapter 10, 5). I consider part of this passage below as a particularly intense and extended instance of Mann's manipulation of perspective in the novel. The character has been reading a volume of Schopenhauer, and finds his own anguish echoed – but also strangely relieved – by what he reads. The passage represents the most critical point in his intellectual development. I quote it extensively here to allow comparison, indicating the discourse status in square brackets in the text with the following numbers: [1] narrative report of a thought act/psycho-narration/*Redebericht*; [2] free indirect discourse/narrated monologue/*erlebte Rede*; [3] direct discourse/quoted monologue/*direkte Rede/*; [4] free direct discourse/ autonomous monologue/*autonome direkte Rede*. The narrative voice shifts between these four modes before settling finally (from the end of the quoted section onwards) into a passage of unmediated direct discourse which is sustained over several paragraphs.

1 *[1] Und siehe da: plötzlich war es, wie wenn die Finsternis vor seinen Augen zerrisse, wie wenn die samtne Wand der Nacht sich klaffend teilte und eine unermeßlich tiefe, eine ewige Fernsicht von Licht enthüllte ...*
   [3] Ich werde leben! [1] sagte Thomas Buddenbrook beinahe laut und
5 *fühlte, wie seine Brust dabei vor innerlichem Schluchzen erzitterte. [3] Dies ist es, daß ich leben werde! Es wird leben ... und daß dieses Es nicht ich bin, das ist nur eine Täuschung, das war nur ein Irrtum, den der Tod berichtigen wird. So ist es, so ist es! ... Warum? [1] Und bei dieser Frage schlug die Nacht wieder vor seinen Augen zusammen. Er sah, er wußte*
10 *und verstand wieder nicht das Geringste mehr und ließ sich tiefer in die Kissen zurücksinken, gänzlich geblendet und ermattet von dem bißchen Wahrheit, das er soeben hatte erschauen dürfen.*
   Und er lag stille und wartete inbrünstig, fühlte sich versucht zu beten, daß es noch einmal kommen und ihn erhellen möge. Und es kam. Mit gefal-
15 *teten Händen, ohne eine Regung zu wagen, lag er und durfte schauen ...*
   [2] Was war der Tod? [1] Die Antwort darauf erschien ihm nicht in armen und wichtigtuerischen Worten: er fühlte sie, er besaß sie zuinnerst. [2] Der Tod war ein Glück, so tief, daß es nur in begnadeten Augenblicken, wie dieser, ganz zu ermessen war. Es war die Rückkunft von einem
20 *unsäglich peinlichen Irrgang, die Korrektur eines schweren Fehlers, die Befreiung von den widrigsten Banden und Schranken – einen beklagenswerten Unglücksfall machte er wieder gut.*
   Ende und Auflösung? Dreimal erbarmungswürdig Jeder, der diese nichtigen Begriffe als Schrecknisse empfand! Was würde enden und
25 *was sich auflösen? Dieser sein Leib ... Diese seine Persönlichkeit und Individualität, dieses schwerfällige, störrische, fehlerhafte und hassenswerte Hindernis, etwas Anderes und Besseres zu sein!*
   War nicht jeder Mensch ein Mißgriff und Fehltritt? Geriet er nicht in eine peinvolle Haft, sowie er geboren ward? Gefängnis! Gefängnis!

30 *Schranken und Bande überall! [4] Durch die Gitterfenster seiner
Individualität starrt der Mensch hoffnungslos auf die Ringmauern der
äußeren Umstände, bis der Tod kommt und ihn zu Heimkehr und Freiheit
ruft ...
   Individualität! ... Ach, was man ist, kann und hat, scheint arm, grau,
35 unzulänglich und langweilig; was man aber nicht ist, nicht kann und
nicht hat, das eben ist es, worauf man mit jenem sehnsüchtigen Neide
blickt, der zur Liebe wird, weil er sich fürchtet, zum Haß zu werden
   Ich trage den Keim, den Ansatz, die Möglichkeit zu allen Befähigungen
und Betätigungen der Welt in mir ... Wo könnte ich sein, wenn ich
40 nicht hier wäre? Wer, was, wie könnte ich sein, wenn ich nicht ich
wäre, wenn diese meine persönliche Erscheinung mich nicht abschlösse
und mein Bewußtsein von dem aller derer trennte, die nicht ich sind!
Organismus! Blinde, unbedachte, bedauerliche Eruption des drängenden
Willens! Besser, wahrhaftig, dieser Wille webt frei in raum- und zeitloser
45 Nacht, als daß er in einem Kerker schmachtet, der von dem zitternden und
wankenden Flämmchen des Intellektes notdürftig erhellt wird!
   In meinem Sohn habe ich fortzuleben gehofft? In einer noch ängstli-
cheren, schwächeren, schwankenderen Persönlichkeit? Kindische,
irregeführte Torheit! Was soll mir ein Sohn? Ich brauche keinen Sohn!
50 ... Wo ich sein werde, wenn ich tot bin? Aber es ist so leuchtend klar, so
überwältigend einfach! In allen denen werde ich sein, die je und je Ich
gesagt haben, sagen und sagen werden: besonders aber in denen, die
es voller, kräftiger, fröhlicher sagen ...* (GW I, 656–7).

The initial (highly impressionistic) thought processes reported by the omniscient narrator – a classic piece of '*Gedankenbericht*' – are interrupted in line 4 by a brief exclamation of direct discourse. The verbum dicendi, first person pronoun and indicative future verb are all consistent with direct speech here, but the adverbial 'beinahe laut' holds this part of the text in an indistinct territory between direct speech and direct thought. It is perhaps for this reason that Mann does not place the quoted sentence in quotation marks, and chooses to emphasize it instead: with the sole exception of Thomas's monologue at his uncle Gotthold's deathbed (Chapter 5, 4), other passages of direct thought in the novel are similarly not identified by inverted commas. The direct discourse continues – now without emphasis – in lines 6–8 in the same exclamatory tone: the character's forceful certainty (or is it a desperate attempt at self-persuasion?) is encapsulated in repetitions and compressed clauses which culminate in the desperate question '*Warum?*'. After a further passage of diegetic narrative reportage (lines 8–15), the discourse clearly moves into the free indirect mode (line 16), indicated by the absence of a reporting verb, the shift to the past tense and the question mark, which brings the perspective close to the consciousness of the questioning character. This mode is sustained after a brief passage of narratorial reporting until line 30. In fact, the earlier part of this section, beginning *'Der Tod war ein Glück* [...]', has a transitional status: it is at this point still a relatively controlled reflection on the meaning of death, which is not yet entirely divorced from the voice of the narrator. The intrusion of the character's perceptions is, however, signalled by the evaluative *'so'* in *'so tief'*, the proxemic deictic pronoun *'wie dieser'* (lines 18 and 19), and the introduction of lexical items (*'Banden und Schranken'*, line 21) that are picked up subsequently in discourse that is clearly that of the character (line 30).

The urgently elliptical *'Ende und Auflösung?'* (line 23) opens what is evidently a passage of free indirect discourse, with every sentence marked by an exclamation or question mark. Here we are granted privileged access to the thought processes of a man in extremis, though these processes are still not free from the mediating presence of the narrator. The striking formulations *'dieser sein Leib ... Diese seine Persönlichkeit'* (line 25) dramatically underline the dualism of the narrative voice in their juxtaposition of the proxemic determiner *'dies'* (strongly mimetic perspective) and the third-person pronoun *'sein'* (distancing diegetic mode). Thomas poses and answers his own questions, apparently struggling for conviction and certainty as he seeks to resolve the ultimate issues. At this point, as Hoffmeister notes, Buddenbrook faces the *'quälende Problematik der Reflexion'* (62): the tone is angry, cynical, ironic to the point of sarcasm.

But a further development in the narrative voice now occurs. The exclamatory *'Gefängnis! Gefängnis! Schranken und Bande überall!'* (lines 29–30) marks the shift from free indirect discourse to free direct discourse, indicated by the consistent use of the present tense. It, too, opens with a transitional passage, a generalized comment on the plight of humankind (*'der Mensch'*, *'man'*) interspersed with exclamations, before progressing to unambiguously direct representation with the first-person pronoun (line 38). From this stage onwards the passage, sustained in Mann's text over five long paragraphs, assumes the status of interior monologue: discourse strings unmediated by verba dicendi or credendi and unmarked by quotation marks (Vogt 2008: 185). Now the character answers his self-addressed questions with a higher degree of self-conviction, expressed apodictically. As Hoffmeister writes, these are words of *'triumphierender Verkündigung'* (1967: 62). Indeed, the final section of the quoted passage presents a flow of thoughts in such an apparently spontaneous and unfiltered form that it might even qualify for the status of 'stream of consciousness'.

Despite a high degree of overall correspondence – especially in the tense structure – the translations show a number of modifications to the

The translation of discourse forms 169

perspective. In Lowe-Porter's version, the amendments pertain more to the lexical cohesion which gives the passage much of its imitative urgency than to the deictic coordinates of the discourse. The latter are undertaken at identical points:

1   [1] And behold, it was as though the darkness were rent from before his eyes, as if the whole wall of the night parted wide and disclosed an immeasurable, boundless prospect of light. [3] 'I shall live', [1] said Thomas Buddenbrook, almost aloud, and felt his breast shaken
5   with inward sobs. [3] 'This is the revelation: that I shall live! For *it* will live – and that *it* is not I is only an illusion, an error which death will make plain. This is it, this is it! Why?' [1] But at this question the night closed in again upon him. He saw, he knew, he understood, no least particle more; he let himself sink deep into the
10 pillows, quite blinded and exhausted by the morsel of truth which had been vouchsafed. He lay still and waited fervently, feeling himself tempted to pray that it would come again and irradiate his darkness. And it came. With folded hands, not daring to move, he lay and looked.
15   [2] What *was* Death? [1] The answer came, not in poor, large-sounding words: he felt it within him, he possessed it. [2] Death was a joy, so great, so deep that it could be dreamed of only in moments of revelation like the present. It was the return from an unspeakably painful wandering, the correction of a grave mistake,
20 the loosening of chains, the opening of doors – it put right again a lamentable mischance.
    End, dissolution! These were pitiable words, and thrice-pitiable he who used them! What would end, what would dissolve? Why, this his body, this heavy, faulty, hateful incumbrance, which
25 prevented him from being something other and better.
    Was not every human being a mistake and a blunder? Was he not in painful arrest from the hour of his birth? Prison, prison, bonds and limitations everywhere! [4] The human being stares hopelessly through the barred window of his personality at the high walls of
30 outward circumstances, till Death comes and calls him home to freedom!
    Individuality? – All, all that one is, can and has, seems poor, grey, inadequate, wearisome; what one is not, can not, has not, that is what one looks at with a longing desire that becomes love because
35 it fears to become hate.
    I bear in myself the seed, the tendency, the possibility of all capacity and all achievement. Where should I be were I not here? Who, what, how could I be, if I were not I – if this my external self, my consciousness, did not cut me off from those who are not I?

40 Organism! Blind, thoughtless, pitiful eruption of the urging will! Better, indeed, for the will to float free in spaceless, timeless night than for it to languish in prison, illuminated by the feeble, flickering light of the intellect!

Have I hoped to live on in my own son? In a personality yet
45 more feeble, flickering, and timorous than my own? Blind, childish folly! What can my son do for me – what need have I of a son? Where shall I be when I am dead? Ah, it is so brilliantly clear, so overwhelmingly simple! I shall be in all those who have ever, do ever, or ever shall say 'I' – *especially, however, in all those who say it*
50 *most fully, potently, and gladly!* (Lowe-Porter, 505–7)

Lowe-Porter's version has a somewhat antiquated flavour, and the opening line of the section is almost Biblical in its use of 'behold' and 'rent'. This quasi-religious idiom is sustained in the use of 'revelation' for the object 'es' in her line 5, a noun which Lowe-Porter had introduced three paragraphs earlier when Thomas refers to the experience as a voice (*'Was habe ich vernommen …?*, 655). Although an addition to the text, this does seem consistent with the experience Thomas undergoes, which is presented very much as a quasi-religious epiphany (*'plötzliche, beseligende Erhellungen seines Inneren'*, 658). In discourse terms, Lowe-Porter follows the lead of Mann's text closely, at least as far as the use of pronouns and verb tense is concerned. Graphologically, however, she is not entirely consistent. She places the first two direct utterances, (line 3, lines 5–7) in quotation marks, presumably prompted by Mann's italics and the verb of speech '*sagte Thomas Buddenbrook beinahe laut*', and does the same a page later in her translation of Mann's (again unmarked): *'Ich werde leben! flüsterte er in das Kissen […]'* (659). At that point, too, Mann omits quotation marks – the only occasion on which he does so in the novel in combination with the verb *'flüstern'*. Earlier, however, at the first appearance of a similarly blurred passage of direct discourse in connection with the reading of Schopenhauer (is the *'fragte er sich'* (655) to be understood as spoken or written?), Lowe-Porter leaves the direct discourse, which is clearly indicated by the first-person pronoun, unmarked, as does Mann: 'What was this? He asked himself … What is it? Have I had a revelation? …' (505). The introduction of speech marks in the longer passage quoted above obscures the half-way status of the passage (*'beinahe laut'*) and renders it as a clear instance of direct speech. Mann, in fact, seems careful at this point to blur the distinction: all other direct spoken discourse in the German original is enclosed between inverted commas. Furthermore, from line 28 onwards in the section quoted above, Lowe-Porter continues the free direct discourse without any quotation marks. This is more than a technical detail: the use of quotation marks is, in fact, an indication of the degree of the 'freedom' of the discourse, i.e. its removal from narratorial control and its mimetic approximation to the mental processes of the character concerned.

Lowe-Porter is concerned to mirror other techniques used by the author to signal the workings of the mind in crisis. She emulates the sense of urgency in Thomas's 'voice' in her distribution of exclamation and question marks, in her extensive use of asyndetic clauses, omission of determiners, and use of ellipsis marks (...). In this respect, her text echoes the distraught mental processes of the original. She is, however, less attentive to the lexical recurrences, which in the original create an intensity of intellectual experience. Thus, Thomas's exclamatory 'Individuality' (line 32) remains without a co-reference in her text, since the word has been omitted in her line 26 and is replaced by 'personality' in line 29, and the *'Banden und Schranken'* (Mann line 21 and 30) are not rendered with any consistency. Both of these modifications are significant: the first because it explicitly relates to the dominant philosophical theme of the text at this point (the Schopenhauerian dualism of individual freedom and the will), the second because it forms part of an extensive metaphorical lexical network of captivity and entrapment in the passages (*'Gefängnis'*, *'Haft'*, *'Gitterfenster'*, *'Ringmauern'*, etc.). Most dramatically of all, perhaps, she transforms the climactic and apodictic *'Ich brauche keinen Sohn!'* (line 49) into a less forceful rhetorical question: 'what need have I of a son?' (line 46), reducing the crescendo of certainty. The overall impression of Lowe-Porter's translation is that it significantly softens the focus and weakens the intensity of the emotional experience.

Let us consider now Woods' version of the same passage:

1 [1] But look – suddenly the darkness seemed to split open before his eyes, as if the velvet wall of night parted to reveal immeasurable deeps, an endless vista of light. [3] *'I'm going to live!'* [1] Thomas Buddenbrook said half aloud and felt his chest jolted by sobs
5 somewhere deep inside. [3] 'That's it – I'm going to live. *It* is going to live ... and thinking that it and I are separate instead of one and the same – that is the illusion that death will set right. That's it, that's it! But why?' [1] He asked the question – and night closed over him again. And he perceived, he knew, he understood not one
10 whit of it now and let his head sink back into the pillow, blinded and exhausted by that smidgen of truth he had been permitted to see.

And he lay there quietly in fervent expectation, was even tempted to pray for truth to return and illumine him again. And it did come. Not daring to stir, he lay there with his hands folded – and was
15 allowed to watch.

[2] What was death? [1] The answer to the question came to him now, but not in poor, pretentious words – instead, he felt it, possessed it somewhere within him. [2] Death was a blessing, so great, so deep that we can fathom it only at those moments, like this one now, when we are reprieved from it. It was the return home from long unspeakably painful wanderings, the correction of a great error, the loosening of tormenting chains, the removal of barriers – it set a horrible accident to rights again.

An end, a dissolution? Empty words, and whoever was terrified by them was a pitiable wretch. What would end, what would dissolve? His body, his personality and individuality – this cumbersome, intractable, defective, and contemptible barrier to becoming something *different and better.*

Was not every human being a mistake, a blunder? Did we not, at the very moment of birth, stumble into agonizing captivity? A prison, a prison with bars and chains everywhere! [4] And, staring out hopelessly from between the bars of his individuality, a man sees only the surrounding walls of external circumstance, until death comes and calls him home to freedom.

Individuality! Oh, what a man is, can, and has seems to him so poor, gray, inadequate, and boring. But what a man is not, cannot, and does not have – he gazes at all that with longing envy – envy that turns to love, because he fears it will turn to hate.

I bear within me the seed, the rudiments, the possibility of life's capacities and endeavors. Where might I be, if I were not here? Who, what, how could I be, if I were not me, if this outward appearance that is me did not encase me, separating my consciousness from that of others who are not me? An organism – a blind, rash, pitiful eruption of the insistent assertion of the will. Far better, really, if that will were to drift free in a night without time or space, than to languish in a prison cell lit only by the flickering, uncertain flame of the intellect.

And I hoped to live on in my son? In another personality, even weaker, more fearful, more wavering than my own? What childish, misguided nonsense! What good does a son do me? I don't need a son. And where will I be once I am dead? It's so dazzlingly clear, so overwhelmingly simple. I will be a part of all those who say 'I': and, most especially, *a part of those who say it more forcibly, joyfully, powerfully.* (Woods, 635–6)

Woods similarly marks the introductory direct discourse in the passage (line 3, lines 5–8) by inserting quotation marks. Like Lowe-Porter, he then continues from line 31 onwards without marks. Three paragraphs earlier, however – and unlike Lowe-Porter – he had placed the first passages of direct discourse in this episode in inverted commas ('"What was that?" he asked himself [...] What happened to me?"' (634). This procedure is consistent at least in so far as the translator identifies direct discourse as spoken wherever it is accompanied by a verb of speech ('asked', 'said', 'asked' again, and 'whispered' later on, 637). Woods is less consistent, however, in his manipulation of the narrative perspective on a number of occasions. In lines 18 ff., where the German original remains firmly within the perspective of free indirect discourse, Woods mixes tenses and pronouns to produce a rather incongruous effect: 'Death was a blessing, so great, so deep, that we can fathom it only at those moments, like this one now, when we are reprieved from it.' The shift towards direct discourse evident here after the first clause, signalled by the unexpected switch to the present from the past, is problematic: there appears to be an unmotivated move from the characteristics of free indirect discourse (the distantiated preterite verb form, the personally evaluative and repeated 'so', the proxemic deictic adverb 'now') to the inclusive/proxemic first-person (plural) pronoun governing the present-tense verb. In the same vein, Mann's carefully balanced *'diese seine Persönlichkeit und Individualität'* is simplified by the omission of *'diese'*, obscuring the striking fusion of demonstrative and personal possessive forms (which evoke distance and proximity respectively) within individual phrases. Several other features stand out in Woods' version. He reduces the spontaneous, highly intense quality of Mann's text in the passage by introducing syndetic relations via the insertion of conjunctions and adverbs: *'Die Antwort darauf erschien ihm nicht in armen und wichtigtuerischen Worten: er fühlte sie, er besaß sie zuinnerst'* (lines 16–17) becomes the smoother and less urgent 'The answer to the question came to him now, but not in poor, pretentious words – instead, he felt it, possessed it somewhere within him' (16–18). At the same time, he removes the pause marks from Mann's text and significantly reduces the number of exclamation marks in this section: while Mann's text has no fewer than 16, Woods has just 5. In itself, perhaps, the mere quantity of such punctuation features is of limited informative value. However, in conjunction with the other techniques outlined above it indicates the extremity of the mental processes represented in Mann's text.

The modifications to the indirect discourse structure outlined above are subtle and, on a local level, of limited impact on our reading of the text as a whole. I do not offer them here as an illustration of avoidable (and thus culpable) translation loss, nor would I wish to suggest that they dramatically alter the meaning potential of the novel in broader terms. On the contrary: overall, both versions of these passages effectively convey the progression Thomas Buddenbrooks undergoes as he moves increasingly towards a defiant acceptance of what he sees as a metaphysical truth. Rather, I quote the examples above as evidence of the kind of translation shift that can obfuscate the careful balance of narrative voices in a literary text, amending the style in subtle ways. Controlled bivocality is an important instrument of reader manipulation in Mann's novel, as the point of view oscillates between various discourse forms. As we have seen, the instability of the narrative perspective ultimately signals an unstable take on the world. Processes of normalization, which have been held to be a central feature – even a universal – in translated texts (Kenny 2001), inevitably dilute that oscillation between diverse perspectives.

Conclusion

The issue of speech and thought representation is, as the above discussion illustrates, a key dimension in the exploration of narrative structures under translation. As a significant parameter of narrative perspective, techniques employed by writers in their endeavour to represent the speech patterns, thoughts and feelings of characters constitute a clear example of the interrelationship between linguistic form (realization) and literary import (meaning potential). As such, they belie the notion that narrative structure is language-independent, that it 'functions independently of specific verbal formulations' (Lodge 1990: 4), and support the claim of stylistics to provide a vital instrumentarium for reliable and replicable textual analysis as an aid to interpretation. The discussion of the manner in which the two translators of Mann's *Buddenbrooks* handle key passages of direct and free direct discourse shows that the (often inevitable) manipulation of the structures of the source text can have significant implications for a reading of the text.

In the absence of clear cross-linguistic correspondences, the translators resort to a variety of compensatory strategies. In both the discourse areas selected for analysis here, the translations show a tendency towards levelling. In the case of direct discourse, the degree of differentiation evident in Mann's text is reduced in both the Lowe-Porter and the Woods versions above all by the dilution of regiolectal forms: the latter are frequently standardized, rendered as geographically neutral but non-standard patterns, transposed into indirect discourse, deleted altogether, or glossed metalinguistically. This, as has been seen, has implications for our understanding of the characters and the cultural contextualization of the action. Lowe-Porter adopts a truly radical translation strategy in this context, freely inventing additional narratorial comment which serves to steer the reader's understanding of the episode concerned. Meanwhile, in the case of the free indirect discourse modes used extensively by Mann to generate an interweaving of the authorial and figural voices, the obfuscation of the perspectives constructed in the original serves to undermine the instability of the narrative as it shifts subtly between points of view. Here, too, discourse management is a crucial factor in psychological character portrayal. The perspectival presentation of internal thought processes – for example of the spiritual crisis experienced by Thomas Buddenbrook in Chapter 10, 5 – is subtly modified in both versions, affecting the reader's perception of the intellectual and emotional development of the character concerned.

7 Translating modes of address as an index of interpersonal dynamics

Preliminary remarks

In a letter to Alfred A. Knopf dated 11 November 1943, Helen Tracy Lowe-Porter set out a number of issues she considered, and had found, particularly problematic in the process of translation (see Chapter 3). In her comments, she explicitly refers to the translation of the 'German second person singular' ('*du*') as 'a tricky thing' (Thirlwall 1966: 60). In doing so, she identifies one of the most notorious structural incompatibilities in translation between English and German: the asymmetry in the pronominal systems of address, a divergence which has often been discussed in work on sociolinguistics (Brown and Levinson 1978/87, Chapter 5) and, less frequently, in studies of the pragmatics of translation (Horton 1996; Albrecht 2005: 192–8; Berger 2005). In respect of literary translation this issue deserves more attention than it has been granted hitherto, since it is much more than a merely technical or localized problem in the process of interlingual transfer. As a key index of social status and developing personal relations, address systems constitute an important dimension of the interpersonal dynamics of literary texts (Horton 1999). They are, first and foremost, a crucial element in text-internal discourse organization at the level of speech representation. But they can also play a part in constructing point-of-view through the device of narratorial address (the apostrophization of characters, and even of the reader), as can be seen in Mann's work, too. Furthermore, in the fictional world of Mann's novels, which are much concerned with the power of behavioural norms and expectations – be they bourgeois (*Buddenbrooks, Der Zauberberg, Doktor Faustus, Felix Krull*) or historical-legendary (*Königliche Hoheit*, the Joseph novels, *Lotte in Weimar, Der Erwählte*) – the pragmatics of social intercourse play an important role. It is hardly surprising, then, that the issue of address behaviour is explicitly thematized in virtually all of Mann's novels.

Thomas Mann's own social interactions were consistently characterized by a high degree of refinement expressed in impeccable manners and a courteous, even formal approach to personal relationships. He was conditioned by his own middle-class upbringing in the social hierarchy of a small Hanseatic city, which instilled in him a catalogue of values amongst which Kurzke emphasizes *'Form- und Stilgefühl, Takt, Diskretion, Wissen um das Gehörige* [...] *Die Umgangsformen sind stets aufs Nuancierteste gewahrt'* (Kurzke 2010: 29). Mann himself wrote: *'Ich bin ein Städter, Bürger, ein Kind und Urenkelkind deutscher bürgerlicher Kultur'* (GW 9: 386), and he was at all times concerned to project a highly respectable image. Simultaneously indebted to and sceptical of the bourgeois world of which he was so much a part – like his Tonio Kröger he was ultimately a *'Bürger auf Irrwegen'* (GW 9: 305) – Mann maintained a cautious distance and a jealously guarded privacy in dealings with others. He was, as his biographers point out, on *'du'* terms with only very few people outside his immediate family, requiring no fewer than 34 years to move onto an intimate footing with his friend and neighbour Bruno Walter (GW 10: 507). And his concern to uphold the standards of propriety and decorum associated with the German *'Bürgertum'* – values which made him a natural target for anti-bourgeois artists and intellectuals from the late 1960s onwards – can be seen in his letters. His correspondence with his future wife, for example, is marked by tortuous politeness formulations before the 'abrupt, triumphant intimacy of the shift from the formal *Sie* to the familiar *du* in the final stages of their premarital exchange' (Winston and Winston 1990: xii).

His correspondence with Lowe-Porter and Knopf, which lasted for many years, provides ample indication of the scrupulousness he devoted in his social contacts. The letters abound in the repertoires of politeness, and show a highly tentative development towards more intimate forms of salutation. Those to Helen Lowe-Porter are marked by a gradual progression from the initial *'Mistress Lowe'*, via *'Sehr verehrte gnädige Frau'*, *'Sehr verehrte Mrs Lowe'* and *'Liebe Mrs Lowe'* to *'Helen'*. The correspondence with Knopf, meanwhile – in which Mann gradually moves from *'Hochgeehrter Herr'* via *'Lieber Herr Knopf'* to *'Alfred'* – provides clear evidence (if evidence were needed) that English first-naming cannot be pragmatically equated with the German *'duzen'*, as is erroneously assumed in some quarters: *'Knopf war einer der wenigen Zeitgenossen, mit dem TM sich duzte; man redete einander auf englisch mit Vornamen an'* (Armbrust and Heine 2008: 140). In fact Mann always retained the *Sie*-form in combination with the use of first names vis-à-vis both correspondents. In all his letters, Mann was careful to cultivate a civil, respectful tone, divulging little of his most intimate preoccupations. As the publication of the diaries has made clear, there was a profound tension between Mann's resolute projection of solid social respectability on the one hand and impulses which constituted a threat to his perceived normality and solidity on the other. As an accomplished social performer racked by the pressures imposed by the need to conform, he was well placed to portray the dynamics, tensions and contradictions of the *'Bildungsbürgertum'* (Lehnert 2004: 11f.). It is no wonder, then, that his literary explorations of the vicissitudes of interpersonal relations focus very much on the formal strategies employed to encode intimacy and distance.

The systemic asymmetries and discourse-conventional divergences between German and English in the pragmatics of politeness are an interesting contrastive feature which inevitably leaves its mark in terms of translator strategy. From a relativistic, structuralist point of view, these cross-linguistic differences constitute an (at least theoretical) 'impossibility of translation' (Lyons 1980; Andermann 1993). Functionalist translation scholarship, on the other hand, has focused instead on the compensation strategies that enable interlingual transactions to operate successfully even where formal divergences prevent 'equivalence' (thus the German functionalist school, for example Nord 1997). A great deal of research has been undertaken in the field of *'Anredeforschung'* or 'politeness research' in sociolinguistics since the 1970s, and the language-specific repertoires have been described in detail (Hoppmann 2009; Bousfield and Grainger 2010). This attention is hardly surprising, given that modes of address are a particularly clear illustration of the correlation between linguistic form and sociocultural context, encoding key information about ideologies, status, relations and attitudes. In the language–pair German/English, the most obvious distinction is in the pronominal system. English has, since the seventeenth century, abandoned its 'thou'-'you' differentiation. Modern German, on the other hand, has retained this so-called T-V dichotomy, while losing other modes of address, such as third-person singular *'Er'* and the singular use of the second-person plural pronoun (*'Ihr'*) in the standard language (Howe 1996). English, then, no longer has the ability to mark socially meaningful pronoun choices which it still had in Shakespeare's time ('I thou thee, thou traitor', Edward Coke to Walter Raleigh, 1603), except in dialectal, poetic and religious usage. Instead, collocutors rely on sophisticated nominal systems to mark such social-psychological phenomena as power/solidarity (reflected in asymmetrical v. reciprocal use) and distance/proximity. These vocative markers of register include naming techniques (first name, last name, nickname, no-naming), the use of kinship terms and of titles (both with and without names), and an entire range of nominal descriptors comprising gender-specific and occupational indicators, as well as terms of endearment and disrespect. As norm-controlled behaviour, the use of address strategies and greeting formulations is sensitive to a number of contextual factors, including group membership, regional identity, age, gender, ideology/religion, educational background and situational parameters (politeness, degree of formality), but it also allows scope for individual behaviour in response to emotion, mood and evaluation. In sum, then: 'The selection of address options is a graphic illustration of the intimate relationship between language variation and interpersonal dynamics in socially defined situations' (Horton 1996: 72).

In the language-pair English/German, the cross-linguistic incompatibilities that arise in translation are relatively limited in scope. In the direction German-English, an important source-language differentiating feature – pronominal variation – is unavailable, resulting in potential translation loss (address reduction). Compensation strategies must be used if the interpersonal dynamics of the original are to be effectively re-encoded in the target language. In English-German translation, on the other hand, the unavoidability of pronominal differentiation in dialogic exchanges means that the translator is required to make choices which are typically not explicitly motivated in the source text (address amplification). In both directions, translators are forced to make an assessment on the basis of their reading of the developing personal interaction. In literary communication, which functions on a non-pragmatic, distantiated level, such an assessment can only be made on the basis of an interpretation of the text at hand. On the nominal level of interpersonal address, meanwhile, the issues in question are not structural, but are subject to cultural, historical and register-specific constraints. Taken as a whole, the interlingual transfer of such pragmatic markers – with all of their connotative implications – can, indeed, strain '*die Grenzen der Übersetzbarkeit*' (Schulze and Kerzel 2004: 939).

The following discussion is concerned to reveal where and how translators adopt compensatory strategies in order to balance out structural asymmetries which have a meaning-constitutive function in Mann's texts. The available strategies in the process of translation from German into English range along a cline of explicitation/textual integration, comprising:

1. the retention of – or, more likely, reference to – source-language forms ('*du*', '*vous*');

2. the adoption of differentiated target-language pronominal forms ('thou', 'ye'), which can carry historical and regional connotations;

3. the compensation of pronominal differentiation through naming strategies, e.g. introduction of first-naming to suggest familiarity or

of title + second-naming to indicate politeness, or no naming (the deletion of names) in cases of uncertainty;

4. the transformation of source-language names into less formal target-language forms (via processes of reduction, diminution, nicknaming: Georg>Georgie), or the contrary (Hans>Johannes);

5. the insertion of nominal/vocative forms to compensate for loss of distance ('Sir', 'Master') or familiarity ('my dear friend'), often in combination with first or last names;

6. the use of alternative linguistic signals in direct speech exchanges to suggest social relations (indications of colloquialism, intimacy, formalism);

7. the insertion of metalinguistic authorial comment on speech processes via the addition of reporting clauses or phrases, verba dicendi, adverbials, drawing attention to specific source-language forms ('he said, using the familiar pronoun');

8. the insertion of paralinguistic information to suggest relations (body language, gesture);

9. the addition of a translator's note (metatextual gloss) explaining the issue;

10. the complete deletion of differentiation (i.e. loss of ST feature).

Virtually all of these techniques are evident in the various translations of Thomas Mann's works, and they are considered below in terms of their impact on textual meaning.

Buddenbrooks

In Mann's work, the most profound and wide-ranging preoccupation with the issue of linguistic address patterns as an index of social relations is, undoubtedly, to be found in *Der Zauberberg* and *Doktor Faustus*, where it assumes leitmotivic significance. It is there that the procedures adopted by translators are most apparent, and are at their most powerful in terms of their interpretive consequences. But the operation of politeness markers in a structured social universe is also apparent in Mann's first novel, as well as in a variety of the short prose texts. In the first of these cases, *Buddenbrooks*, a number of phenomena are relevant in translational terms. At the pronominal level, the forms of address used by the characters serve as an important indication of the changing behavioural norms which operate across the generations in the Buddenbrook family. These changes reflect one of the key themes of the novel: the historical development away from more formalized patriarchal structures (with their ideological and commercial values), which prevail under the aegis of the first Johann Buddenbrook, towards a less structured form of familial intercourse in the second generation (Johann junior, called Jean). In keeping with the conventions of the age (1835), the forms of address used between the generations at the beginning of the novel are asymmetrical in structure: Jean addresses his parents with the polite '*Sie*' (*GW* 1: 12, 14), as does his wife (13), while the parents respond in the '*du*' form (14). This pattern of respectful formulation in contact with the parents is also evident in the letter from the absent son Gotthold to his father, and the same constellation applies in the verbal behaviour of the grandchildren, Thomas, Tony and Christian, towards their grandparents. In the second and third generations of the family, however, that pattern has changed: Jean's children address their parents throughout in the familiar form, as does Hanno his father Thomas, and relationships of generationally conditioned asymmetry no longer apply. This shift to symmetrical forms indicates a historical-social development. Status-conditioned asymmetry, meanwhile, is apparent in all generations of the family: the Buddenbrooks address their domestic staff in the familiar form, and receive the polite form in return. The same is true of lower-status company employees. But address modes can also serve as an instrument of manipulation. As an indication of pseudo-identification with lower-status interlocutors, Jean adopts dialectal forms, receiving the '*Sei*' form ('"*Je, Herr Kunsel, dat seggen Sei woll*"', 192) and in his responses mixes forms as a means of social control ('*Hür mal, Smolz*', '*du*', '*Ji*' and '*Sei*'). In the Woods version of the novel, this pronominal differentiation is lost completely, while Lowe-Porter uses the rather archaic 'ye' form as the mode of upward address in these scenes (Lowe-Porter 1957: 148).

A further (though limited) example of significant pronominal differentiation in *Buddenbrooks* is provided by the deliberate use of asymmetrical patterns as a form of resistance against overfamiliarity. In his forceful courtship of Tony, the persistent Grünlich seeks to impose himself upon Tony not merely physically (he pulls her onto his lap), but also rhetorically '"*Habe ich dich doch erwischt? Habe ich dich doch noch ergattert?*"' (163), to which she replies '"*O Gott, Sie vergessen sich!*"'. In the Lowe-Porter version, this is obscured (126). Woods adopts a compensation strategy (No. 5 above), inserting 'sir' (Woods 1993: 159). Nominal address forms, meanwhile, show no significant variations. In the vast majority of cases, both translators import the address formulations of the original, usually retaining the '*Herr*', '*Frau*', '*Mamsell*' titles in front of official functions (*'Consul'*, *'Senator'*), professional designations (*'Pastor'*) and last names. On a number of occasions Woods inserts *'Herr'* where it is not present in Mann's text, thus understating the familiarity of last-name address forms in the first generation (*'alle Achtung Buddenbrook'*, 22), and omits it in professional epithets (*'Pastor'* for *'Herr Pastor'*, 20). He also transforms a number of instances of *'Herr Konsul'* into *'Herr Buddenbrook'*, apparently to avoid confusion where a number of people involved in the scene share the same title (Woods 36, 95).

Short prose works, *Königliche Hoheit*

A number of significant address patterns, and thus potentially interesting translation issues, are evident in Mann's short prose fiction. Among these are the processes of address transition – almost always, for pragmatic reasons, from polite to familiar forms – and of address instability. Both of these processes are explicitly thematized in an early story which is typically counted among Mann's minor works, since he did not include it in his German anthologies or in his English omnibus edition *Stories of Three Decades*. It was never translated by Lowe-Porter, and it is rarely mentioned in general studies on the author (Vaget 1984: 147). The story *'Gerächt'* (which appeared in *Simplicissimus* in August 1899) deals with the relationship between the young narrator (Anselm) and an emancipated older woman, Dunja Stegemann. The English translator, Peter Constantine, comments in the foreword to his version of the text that the relationship between the two characters 'closely prefigures the intimate yet oddly formal one between the liberated painter Lisaweta Ivanovna and the uptight writer Tonio Kröger in *Tonio Kröger*' (Constantine 1998: 138). While this is undoubtedly true, the interaction between Kröger and Lisoweta is encoded throughout in the polite *'Sie'* form in combination with naming, reflecting a respectful distance between the characters. At the centre of *Gerächt*, on the other hand, stands the tension between platonic and sensual attraction, and this theme is reflected in forms of address which take on complex functions (instability of address). The narrator draws express attention to the fact that the characters vacillate in their dealings between the *'"Sie", das in minder gehobenen Stunden unsere Anrede blieb'* and a *'makellose[s] "Du"'*(*GW* 8: 164) at moments of *'intime Vertrautheit'* (165). When, having convinced himself of the physical unattractiveness of Dunja, the narrator learns that she is sexually experienced, he is uncertain – in his shock – as to the appropriate form of address (crisis of address). *'Ich rief: Du? ... Sie?'*. Succumbing to lust, he makes forceful advances (*'"Was zierst du dich denn?"'*, 166). She resists via a consistent reversion to the *'Sie'* form: *'"Nehmen Sie sich zusammen [...] Sie sind ganz außer sich!"'* (167). The distribution of the carefully differentiated forms in Mann's text (nine *'Sie'* forms and nine *'du'* forms) cannot be translated by grammatical means: Constantine, the only translator of this text to date, deletes the explicit reference in Mann's text to the use of the polite and familiar forms, and flattens all other instantiations.

In Mann's short fiction there are various examples of pronoun transition and switching. In systemic terms, these are all obscured in translation. However, in many cases the translators use compensatory techniques, or rely on other indications of distance/proximity in the source text to encode the dynamics of interaction.

The narrator's adoption of the *'du'* to signal his love for the actress Irma in *Gefallen* is relatively unproblematic, since unfolding relations in this text are also encoded in nominal forms of address which signal increasing intimacy: as relations become more intimate, there is a clear shift in the narrator's discourse from *'gnädiges Fräulein'* to *'Fräulein Weltner'* to *'Fräulein Irma'* and finally to *'Irma'*: in Constantine's translation, the first of these forms is omitted, while the forms *'Fräulein Weltner'*, *'Fräulein Irma'* and *'Irma'* are retained as in German. The actual moment of transition, in the middle of a highly emotional scene, is obscured, since no naming is used at that point.

As an expression of Detlef's brotherly solidarity with the beggar in *Die Hungernden* (*'Du irrst, Freund* […]*'* (GW 8: 212), the concomitant use of the nominal forms *'Freund'* and *'Kamerad'* in Mann's text means that translation 'loss' is kept to a minimum.

Address transition operates as an element of romantic confession in the later story *Die Betrogene*, where the protagonist initially refers to the American object of her affections in the third person as *'Mr Keaton'* and later switches to the familiar form in a moment of passion: *'"Ken, Ken* […] *ich liebe dich, ich liebe dich"'* (GW 8: 945). Here, Rosalie's adoption of the first name in the English version does not appear sufficient to suggest the truly taboo-breaking declaration of love for a much younger man expressed through the use of the intimate pronoun.

The situation is more complex in *Mario und der Zauberer*, where the hypnotist-performer Cipolla exploits the use of pronouns strategically as means of intimidation and power. While he addresses members of the audience of upper (*'der junge Herr'*) and middle-class status (Signora and Signor Abgiolieri) respectfully as *'Sie'*, he does not hesitate to use the downward form of address to the *'Volk'*, to the unnamed young man, and to Mario. This reflects the overall strategy pursued by the manipulator: *'Cipolla hütete sich, den vornehmen Teil seines Publikums zu belästigen. Er hielt sich an das Volk'* (GW 8: 681). Thus he addresses the unnamed young man with the informal noun *'giovanotto'*, and to Mario applies the form *'ragazzo mio'* before asking his name *'("Nur den Vornamen will ich wissen"'*, 706) and calling him at various stages in the proceedings *'mein Mario'*, *'mein Lieber'*, *'mein Freund'*, *'mein Sohn'*.

Such forms of mock intimacy function as a means of control, as can be seen in the case of the *'junger Herr'*, where the hypnotist switches to the *'du'* as a form of manipulation and degradation: *'"Nennst du es Freiheit – diese Vergewaltigung deiner selbst?"'* (702). All of these characters respond with *'Sie'*, in Mario's case accompanied by the title 'Signore'. In the translation, Lowe-Porter (the only translator of *Mario*) uses 'ye' on one occasion for Cipolla to Mario ('"hark ye, my friend"', Lowe-Porter 1936: 542) and otherwise flattens the differentiations in address (including those for the *'junger Herr'*). In the mock love scene, where Cipolla parodies Mario's Silvestra, Lowe-Porter uses 'thee' (566). The historicizing quality of these obsolete pronouns in English has already been noted.

One interesting compensatory technique (No. 9 above) which is unique in the translation of Mann's works is evident in the English version of *Königliche Hoheit*, a novel of courtly life characterized by highly ritualized forms of address. In Mann's novel, the *'Sie'* form is inevitably used in all extra-familial dealings, where it occurs with a wide variety of nominal titulations indicating status, rank, and profession (*'Königliche Hoheit'*, *'Exzellenz'*, *'Teuerster Baron'*, *'Herr Hauptmann'*, *'Herr Generalarzt'*, *'Großherzogliche Hoheit'*). The latter are translated literally into English. The issue of familiar forms of address – *'duzen'*– becomes relevant above all in contexts where Prince Klaus Heinrich has regular contact with commoners and the usual norms of status-driven address behaviour are suspended in favour of markers of solidarity. Thus the reciprocal use of familiar pronouns despite status differences is explicitly mentioned in connection with Klaus Heinrich's school days (*GW* 2: 92), and also with his membership of a university student association (117). In both cases, address uncertainty is evident. In the original Cecil Curtis translation of this text (1916) the issue of pronominal differentiation is circumvented by the use of first-naming ('to be on Christian name terms with Klaus Heinrich. For the use of Christian names was ordered', 80), and the hesitation on the part of the prince's classmate is signalled by the insertion of a nominal form ('Your Highness') to indicate the inadvertent use of the German *'Sie'* form. The same technique of first-naming is used in the student *'Korps'* scene. Here, though, it is combined with an explanatory insertion (italics) which makes explicit values that in German are inherent in the pronoun: 'The use of Christian names was *the bond of union* between Klaus Heinrich and his corps brothers as the expression and basis of spontaneous comradeship' (105, my italics). In her 1962 revision of the Cecil Curtis translation (a truly extensive rewriting which leaves virtually no sentence unchanged) the translator Constance McNab employs a strategy which is not seen anywhere else in the body of Mann's work in English. In the first instance cited above, she retains the German *'per du'* and adds a footnote (McNab 1962: 81): 'In German there are two nouns [sic]: *'Sie'* and *'Du'*, the formal and the intimate address, corresponding to the French *'vous'* and *'tu'* – Translator's note'. The use of this note enables her to repeat the German pronoun *'du'* on the second occasion it is used (103). The use of footnotes in literary texts is often regarded as the solution of last resort, since it implies the addition of paratextual material which is not integral to the original text, and thus introduces a metatextual dimension to the fiction (Landers 2001: 93 ff.).

Der Zauberberg

Nowhere in Mann's work does the issue of interpersonal address assume such significance as it does in *Der Zauberberg*, where the differentiation of forms is not merely a subtle and carefully exploited device in the interpersonal dynamics of the text, but also forms part of the leitmotivic structure of the novel. As such, it is at this point that the much-lamented 'untranslatability' of pronouns of address becomes most critical. The way in which the two translators handle this phenomenon – and there are major differences – thus sheds an interesting light on their translation technique, and raises questions about the impact of such techniques on the orientation and meaning potential of their versions.

As we saw in Chapter 4, Mann's use of the celebrated 'leitmotif' technique plays a key role in establishing associative thematic connections between scenes in the novel, creating a level of extra texture which is of major hermeneutic significance. The antithetical structure of the chains of motifs has been much discussed in the literature (Kristiansen 1978; see also Liewerscheidt 2006). The socially regulated linguistic behaviour of the characters in terms of address patterns is seen by commentators as part of this dichotomous scheme (Kurzke 2010: 203). The dualism of *'Siezen'* and *'Duzen'* thus reflects the underlying tension between bourgeois form (*'Flachland'*) and anarchic formlessness (*'Berg'*), and within the text itself the humanist Settembrini interprets its wider symbolic ramifications in precisely the same way. The dialogue between Castorp and Settembrini early in the *'Walpurgisnacht'* episode prepares the reader for the significance of the discourse forms employed in the exchange between Castorp and Clawdia Chauchat which is to follow, and even establishes the framework within which that latter dialogue is to be read. Horrified by Castorp's adoption of the familiar pronominal form during the mardi gras festivities, Settembrini sets up a metaphysical dualism of civilization (the west) and barbarism (the east), of which the unsolicited *'du'* is an expression: *'"Das 'Du' unter Fremden, das heißt unter Personen, die einander von Rechtes wegen 'Sie' nennen, ist eine widerwärtige Wildheit, ein Spiel mit dem Urstande, ein liederliches Spiel, das ich verabscheue, weil es sich im Grunde gegen Zivilisation und entwickelte Menschlichkeit richtet – sich frech und schamlos dagegen richtet"'* (*GW* 3: 457). Settembrini sees Clawdia Chauchat in her influence on Hans Castorp as an embodiment of this destructive impulse, and the motifs which are used in connection with her – her Kirgisian eyes (the Asian principle), her slamming of doors, feline movement, chewed fingernails, inner decay (*'wurmstichig'*), promiscuity, identification with Lilith within the mythological framework of the Walpurgis scene – confirm Settembrini's view that she represents the forces of chaos which Castorp actively embraces in his persistent use of '*du*' and his ultimate confession of love for her. The latter culminates in his vision of the *'Liebestod'*, where the principles of Eros and Thanatos are brought together in Castorp's *'Sympathie mit dem Tode'*. Castorp's refusal to heed Settembrini's warnings – '"*Ma è matto questo ragazzo!*"' (462) – is, then, a signal of his descent into the underworld of the sanatorium (Hades echoes) and its value structure. The '*du*' has become far more than a grammatical component within a sociolinguistic framework: it has assumed significant literary meaning. Castorp's violation of linguistic conventions reflects his abandonment of the ordering principles of the bourgeois world.

Castorp's sensitivity in matters of linguistic decorum – which makes his 'descent' into the 'du' vis-à-vis unrelated persons all the more dramatic – is indicated at the opening of the novel, where the narrator comments on his relationship with Joachim Ziemssen. Governed by the *'kühle und spröde Sitten'* and a *'Scheu vor zu großer Herzenswärme'* (*GW* 3: 15) which are considered characteristic of their north German origins, the cousins avoid the use of first names and address each other (as relatives) in the familiar pronominal form. This observation on the part of the narrator points to an important discourse feature of the novel: in the fictional world of Mann's text, the use of first names cannot be considered to be an automatic concomitant of the '*du*' form. Indeed, the use of Christian names marks a significant further step on the scale of intimacy, confirming that the use of '*du*' in German and of first names in English cannot be regarded as 'equivalent' across the languages.

The two English versions of these early passages anticipate the techniques which the respective translators adopt throughout the novel. Lowe-Porter writes: 'And, as they could not well address each other by their last names, they confined themselves, by established custom, to the thou' (Lowe-Porter 1960: 6). This use of the 'thou' form is problematic. It is an archaic pronoun, and reinforces the antiquated tone of the Lowe-Porter translations as a whole (see Chapter 4). Indeed, as early as 1785 the German satirist Georg Christoph Lichtenberg lamented the loss of the familiar form – the *'seelenverbindendes Du […]'* – in English: 'Thou *ist entweder feierlich wie im Gebet, oder dichterisch, oder drollig oder quäkerhaft'* (quoted in Zuschlag 2001: 137). The 'thou' form had become infrequent by the time the *Zauberberg* action is set (1907), and even more so by the time Lowe-Porter began her work on the translation (1925). A one-million word corpus of English texts published between 1910 and 1925 by Forster, Lawrence and Galsworthy shows that the form occurs essentially only in dialectal and religious usage, and virtually never appears as an index of familiarity in standard usage. It is for this reason, presumably, that Lowe-Porter, while resuming the 'thou' form at later strategic points in her text, does not use it consistently: she reverts to 'you' once the 'thou' has been introduced. It is unsustainable, as Lyons comments in his essay on English translations of Russian texts: 'It is not difficult to imagine the incongruity of the English that would be produced by the systematic and consistent employment of what is for most people nowadays either an archaic or a rustic pronoun of address to translate the Russian T-form' (Lyons 1980: 245).

Woods, by contrast, adopts from the outset a metalinguistic approach to the problem of pronominal differentiation, explicitly thematizing the grammatical forms employed: 'And since they could not very well address one another by their last names, they confined themselves to the use of familiar pronouns – now a deeply rooted habit between the two cousins' (Woods 1995: 6). Woods does this frequently in the text, variously drawing attention to the use of 'formal', 'informal', 'personal', or 'familiar' pronouns. This technique of explicit grammatical reference becomes especially cumbersome – and arguably unnatural – in extensive exchanges where the characters explicitly refer to the dualism of '*Duzen*' and '*Siezen*'. In the opening exchange between Castorp and Ziemssen, both translators are at pains to suggest the familiar character of the discourse by using compensatory informal registers (technique No. 5 above): thus Lowe-Porter has '"Hullo – It's all right – give us [=me] your things"' (5), while Woods has '"Hello there – Sure you are – I've got a carriage"' (5). In Chapter 6, where Ziemssen suddenly adopts first-naming in his farewell to Hans Castorp rather than the simple '*du*' or nominal epithet '*Mensch*' ('*aller Sittenspröhdigkeit zum Trotz und peinlichst überschwenglicherweise*', GW 3: 587), Lowe-Porter refers once again to the 'thou', adding an additional indicator of familiarity ('old fellow'), while Woods again comments metalingusitically on the use of 'informal pronouns' (417).

As the action develops and the patterns of discourse come to assume more fundamental importance, both translators find themselves forced to diversify their techniques. Thus, in the Settembrini scene on '*Walpurgisnacht*', in which address forms become a point of conflict between the interlocutors, Lowe-Porter introduces metalinguistic references to 'third person' and 'second person' forms: 'When strangers, who would regularly use the third person, speak to each other in the second, it is an objectionable freedom, it is wantonly playing with the roots of things, and I despise and condemn it' (328). Having introduced this reference to pronominal forms, Lowe-Porter is subsequently able to refer simply to 'this form' or the 'other form'. But she continues to use the 'thou', which leads her to the odd formulation: '"I find it perfectly easy and natural to say thou to you"' (328), and even uses 'ye' in Settembrini's acerbic rejection of Castorp's overfamiliar behaviour (328). On this occasion, the 'ye' form seems to function as an explicit contradiction of Castorp's 'thou'. Woods, meanwhile, continues with his references to pronouns, but from this point onwards adopts an additional technique, inserting first names where these are not present in the original: 'For people to use informal pronouns or first names when they have no real reason to do so is a repulsively barbaric practice, a slovenly game, a way of playing with the givens of civilization and human progress' (322). Thus Woods has Castorp addressing Settembrini as 'Lodovico' (three times in the text), inserts the warning 'No first names', and renders Castorp's closing words in this exchange – which in Mann's text are carefully suspended between familiarity and formality ('"*Dein Wohl, Herr Settembrini, sollst leben*"', 454) – as '"To your health, Lodovico – I wish you a long life"' (324). In Mann's original text, in fact, the use of first-naming is extremely limited, as the opening meeting between Castorp and Ziemssen shows. It is by no means accidental that the only consistent use of first names in Mann's entire text is that by Castorp vis-à-vis Clawdia, where the former adopts it as a persistent and invasive strategy in a relationship that he considers to be beyond social norms. In both English versions, Settembrini's persistent refusal to shift to familiar forms in his '*Fastnacht*' exchange with Castorp is obscured. For Mann's '"*Hören Sie, Ingenieur*"' (456) Lowe-Porter has '"Why, Engineer"' (329), while Woods uses '"My good engineer"' (324). Towards the end of the novel, when Settembrini says farewell to the departing Castorp in an uncharacteristically emotional fashion, first-naming him as '*Giovanni*' and adopting the '*du*' (989) – a different quality of '*du*' from that diagnosed earlier – Lowe-Porter resumes the 'thou' ('spoke to him with the thou', 712), while Woods again has 'informal pronouns' (702).

In the extensive exchange with Clawdia Chauchat in the same scene, Castorp's linguistic behaviour confirms – as he later concedes to Peeperkorn (848) – the '*Unvernunft*' about which Settembrini has warned him ('"*Un po' di ragione, sa!*"', 462). Castorp has realized from the outset that any relations with Clawdia Chauchat, at least in the sense of '*gesittete Beziehungen, bei denen man "Sie" sagte* […]' (335), would be inconceivable in the normal world. In his besotted state, normal judgements are suspended ('*bei der Verliebtheit kommt das ästhetische Vernunfturteil sowenig zu seinem Recht wie das moralische'*, 336). Under the cover of the mardis gras, then, Castorp approaches Clawdia, engaging her for the first time in conversation and quickly moving to a confession of love. The exchange between the two is conducted predominantly in French, and is thus thrice removed from quotidian reality: it takes place within the hermetic world of the sanatorium, is located within the extra-societal context of the mardi gras, and is conducted for the most part in what is for both interlocutors a foreign language. Castorp immediately adopts the *'du'* (*'"Hast* du *nicht vielleicht einen Bleistift?"'*, 463). Clawdia responds hesitantly in the same form, before switching to French and combining the T/V forms: '"*Prenez garde, il est un peu fragile* [...] *C'est à visser, tu sais*"' (464). In the opening turns of the exchange, Clawdia is reluctant to move to the familiar form, but succumbs under Castorp's pressure, which also embraces the shift to first names on his part. To the very end of the scene, where she shifts back to the *'vous'* as a signal of return to the real world when the party draws to a close – ('"*Vous connaissez les conséquences, monsieur*"', 474); '"*N'oubliez pas de me rendre mon crayon*"', 478) – he steadfastly clings to the informal form, which he considers the ultimate expression of his love for her ('"*tu es le Toi de ma vie*"', 476). The scene is repeatedly defined as a dream, an escape (for Castorp) from the *'pédanterie'* of the *'Occident cultivé'* (474) into the world of formlessness and unconvention (Castorp to Peeperkorn, 847). As Castorp's closing speech makes clear, he has embraced the principle of the inseparability of *'Leib, Liebe, Tod'* – corporeality, Eros, Thanatos – which marks the nadir of his self-abandonment to the values of the Berghof world: '"*et laisse moi périr, mes lèvres aux tiennes*"' (477). The use of the familiar form is a key symbolic index of this process.

In all of the French exchanges, Lowe-Porter takes over Mann's text verbatim, which enables her to retain the dynamics of the original. For Castorp's opening gambit: '"Do *you* happen to have a pencil?"' (332), she adds a metalinguistic comment: 'He had used the second person singular' (332), but does not indicate the informal form Clawdia uses in reply. Woods, by contrast, translates all of the extensive French exchange – with one notable exception – into English. This was done, as was mentioned in Chapter 4, at the instigation of the publisher, and was the option least preferred by Woods himself. The wider consequences of this interlingual strategy have also been indicated above. In using a foreign tongue, Castorp claims, he has suspended reality and can talk without saying anything. In the opening exchange, as elsewhere, Woods draws attention to the modes of address by inserting metalingusitic information: '"Do you mean me?" the bare-armed patient replied, in response to the familiar pronoun in his question' and 'she said, likewise using personal pronouns' (327). Only on one important occasion does Woods take over Mann's French: '"*Prenez garde, il est un peu fragile* [...] *C'est a visser, tu sais*"' (327). It is not clear from the text whether Woods seeks to imply, with this French sentence, that all the remainder of the italicized discourse is to be perceived by the reader as French, but it certainly suggests the instability which is to mark Clawdia's utterances in the early parts of the exchange. Throughout the scene, Woods otherwise relies on the use of the nominal forms in the original text (Castorp's first-naming of Clawdia, her use of *'monsieur'*) to express the dynamics of the exchange: to compensate for potential loss, he on one occasion inserts a 'sir' (330) and translates '*Klein, aber dein*' (464) with an adapted idiomatic expression (from *As You Like It*): 'A poor thing, but thine own' (328), exploiting the familiarity of the 'thou' pronoun by placing it in an archaic-humorous context. The extensive use of metalevel substitution in Woods' version can have an awkward effect, drawing attention to lexico-grammatical phenomena which seem to have no real place in the discourse of a literary work:

> "Besides," Hans Castorp said, "if I had spoken to you before this, I would have had to use the formal pronoun."
> "I see. Do you intend to use only the informal with me from now on?"
> "But of course. I've used it with you all along, and will for all eternity."
> "That's a bit much, I must say. In any case, you won't have the opportunity to use informal pronouns with me for much longer. I'm leaving." (331)

The same interpersonal dynamic is evident when Clawdia returns to the sanatorium two years later (Castorp has waited for her). Again Castorp insists on the inviolability of the familiar form, while she on this occasion adopts a range of strategies to maintain a distance: the '*Sie*' form, the highly formal use of *'monsieur'* with a third-person verb ('"*Und Monsieur ist nicht einmal zum Begräbnis des Vetters gefahren?*"', 773), the circumlocutory pronoun *'man'* (774). Only with some protest – *'Mais c'est un sauvage'* (774), *'närrische Hartnäckigkeit'* (825) – does she succumb to the familiar form. Lowe-Porter adopts an interesting and apparently quite radical technique here: she translates six passages of Mann's German not into English, but rather into French, which enables her to indicate the T/V interplay in the scene, and in one instance inserts additional information which enables her to bring out the linguistic processes at work: '"*Toujours ce tutoyer*" ' (559). At the same time, the adoption of French discourse creates a direct link back to the Walpurgis scene some three hundred pages earlier, maintaining the unreal character of the situation. Indeed, Lowe-Porter adopts the compensatory technique of inserting a further sentence which explicitly makes this point: 'And Hans Castorp answered as he had vowed and dreamed: *"Tu l'a su,"* he said' (558). In this scene once again, Lowe-Porter reverts on one occasion to the 'thou' (559). Woods, meanwhile, employs a quite different technique: first-naming. He inserts Clawdia's first name in four positions (it does not appear in Mann's text at this point). On the scale of address modes, as noted above, this use of first name appears to amplify the intimate status of the discourse, suggesting the degree of Castorp's self-abandonment. However, during one later exchange between the two, Woods goes a step further: he also introduces first-naming in the opposite direction: '"That's not a stupid way to put it, Hans"' (588), something that Mann does not do at all in his text. It is difficult to assess the force of this strategy. It seems in Woods' text as if Clawdia uses 'Hans' to Castorp (she uses it three times, on the first occasion in combination with his surname) not as the first name of romantic adulation, but as the first name of friendship: it occurs in the exchange during which she proposes a pact of friendship with him, a process which culminates in the highly ambivalent *'russischer Kuß'* (831). In this latter position, too, Lowe-Porter occasionally translates into French (595ff.).

Viewed in the context of the symbolic significance of Castorp's sustained *'Duzen'* of Clawdia Chauchat, which is rendered by the translators in various ways, the protagonist's adoption of the *'Sie'* form vis-à-vis Clawdia following the death of Peeperkorn is an important move. The unexpected and dramatic shift in modes of address is, at this stage, the only indication of the development in their relations, and thus takes on great literary significance. Clawdia has called Castorp to Peeperkorn's deathbed, and addresses him in the polite form: '"*Sie hatten ein Anrecht darauf, daß ich Sie rufen ließ*"' (867). He replies without hesitation: '"*Es war sehr gütig von Ihnen*"'. The new quality of the relationship – a conscious distancing from what Clawdia calls *'unsere Torheit'* – is confirmed by the fact that Castorp is now able to give her the *'Stirnkuss'* he declined during his period of infatuation. As Kurzke comments, the kiss marks the final stage in the process of the *'Enterotisierung'* of their relations (Kurzke 2010: 190). Both translators, recognizing the import of this scene, resort to metalinguistic strategies at this point.

Lowe-Porter has: '"It was kind of you", he answered, "and you are right." He availed himself of the third person plural as used by the peoples of the cultured West' (624), while Woods writes: '"Very kind of you," he said, adopting formal pronouns himself, "and it was the correct thing to do"', 556). Lowe-Porter's addition here 'as used by the peoples of the cultured West' explicitates the link between this statement and the earlier discussion on modes of address, underlining the magnitude of the move which has been made. Lowe-Porter here echoes a number of references in the text to the notion of the 'civilized', 'cultured' or 'educated' West, which is set up by Settembrini as the antithesis of the wild East, associated with force, tyranny, superstition, barbarism and lethargy, and she uses the same formulation later in Settembrini's farewell to Castorp (712). The two versions of Peeperkorn's '*Brüderschaft des Du*' once again highlight the key divergence between the strategies of the translators, and also illustrate the intractability of the task facing them. Woods has the lexico-grammatical reference 'brotherhood of informal pronouns', while Lowe-Porter prefers the obsolete pronoun 'the brotherly thou' (565).

One final aspect of address behaviour in *Der Zauberberg* deserves attention, which functions quite apart from the internal discourse processes between characters involved in the action. In the text, the narrator frequently shifts perspective on the action, moving tantalizingly between omniscience and limitation, proximity and distance, and on numerous occasions enters deictically into the fictional world (the use of the inclusive '*wir*', of the '*hier oben*'). At the end of the text – for the first time – he addresses Castorp directly, switching from third person narration, in which he acts as an observer despite personal involvement ('*Da ist unser Bekannter, da ist Hans Castorp!*', 993), to a closing valediction which is notable for its ambivalence ('*Lebewohl, Hans Castorp*', 994). In this narrative apostrophe, the narrator resumes a series of motifs from the opening paragraph of the '*Vorsatz*', addressing his 'acquaintance' this time in the '*du*' form rather than reporting in the third person. In the final paragraph of her version, Lowe-Porter resumes the use of 'thou' – one paragraph later than Thomas Mann – and applies it for the first time with complete consistency, responding to the archaism of Mann's diction in his last paragraph ('*Fahr wohl – du lebest nun oder bleibest! Deine Aussichten sind schlecht*', 994): 'Farewell – and if thou livest or diest. Thy prospects are poor' (716). She uses forms of the archaic pronoun ten times in seven sentences. The elevated tone of her paragraph, with its marked word order ('will last yet many a sinful year'), subject-complement inversion ('Moments there were'), and archaic verb forms ('couldst', 'tookest') creates a finale which takes on a markedly poetic and apocalyptic tone (congruent with Mann's '*Weltfest des Todes*', '*Fieberbrunst*') and moves coherently towards the pretentiousness of the closing 'FINIS OPERIS'. Newmark praises this as 'a beautiful lyrical translation' (2000: 908). Lowe-Porter's 'thou' appears here not as a marker of familiarity, but rather as a quasi-Biblical mode of address, which amplifies one stylistic dimension of Mann's paragraph. The original author, in fact, mixes registers at this point, combining archaisms (syntactic structures such as '*worein du gerissen bist*', '*Abenteuer im Fleische*') with neologisms ('*Sündenjährchen*', '*Körperunzucht*') and almost informal elements ('*davonkommen*', '*lassen wir ziemlich unbekümmert die Frage offen*'). Lowe-Porter's technique here prefigures the style she was to adopt for the *Joseph* tetralogy, where she consistently employs a pseudo-archaic diction, characterized by similarly obsolete verb morphologies, syntactic structures and lexical forms. In her translation of Mann's monumental tetralogy, Lowe-Porter uses the 'thou' form consistently for Mann's '*du*' between members of the same ethnic community, employing the 'you' form in plural contexts (where Mann has '*ihr*') and also for individual address situations between members of different ethnic-religious groups. In his version of the Joseph novels, Woods by contrast uses 'you' in combination with modern verb forms throughout, commenting in his Introduction that Lowe-Porter limits 'herself, and Mann, to a diction modeled on the King James Bible [...] But it is not Mann's language' (xv). The latter Woods describes as 'an exuberant hodgepodge, happily at home with both anachronisms and archaisms, now elegantly sublime, now comically coarse.'

At the end of *Der Zauberberg*, Woods provides an unmarked version of the closing paragraphs, avoiding archaisms completely and compensating for the '*du*' in Mann's paragraph via the insertion of a 'Hans' at the beginning of the last section. This technique raises the same question as the use of first-naming elsewhere in the text: throughout, Mann refers to his protagonist exclusively by first and last name combined. This form of reference is striking in Mann's text, since all other characters are referred to by Christian name only (Joachim), last name only (Settembrini, Naphta), title plus surname (*Frau Stöhr, Hofrat Behrens*) or title only (*Der Hofrat*). Mann sustains the '*Hans Castorp*' form of reference until the very end, i.e. to the penultimate paragraph of the novel. The use of Christian name only, limited otherwise in Mann's text to Castorp's address of Clawdia, is thus a clearly marked feature in Mann's text. The difference between the two translations is especially evident in their versions of the final paragraph:

Farewell – and if thou livest or diest! Thy prospects are poor. The desperate dance, in which thy fortunes are caught up, will last yet many a sinful year; we should not care to set a high stake on thy life by the time it ends. We even confess that it is without great concern we leave the question open. Adventures of the flesh and in the spirit, while enhancing thy simplicity, granted thee to know in the	Farewell, Hans—whether you live or stay where you are! Your chances are not good. The wicked dance in which you are caught up will last many a little sinful year yet, and we would not wager much that you will come out whole. To be honest, we are not really bothered about leaving the question open. Adventures in the flesh and spirit, which enhanced and heightened your ordinariness,

spirit what in the flesh thou scarcely couldst have done. Moments there were, when out of death, and the rebellion of the flesh, there came to thee, as thou tookest stock of thyself, a dream of love. Out of this universal feast of death, out of this extremity of fever, kindling the rain-washed evening sky to a fiery glow, may it be that Love one day shall mount? (Lowe-Porter, 716)	allowed you to survive in the spirit what you probably will not survive in the flesh. There were moments when, as you "played king," you saw the intimation of a dream of love rising up out of death and this carnal body. And out of this worldwide festival of death, this ugly rutting fever that inflames the rainy evening sky all round—will love someday rise up out of this, too? (Woods, 706)

Doktor Faustus, Felix Krull

The second novel in which modes of address assume a key thematic significance is *Doktor Faustus*, where once again they are an important projection of the erotic theme. Where the Castorp-Chauchat relationship gained an implied homoerotic dimension through various leitmotifs and the association of Chauchat with Hippe (underpinned biographically by the Wiliram Timpe episode), the Leverkühn-Schwerdtfeger relationship is more explicitly cast as homoerotic, and echoes the Paul Ehrenberg chapter in Mann's life. The narrator, Serenus Zeitblom, is jealously protective of his unique and long-standing relationship with the composer Adrian Leverkühn, who is presented as a charismatic and fascinating figure but is, at the same time, cold, cynical and remote. Zeitblom is intensely proud to be the protagonist's only '*Duzfreund*'. He is envious of other suitors for Leverkühn's affections, such as Rüdiger Schildknapp and Rudolf Schwerdtfeger, and monitors their efforts to win the composer's friendship closely and grudgingly (and, in the view of many commentators, not without sublimated desires of his own). For the narrator, patterns of address are the key indicator of intimacy, and he observes the way in which his rivals seek to exploit them with an enormous attention to pragmalinguistic detail: hardly surprisingly, in view of his philological background. The struggle for Leverkühn's affections is thus presented as a battle for the right to use first names and informal patterns of address. Thus we are told that Zeitblom and Leverkühn have been on '*du*' terms since their early childhood (*GW* 6: 229), sharing a '*Kindheits-Du*' which gives the former an advantage over Schildknapp: '*Kaum brauche ich hinzuzufügen, dass sie einander allezeit mit Nachnamen und mit "Sie" anredeten*' (229). The violinist Schwerdtfeger is the only one who succeeds in advancing to more familiar terms with the protagonist. This is achieved only as a result of persistent attempts which are long resisted by Leverkühn, including a *'karnevalistisches Du'*, an attempt to achieve familiarity during a musical soirée, and a visit to the sick Leverkühn which is described in some detail by the narrator:

> [er] redete Adrian zu Beginn seines Besuches zweimal mit Du an, um sich erst beim dritten Mal, da jener nun einmal nicht darauf einging, zu verbessern und es beim Vornamen mit dem Sie sein Bewenden haben zu lassen. Gewissermaßen zum Trost und experimentierender Weise nannte auch Adrian ihn gelegentlich mit Vornamen, wenn nicht in der traulich verkleinerten, bei Schwerdtfeger allgemein üblichen Form, so doch in der vollen, also Rudolf, kam aber gleich wieder davon ab (462).

Leverkühn's reluctance to move to familiar terms is an index of his inaccessibility, while Schwerdtfeger's determination to penetrate the protective shield of impersonality is implicitly articulated as an assault, an *'Anschlag der Zutraulichkeit'* (467). Only after an intimate correspondence and a joint stay in Hungary – the implied transition to homosexual relations – is the familiar form of discourse established: *'Als sie von dort zurückkehrten, erfreute sich Rudolf sich des Prärogativs, das bisher, von Kindheits wegen, ausschließlich mir gehört hatte: er und Adrian nannten einander du'* (552). It is, as Zeitblom comments, to prove an *'unseliges "Du"'* (553). Schwerdtfeger is murdered by a jealous lover after becoming embroiled in a romantic mission on Leverkühn's behalf.

The way in which the two translators handle the thematically significant interplay of naming systems and pronominal forms of address provides in this case too an interesting insight into their technique. Woods maintains the approach he had adopted in his earlier versions, providing stylistic information on the quality of the pronouns used (formal, intimate, familiar), thus shifting the issue of address to a metalinguistic, almost extraneous level. This procedure is at its most awkward in the latter instance cited above, where Woods has to define further the 'you' which he uses at this point: 'Luckless "you"! Neither did that familiar "you" befit the blue-eyed inconsequentiality that had won it for itself, nor could he who had designed to grant it help avenging the abasement [...]' (Woods 1997: 437). Lowe-Porter adopts a more radical procedure here. In a dramatic abandonment of her earlier translation solutions, she retains the German *'du'* and *'Sie'* forms on all six occasions where the dichotomy is thematized. She does so without notes or explanation, and without additional intratextual explicitation of any kind: her strategy is thus markedly foreignizing, assuming on the part of the reader the ability to interpret what is going on. She sees this technique justified, presumably, by an early intratextual reference in the original to the combination of familiar pronoun and first naming:

'It was the time in which our *du* was rooted, the time when he too must have called me by my Christian name.' (Lowe-Porter 1968: 23). Henceforth, she retains the '*du*' and '*Sie*' without comment, translating the '*Kindheits-Du*' with 'our childhood tie, our "*du*"' (171) – a subtle form of explicitation – and even referring at the point of transition between Leverkühn and Schwerdtfeger to the fact that they were now '*per du*'. (461). It is, then, logical that she should write on the last occasion: 'Unhappy "*Du*"!'. But Lowe-Porter has not abandoned the 'thou' and 'ye' forms entirely in her version. In the conversation between the Devil and Leverkühn, in which the former adopts for long passages the antiquated style of the chapbooks, she initially retains the differentiation between the Devil's use of 'thou' (Leverkühn protests: 'Who says thou to me?', 223) and Leverkühn's responses in the 'ye' as a marker of the historical register, significantly amplifying the archaism of Mann's text:

> "I," he says. "I, by your leave. Oh, thou meanest because thou sayst to nobody thou, not even to thy jester gentilman, but only to the trusty play-fere, he who clepes thee by the first name but not thou him. No matter." (217)

Woods also employs a historical register for these passages, but does not imitate the forms of address, once again preferring instead to introduce an adverbial of manner ('"Who speaks familiarly with me?"' 239).

The final text in which modes of address assume thematic significance is the English *Confessions of Felix Krull, Confidence Man*. *The Beloved Returns/Lotte in Weimar* and *The Holy Sinner* are not of interest in the present context. In the Krull novel, we see once again asymmetry and instability of address forms, and it is interesting to note how these are handled by a translator who undertook only one translation commission for Knopf: Denver Linley. In this novel, too, linguistic behaviour is an important aspect of the text: not because it functions as a symbolic index of underlying thematic concerns, but because rhetorical facility is a key attribute of the manipulative pseudo-bourgeois protagonist, who prizes linguistic decorum as an instrument in his repertoire of simulation and dissembling. Krull's determination to maintain distance and propriety in his interpersonal dealings results in a number of situations in which he persistently declines to adopt familiar forms despite pressure from his interlocutors (Stanko and the watchmaker). Thus he seeks to insist that his colleague Stanko should show him the appropriate courtesy in their exchanges ('"*Wollen Sie mich, bitte, nicht duzen*"', *GW* 7: 401 becomes '"Don't speak familiarly with me, please"', Linley 1955: 119), and – noting the consistency with which his interlocutor uses the '*du*' form – clings doggedly to the '*Sie*'. This sustained asymmetry is obscured in the translation, as is that in the exchange between Krull and the watchmaker who buys his stolen jewellery. Most interesting is the scene with Madame Houpflé, who demands that Krull (whom she casts in the role of Hermes) should debase her: her sexual subservience is, then, reflected in the linguistic roles adopted in the scene: *'"Duze mich derb zu meiner Erniedrigung! J'adore d'être humiliée! Je l'adore! Oh, je t'adore, petit esclave stupide qui me déshonore"'* (442). Houpflé's intermittent use of French in this exchange enables the translator to retain the transition to familiar forms ('"Call me *tu*! [...] Be familiar with me, degrade me!"' (155), and by inserting additional references to the French T form, the translator is able at least to suggest that Krull has assumed the desired role, an assumption which is reinforced by Krull's consistent use of her first name (Diane).

Conclusion

The variety of solutions adopted by translators in response to the anisomorphism of address pronouns effectively demonstrates the challenges translators face when confronted with interlingual incompatibilities. The techniques employed vary from direct transfer of source-language forms at one end of the scale to deletion of all differentiation at the other. Our discussion has demonstrated that the absence of pronominal distinctions in English constitutes an 'impossibility of translation' only in structural terms. For the most part, the English versions of Thomas Mann's texts demonstrate how compensatory strategies are able to redress formal asymmetries between languages in a functionally effective manner. We have seen that in selecting options the translators are generally responsive to contextual and cotextual clues. Indeed, they have to be: the complexity of address modes as a layer of extra pragmatic significance in literary texts means that the social and individual variables which condition the behaviour of participants in the discourse must be viewed within an overall interpretation of the interpersonal dynamics unfolding in texts. Furthermore, as we have noted, the linguistic phenomenon of address can – and in Mann's works often does – assume symbolic significance (beyond the level of 'characterization') as a key index of literary meaning, generating important thematic networks and pointing to the author's underlying intellectual concerns. It is, in short, leitmotivic. On this level, it is perhaps inevitable that there will be distortion, dilution or even loss of coordinates visible in the original, and to that extent it is extremely difficult for the translators to offer access to the full meaning potential of the source text.

What are the consequences of the incompatibilities in thematic terms? As we have seen, the address reduction or amplification occasioned by the under- or overdetermination of pragmatic indicators in the translations impacts subtly on attitudinal nuances. Thus Woods' oversubscription to the technique of first-naming modifies the quality of the Castorp-Chauchat and Castorp-Settembrini exchanges at decisive points in the text, colouring our reading in ways which diverge from the original. Furthermore, his extensive use of metalinguistic explicitation adds a level of extraneous lexicogrammatical detail to the text which is absent in the original, and is perhaps anomalous in a fictional text. Lowe-Porter's recurrent use of antiquated pronouns, meanwhile, frequently strains the naturalness of her versions, diverging from the norms of English operative at the time and infusing the text with an at times archaic quality. Her most interesting intervention in strategic terms, though, is her rendition of parts of Mann's text not in English, but in French. However, this radical modification (a complete substitution of semiotic systems) is imbued with intratextual coherence by the heteroglossic qualities evident in certain scenes in Mann's text. There could hardly be a clearer illustration of a translator's departure from superficial equivalence in the interest of functional efficacy.

8 Syntactic form and literary meaning in translation

Preliminary remarks

In much recent literary translation research, the focus has been on the broader historical perspective, on systems, norms and institutional contexts. Where literary Translation Studies has dealt with actual processes of textual transfer on the micro-level, it has tended to concentrate on phenomena such as lexical semantics, contrastive grammatical typologies, pragmatic features, and rhetorical devices such as metaphor and wordplay, while much less attention has been devoted to questions of syntactic structure. In non-literary Translation Studies, on the other hand, the consideration of syntactic questions has a long tradition, with a strong (and generally prescriptive) focus on the shifts and transpositions necessitated by interlingual incompatibilities (Albrecht 2005; Stolze 2008). Thus, in his pioneering work on literary translation, Levy deals somewhat peremptorily with questions of sentence structure (Levy 1969). And years later, Lefevere does the same, viewing syntax as a linguistic given that carries little stylistic value, rather than as an area of significant translational optionality: 'Syntax is perhaps the most stringent and least flexible of all the constraints translators must work under since it regulates the order of the words to be translated and because few liberties can be taken with that order before the text veers into the unintelligible' (Lefevere 1992a: 78). The issue of syntax in literary translation has remained underrepresented in the field, as can be seen in the twelve volumes published by the Göttingen group, as well as in the leading academic journals. This neglect is somewhat surprising in view of the fact that intralingual linguistic studies of literature have long focused on sentence structure as a semiotic system (Fowler 1996; Leech and Short 2007). In stylistics, the fundamental assumption that literary texts create meaning (partly) via the semanticization of form has led to extensive investigations of processes of segmentation, sequencing and relative salience – the linear organization and hierarchization of information in the sentence – as primary contributors to textual meaning (Jeffries and McIntyre 2010, Chapter 2).

In the present chapter, I would like to consider some of the interpretive implications that arise from the interlingual transfer of syntactic structures in the literary text, using two translations of the opening of Mann's *Der Tod in Venedig* as an illustration. Even the most cursory glance at a translation corpus shows that translators – subject to language-typological constraints in syntactic possibilities (for English-German see Hawkins 1986; König and Gast 2007) – are generally concerned to mirror the sentence structures of the source text in the syntactic composition of their target versions. Deviations from this principle are generally criticized on normative grounds as a distortion of key stylistic values. For example, Levy writes: '*Beim Übersetzen geht es darum, die Grundtendenz des zu übersetzenden Textes zu wahren bzw. Abweichungen an den Stellen des Textes zu meiden, wo die syntaktische Geschlossenheit oder Auflockerung stilistisch wirksam ist.*' (Levy 1969: 120). However, where the degree of syntactical organization in a text is particularly high, questions of transferability inevitably arise, and changes in patterns of information structure can impinge decisively on the potential meanings of the text. I focus here on Mann's Venice story because this text has frequently been singled out as an example of extreme syntactic sophistication (Frizen 1993: 87ff.). My selection of the opening passage of the story, which introduces the protagonist Gustav von Aschenbach, requires little justification, as the narrative onset to a linguistically complex and highly structured text.

The linguistic sophistication of Mann's writing, and the implications it has for translation, have been outlined in previous chapters of the present study. As was pointed out in Chapter 4, much of that sophistication derives from his use of expansive syntactic structures – both complex and compound – which play a key role in the generation of meaning. Yet it is possible to read studies of English Thomas Mann translations without gaining any sense that his structures are anything more than pure form, a virtuoso display of verbal dexterity that must be copied as closely as possible. As noted earlier, discussion of the English versions of Thomas Mann's works has largely exhausted itself in an extended diatribe against the established, 'authorized' versions of Helen Tracy Lowe-Porter. Beyond a doubt, Lowe-Porter's versions are marred by numerous overt errors and distortions, in many cases born out of a simple misunderstanding of the original. To that extent, they are clearly 'badly flawed versions' (Buck 1996: 918). But even in the case of the two most frequently identified structural modifications in her *Death in Venice* – her reversal of the order of clauses in the long and much-discussed sentence which opens Chapter 2 of the story, and her omission of the last sentence of the text's penultimate paragraph – commentators have criticized the changes without seeking to assess their impact. Although it has frequently been referred to, the sensitive and non-hortatory early work by Koch-Emmery on Lowe-Porter's handling of Mann's syntax, for example, has never been followed up in any detail. There, it is rightly pointed out that the translator faced with 'a word texture so closely knit, so deliberately shaped' tends to concentrate 'on detail, on word-translation, but is inclined to overlook the major principle that underlies the sentence structure in the original' (Koch-Emmery 1952/3: 276).

The widely held view that Lowe-Porter tends to undertake significant amendments to Mann's syntax is undoubtedly correct. Time and again in her translations, she reduces the structural sophistication of the original texts (Horton 2010). She does this as a matter of translation strategy, in the conviction that English norms will not tolerate the sheer dimensions or complexity of units that German allows. As noted in Chapter 3, she makes this very point in her essay 'On translating Thomas Mann' (Lowe-Porter 1996). Lowe-Porter also undertakes extensive redistribution operations, and in so doing goes much further than would seem necessary to generate the simpler structures which she sees as constitutive of English textual norms. Indeed, in all her versions, she recasts the sentences of the originals to a far greater extent than any other translator of Thomas Mann's works. But her strategy differs from that of her fellow translators only in degree. Even Luke, whose translations are often cited as especially close, accurate and idiomatic renderings of Mann's texts – and more specifically as a significant improvement on Lowe-Porter's versions – does not shy away from comprehensive restructuring. The extent to which structures can be replicated (idiomatically) across languages will naturally remain subject to personal judgment, intuition and non-empirical assumptions concerning the limits of acceptability. Notions of what is 'equivalent' will inevitably vary, and Luke's use of the term in his criticism of Lowe-Porter raises more questions than it answers: 'Because of the inherent differences between the languages, a translator's equivalent English sentences should not try to follow the structure of Mann's German sentences too closely, or they will cease to be equivalent' (Luke 1988: l). The degree of divergence in a translated text must be seen in terms of the translation's potential to provide a view of the stylistic values of the original, which in itself depends critically on the semantic values attributed to the linguistic structure of that original via a process of interpretation. It is not the surface structure of the text, but rather its 'cognitive core', that matters in the process of translation (Gutt 2005).

The opening paragraph of Mann's *Der Tod in Venedig*

I would like to consider the opening paragraph of *Der Tod in Venedig* as a case in point, focusing on the two established translations cited above. Mann's first paragraph reads as follows:

> *Gustav Aschenbach oder von Aschenbach, wie seit seinem fünfzigsten Geburtstag amtlich sein Name lautete, hatte an einem Frühlingsnachmittag des Jahres 19.., das unserem Kontinent monatelang eine so gefahrdrohende Miene zeigte, von seiner Wohnung in der Prinzregentenstraße zu München aus allein einen weiteren Spaziergang unternommen. Überreizt von der schwierigen und gefährlichen, eben jetzt eine höchste Behutsamkeit, Umsicht, Eindringlichkeit und Genauigkeit des Willens erfordernden Arbeit der Vormittagsstunden, hatte der Schriftsteller dem Fortschwingen des produzierenden Triebwerks in seinem Innern, jenem 'motus animi continuus', worin nach Cicero das Wesen der Beredsamkeit besteht, auch nach der Mittagsmahlzeit nicht Einhalt zu tun vermocht und den entlastenden Schlummer nicht gefunden, der ihm, bei zunehmender Abnutzbarkeit seiner Kräfte, einmal untertags so nötig war. So hatte er bald nach dem Tee das Freie gesucht, in der Hoffnung, daß Luft und Bewegung ihn wiederherstellen und ihm zu einem ersprießlichen Abend verhelfen würden.*

(GW 8: 444)

Some purely quantitative data may be cited to provide an initial indication of the linguistic characteristics of the passage, since this can shed light on one of the most celebrated features of Mann's sentence structure: its length. The paragraph consists of three sentences composed of a total of 142 words (44–71–27). The average sentence length here is thus 47.67 words, almost twice as high as the 24.74 calculated for *Der Tod in Venedig* in its entirety (Hassan 1967: 75). Even by the standards of the first chapter of the novella as a whole – which has a greater sentence length than any other of the chapters, with 39.3 words per sentence – the opening paragraph shows a pronounced degree of sentential expansion. Overall, sentence length in *Der Tod in Venedig* is slightly higher than the average for Mann's short prose narratives (which Hassan puts at 21.59 words), and the sentence length in the first chapter of *Der Tod in Venedig* is higher than even that of Mann's later novels. Statistical analyses of Mann's texts have established a gradual increase in sentence length in the writer's oeuvre, from 21.6 in *Buddenbrooks* to 32.9 words in the *Joseph* tetralogy and 34.7 in *Doktor Faustus* (Lawson 2000: 164).

Such information is helpful as a general guideline, and the application of readability formulas can provide useful statistical information on the relative understandability of texts (see Chapter 4). Thus the

Syntactic form and literary meaning in translation   203

lexical variety of the passage (the ratio of different words to the total number of words) is 75.5 per cent and the LIX 'readability' index shows a score of 81.23. Of the 142 words, 77 are content words: the lexical density (according to the common definition, i.e. number of content words divided by the total number of words × 100) is thus 54 per cent. However, such formulas are surface-oriented and purely mechanical. To gain a fuller grasp of the mental processability of text, consideration of deeper syntactic and semantic structures is required. The specific linguistic texture of the introductory section of Mann's text is not, after all, the product of quantitative features alone. In terms of its qualitative intricacy, too, the first paragraph of *Der Tod in Venedig* is striking. The high level of sophistication derives principally from four sources:

a. Hypotaxis. The paragraph contains a number of complex clause structures. The first sentence (44 words) contains two subordinate clauses, the second (71 words) three, and the shorter third sentence (27 words) has one subordinate clause. The clauses are of different types: finite and non-finite, adverbial, relative, participial and complementary. In some cases they are inserted as anticipatory constituents, in others as trailing structures. The sequence 2–3–1 in terms of subordinate clauses underlines the weight of the central sentence, and the paragraph closes with a much shorter sentence of reduced syntactical complexity. This latter sentence is the only one with a short initial main clause uninterrupted by retarding parenthetical constituents.

b. Complex nominal groups. Virtually all the head nouns in the three sentences are qualified by extensive pre-posed or post-posed modifying structures. The nouns '*Gustav Aschenbach*', '*des Jahres 19..*', '*Triebwerk in seinem Innern*', and '*Schlummer*' are especially heavily postmodified, while '*der Schriftsteller*' and '*Arbeit*' are preceded by very extensive modifiers. The paragraph is, then, a clear example of the heavily adjectival, attributive style which is considered typical of Thomas Mann (Schröder 1972). The second sentence shows especially extensive modification, while the final sentence is again marked by the virtual absence of qualifying structures (only one adjective). Much of the modifying information contained in these three sentences occurs in the form of parenthetical elements which interrupt the flow of the main clauses in each case. Far more than the mere presence of subordinated constituents, the extent of modification serves to increase the intricacy of the text via large-scale noun phrases.

c. Frequency of adverbial structures. The syntax of Mann's opening passage is characterized by a high frequency of adverbials. The first sentence contains seven, the second sentence has five, and the third sentence has three. These adverbials fulfil a retarding function, delaying the introduction of the main verb – and thus the completion of the semantic unit – in each case. The first sentence is particularly marked in this regard, inserting extensive adverbials of time and place, and an adverb of manner (*'allein'*), between the auxiliary verb and the direct object of its main clause, while the parenthetical *'wie'* clause contains two adverbials between the subject and the auxiliary verb. Two adverbials in this opening sentence – *'amtlich'* and *'allein'* – are placed in marked positions (Rossbach 1988: 243). The heavy second sentence, meanwhile, exploits a different retarding device, fronting a highly complex (past) participial structure in which the head noun *'Arbeit'* is premodified by two adjectives and a (present) participial modifier containing four object nouns before the main clause follows. The latter itself features an extensive object, a further adverbial of time, and a relative clause containing two further adverbial structures. The third sentence, finally, opens with the causal adverb *'so'*, inserts a short adverbial of time into the main clause, and closes with the extensive subordinated adverbial construction headed *'in der Hoffnung'*. In this third sentence, the principle of retardation is abandoned: the introductory *'so'* signals cohesive resolution by underlining the explanatory force of the preceding sentence, and the greater part of the information contained in this shorter structure appears as a trailing adverbial constituent following the main verb *'gesucht'*, rather than as an anticipatory or interpolated structure inserted before the main verb.

d. Lexical variety. The above-mentioned syntactic features contribute to a style in which numerous pieces of information are held in view in an integrated form, rather than presented in a cumulative sequence. The structure is dense. The same applies to the lexical composition of the passage. Particularly striking in this connection is the second sentence, with its accumulation of abstract adjectives and nouns qualifying *'Arbeit der Vormittagsstunden'*. The four nouns *'Behutsamkeit'*, *'Umsicht'*, *'Eindringlichkeit'*, and *'Genauigkeit'* are all semantically close, and constitute an example of the process of cumulative lexical definition that is so typical of Mann's writing. There are five *'-keit'* nouns in the second sentence alone. Finally, the cohesion of the passage is tight. The name of the subject Gustav Aschenbach is indicated only in the first sentence, and is subsequently substituted via nominal variation (*'der Schriftsteller'*) and by a pronominal reference. Aschenbach appears in the central subject role in each of the three sentences.

After this initial characterization I would like to turn to the qualitative effects – the stylistic value – of Mann's opening paragraph. It is this, after all, rather than the formal structures in themselves which will typically be considered important in the process of translation. The text opens in the formal stylistic register that is to be sustained throughout. Its highly wrought style bears, as Mann himself stressed in a letter to Paul Amann dated 10 September 1915 (*DüD* 1: 406), unmistakable features of a neoclassical diction through which the narrator mimics

– and even parodies – Aschenbach's own erudite style, to which the narrator later applies such epithets as *'das Mustergültig-Feststehende, Geschliffen-Herkömmliche, Erhaltende, Formelle, selbst Formelhafte'* (GW 8: 456). The complex structure of the first paragraph allows the author to integrate a large amount of information in a carefully sequenced and segmented exposition to the text as a whole, and from the very first sentence onwards, the narrative voice orders and weights segments in a consciously hierarchical manner. Structurally, the essential feature of the opening paragraph is its tripartite segmentation. The relative length and complexity of the three sentences is carefully balanced, ordering the various elements of the exposition in a rhythmical process of expansion and contraction.

The first sentence is marked by a high degree of deictic density, comprehensively locating the narrative in time and space. In its structure $SA_1(A)(A)VA_2(A)A_3A_4O$, its sequence of adverbials provides the kind of situational information ('circumstantia') typically elicited in classical rhetoric via the determinate questions *quis, quid, quando, ubi, cur, quem,* etc., which have found their way into modern communication theory through the Lasswell formula. The sentence sets the stage for an apparently realistic narrative unfolding within clearly defined coordinates. The text presents this information in a dense package in which the narrative voice, opening with the extended subject, twice interrupts its flow before the predicate of the sentence is revealed. We learn about the 'who' (Aschenbach's private and public personas, approximate age), the 'when' (the time of day and year, an indication of the historical situation), the 'where' (the precise location of the action), and 'how' (alone) of the situation – in that order – before the 'what' (a long walk) is defined. Only the 'why' is left unanswered at this point, pointing forward to the third sentence. With this opening, the authorial voice is apparently preparing the reader for a narrative in the nineteenth-century realist tradition. Yet even at this stage, what appears to be a documentary naturalism is undermined by hints of disturbance and inconsistency, undermining the reader's expectations (Adolphs 1985: 23–30). Aschenbach's name is immediately qualified by an alternative definition, the year remains strangely unspecified, and the historical context is referred to only nebulously, personified in a metaphor of threat and unease (*'gefahrdrohende Miene'*). Aschenbach's loneliness is placed in a position of some prominence by the placement of the adverbial *'allein'*, and he sets out on a walk which is described as *'weiter'*, perhaps suggesting the need for relief and release. Furthermore, the narrator, who launches his exposition in a spirit of objective description, quickly introduces an element of personal involvement. He uses the inclusive first-person pronoun *'unser'* in relation to the continent of Europe, and inserts the subjective and appellative intensifier *'so'* in referring to the threatening clouds that characterize the political situation. His position of detachment begins to look ambivalent, as he mixes an authorial perspective of distance from the action with an element of proximity to it (Cohn 1983; Reed 1994; Lorenzen-Peth 2008). Much of the expository information in the opening sequence is sandwiched between the auxiliary verb and the main verb, which is the last word in the sentence. The sentence opens and closes with references to Aschenbach's private activities, embedding the historical-geographical information in the extensive central adverbials.

The long second sentence shifts the focus from a quasi-objective determination of the situational context to the inner life of the protagonist, whose personal crisis – the two negated main verbs (*'Einhalt tun'*, *'finden'*) explicitly formulate his inability to control developments – reflects the threat suggested in the world outside (a parallelism is established in the modified recurrence *'gefahrvoll'*-*'gefährlich'*). In this sentence, the narrator gives us access from a position of external omniscience to the protagonist's mental processes, doing so through what appears to be a purely homodiegetic process of narration. However, here too a suggestion of the character's own viewpoint on the narration is again introduced through the adverbial *'eben jetzt'*. This phrase introduces a perspective of actuality into the remote narrative time, and points to the character's own assessment of the difficulties he faces in his work. It hints – like the introduction of another *'so'* in *'so nötig'*– at a personal, internal perspective within the text, and prepares the ground for the increasingly mimetic dimension of the narrative that is expressed through extensive free indirect discourse as the text progresses. The syntactic structure of this long sentence is, as outlined above, highly intricate, and might be held to have an iconic dimension. The principle of syntactical linearity is completely undermined here via the interdependencies Mann sets up. Indeed, it might not be going too far to suggest that the pressure under which Aschenbach finds himself is encapsulated syntactically. He, the subject (*'der Schriftsteller'*), is positioned after the highly complex introductory clause which defines his mental state and builds up an anticipatory syntactic pressure through the process of retardation. The syntax here appears to mirror both his mental stress and the elevated diction which, we learn later, is characteristic of his own writings. And the subject is positioned before the two (also complex) object clauses which describe his inability to find relief. The principle here is one of accumulation rather than addition, and the sentence ends on an unresolved moment of suspense. The *'Entlastung'*, which is so necessary for a man of his waning powers, is unattainable.

The third sentence completes the miniature drama of Aschenbach's mental state at the beginning of the story by providing the resolution.

It does so by referring back to the final section of the first sentence, now making explicit a connection the reader may well have inferred by filling in the gap between the first and second sentences. As we had suspected, the reason for Aschenbach's *'weiterer Spaziergang'* is the search for relief and restoration (*'wiederherstellen'*). In other words, this sentence functions as an exposition within the exposition, and retrospectively provides information that is required for a full understanding of what is going on. The macrotextual coherence of the opening paragraph is now completed, and is carefully underpinned by a sequence of time references. The first sentence states that Aschenbach takes a walk on a *'Frühlingsnachmittag'*. The second takes us back, referring to the work he found so frustrating during the *'Vormittagsstunden'* and the fact that he was unable to find relaxation even after the *'Mittagsmahlzeit'*. And the third tells us that he set out shortly after his *'Tee'*, explains the rationale of the *'weiterer Spaziergang'* of the first sentence (*'So hatte er ...'*) via the rather inflated circumlocution *'das Freie suchen'* (which also has a symbolic dimension, in its reference to freedom, release, the open), and looks forward in the conditional to the *'Abend'*. While the consistent use of the past perfect tense throughout the passage initially obscures the chronological relations of the three sentences – all the events are, at the moment of their introduction, undifferentiated anteriority, as later becomes clear – we now realize that the second and third sentences precede the first in terms of narrated time, in the sequence *'Vormittagsstunden – Mittagsmahlzeit – Tee – (Frühlings)Nachmittag'*. The third sentence thus rounds off the information of the first two. Yet while it resolves the details of the situation, it creates suspense about what will happen next. The past perfect structure of the opening paragraph (each sentence contains one *'hatte'*, which in the second sentence governs two participles) must, surely, lead us to the present time of the narrative, which will find expression in the preterite. This is indeed the case: after the continuation of the past perfect narration in the second paragraph, the use of the preterite *'erwartete'* brings the condensed report of the pre-story to the point where the action proper begins. At that point, yet another level of exposition comes to an end and we are brought to the present of the narrative: Aschenbach waits for the tram.

In their varying length and intricacy, the first three sentences of Mann's text are carefully weighted, and develop a striking rhythm and momentum. Creating an interplay of statement and qualification, progression and retardation, they might be held to create a symbolic syntactical reflection of the process of expansion and contraction (the systolic and diastolic) which is so central to the text, and which finds its most concise thematic symbol in Aschenbach's clenched fist. Constricted by his inability to progress with his work, Aschenbach seeks mental renewal in *'das Freie'*. Scenes and images of attempted escape (the walk, the holiday, the decision to change the location of his vacation, the abortive flight from Venice) and subsequent further entrapment permeate the story. The process of *'Ausweitung'* is invariably followed by one of *'Erstarrung'*, until final release is found in the *'Liebestod'* at the end (Frizen 1993: 28ff). The dualism of anticipation and resolution is, of course, explicit in the rhetorical organization of the discourse itself. The text opens in (apparently) detached reporting mode in the first sentence, raises questions and expectations by adumbrating problems in the second (*'Überreizt'*, *'schwierig und gefährlich*, *'Abnutzbarkeit seiner Kräfte'*), and provides the explicit resolution in the third. But the dualism of accumulation and release is also presented syntactically. As noted above, the first sentence with its 44 words is already long by Mann's standards. It is the only sentence of the three to contain an extended subject, and the other clause elements are relatively compact. The second (71 words), built around highly expanded modifying structures, is significantly more expansive, and features a single-noun substitute subject, while its other constituents are heavily modified. Finally, the third, with just 28 words, is almost two-thirds shorter, and is virtually free of modifications.

Lowe-Porter's version

I have not dwelt in such detail on the opening passage of Mann's work because I wish to suggest that it constitutes an inviolable object of determinate meaning against which any translation must be measured, and will necessarily fail. Indeed, the interpretive inferences I have made between structures which are visible in the text and their potential to suggest literary significance within the unfolding narrative are open to debate, and other readers may well make different inferences. The selection of features for analysis, the assessment of the salience of those features relative to others, the implicatures derived from them – all of these variables are subject to individual judgement. Even the most mechanistic of analytical procedures is ultimately unable to circumvent the interpretive phase, where the observer is 'weighing and weighting different parts of the evidence, bringing together diverse features to show how they form a coherent, integrated pattern, and making judgements about the significance of such patterns in relation to the context of the work as a whole' (Halliday 1983: x). Through their high level of organization, Mann's sophisticated structures certainly invite us to seek 'extra significance'. They create different points of focus, develop areas of relative salience and prominence, and throw up ambiguities and uncertainties. The connections I have made do, I believe, make sense within the text as a whole – but only in terms of the text as a whole. It would be misleading to suggest that communicative clues can be read off consecutively as they appear in the text. Their contribution to potential textual meaning is constituted only by the progressive establishment of suggestive patterns, and only becomes apparent through a process of hermeneutic inference and revision as we pass through the text. Bearing this in mind, it is instructive to turn now to Lowe-Porter's version of the text, with its extensive modifications.

Lowe-Porter replaces Mann's three sentences with five, and relocates large sections of information within the paragraph as a whole. She herself comments specifically on her reworking of this passage in a letter dated 30 March 1934 to the publisher Alfred A. Knopf (Thirlwall 1966: 31). Discussing fundamental approaches to translation, she states that she belongs to the school of translators who feel 'that it is insulting to an author who is worth translating to render his style into a sort of bastard English', and continues: 'As a matter of fact, in translating much of Dr Mann, I have felt it sensible to break up the sentences or even to transpose them – the beginning of *Death in Venice* is a good example.' Her paragraph reads thus:

> GUSTAVE ASCHENBACH – or von Aschenbach, as he had been known officially since his fiftieth birthday – had set out alone from his house in Prince Regent Street, Munich, for an extended walk. It was a spring afternoon in that year of grace 19-, when Europe sat upon the anxious seat beneath a menace that hung over its head for months. Aschenbach had sought the open soon after tea. He was overwrought by a morning of hard, nerve-taxing work, work which had not ceased to exact his uttermost in the way of sustained concentration, conscientiousness, and tact; and after the noon meal found himself powerless to check the onward sweep of the productive mechanism within him, that *motus animi continuus* in which, according to Cicero, eloquence resides. He had sought but not found relaxation in sleep – though the wear and tear upon his system had come to make a daily nap more and more imperative – and now undertook a walk, in the hope that air and exercise might send him back refreshed to a good evening's work.
>
> (Lowe-Porter 1955: 7)

This passage has been singled out for comment in a number of previous discussions of Lowe-Porter's work (Hayes 1974; Sixel 1994; Barter 2007). Most of the attention devoted to it hitherto has focused on the lexical features of her version, as well as on her additions and deletions. Thus commentators have dwelt on the spelling of the protagonist's name, the translation of the street name, the insertion of the 'year of grace', the somewhat expansive 'sat upon the anxious seat beneath a menace that hung over its head for months', the substitution of 'Europe' for *'unser Kontinent'*, the use of the word 'house' for *'Wohnung'*. However, the impact of Lowe-Porter's transpositions on the reader's processing of the text has hardly been explored. It is on the structure of the passage, rather than its lexical composition, that I would like to focus in the following observations.

The redistribution of information in this version is so extensive that it can be aligned with Mann's original only through careful comparison. Lowe-Porter clearly subordinates any attempt at syntactical replication to her superordinate aim of creating a more easily readable text in the target language. Superficially, she certainly achieves this in terms of ease of mental processing, as the application of standard readability measures to her opening paragraph shows. Her version of the opening paragraph is significantly longer than Mann's. Its five sentences (one of them punctuated with a semicolon which marks the division between two coordinated main clauses) contain 175 words, producing an average sentence length of 35 words. If the highly wrought style of Mann's opening is to be seen as a reflection (or parody) of Aschenbach's own diction, then Lowe-Porter's reduction clearly denies the reader access to an important dimension of the text – at least in terms of surface-oriented measures. Thus, the LIX score for her version is 53.29, the lexical variety measure is 67.4 per cent, both of which are significantly lower than Mann's, while the lexical density is slightly lower, at 52.5 per cent.

However, Lowe-Porter's relocation of the various semantic units into independent sentences does not enable her to reduce the hypotaxis of her text to the extent one would expect. Her five sentences (comprising 31–28–8–58–50 words respectively) contain 1–2–0–4–3 subordinate clauses. Lowe-Porter's version even contains an instance of secondary-level subordination, a device which is not present at all, even in Mann's opening section: *'when* Europe sat upon the anxious seat beneath a menace *that* hung over its head for months'. This expansive translation of Mann's *'gefahrdrohende Miene'* also serves to intensify the complexity of Lowe-Porter's text in a number of other ways. Not only does it involve an additional stratum of subordination and significantly increase the number of words in the text: it also introduces a multiply metaphorical circumlocution that increases the semantic complexity (Europe sits upon a seat, the seat is anxious, a menace hangs over Europe's head, etc.). Thus, while she explodes Mann's opening sentence into two separate units by casting the extensive adverbial of time as a new sentence, thus securing a degree of simplification, her expansionary translation significantly increases the amount of interpretive effort involved in reading. And, in terms of the information perspective, it makes a highly significant change: it raises what in the

German is one embedded retarding unit in a carefully constructed sequence of adverbials (the time phrase) to the level of an independent sentence, thus enhancing its status.

The only simple sentence Lowe-Porter creates – her third – is a constituent brought forward from the beginning of Mann's third sentence. The relocation of this constituent has significant consequences for the interpretive possibilities suggested above. First, it deletes the explicit causal link between Aschenbach's creative crisis and his decision to take a walk (by reversing the order of those two units of information), thus weakening the sense of resolution suggested in the original. And second, it disrupts the chronological relations of Mann's text, bringing 'soon after tea' into a position prior to 'a morning of hard ... work'. Problems of coherence arise here, too: Lowe-Porter's string of sentences lacks any clear thematic development or cohesive ties. Mann's carefully structured and integrated whole, in which units of information are stacked up in an increasingly complex network, is replaced by an additive sequence of isolated ideas which lack conjunctive relationships. The fact that she separates units in two of her sentences with the aid of dashes, and in one instance with a semicolon (where Mann uses commas throughout), reinforces this impression of non-cohesion.

Lowe-Porter's final two sentences, by contrast, are relatively long and complex, and her shifting of large elements from Mann's penultimate sentence into her final sentence serves to redistribute the weight of those two units, undermining the effect of shortness/release caused by Mann's 27-word final sentence. Furthermore, her fragmentation of Mann's larger integrated structures into sequential components forces her to add a complete phrase to her final sentence – 'and now he undertook a walk' – in order to create a cohesive link with information that is placed in her short third sentence, although the causal conjunctive connection (Mann's 'so') remains absent. While in Mann's text the two references to Aschenbach's walk act as a bracket around the central sentence depicting his frame of mind, Lowe-Porter thus refers at three points to the walk ('set out for ... an extended walk' – 'sought the open' – 'undertook a walk'). Her treatment of the extensive *'überreizt'* clause is also interesting here. Of course, such extensive premodifiers are not possible in English, and must be restructured. Lowe-Porter raises the participial *'überreizt'* hierarchically to the status of a main clause, placing the verb in the imperfect tense ('He was overwrought'). In doing so, she further undermines the consistent anteriority of the original. Where Mann's text places all verbs relating to the protagonist's actions and mental state in the past perfect, or in (non-tensed) participial form – creating anticipation – she mixes her tenses ('he had set out', 'he was overwrought', 'he found himself').

In her version, the clause 'he was overwrought' seems to apply to Aschenbach's state of mind as he walks, rather than to the mental state of the second sentence. In her treatment of the postmodifiers, she places the two adjectives before the noun 'work', and then repeats the noun and postmodifies it with the noun sequence in a relative clause.

In the patterns of grammatical construction in Lowe-Porter's sentences there is a further disruption of the intricacy of Mann's opening. All five of them open with their subject, in four cases with the name 'Aschenbach' and on one occasion with the pronominal substitute 'he'. The segmentation of Mann's tripartitite opening (situation – state of mind – resulting walk) is obscured, replaced by a sequence of units that are both syntactically and thematically independent: once again, Mann's complex vision has been dissolved into a series of semantically unconnected statements, which lack any variation in connection. Her sentences, all of which have a SV structure, begin 'Aschenbach' – 'It' – 'Aschenbach' – 'He' – 'He' respectively. This lack of syntactic variety is, perhaps, the reason why she chooses not to take over the reference pattern of Mann's paragraph, preferring to repeat the protagonist's name as the subject of her short third sentence rather than to translate the occupational substitute noun *'der Schriftsteller'*. This means above all, of course, that the information structure is changed. Important information about the protagonist is simply omitted, and the nature of his taxing and frustrating work is not defined at the opening of the story. Indeed, it becomes clear only in the second chapter of Lowe-Porter's version that Aschenbach is a writer. Furthermore, this arrangement omits the first link in a protracted chain of nouns which are applied to Aschenbach throughout the text. This move, too, has various consequences, as will be seen more clearly in the discussion of Luke's version.

Luke's version
This is Luke's rendering of the same passage:

> On a spring afternoon in 19-, the year in which for months on end so grave a threat seemed to hang over the peace of Europe, Gustav Aschenbach, or von Aschenbach as he had been officially known since his fiftieth birthday, had set out from his apartment on the Prinzregentenstrasse in Munich to take a walk of some length by himself. The morning's writing had overstimulated him; his work had now reached a difficult and dangerous point which demanded the utmost care and circumspection, the most insistent and precise effort of will, and the productive mechanism in his mind – that *motus animi continuus* which according to Cicero is the essence of eloquence – had so pursued its reverberating

rhythm that he had been unable to halt it even after lunch, and had missed the refreshing daily siesta which was now so necessary to him as he became increasingly subject to fatigue. And so, soon after taking tea, he had left the house hoping that fresh air and movement would set him to rights and enable him to spend a profitable evening.

(Luke 1988: 195)

Luke has retained the three sentences of Mann's original, although he has divided the second sentence into two major parts by inserting a semicolon to mark the end of his opening main clause. The continuation of this sentence after the semicolon with a new subject, verb and object suggests that it is really a fully independent sentence, whose cohesion is secured by the referential connection between the two nouns 'writing' and 'work'. The semicolon is clearly intended to suggest an adverbial (causal) connection between the two clauses, though it could easily be replaced by a full stop. In its three-sentence form, Luke's paragraph has 180 (61–89–30) words, producing an average sentence length of 60 words, significantly higher than Mann's (which is 47.67). It uses 115 different words, generating a lexical variety index of 63.89 per cent (lower than both Mann's and Lowe-Porter's), and a LIX score of 79.44, largely on account of its greater sentence length. The near-30 per cent expansion in Luke's text compared with Mann's is due principally to his treatment of the first two sentences, where he selects complex options for what in Mann's original are simple groups. Furthermore, he adds significantly to the length of the text by making major transpositions.

Once again, the actual intricacy of the text here is more than just a function of surface-level characteristics. Morphological, lexical, syntactic, semantic and discourse features combine in their contribution to the sophistication of text. In terms of the descriptors outlined above, Luke's text is significantly more hypotactic than Mann's original, with thirteen subordinated constituents to Mann's seven. Luke's three sentences have 4–6–3 subordinated constituents respectively; Mann has 2–4–1. Here too, though, absolute figures are deceptive. While Mann's hypotactic structures are largely due to subordinated modifying constituents – he has a total of three relative clauses, an adverbial clause, the complex participial clause in the second sentence, and two complement clauses – Luke's thirteen subordinate structures comprise four relative clauses, four adverbial clauses and five complement clauses. Much of the additional hypotaxis in Luke's version stems from his translation of two of Mann's prepositional phrases ('*bei zunehmender Abnutzbarkeit*', '*in der Hoffnung ...*') with participial groups, and from his tendency to use verbs with infinitive complementation where German has simple verbs. Unsurprisingly, the crude readability measures mentioned above do not fully reflect this dimension of the text.

Luke's syntactic structures certainly capture the intricacy and sophistication of Mann's syntax. In fact he significantly expands it, though without apparently overstraining the ability of English syntax to accommodate so much information. Naturally, given the necessity of transposing structures across the two languages, he can only do so by undertaking major shifts in grammatical relations. However, an examination of these shifts in Luke's version demonstrates that he does not merely undertake the kind of obligatory shifts which are unavoidable even in very close translation, but on two occasions also undertakes significant additional transpositions.

The first example of extensive syntactical transformation is the opening. While Mann begins by naming the protagonist, Luke brings the extended adverbial clause elements of time into initial position. The rationale for this is presumably that he wishes to avoid what might otherwise appear to be an unidiomatic accumulation of adverbials in medial position. Adverbial pre-positioning is one method of achieving this. Another, as was seen in Lowe-Porter's version, is to relocate constituents in other sentences, or perhaps to separate them out in an independent sentence. Both solutions have significant consequences in terms of salience. Lowe-Porter's technique, as we have seen, isolates the information in a construction that necessitates a new (impersonal) subject, elevating the information to the level of a new compound sentence, and raises questions of cohesion. Luke's strategy enables him to retain the unit as part of the same sentence, but also has significant consequences in terms of the information structure. While Luke places the temporal adverbial in a position of marked focus, Mann's sentence provides a clear example of sentence-initial subject focalization: the name of the protagonist appears in what is 'cognitively speaking an eminently salient position' (Lambrecht 1996: 201). More than this: the text-initial status of this sentence further enhances the salience of the opening constituent, since the 'topic-first principle' cannot apply in this position. Indeed, the overwhelming centrality of the subject in the information structure of Mann's sentence is further underlined by its weight (extensive postmodification through the parenthetical clause) and by the fact that it opens the sentence brace which envelops all the information contained in the other clause elements between the subject and the lexical verb (*'Gustav ... unternommen'*). Mann's text, then, clearly rhematizes Aschenbach, while Luke's gives prominence to the temporal context by removing it from the sentence brace. Highly important though that situational information is in the context of the exposition (the spring afternoon, which turns out to be a false spring; the ominous and tantalizingly unspecified year; Aschenbach's official status, age and place of residence), it is, in Mann's text, placed in a position of secondary prominence, rather than pre-positioned.

It should be added that Mann does not place the name of his protagonist at the beginning of his text as a matter of routine. In Mann's entire fictional oeuvre, *Der Tod in Venedig* is the only text to open in this way. Second, as we have seen above, it is significant in thematic terms that this unique *'personeller Erzähleinsatz'* (figural narrative opening) does not merely name the character, but immediately draws attention to the dualism of his persona – the private and public identities – which will play such a key role as the story develops. And third, in a text which abounds in literary and mythological allusions, references and quotations, the opening sentence echoes the beginning of a novel which Mann claimed to have read five times during the composition of his story: Goethe's *Die Wahlverwandtschaften*. The influence of Goethe's novel on *Der Tod in Venedig* remains a matter of some controversy in the literature, though attention has frequently been drawn to the parallels in the classical style of both works (Hinton Thomas 1955; Vaget 1973). Of special interest here is the opening of *Die Wahlverwandtschaften*: Goethe begins with a sentence which, despite major thematic differences, resembles Mann's narrative onset: *'Eduard – so nennen wir einen reichen Baron im besten Mannesalter – Eduard hatte in seiner Baumschule die schönste Stunde eines Aprilnachmittags zugebracht, um frisch erhaltene Propfreiser auf junge Stämme zu bringen'* (Goethe 1968: 242). By shifting the subject into medial position, Luke undermines both the thematic focus and intertextual resonance in his apparent attempt to loosen the dense sequence of clause elements.

In the second sentence, too, Luke is at pains to integrate precisely the same information as Mann. However, he again significantly modifies the sequence and segmentation of the original. None of the semantic units is relocated to other sentences, but the overall composition of the sentence is changed. My aim in establishing such divergences is, once again, not to register complaint, but rather to note the subtle shifts in meaning potential that Luke's recasting triggers. The most significant of the changes is to the agency pattern and mood of the sentence. Luke undertakes a number of transpositions in the grammatical relations in this sentence, all of which serve to diminish the position of the protagonist as its subject by introducing additional clause elements. The passive subject *'Arbeit der Vormittagsstunden'*, which is delayed by such heavy premodification in the German, is raised in Luke's version to the level of an active subject without modifiers, and isolated in a very short introductory main clause. The centrally positioned subject of Mann's sentence – the important *'der Schriftsteller'* – must therefore now be cast in the role of object: 'The morning's writing had overstimulated him.' The isolation of this nominal group in initial subject position as a simple subject-verb-object structure means, of course, that all the modifiers must now appear in Luke's second clause. However, like Lowe-Porter Luke chooses not to arrange these modifiers in an uninterrupted sequence. Where the former had repeated the noun 'work', using the second occurrence of the noun as the antecedent of the following relative clause ('... work, work which ...'), Luke breaks up Mann's sequence further by introducing a substitute subject 'his work' after the semicolon, effectively translating '*Arbeit*' twice: 'The morning's writing had overstimulated him; his work had now reached ...'. This noun refers back to 'writing' and governs a new clause which appears as an extensive reformulation of Mann's adverbial '*eben jetzt*': Luke introduces a new verb and noun ('had reached ... a point'), and relaxes the cumulative tension of Mann's premodifying sequence by inserting the two adjectives ('*schwierig, gefährlich*') before the new object noun. This in turn becomes the subject of a relative clause containing the four abstract nouns which take the role of object to 'demand'.

This is a truly extensive reformulation, and is reminiscent of the realignment so frequently carried out by Lowe-Porter. One of its consequences is that it removes Aschenbach from the sustained subject position that he occupies throughout Mann's opening paragraph. In the latter, Aschenbach completely dominates the information focus via his agentive role. This text is clearly to be about him. Introduced in initial position as the named subject (twice) in the first sentence, he appears as the delayed subject in central position in the second and close to the beginning of the third. In other words, the skeletal structure of Mann's paragraph is: '*Aschenbach* [...] *der Schriftsteller* [...] *er*'. In Luke's version of the text, Aschenbach's semantic role is changed. He becomes the direct object of the 'morning's work' in the first clause, and is further removed from the dominant agentive position by the insertion of a series of other subject roles that are not present in the German: 'his work had ... reached a point', 'which demanded the utmost', and – in what is a very clear shift in focus – the '*Triebwerk*' which Aschenbach is unable to halt becomes the subject of a further verb ('pursued its reverberating rhythm'). The referential density of Mann's opening section, which follows on in a process of tight cohesion from the narrative opening, is relaxed: the focus oscillates between a variety of subjects.

A further consequence of Luke's recasting is connected to these transformations. We saw above that Lowe-Porter simply repeats the name of the protagonist in her third sentence, and fails to identify Aschenbach's profession. Luke retains a reference to the nature of Aschenbach's work, but he does so in the form of a process noun ('the morning's writing'). The reader here infers the protagonist's status by inferentially combining the values of 'work' and 'writing'. In Mann's text, though,

'*Schriftsteller*' is the initial entry in a long series of substitute nouns which are carefully sequenced and variously repeated throughout the story. The name of the protagonist occurs 97 times in Mann's text. However, on an approximately equal number of occasions, it is substituted, and the chain of nouns which the author uses shows a striking development and consistency. In the first two chapters of the story (and especially in the second) the focus is on Aschenbach's image and self-perception as an artist. The nouns here include, after the opening '*Schriftsteller*' (which appears in two other instances in the text), '*Autor*' (three occurrences), '*Künstler*' (nine), '*Schöpfer*' (two), '*Verfasser*' (one), and he is ultimately elevated to the level of '*Dichter*' (five). Following the protagonist's fall, that identity is ironized in the fifth chapter by the narrator (or are these Aschenbach's internal thoughts, presented through free indirect speech?). Here, the sequence reads '*Meister*' – '*Künstler*' – '*Autor*', and progresses to the sarcastic '*Hochgestiegener*'. As the story unfolds, other sequences of nouns move to the fore, and adjectival and participial nouns increasingly take over from full morphological ones: in the third chapter Aschenbach is presented as the traveller '*Reiselustiger*', '*Reisender*', and the observer '*Schauender*', '*Betrachtender*'. Towards the end of the third, during his abortive attempt to leave Venice, he becomes the '*Gequälter*', an epithet which ushers in the long series of nouns with which the narrator increasingly distances himself from the protagonist, culminating in the ambiguous '*Hinabgesunkener*' at the very end. Luke's deletion of the '*Schriftsteller*' noun, then, undermines the referential coherence of Mann's text, which can be traced through the extensive series of nouns, by removing the first link in the chain.

Conclusions

An investigation of the structures employed by two translators of the first paragraph of Mann's *Der Tod in Venedig* serves as a useful corrective to Luke's assumption that translation solutions can be in any way 'equivalent' to the original at the level of complex syntax. Despite Luke's criticism of Lowe-Porter's 'cavalier treatment' of Mann's complex sentence structures, we have noted significant non-obligatory shifts in his version too. Indeed, two further points should be made about the opening of the two English translations, and they both concern the deictic framework of the narrative. Inevitably, then, they have consequences for the positioning of the narrative voice relative to the action.

In both versions examined here, the translators delete the first-person pronominal identification with the continent of Europe, '*unser Kontinent*', in the first sentence (personal deixis). As mentioned above, this inclusive perspective serves to place the narrator in a position of situational identity with the reader. It paves the way for the frequent shifts in point of view which permeate Mann's text, as the narrator adopts various stances between the poles of diegetic and mimetic presentation, omniscience and limitation, commentary and report. In the English texts, this introductory signal of instability is absent.

The second point relates to the localization of the narrated action in time (temporal deixis). As noted above, Mann's text opens in the past perfect tense. This establishment of an anticipatory temporal frame is clearly designed to raise expectations: all the expository information provided in the first two paragraphs seems to be functioning as a preamble to the start of the action, which will (presumably) be narrated in the preterite. The past tense verb, when it does arrive, is '*erwartete*': Aschenbach has completed his walk through the park and is now waiting at the cemetery for a tram to take him home. This is where the story proper begins, and it is clearly marked through the pattern of tenses: from this point on all the verbs in the following sections are in the preterite (and three other imperfect verbs follow very closely upon the '*erwartete*', as if to drive this point home). Aschenbach sees the wanderer, and the thought processes which ultimately lead to his decision to take a holiday are triggered. All the internal processes presented in this first chapter (and they are crucial pointers to what will follow) are placed between the '*erwartete* [...] *die Tram*' (501) and the final paragraph of the chapter: '*So dachte er, während der Lärm der elektrischen Tram die Ungererstraße daher sich näherte* ...' (507). The '*erwartete*' is a pivotal moment. In Lowe-Porter's version, there is no consistency in the treatment of time. In her opening section she switches between the past perfect and the preterite, and the key moment is obscured, simply appearing as another link in a sequence of preterite verbs: 'so he waited at the stopping-place for a tram ...' (7). Indeed, in Lowe-Porter the placement of a simple past verb at the end of the first paragraph ('now undertook a walk') raises the expectation that the exposition is complete – and the plot about to commence – at this point. But Luke's version, too, diverges from the structures of the original at this point. He consistently maintains the past perfect structure of the first two paragraphs, and sustains it to include even the '*erwartete*': 'he had stopped by the North Cemetery to wait for the tram ...' (195). Here, too, a clearly marked caesura in the developing text is obscured by the failure to shift tense. While Mann's text uses a change in verb form to focalize Aschenbach as he stands waiting, and to arouse the expectation that something is about to happen, Luke's tense pattern is unable to create the same expectant atmosphere.

The kinds of changes identified above belie the notion that Luke's version mirrors the structures of Mann's text 'as closely as possible'. His modifications are not motivated simply by a concern to create sentences which are 'as complex as is consistent with what sounds natural for a single sentence by English standards' (Luke 1988: 1) – however that might be defined. Rather, the forms he selects significantly amend the information focus, agency patterns and cohesion of the original, inevitably impacting on the literary meaning in subtle ways. It is interesting to note that T. J. Reed, when quoting from the text in his monograph on Mann's story, feels the need to make 'slight changes to [Luke's] English, tacitly or expressly, so as to get closer to the effect of the original' (Reed 1994: ix). Lowe-Porter's notorious reformulations – born out of a highly translator-centred, target-language-oriented concept of the translator's task – are undoubtedly problematic in terms of the artistic unity and meaning potential of Mann's structures. Her version of the opening of Mann's story undertakes more wide-ranging transformations than any other version available to date. Yet, on closer examination, even a translation whose 'stated and manifestly achieved aim is to translate more accurately [...] and to reflect, as far as possible, the story's elevated diction and the complexity of Mann's prose' (Buck 2002: 240) shows traces of elective textual manipulation that can materially affect the reader's response to the unfolding fiction.

9 Conclusion

'Nobel Prize winner Thomas Mann (1875–1955) is not only one of the leading German novelists of the twentieth century, but also one of the few to transcend national and language boundaries to achieve major stature in the English-speaking world.' These words, which preface Todd Kontje's recent *Cambridge Introduction to Thomas Mann* (2011), constitute a typical assessment of the author's status. The process by which Mann's works came to form part of the world-literary canon through the medium of English has been traced above, and insights have been provided into the ways in which selected aspects of his works have been handled in translation. As was noted, the English versions of Mann's works as they appeared during his own lifetime were by no means subject to the kind of institutional pressures that are sometimes seen in processes of intercultural transfer. Although the publisher Knopf was always at great pains to shape the receptive context in which his author was read, and certainly had very strong views on marketing procedures, he did not intervene in the composition of the texts. Nor did Mann himself propose to his 'official' English translator anything more than the occasional tentative corrections or improvements. Mann's 'major stature in the English-speaking world' is, then, to a very large extent the direct result of the efforts of his authorized translator.

The name of Helen Tracy Lowe-Porter continues to dominate perceptions of Mann in the English-speaking world. While many recent discussions of her work in English cite the Woods versions as undoubtedly more accurate renderings of Mann's novels, Lowe-Porter's versions (which are still frequently re-issued, often in licensed editions) remain the classic texts. Despite the intense focus on the defectiveness of her versions in recent years she was, it must ultimately be conceded, eminently successful within the terms she had set herself – those of transparent domesticating translation and translator authorship. Certainly, the commercial return on Mann's books in English surpassed all expectations. Lowe-Porter was firmly convinced of the importance of her own contribution to the author's global standing, once claiming: 'his books would not have made money in English translation if they had not – out of my profound respect for the English tongue – been "easily readable"' (Heilbut 1995: 466). Furthermore, as was also noted above, the English versions published by Knopf were frequently honoured as Book-of-the-Month Club selections, and enjoyed highly favourable reviews. In considering Lowe-Porter's achievement, we would do well to bear in mind that early twenty-first-century reader expectations of English fictional prose style cannot do justice to her versions, which were produced well over half a century ago. We would also do well to remember that Lowe-Porter translated Mann 'hot-off-the-press'. In some cases, as we have seen, she found herself under the very considerable pressure of working simultaneously with Mann as he produced the original texts. She had no access to the author's extensive personal documents – the letters and notebooks – which have been systematically collected and edited since his death. She had no knowledge of the diaries, which were first published from 1977 onwards and triggered a reconsideration of many aspects of his work. And she had no access to a body of highly developed Thomas Mann scholarship such as that which has grown since the 1960s. Given such constraints, her achievement as an interpreter and mediator of Mann is nothing less than impressive. The continuing paradox with regard to the quality of her renderings is that of their unevenness: while she was able on countless occasions to understand and transfer elegantly into English the most complex passages written by one of the most difficult German authors – passages that constitute a challenge even to native speakers of German – she also committed a large number of fundamental errors.

However, despite Lowe-Porter's free and markedly target-oriented approach to translation, Mann's reputation in the USA was that of a wordy, overly intellectual writer, an image that was even more marked in Britain. He often complained that he had been misrepresented in his English versions, which, he feared, obscured the humour that he considered to be his hallmark as a writer. In a long letter to Irita van Doren, in which he sought to deflect the widespread criticism that his works were 'olympic', 'pompous' and 'ponderous', he spoke of general '*Mißverständnisse*' concerning his output: '*Tatsächlich fühle ich mich in erster Linie als Humorist – und das ist eine Art von Selbstgefühl, das mit dem Olympischen und Pompösen schlecht zusammenreimt*' (28 August 1951, *Br* 3: 220). The same protests, in very similar formulations, are to be found in his letter to Knopf of 3 February 1949 (*DüD* 3: 218). He stresses the role of irony and parody, even self-parody, in his work, presenting himself as an '*ironischer Konservativer*'. This self-assessment is, naturally, a simplification. Elsewhere, Mann was keen to stress that he had developed the intellectual novel as a vessel of profound cultural, political and philosophical concerns. But if there is a distinct translation loss in Lowe-Porter's versions of Mann's texts, it is undoubtedly here – in her treatment of Mann's ironic ductus. As early as 1958, Erich Heller noted in connection with *Death in Venice* that 'In English, alas, the ironically draped velvet and silk often look like solemnly donned corduroy and tweed.' (Heller 1958: 103), and this sentiment has been widely echoed in more recent studies (Robertson 2002: xiii). This apparent distortion of the lightness of Mann's tone (despite its great syntactic and lexical complexity) is, though, an unconscious defect in her renditions. As was noted in connection with her translation of *Der Zauberberg* (Chapter 4), it is the sum total of individual translation decisions at the level of lexis and syntax rather than the outcome of a systematic translation strategy. Nowhere in Lowe-Porter's renditions of Mann's oeuvre is there, I believe, any real evidence of conscious and consistent manipulation. The foregoing analyses of key dimensions of Mann's work in English demonstrate the processes of transformation and modification that are by definition inherent in the translation process: and these are evident, to a greater or lesser degree, in all the versions.

Despite the vicissitudes of Mann's fortunes in the latter half of the twentieth century – both in Germany and abroad – his global status remains undiminished to this day. His reception by other creative writers has been described as virtually non-existent (Vogt 2008: 245), and it is certainly true that his predilection for traditional narrative forms and his rootedness in the classical German '*bürgerlich*' tradition have found few emulators, despite markedly postmodern elements (Pütz 1976; Ridley and Vogt 2009, Chapter 11; Kurzke 2010). In this regard, Mann's hopes that the words of one critic writing in 1948 – 'Thomas Mann is a writer's writer. Under cover of a conventional use of language, he has been perhaps as adventurous and persistent an innovator as Joyce' – might prove prophetic have been frustrated. (Charles R. Rolo, quoted in *AEM* 1066). Kafka, Musil, Döblin and Brecht have fared much better. But there is plentiful evidence that Mann remains a central figure in European letters, as well as in 'Western civilization at large' (Lubich 1999: xxiii), on the strength of his translated works. Like his reception in the German-speaking countries, his standing in the English-speaking world has been reinvigorated by the publication of his diaries from 1977 onwards and by the emergence of sexually-oriented literary studies. It has been further underpinned by the fact that, of the four major biographies to appear in the mid–1990s, no fewer than three were in English (Hayman, Heilbut and Prater, all 1995). And the new millennium has seen the publication of an entire series of introductions and companions written for an English-speaking readership (Robertson 2002; Bloom 2003; Lehnert 2004; Mundt 2004; Kontje 2011). Thus, as Mann's texts continue to play a key role in comparative literature courses around the world, their understanding is underpinned by an extensive body of scholarship in the English language.

The retranslation of the majority of Thomas Mann's texts over the last twenty-five years has, of course, been prompted in part by the perceived inaccuracies in Lowe-Porter's work, and vociferous critics like Luke and Buck are right to draw attention to the distortions her versions contain. The need for more accurate versions has always been a mainspring behind the retranslation of major works of literature. But so, too, have changes in tastes and expectations in terms of what a translation should be: for while original literature endures, translations have a limited life expectancy. As responses to the more recent Thomas Mann translations show, it should not be assumed that later versions, for all their enhanced accuracy and integrity, are necessarily 'better' than the texts they are intended to replace. They are, however, different in subtle ways. Our exploration of various dimensions of Thomas Mann's oeuvre in English – intertextual, paratextual, macrostylistic, pragmatic and microstylistic – has, it is hoped, illustrated some of the ways in which literary meaning is inevitably affected by the process of interlingual and intercultural transfer.

Bibliography

Thomas Mann's works, letters, diaries

References to Thomas Mann's works, letters and diaries are provided in the main text using the following abbreviations. Where the work consists of more than one volume, reference is made to the volume and page number:

GW
Thomas Mann, *Gesammelte Werke in dreizehn Bänden* (Frankfurt am Main: Fischer, 1974).

Br
Thomas Mann. Briefe, 1889–1955, 3 vols, (ed.) E. Mann (Frankfurt am Main: Fischer, 1961–65).

DüD
Dichter über ihre Dichtungen 14: Thomas Mann, (1: 1889–1917, II: 1918–43; III: 1944–55), (ed.) H. Wysling with the collaboration of M. Fischer (Munich and Frankfurt am Main: Heimeran/Fischer, 1975, 1979, 1981).

Reg
Die Briefe Thomas Manns. Regesten und Register, (eds) H. Bürgin and H.-O. Mayer, 5 vols (Frankfurt am Main: Fischer, 1976–87).

TB
Thomas Mann, *Tagebücher*, (ed.) P. de Mendelssohn (5 vols, 1918–43) and Inge Jens (5 vols, 1943–55) (Frankfurt am Main: Fischer, 1977–95).

AEM
Thomas Mann – Agnes E. Meyer: Briefwechsel, (ed.) H. R. Vaget (Frankfurt am Main: Fischer, 1992).

GBF
Thomas Mann. Briefwechsel mit seinem Verleger Gottfried Bermann Fischer 1932–1955, (ed.) P. de Mendelssohn (Frankfurt am Main: Fischer, 1973).

English versions of Mann referred to in the text

Appelbaum, S. (1995), *Death in Venice*. New York: Dover Publications.
Burke, K. (1925), *Death in Venice*. New York: Alfred A. Knopf.
Cecil Curtis, A. (1916), *Royal Highness*. London: Sidgwick and Jackson.
Chase, J. S. (1999), *Death in Venice and Other Stories*. New York: Signet.
Constantine, P. (1998), *Six Early Stories*. Los Angeles: Sun & Moon.
Doege, M. (2010), *Death in Venice*. CreateSpace BoD.
Faber, M. and S. Lehmann (2010), *The Tables of the Law*. London: Haus Publishing.
Heim, M. (2004), *Death in Venice*. New York: Harper Collins.
Koelb, C. (1994), *Death in Venice*. New York: Norton.
Lewisohn, L. (1923), *Hungry Souls*. Nation 117: 318–19.
Linley, D. (1955), *Confessions of Felix Krull, Confidence Man*. Harmondsworth: Penguin (first published in 1955, New York: Alfred A. Knopf).
Lowe-Porter, H. T. (1955), *Death in Venice, Tristan, Tonio Kröger*. Harmondsworth: Penguin (first published in 1928, London: Secker&Warburg).
—(1936), *Stories of Three Decades*. New York: Alfred A. Knopf.
—(1957), *Buddenbrooks*. Harmondsworth: Penguin (first published in 1924, New York: Alfred A. Knopf).
—(1960), *The Magic Mountain*. Harmondsworth: Penguin (first published 1927, New York: Alfred A. Knopf).
—(1968), *Doctor Faustus*. Harmondsworth: Penguin (first published 1948, New York: Alfred A. Knopf).
Luke, D. (1970), *'Tonio Kröger' and Other Stories*. New York: Bantam.
Luke, D. (1988), *'Death in Venice' and Other Stories*. New York: Bantam.
McNab, C. (1962), *Royal Highness*. London: New English Library.
Morgan, B. Q. (1914), *Tonio Kröger* in H. Francke (ed.), *The German Classics of the 19th and 20th Centuries*, Vol. 19. New York: German Publications Society, pp. 184–250.
Neugroschel, J. (1998), *'Death in Venice' and Other Tales*. New York: Viking Penguin.
Robertson, R. (1999), *The Blood of the Volsungs*, in R. Robertson (ed.), *The German-Jewish Dialogue: An Anthology of Literary Texts, 1749–1993*. Oxford: Oxford University Press, pp. 152–78.
Robinson, A. (ed.) (1943), *The Ten Commandments: Ten Short Novels of Hitler's War against the Moral Code*. New York: Simon & Schuster.
Scheffauer, H. G. (1928), *Children and Fools*. New York: Alfred A. Knopf.
Trask, W. (1955), *The Black Swan*. New York: Alfred A. Knopf.
Winston, R. and C. Winston (eds) (1990), *Letters of Thomas Mann, 1889–1955*. Berkeley: University of California Press.
Woods, J. E. (1993), *Buddenbrooks*. New York: Alfred A. Knopf.
—(1995), *The Magic Mountain*. New York: Alfred A. Knopf.
—(1997), *Doctor Faustus*. New York: Alfred A. Knopf.
—(2005), *Joseph and His Brothers*. New York: Alfred A. Knopf.

Other works and translations referred to the text

Goethe, J. W. (1886), *Faust: A Dramatic Poem*, translated by T. Martin. Edinburgh and London: William Blackwood.
—(1968), *Werke in 14 Bänden*, Vol 6. B. von Wiese and E. Trunz (eds). Hamburg: Christian Wegner.
Kafka, F. (2009), *'The Metamorphosis' and Other Stories*, translated by J. Crick. Oxford: Oxford University Press.

Mann, H. (1998), *The Loyal Subject*, translated by H. Peitsch. New York: Continuum.

Secondary literature

Adolphs, D. (1985), *Literarischer Erfahrungshorizont: Aufbau und Entwicklung der Erzählperspektive im Werk Thomas Manns*. Heidelberg: Carl Winter.

—(1990), 'Thomas Manns Einflussnahme auf die Rezeption seiner Werke in Amerika'. *Deutsche Vierteljahrsschrift für Literaturwissenschaft und Geistesgeschichte* 64: 560–82.

Albrecht, J. (1998), *Literarische Übersetzung: Geschichte, Theorie, kulturelle Wirkung*. Darmstadt: Wissenschaftliche Buchgesellschaft.

—(2005), *Übersetzung und Linguistik*. Tübingen: Gunter Narr.

Alter, R. (2010), 'How to Hiss and Huff: *The Tables of the Law* by Thomas Mann, translated by Marion Faber and Stephen Lehmann'. *London Review of Books*, 2 December, pp 23–4.

Ammann, M. (1990), 'Anmerkungen zu einer Theorie der Übersetzungskritik und ihrer praktischen Anwendung'. *TextconText* 5: 209–50.

Andermann, G. (1993), 'Untranslatability: The case of pronouns of address in literature'. *Perspectives: Studies in Translatology* 1: 57–67.

Apel, F. and A. Kopetzki, A. (2003), *Literarische Übersetzung* (2nd edn). Stuttgart: Metzler.

Apter, E. (2008), 'Untranslatables: A world system'. *New Literary History* 39: 581–98.

Arens. H. (1964), *Analyse eines Satzes von Thomas Mann*. Düsseldorf: Pädagogischer Verlag Schwann.

Armbrust, H. and G. Heine (2008), *Wer ist wer im Leben von Thomas Mann? Ein Personenlexikon*. Frankfurt am Main: Vittorio Klostermann.

Baker, M. and G. Saldanha (eds) (2009), *Routledge Encyclopedia of Translation Studies*. London: Routledge.

Banfield, A. (1982), *Unspeakable Sentences: Narration and Representation in the Language of Fiction*. Boston and London: Law Book Company of Australasia.

Barter, R. (2007), *Deaths in Venice: Readings in Comparative Translation*. Saarbrücken: Verlag D. Müller.

Bassnett, S. and A. Lefevere, A. (eds) (1990), *Translation, History and Culture*. London: Routledge.

Bassnett-McGuire, S. (1980), *Translation Studies*. London: Methuen.

Bauer, R. (1993), 'Der Unpolitische und die Décadence', in E. Heftrich et al. (eds), *Wagner – Nietzsche – Thomas Mann*. Frankfurt am Main: Vittorio Klostermann, pp. 279–97.

Baumgart, R. (1966), *Das Ironische und die Ironie in den Werken Thomas Manns* (2nd edn). Munich: Carl Hanser.

Belloc, H. (1931), *On Translation*. Oxford: Oxford University Press.

Berger, T. (2005), 'Zur Problematik der Übersetzung pronominaler und nominaler Anredeformen', in S. Kempgen (ed.), *Slavistische Linguistik 2003*. Munich and Berlin: Otto Sagner, pp. 9–35.

Berlin, J. B. (1992), 'On the Making of the *Magic Mountain*: The Unpublished Correspondence of Thomas Mann, Alfred A. Knopf, and H. T. Lowe-Porter'. *Seminar* 28: 283–320.

—(2001), '"Ihr Gedanke, dieser Äußerung in Amerika noch eine etwas weitere Publizität zu verschaffen, ist mir sehr sympathisch" – Thomas Mann's

Unpublished Correspondence from 5 January 1936 to 3 May 1936 with Alfred A. Knopf and H. T. Lowe Porter'. *Euphorion* 95: 197–210.
—(2005a), 'On the nature of letters: Thomas Mann's unpublished correspondence with his American publisher and translator, and unpublished letters about the writing of *Doctor Faustus*'. *European Journal of English Studies* 9: 61–73.
—(2005b), 'Additional reflections on Thomas Mann as a letter-writer'. *Oxford German Studies* 34: 123–57.
Berlin. J. B and J. M. Herz (1994), '"Ein Lese- und Bilderbuch von Menschen": Unpublished Letters of Thomas Mann, Alfred A. Knopf, and H. T. Lowe-Porter, 1929–1934, with Special Reference to the *Joseph*-Novels'. *Seminar* 30: 221–75.
—(1996), '"Antwort auf Knopfs Warnungen": Unpublished letters of Thomas Mann and Alfred A. Knopf (March 1939–June 1940)'. *Seminar* 32: 189–220.
Berman, A. (2009), *Toward a Translation Criticism: John Donne*. Kent, OH: Kent State University Press.
Bloom, H. (1999), 'Foreword', in F. Lubich (ed.), *Thomas Mann: 'Death in Venice', 'Tonio Kröger' and Other Writings*. New York: Continuum, vii–xvi.
Boase-Beier, J. (2006), *Stylistic Approaches to Translation*. Manchester: St. Jerome.
—(2011), *A Critical Introduction to Translation Studies*. London and New York: Continuum.
Bouchehri, R. (2008), *Filmtitel im interkulturellen Transfer*. Berlin: Frank & Timm.
Bousfield, D. and K. Grainger (2010), 'Politeness Research: Retrospect and Prospect'. *Journal of Politeness Research: Language, Behaviour, Culture* 6: 161–82.
Brown, G. (1983), *The Dial: Arts and Letters in the 1920s*. Amherst: University of Massachusetts Press.
Brown, P. and S. Levinson (1987), *Politeness: Some Universals in Language Usage*. Cambridge: Cambridge University Press.
Brownlie, S. (2006), 'Narrative theory and retranslation theory'. *Across Languages and Cultures* 7: 145–70.
Bruckner, D. J. R. (1995) 'They're Speaking English Up There Now'. *New York Times*, 22 October (online edition).
Buck, T. (1995), 'Neither the letter nor the spirit'. *Times Literary Supplement*, 13 October, p. 17.
—(1996), 'Loyalty and licence: Thomas Mann's fiction in English translation. *Modern Language Review* 91: 898–921.
—(1997), 'Retranslating Mann: A fresh attempt on *The Magic Mountain*'. *Modern Language Review* 92: 656–9.
—(2002), 'Mann in English', in R. Robertson (ed.), *The Cambridge Companion to Thomas Mann*. Cambridge: Cambridge University Press, pp. 235–48.
Bulhof, F. (1966), *Transpersonalismus und Synchronizität: Wiederholung als Strukturelement in Thomas Manns 'Zauberberg'*. Groningen: Drukkerij van Denderen.
Bürgin, H. (1959), *Das Werk Thomas Manns*. Frankfurt am Main: Fischer.
Burnett, L. (2000), 'Fedor Dostoevskii', in O. Classe (ed.), *Encyclopedia of Literary Translation into English*, Vol 1. London: Fitzroy Dearborn, pp. 365–71.
Chakhachiro, R. (2009), 'Analysing irony for translation'. *Meta* 54: 32–48.
Chesterman, A. (1997), *The Memes of Translation*. Amsterdam and Philadelphia: John Benjamins.
Classe, O. (ed.) (2000), *Encyclopedia of Literary Translation into English*. 2 vols. London: Fitzroy Dearborn.

Cohn, D. (1978), *Transparent Minds. Narrative Modes for Presenting Consciousness in Fiction*. Princeton: Princeton University Press.
—(1983), 'The second author of *Death in Venice*', in B. Bennett et al. (eds), *Probleme der Moderne*. Tübingen: Max Niemeyer, pp. 223–45.
Craven, P. (2007), 'Lost in translation'. *The Australian* (online edition), 13 January, no page number.
Crisafulli, E. (2002), 'The quest for an eclectic methodology of translation description, in T. Hermans (ed.), *Crosscultural Transgressions*. Manchester: St. Jerome, pp. 26–43.
Czennia, B. (1992), *Figurenrede als Übersetzungsproblem: Untersucht am Romanwerk von Charles Dickens und ausgewählten deutschen Übersetzungen*. Frankfurt am Main: Peter Lang.
—(2004a), 'Erzählweisen in literarischer Prosa und ihre Übersetzung', in H. Kittel et al. (eds), *Ein internationales Handbuch zur Übersetzungsforschung*, Vol 1. Berlin and New York: de Gruyter, pp. 987–1007.
—(2004b), 'Dialektale und soziolektale Elemente als Übersetzungsproblem', in H. Kittel et al. (eds), *Ein internationales Handbuch zur Übersetzungsforschung*, Vol 1. Berlin and New York: de Gruyter, pp. 505–12.
de Wilde, J. (2010), 'The analysis of translated literary irony: Some methodological issues', in K. Lievois and P. Schoentjes (eds), *Translating Irony*. Antwerp: Linguistica Antverpiensa, pp. 25–44.
Dirks, M. (2003), *Studien zu Mythos und Psychologie bei Thomas Mann*. Frankfurt am Main: Vittorio Klostermann.
Doran, G. (1952), *Chronicles of Barabbas 1884–1934. Further Chronicles and Comment*. New York: Rinehart & Company.
Dowden, S. (2001) (ed.), *A Companion to Thomas Mann's 'The Magic Mountain'*. Columbia: Camden House.
Drosdowski, G. et al. (1984), *Duden. Die Grammatik*. Mannheim: Duden-Verlag.
Durrani, O. (2002), 'Editions, translations, adaptations', in J. Preece (ed.), *The Cambridge Companion to Kafka*. Cambridge: Cambridge University Press, pp. 206–25.
Eco, U. (1991), *The Limits of Interpretation*. Bloomington, IN: University of Indiana Press.
Erben, J. (2006), 'Bemerkungen zum Sprachbewusstsein und sprachreflexiven Stil Thomas Manns'. *Zeitschrift für deutsche Philologie* 125: 61–90.
Eroms, H.-W. (2008), *Stil und Stilistik: Eine Einführung*. Berlin: Schmidt.
Fehlauer-Lenz, I. (2008), 'Von der übersetzten Ironie zur ironischen Übersetzung'. Unpublished doctoral thesis, Martin-Luther-Universität Halle-Wittenberg.
Ferguson, S. (1997), *Language Assimilation and Crosslinguistic Influence: A Study of German Exile Writers*. Tübingen: Gunter Narr.
Fischer, B-J. (2002), *Handbuch zu Thomas Manns Josephromanen*. Tübingen: A. Francke.
Fix, U. et al. (eds) (2010), *Handbuch Rhetorik und Stilistik: Ein internationales Handbuch historischer und systematischer Forschung*, Vol 1. Berlin: Walter de Gruyter.
Fludernik, M. (2008), *Erzähltheorie: Eine Einführung* (2nd edn). Darmstadt: Wissenschaftliche Buchgesellschaft.
Fowler, R. (1996), *Linguistic Criticism* (2nd edn).Oxford: Oxford University Press.
France, P. (ed.) (2000), *The Oxford Guide to Literature in English Translation*. Oxford: Oxford University Press.

Frank, A. P. (1984), 'Theories and Theory of Literary Translation', in J. P. Strelka (ed.), *Literary Theory and Criticism: Part 1: Theory*. Frankfurt am Main and Bern: Peter Lang, pp. 203–21.

—(1987), 'Einleitung', in B. Schulze (ed.), *Die literarische Übersetzung. Fallstudien zu ihrer Kulturgeschichte*. Berlin: Erich Schmidt, pp. ix–xvii.

Frank, A. P. and H. Kittel (2004), 'Der Transferansatz in der Übersetzungsforschung', in A. P. Frank and H. Turk (eds), *Die literarische Übersetzung in Deutschland: Studien zu ihrer Kulturgeschichte in der Neuzeit*. Berlin: Erich Schmidt, pp. 3–67.

Frank, A. P. and B. Schultze (1990), 'Normen in historisch-deskriptiven Übersetzungsstudien', in H. Kittel (ed.), *Die literarische Übersetzung: Stand und Perspektiven ihrer Erforschung*. Berlin: Erich Schmidt, pp. 96–121.

Frères, E-P. (1949), 'Lettre adresseé à Mme Yanette Deletang-Tardif, par T. Mann', in E-P. Frères (ed.), *Hommage à Maurice Betz*. Paris: E. P. Frères.

Freudenberg, R. (2001), 'Thomas Mann auf Englisch', in A. Braun (ed.), *Beiträge zu Linguistik und Phonetik*. Stuttgart: Steiner, pp. 366–91.

Frizen, W. (1993), *Thomas Mann: 'Der Tod in Venedig'*. Munich: Oldenbourg.

—(2001), 'Thomas Manns Sprache', in H. Koopmann (ed.), *Thomas-Mann-Handbuch* (3rd edn). Stuttgart: Kröner, pp. 854–74.

Gambier, Y. (1994), 'La retraduction: Retour et Détour'. *Meta* 39: 413–17.

Gauger, H-M. (1975), 'Der Zauberberg – ein linguistischer Roman'. *Die Neue Rundschau* 86: 217–45.

Genette, G. (1988), 'Structure and Functions of the Title in Literature'. *Critical Inquiry* 14: 692–720.

Gentzler, E. (2001), *Contemporary Translation Theories* (2nd edn). Clevedon: Multilingual Matters.

Gildhoff, H. (2001), 'Thomas Mann und die englische Sprache'. *Thomas-Mann-Jahrbuch* 14: 143–67.

Glass, D. (2000), 'German: Literary Translation into English', in O. Classe (ed.), *Encyclopedia of Literary Translation into English*, Vol 1. London: Fitzroy Dearborn, pp. 512–20.

Gledhill, J. (2007), *How to Translate Thomas Mann's Works: A Critical Appraisal of Helen Lowe-Porter's Translations of 'Death in Venice', 'Tonio Kröger' and 'Tristan'*. Saarbrücken: Verlag Dr. Müller.

Gloystein, C. (2001), *Mit mir aber ist es was anderes. Die Ausnahmestellung Hans Castorps in Thomas Manns Roman 'Der Zauberberg'*. Würzburg: Königshausen & Neumann.

Gooderham, W. (2011), 'Winter reads: The Magic Mountain by Thomas Mann', *The Guardian*, 14 December.

Gray, R. (1977), 'But Kafka Wrote in German', in A. Flores (ed.), *The Kafka Debate: New Perspectives for Our Time*. New York: Gordian Press, pp. 242–52.

Greenberg. M. (1999), 'Thomas Mann in English: On the difficulties of translation'. *New Criterion* 17: 21–8.

Greiner, N. (2004), *Übersetzung und Literaturwissenschaft*. Tübingen: Gunter Narr.

Grieve, J. (1992), 'On Translating Proust'. *Journal of European Studies* 12: 55–67.

Grimm, C. (1991), *Zum Mythos Individualstil: Mikrostilistische Untersuchungen zu Thomas Mann*. Würzburg: Königshausen & Neumann.

Guess, J. C. (1977), *Thomas Manns englische 'Lotte': Eine übersetzungskritische Untersuchung der englischen Übertragung von Thomas Manns 'Lotte in Weimar' unter Anwendung eines Rahmenmodells der Übersetzungskritik*. Munich: Reprographischer Betrieb W. u. J. M. Salzer.

Gutt, E-A. (2005), 'On the Significance of the Cognitive Core of Translation'. *The Translator* 11: 25–49.
Halliday, M. (1983), 'Foreword', in M. Cummings and R. Simmons, *The Language of Literature*. Oxford: Pergamon, pp. vii–xiv.
Hardt, R. (1957), 'Über Thomas Manns Sprachmeisterschaft im *Zauberberg*'. *Muttersprache* 67: 426–28.
Harman, M. (1994), 'A conversation with John E. Woods'. *Translation Review* 44/45: 4–7.
—(1995), 'The Artist and His Demons'. *Book World*, 26 November, p. 5.
—(1996), '"Digging the Pit of Babel": Retranslating Franz Kafka's *Castle*'. *New Literary History* 27: 291–311.
Harpprecht, K. (1995), *Thomas Mann – Eine Biographie*. Reinbek: Rowohlt.
Harvey, K. (1995), 'A Descriptive Framework for Compensation'. *The Translator* 1: 65–86.
Hassan, A. (1967), 'Satz und Absatz bei Thomas Mann: eine syntaktisch-stilistische Untersuchung zu der Novelle *Der Tod in Venedig*'. Unpublished doctoral thesis, University of Munich.
Hatfield, H. (1990), 'Literature in Translation. *Die Unterrichtspraxis* 23: 192.
Hawkins, J. (1986), *A Comparative Typology of English and German: Unifying the Contrasts*. London: Croom Helm.
Hayes, J. (1974), 'A Method of Determining the Reliability of Literary Translations: Two Versions of Thomas Mann's *Der Tod in Venedig*'. Unpublished doctoral thesis, University of Massachusetts.
Hayman, R. (1995), *Thomas Mann – A Biography*. London: Bloomsbury.
Heilbut, A. (1995), *Thomas Mann: Eros and Literature*. New York: Knopf.
Heim, M. (2008), 'Function as an Element in Conveying Cultural Difference in Literary Translation'. *Yearbook of Comparative and General Literature* 54: 74–82.
—(2009), 'A Life in Translation'. Oregon State University Horning Lecture, 5 November 2009 (available online).
Heller, E. (1958), *Thomas Mann, the Ironic German*. London: Secker & Warburg.
Henderson, C. and R. W. Oram (2010), *Dictionary of Literary Biography: The House of Knopf 1915–1960*. Michigan: Gale.
Henjum, K. B. (2004), 'Gesprochensprachlichkeit als Übersetzungsproblem', in H. Kittel et al. (eds), *Ein internationales Handbuch zur Übersetzungsforschung*, Vol 1. Berlin and New York: de Gruyter, pp. 512–20.
Hermans, T. (ed.) (1985a), *The Manipulation of Literature: Studies in Literary Translation*. London: Palgrave Macmillan.
—(1985b), 'Translation studies and a new paradigm', in T. Hermans (ed.), *The Manipulation of Literature: Studies in Literary Translation*. London: Palgrave Macmillan, pp. 7–15.
—(1996), 'The Translator's Voice in Translated Narrative'. *Target* 8: 23–48.
—(1999), *Translation in Systems*. Manchester: St. Jerome Publishing.
—(2000), 'Norms of Translation', in P. France (ed.), *The Oxford Guide to Literature in English Translation*. Oxford: Oxford University Press, pp. 10–15.
Hervey, S. et al. (1995), *Thinking German Translation*. London: Routledge.
Hewson, L. (2011), *An Approach to Translation Criticism*. Amsterdam and Philadelphia: John Benjamins.
Hilscher, E. (1955), 'Thomas Mann als Sprachkünstler'. *Neue deutsche Literatur* 3: 56–71.
Hinton Thomas, R. (1955), '*Die Wahlverwandtschaften* and Mann's *Der Tod in Venedig*'. *Publications of the English Goethe Society* 24: 101–30.

Hoek, L. H. (1982), *La marque du titre*. The Hague and New York: Mouton.
Hoffmann, M. (2009), 'Mikro- und Makrostilistische Einheiten im Überblick', in U. Fix et al. (eds), *Handbuch Rhetorik und Stilistik: Ein internationales Handbuch historischer und systematischer Forschung*, Vol 1. Berlin: Walter de Gruyter, pp. 1529–45
Hoffmeister, W. (1967), *Studien zur erlebten Rede bei Thomas Mann und Robert Musil*. The Hague and London: Mouton.
Holmes, J. (1988), 'Describing literary translations: Models and methods', in J. Holmes (ed.), *Translated! Papers on Literary Translation and Translation Studies*. Amsterdam: Rodopi, pp. 80–91.
Hoppmann, M. (2009), 'Pragmatische Aspekte der Kommunikation: Höflichkeit und Ritualisierung', in U. Fix et al. (eds), *Rhetorik und Stilistik. Ein internationales Handbuch*. Berlin: Walter de Gruyter, pp. 826–36.
Horrocks, D. (2000), 'Hermann Hesse', in O. Classe (ed.), *Encyclopedia of Literary Translation into English*, Vol 1. London: Fitzroy Dearborn, pp. 639–41.
Horton, D. (1996), 'Modes of address as a pragmastylistic aspect of translation', in A. Lauer et al. (eds), *Übersetzungswissenschaft im Umbruch: Festschrift für WolframWilss*. Tübingen: Gunter Narr, pp. 69–83.
—(1998), 'Non-standard language in translation: Roddy goes to Germany'. *German Lifae and Letters* 51: 415–30.
—(1999), 'Social deixis in the translation of dramatic discourse'. *Babel* 45: 53–73.
—(2010), '"'An acceptable job"? The First English Translation of Thomas Mann's *Das Gesetz*'. *Modern Language Review* 105: 149–70.
Howe, S. (1996), *The personal pronouns in the Germanic languages: a study of personal pronoun morphology and change in the Germanic languages from the first records to the present day*. Berlin: Walter de Gruyter.
Huddlestone, R., G. Pullum et al. (2002), *The Cambridge Grammar of the English Language*. Cambridge: Cambridge University Press.
Jacob, D. (1988), 'Englische Leser Kafkas. Werk und Übersetzung: Ästhetische Erwartungen und Erfahrungen im Kontext der fremden Sprache'. *Euphorion* 82: 89–103.
Jahrhaus, O. (2004), *Literaturtheorie: Theoretische und methodische Grundlagen der Literaturwissenschaft*. Tübingen and Basel: A. Franke.
Jeffries, L. and D. McIntyre (2010), *Stylistics*. Cambridge: Cambridge University Press.
Jürgensen, C. (2007), *"Der Rahmen arbeitet": paratextuelle Strategien der Lektürelenkung im Werk Arno Schmidts*. Göttingen: Vandenhoeck & Ruprecht.
Katz, J. J. (1990), *The Metaphysics of Meaning*. Cambridge and Massachusetts: MIT Press.
Keenon, R. et al. (1997), *The Babel Guide to German Fiction in English Translation: Austria, Germany, Switzerland*. London: Boulevard.
Kelly, C. (2000), 'Dostoevsky', in P. France, (ed.), *The Oxford Guide to Literature in English Translation*. Oxford: Oxford University Press, pp. 594–8.
Kelly, L. (1979), *The True Interpreter: A History of Translation Theory and Practice in the West*. Oxford: Basil Blackwell.
Kenny, D. (2001), *Lexis and Creativity in Translation: A Corpus-based study*. Manchester: St. Jerome.
Kinkel, E. (2001), *Thomas Mann in Amerika: Interkultureller Dialog im Wandel?* Frankfurt am Main and Bern: Peter Lang.
Knopf, A. (1975), 'On publishing Thomas Mann'. *The American Pen: An International Quarterly of Writing* 7: 1–9.

Koch- Emmery, E. (1952/3), 'Thomas Mann in English translation'. *German Life and Letters* 6: 275–84.

Koepke, W. (1992), 'Lifting the Cultural Blockade: The American Discovery of a New German Literature after World War 1 – Ten Years of Critical Commentary in the *Nation* and the *New Republic*', in W. Elfe et al. (eds), *The Fortunes of German Writers in America: Studies in Literary Reception.* Columbia, SC: University of South Carolina Press, pp. 81–98.

König, E. and V. Gast (2007), *Understanding English-German Contrasts.* Berlin: Erich Schmidt.

Kontje, T. (2011), *The Cambridge Introduction to Thomas Mann.* Cambridge: Cambridge University Press.

Koopmann, H. (2001), 'Humor und Ironie', in H. Koopmann (ed.), *Thomas-Mann-Handbuch* (3rd edn). Stuttgart: Kröner, pp. 836–53.

Koster, C. (2000), *From World to World: An Armamentarium for the Study of Poetic Discourse in Translation.* Amsterdam: Rodopi.

Kreimeier, K., G. Stanitzek and N. Binczek (2004), *Paratexte in Literatur, Film, Fernsehen.* Berlin: Akademie-Verlag.

Kristiansen, B. (1978), *Thomas Manns 'Zauberberg' und Schopenhauers Metaphysik.* Copenhagen: Akademisk Forlag.

Kurzke, H. (2010), *Thomas Mann: Epoche – Werk – Wirkung* (4th edn). Munich: C. H. Beck.

Lambert, J. and H. van Gorp (1985), 'On describing translations', in T. Hermans (ed.), *The Manipulation of Literature: Studies in Literary Translation.* London: Palgrave Macmillan, pp. 42–53.

Lambrecht, K. (1996), *Information Structure and Sentence Form: Topic, Focus, and the Mental Representations of Discourse Referents.* Cambridge: Cambridge University Press.

Lämmert, E. (2004), *Bauformen des Erzählens* (9th edn). Stuttgart: Metzler.

Landers, C. (2001), *Literary Translation: A Practical Guide.* Clevedon: Multilingual Matters.

Latta, A. (1987), 'The Reception of Thomas Mann's *Die Betrogene*: Tabus, Prejudices and Tricks of the Trade'. *Internationales Archiv für Sozialgeschichte der deutschen Literatur* 12: 237–72.

—(1993), 'The Reception of Thomas Mann's *Die Betrogene*: Part II: The Scholarly Reception'. *Internationales Archiv für Sozialgeschichte der deutschen Literatur* 18: 123–56.

Lawson, A. (2000), '"Die schöne Geschichte": A Corpus-based Analysis of Thomas Mann's *Joseph und seine Brüder*', in B. Dodd (ed.), *Working with German Corpora.* Birmingham: University of Birmingham Press, pp. 161–80.

Lecercle, J-J. (1999), *Interpretation as Pragmatics.* London: Macmillan.

Lee, C-H. (1994), 'Die Wiedergabe gesprochener und gedachter Rede in Thomas Manns *Buddenbrooks*'. Unpublished doctoral thesis, University of Marburg.

Leech, G. and M. Short (2007), *Style in Fiction* (2nd edn). London: Pearson Education.

Lefevere A. (1992a), *Translating Literature: Practice and Theory in a Comparative Literature Context.* New York: Modern Language Association.

—(1992b), *Translating, Rewriting and the Manipulation of Literary Fame.* London: Routledge.

Lehnert, H. (1969), *Thomas-Mann-Forschung.* Stuttgart: Metzler.

Lehnert, H. and E. Wessel (eds) (2004), *A Companion to the Works of Thomas Mann.* New York: Camden House.

Levin, H. (1948), 'Dr. Mann versus a Teutonic Mephisto', *New York Times Book Review*, 31 October, p. 5.
Levy, J. (1969), *Die literarische Übersetzung. Theorie einer Kunstgattung*. Frankfurt am Main: Athenäum.
Lewisohn, L. (1917), *The Spirit of Modern German Literature*. New York: W. B. Huebsch.
Liewerscheidt, D. (2006), 'Lebensfreundliche Illumination und erschöpfte Ironie. Zu Thomas Manns *Zauberberg*. *Revista de Filología Alemana* 14: 67–80.
Lodge, D. (1990), *After Bakhtin: Essays on Fiction and Criticism*. London: Routledge.
Lorenzen-Peth, J. (2008), *Erzählperspektive und Selbstreflexion in Thomas Manns Erzählungen*. Kiel: Ludwig.
Lowe-Porter, H. (1933), 'Foreword', in *Thomas Mann. Past Masters and Other Papers*. New York: Alfred A. Knopf.
—(1966), 'On translating Thomas Mann', in J. C. Thirlwall (ed.), *In Another Language: A Record of the Thirty-Year Relationship between Thomas Mann and His English Translator, Helen Tracy Lowe-Porter*. New York: Alfred A. Knopf, pp. 178–209.
Lubich, F. (1994), 'Thomas Mann's Sexual Politics – Lost in Translation'. *Comparative Literary Studies* 31:107–27.
—(1999), 'Introduction', in F. Lubich (ed.), *Thomas Mann: 'Death in Venice', 'Tonio Kröger' and Other Writings*. New York: Continuum, pp. xvii–xxvi.
Lyons, J. (1980), 'Pronouns of Address in Anna Karenina: The Stylistics of Bilingualism and the Impossibility of Translation', in S. Greenbaum et al. (eds), *Studies in English Linguistics. For Randolph Quirk*. London: Longman, pp. 235–49.
MacKenzie, I. (2002), *Paradigms of Reading: Relevance Theory and Deconstruction*. London: Palgrave Macmillan.
Mahlberg, M. (2007), 'Bridging the gap between linguistic and literary studies', in M. Hoey et al. (eds), *Text, Discourse and Corpora: Theory and Analysis*. London: Continuum, pp. 219–46.
Malmkjaer, K. (2004), 'Translational Stylistics: Dulcken's translations of Hans Christian Andersen'. *Language and Literature* 13: 13–24.
—(2011), 'Translation universals', in K. Malmkjaer and K. Windle (eds), *The Oxford Handbook of Translation Studies*. Oxford: Oxford University Press, pp. 83–93.
Mandel, S. (1982), 'Helen Tracy Lowe-Porter: Once a translator, always a translator'. *Denver Quarterly* 17: 29–39.
Martinez, M. and M. Scheffel (2007), *Einführung in die Erzähltheorie* (7th edn). Munich: Beck.
Mater, E. (1962), 'Zur Wortbildung und Wortbedeutung bei Thomas Mann', in G. Wenzel (ed.), *Vollendung und Größe Thomas Manns*. Halle: Verlag Sprache und Literatur, pp. 141–8.
Mathews, A. (2000), 'Franz Kafka', in O. Classe (ed.), *Encyclopedia of Literary Translation into English*, Vol 1. London: Fitzroy Dearborn, pp. 747–51.
Matthias, K. (1967), 'Zur Erzählweise in den *Buddenbrooks*', in K. Mathias, *Studien zum Werk Thomas Manns*. Lübeck: Schmidt-Römhild, pp. 7–54.
McLean, H. (2008), *In Quest of Tolstoy*. Brighton / Massachusetts: Academic Studies Press.
Mellown, E. W. (1964), 'The development of a criticism: Edwin Muir and Franz Kafka'. *Comparative Literaure* 16: 310–21.
Miller, G. (2000), 'Thomas Mann: *Buddenbrooks*', in O. Classe (ed.), *Encyclopedia of Literary Translation into English*, Vol 2. London: Fitzroy Dearborn, pp. 904–6.

Miltenberger, A. (2000). *Verborgene Strukturen in erzählenden Texten von 1900–1950*. Munich: Utz.
Mitchell, B. (1998), 'Afterword: The Translator's Trial'. *Conjunctions* 30, Spring 1998, online edition www.conjunctions.com/archives/c30-fk.htm [Last accessed 1 January 2013].
Moenninghoff, B. (2000), *Goethes Gedichttitel*. Berlin and New York: de Gruyter.
Morgan, B. Q. (1946), 'On translating *Tonio Kröger*'. *German Quarterly* 18: 220–5.
—(1965), *A Critical Bibliography of German Literature in English Translation* (2nd edn). New York: Scarecrow Press.
Moulden, K. and G. von Wilpert (eds) (1988), *Buddenbrooks-Handbuch*. Stuttgart: Kröner.
Müller, F. (1998), *Buddenbrooks*. Munich: Oldenbourg.
Müller, M. (1995), *Die Ironie: Kulturgeschichte und Textgestalt*. Würzburg: Königshausen & Neumann.
Munday, J. (2007), *Style and Ideology in Translation. Latin American Writing in English*. London: Routledge.
—(2008), *Introducing Translation Studies: Theories and Applications* (2nd edn). London: Routledge.
Mundt, H. (2004), *Understanding Thomas Mann*. Columbia, South Carolina: University of South Carolina Press.
Neider, C. (ed.) (1947), *The Stature of Thomas Mann*. New York: New Directions.
Newmark, P. (1982), *Approaches to Translation*. Oxford: Pergamon.
—(1991), *About Translation*. Clevedon: Multilingual Matters.
—(2000), 'Thomas Mann: The Magic Mountain', in O. Classe (ed.), *Encyclopedia of Literary Translation into English*, Vol 2. London: Fitzroy Dearborn, pp. 907–9.
Nord, C, (1993), *Einführung in das funktionale Übersetzen: Am Beispiel von Titeln und Überschriften*. Tübingen and Basle: Francke.
—(1997), *Translating as a Purposeful Activity: Functionalist Approaches Explained*. Manchester: St. Jerome.
—(2004), 'Die Übersetzung von Titeln, Kapiteln und Überschriften in literarischen Texten', in H. Kittel et al. (eds), *Ein internationales Handbuch zur Übersetzungsforschung*, Vol 1. Berlin and New York: de Gruyter, pp. 908–14.
Ormsby, E. (1998), 'Franz Kafka and the trip to Spindelmühle'. *New Criterion* 17: 32–8.
Parkes, T. (2007), *Translating Style* (2nd edn). Manchester: St. Jerome.
Pascal, R. (1977), *The Dual Voice. Free Indirect Speech and its Functioning in the Nineteenth-century European Novel*. Manchester: Manchester University Press.
Pavlovskis-Petit, Z. and H. Rappaport (2000), 'Anton Chekhov', in O. Classe (ed.), *Encyclopedia of Literary Translation into English*, Vol 1. London: Fitzroy Dearborn, pp. 268–73.
Pinkard, T (2001), *Hegel: A Biography*. Cambridge: Cambridge University Press.
Potempa, G. (1997), *Thomas Mann-Bibliographie: Übersetzungen/Interviews*. Morsum and Sylt: Cicero.
Prater, D. (1995), *Thomas Mann: A Life*. Oxford: Oxford University Press.
Prendergast, C. (1993), 'English Proust', *London Review of Books*, 8 July, p. 21.
Prescott, O. (1944), 'Books of the Times', *The New York Times*, 26 June, p. 13.
—(1948), 'Books of the Times', *The New York Times*, 29 October, online edition.
Prunc, E. (2007), *Entwicklungslinien der Translationswissenschaft*. Berlin: Frank & Timme.
Pugliese, R. (2010), 'Ironie also kultureller Stolperstein – Grass' *Beim Häuten der Zwiebel* im Spiegel der italienischen Übersetzung', in K. Lievois and

P. Schoentjes (eds), *Translating Irony*. Antwerp: Linguistica Antverpiensa, pp. 45–61.
Pütz, P. (1976), 'Thomas Manns Wirkung auf die deutsche Literatur der Gegenwart', in H. L. Arnold (ed.), *Text und Kritik: Sonderband Thomas Mann*. Munich: edition text + kritik, pp. 169–79.
Pym, A. (2008), 'On Toury's laws of how translators translate', in A. Pym et al. (eds), *Beyond Descriptive Translation Studies. Investigations in Homage to Gideon Toury*. Amsterdam/ Philadelphia: John Benjamins, pp. 311–27.
—(2010), *Exploring Translation Theories*. London: Routledge.
Rabassa, G. (2005), *If This Be Treason: Translation and its Dyscontents*. New York: New Directions.
Ray, W. (1984), *Literary Meaning: From Phenomenology to Deconstruction*. Oxford: Oxford University Press.
Reed, T. J. (1983), *'Der Tod in Venedig': Text, Materialien, Kommentar mit den bisher unveröffentlichten Arbeitsnotizen Thomas Manns*. Munich: Carl Hanser.
—(1994), *'Death in Venice': Making and Unmaking of a Master*. New York: Twayne.
—(1996), *Thomas Mann: The Uses of Tradition* (2nd edn). Oxford: Oxford University Press.
Reichart, W. A. (1945), 'Thomas Mann: an American bibliography'. *Monatshefte* 37: 389–408.
Reitter, P. (2006), 'That other Metamorphosis'. *German Quarterly* 81: 87–95.
Ricoeur, P. (1981), *Hermeneutics and the Human Sciences*. Cambridge: Cambridge University Press.
Ridley, H. (1987), *Thomas Mann: 'Buddenbrooks'*. Cambridge: Cambridge University Press.
Ridley, H. and J. Vogt (2009), *Thomas Mann*. Stuttgart: UTB.
Riley, A. (1967), *'Das Glasperlenspiel* in English translation (with an unpublished letter of Hermann Hesse's)'. *Monatshefte* 59: 344–50.
Robertson, R. (ed.) (2002). *The Cambridge Companion to Thomas Mann*. Cambridge: Cambridge University Press.
Roche, M. W. (1986), 'Man of Straw *(Der Untertan)* by Heinrich Mann, Trans. Ernest Boyd'. *The German Quarterly* 59: 492–4.
Rodríguez Rodríguez, B. M. (2007), *Literary Translation Assessment*. Munich: Lincoln Europa.
Roffmann, A. (2003), *'Keine freie Note mehr': Natur im Werk Thomas Manns*. Würzburg: Königshausen & Neumann.
Rossbach, B. (1988), 'Der Anfang vom Ende: Narrative Analyse des ersten Kapitels der Novelle *Der Tod in Venedig* von Thomas Mann', in W. Brandt (ed.), *Sprache in Vergangenheit und Gegenwart*. Marburg: Hitzeroth, pp. 237–49.
Rothe, A. (1986), *Der literarische Titel: Funktionen, Formen, Geschichte*. Frankfurt am Main: Vittorio Klostermann.
Round, N. (2005), 'Translation and its Metaphors: the (N+1) wise men and the elephant'. *Skase Journal of Translation and Interpretation* 1: 47–69.
Schmidgall, G. (2001), 'Suppressing the gay: Whitman in America: Translating Thomas Mann'. *Walt Whitman Quarterly Review* 19: 18–39.
Schmidt-Schütz, E. (2003), *Doktor Faustus zwischen Tradition und Moderne*. Frankfurt am Main: Vittorio Klostermann.
Schröder, W. (1972), 'Zum Gebrauch des Beiwortes bei Thomas Mann'. *Der Deutschunterricht* 24: 88–96.

Schulze, B. and M. Kerzel (2004), 'Anrede und Titulatur in der Übersetzung', in H. Kittel et al. (eds), *Ein internationales Handbuch zur Übersetzungsforschung*, Vol 1. Berlin and New York: de Gruyter, pp. 936–48.

Semino, E. and M. Short (2004), *Corpus Stylistics: Speech, Writing and Thought Presentation in a Corpus of English Writing*. London: Routledge.

Shookman, E. (2004), *Thomas Mann's 'Death in Venice': A Reference Guide*. Westport, Co: Greenwood Press.

Simon, E. (2009), 'On translating Thomas Mann'. *Scripta Judaica Cracoviensa* 7: 111–42.

Sixel, F. W. (1994), 'What is a good translation? Some theoretical considerations plus a few examples'. *Meta* 39: 342–61.

Snell-Hornby, M. (1997), 'The integrated linguist: On combining models of translation critique', in G. Wotjak and H. Schmidt (eds), *Modelle der Translation/ Models of Translation* (Festschrift für Albrecht Neubert). Frankfurt am Main: Peter Lang, pp. 73–88.

—(2006), *The Turns of Translation Studies*. Amsterdam and Philadelphia: John Benjamins.

Sprecher, T. (ed.) (2004), *Liebe und Tod in Venedig und anderswo*. Frankfurt am Main: Vittorio Klostermann.

Stanzel, F. K. (2008), *Theorie des Erzählens* (8th edn). Göttingen: Vandenhoeck & Ruprecht.

Steiner, G. (1992), *After Babel* (2nd edn). Oxford: Oxford University Press.

Stolze, R. (2008), *Übersetzungstheorien: Eine Einführung* (5th edn). Tübingen: Gunter Narr.

Stubbs, M. (2005), 'Conrad in the computer: examples of quantitative stylistic methods'. *Language and Literature* 14: 5–24.

Swales, M. (1991), *'Buddenbrooks': Family Life as the Mirror of Social Change*. Boston: Twayne.

Tebbel, J. W. (1975), *A History of Book Publishing in the United States, Vol 2: The Expansion of an Industry, 1865–1919*. New York: Bowker.

—(1978), *A History of Book Publishing in the United States, Vol 3: The Golden Age Between Two Wars, 1920–1940*. New York: Bowker.

—(1981), *A History of Book Publishing in the United States, Vol 4: The Great Change, 1940–80*. New York: Bowker.

Thirlwall, J. C. (1966), *In Another Language: A Record of the Thirty-Year Relationship between Thomas Mann and His English Translator, Helen Tracy Lowe-Porter*. New York: Alfred A. Knopf.

Thome, G. (2002), 'Methoden des Kompensierens in der literarischen Übersetzung', in G. Thome et al. (eds), *Kultur und Übersetzung: Methodologische Probleme des Kulturtransfers*. Tübingen: Günter Narr, pp. 299–317.

Toury, G. (1995), *Descriptive Translation Studies and Beyond*. Amsterdam and Philadelphia: John Benjamins.

Turner, C. (2003), *Marketing Modernism: Between the Two World Wars*. Amherst and Boston: University of Massachusetts Press.

Vaget, H. R. (1970), 'Der Dilettant. Eine Skizze der Wort- und Bedeutungsgeschichte'. *Jahrbuch der deutschen Schillergesellschaft* 14: 131–58.

—(1973), 'Thomas Mann und die Neuklassik: *Der Tod in Venedig* und Samuel Liblinskis Literaturauffassung'. *Jahrbuch der deutschen Schiller-Gesellschaft* 17: 432–54.

—(1984), *Thomas-Mann-Kommentar: zu sämtlichen Erzählungen*. Munich: Winkler.

—(1992), 'Hoover's Mann: Gleanings from the FBI's Secret File on Thomas Mann', in W. Elfe et al. (eds), *The Fortunes of German Writers in America: Studies in Literary Reception*. Columbia South Carolina: University of South Carolina Press, pp. 131–44.

—(2001a), 'Schlechtes Wetter, gutes Klima: Thomas Mann in Amerika', in H. Koopmann (ed.), *Thomas-Mann-Handbuch* (third edn). Stuttgart: Kröner, pp. 68–77.

—(2001b), '*Die Betrogene*', in H. Koopmann (ed.), *Thomas-Mann-Handbuch* (3rd edn). Stuttgart: Kröner, pp. 235–56.

Van den Broeck, R. (1985), 'Second thoughts on translation criticism: A model of its analytic function', in T. Hermans (ed.), *The Manipulation of Literature: Studies in Literary Translation*. London: Palgrave Macmillan, pp. 54–62.

Van Leuven-Zwart, K. (1989), 'Translation and original. Similarities and dissimilarities, I'. *Target* 1: 151–82.

—(1990), 'Translation and original. Similarities and dissimilarities, II'. *Target* 2: 69–96.

Venuti, L. (2004), 'Retranslations: the creation of value', in K. M. Faull (ed.), *Translation and Culture*. Cranbury, NJ: Associated University Presses, pp. 25–38.

—(1998), *The Scandals of Translation: Towards an Ethics of Difference*. London: Routledge.

—(2008), *The Translator's Invisibility: A History of Translation* (2nd edn). London: Routledge.

Viezzi, M. (2011), 'The translation of book titles: Theoretical and practical aspects', in P. Kujamäki et al. (eds), *Beyond Borders – Translation Moving Languages, Literatures and Cultures*. Berlin: Frank & Timme, pp. 183–95.

Vogt, J. (1995), *Thomas Mann: 'Buddenbrooks'* (2nd edn). Munich: W. Fink.

—(2008), *Aspekte erzählender Prosa* (10th edn). Munich: W. Fink.

Von Gronicka, A. (1948), 'Ein "symbolisches Formelwort" in Thomas Manns *Zauberberg*'. *Germanic Review* 23: 125–30.

Von Wiese, B. (1964), 'Thomas Mann: *Der Tod in Venedig*', in *Die deutsche Novelle von Goethe bis Kafka*, Vol 1. Düsseldorf: Bagel, pp. 304–24.

Von Wilpert, G. (1988), 'Sprachliche Polyphonie: Sprachebenen und Dialekte', in K. Moulden, and G. von Wilpert (eds) (1988), *Buddenbrooks-Handbuch*. Stuttgart: Kröner, pp.145–56.

Wagener, H. (2001), 'Thomas Mann in der amerikanischen Literaturkritik', in H. Koopmann (ed.), *Thomas-Mann-Handbuch* (third edn). Stuttgart: Kröner, pp. 925–40.

Waldmüller, H. (1980), 'Thomas Mann: Zahlen, Fakten, Daten seiner Rezeption'. *Aus dem Antiquariat* 3, A 97– A 111.

Wandruszka, M. (1984), '"Sprachkontakte" bedeutet Sprachmischung', in E. Oksaar (ed.), *Spracherwerb – Sprachkontakt – Sprachkonflikt*. Berlin: de Gruyter, pp. 65–75.

Weigand, H. (1965), *Thomas Mann's Novel 'Der Zauberberg': A Study* (2nd edn). Chapel Hill: University of North Carolina Press.

Weinrich, H. (2000), 'Titel für Texte', in J. Mecke and S. Heiler (eds), *Titel-Text-Kontext. Randbezirke des Textes*. Glienicke, Berlin: Galda und Wilch, pp. 3–19.

Weiss, W. (1987), 'Thomas Manns Metaphorik'. *Thomas-Mann-Studien* 7: 311–28.

Whitton, J. (1991), 'H. T. Lowe-Porter's *Death in Venice*', in J. Whitton, *Collected Essays in German Literature*. Frankfurt am Main: Peter Lang, pp. 235–59.

Winston, R. (1975), 'On translating Thomas Mann'. *The American Pen: An International Quarterly of Writing* 7: 15–22.

Wirtz, E. (1962), 'Die Bedeutung des Sprachspiels für den Sinnzusammenhang in Thomas Manns *Zauberberg*'. *Wirkendes Wort* 12: 161–7.

Wolf, M. and A. Fukari, (eds) (2007), *Constructing a Sociology of Translation*. Amsterdam and Philadelphia: John Benjamins.

Wood, D. (ed.) (1993), *Of Derrida, Heidegger and Spirit*. Evanston/Illinois: Northwestern University Press.

Wood, M. (2003), 'Impossible Wishes'. *London Review of Books*, 6 February, p. 4.

Woods, J. E. (2002) 'A Matter of Voice'. *Translation Review* 63: 86–8.

Wysling, H. (1965), 'Aschenbachs Werke: Archivalische Untersuchungen zu einem Thomas Mann-Satz'. *Euphorion*, 59: 272–314.

Zerner, M. (1945), 'Thomas Mann in standard English anthologies'. *German Quarterly* 18: 178–88.

Zuschlag, K. (2002), *Narrativik und literarisches Übersetzen*. Tübingen: Gunter Narr.

Zybatow, L. (2008), 'Literaturübersetzung im Rahmen der Allgemeinen Translationstheorie', in W. Pöckl (ed.), *Im Brennpunkt: Literaturübersetzung*. Frankfurt am Main: Peter Lang, pp. 9–42.

Index

address modes 194
  challenges 176, 177, 185, 192, 197
  complexity 197
  constraint 177
  contemporariness and 181, 184, 186–7, 192–4, 196, 198
  control and 183–4
  dialects 181
  disparities 178, 179, 181, 187–8, 190, 194–5, 196–8
  French terms 189–91, 197, 198
  limitations 187
  metaphor and symbolism 185–6, 189, 191–2, 197
  notes and 184–5
  personal names and 178, 179–80, 181–2, 183, 184, 186, 188, 191, 193, 195–6, 198
  primacy 176, 180–1
  scope 176, 178–9, 180, 182–3, 184, 185, 187, 188–9, 191, 192, 196, 197
  stresses 177–8
  uncertainty 182
advertising 31, 32
alienation 164–5
America *see* United States
American Peace Crusade, The 38–9
annotation 45
  limitations 185
  uniqueness 184–5

anti-fascism 2, 37–8, 39
  control and 37
Apel, F. 17–18
Appelbaum, S. 47
articles *see* determiners

Bajazzo, Der 137, 146
Barter, R. 10–11
Bashan and I 29
Bassnett, S. 20
Bassnett-McGuire, S. 98
Bekenntnisse des Hochstaplers Felix Krull see Felix Krull
Belloc, J. H. P. R. 55–6, 69–70
  fidelity and 61
Berlin, J. B. 54
  editorial control and 35
  titles 36
Betrachtungen eines Unpolitischen 1, 37
Betrogene, Die 40
  address modes 183
  declined 40
  titles 134–6, 146
Betz, M. 76
Black Swan, The (Die Betrogene)
  address modes 183
  declined 40
  titles 134–6, 146
Book-of-the-Month Club 3
Borzoi books 31, 32
Boyd, E. 74

Index

Buck, T. 7–8
 Der Zauberberg 83
Buddenbrooks 1, 30
 address modes 180–2
 dialects 155
 disparities 148
 episodes 147–8
  metaphor and symbolism 148
 irony and 148
 limitations 52
 scope 147, 148
 speech 149, 152–3, 155–64, 167, 170, 172–3, 174
 thought and narrative form 148–9, 162–75
 titles 137
Burke, K. 28
 Der Tod in Venedig 6
Burnett, L. 70

calquing 101–2, 105–6, 120
Cecil Curtis, A. 26–7, 184
Cervantes, M. de 76–7
Chase, J. S. 46–7
communism 38–9
connectives 94
Constantine, P.
 Gefallen 183
 Gerächt 182–3
corpus stylistics 84
Craven, P. 10
Crick, J. 73
Cunningham, M. 48
Czennia, B. 152

Death (Der Tod) 130–1
Death in Venice see *Tod in Venedig, Der*
design of books 31, 32
determiners
 challenges 130, 131–2
 disparities 130, 131, 132, 137–8
 limitations 132
 scope 130–1, 133

Dial, The 2
 financial factors 28–9
 scope 28
dialects 153
 challenges 153–4, 158, 161–2
 constraint 154
 disparities 154–5, 158, 159, 160–1, 162–4, 181
 humour and 157, 162–4
 idiosyncrasies and 157
 limitations 155, 159, 160, 162, 174
 scope 155, 157, 158–60
direct speech *see* speech
discourse 22
 constraint 154
 disparities 55
 limitations 83–4
 see also individual terms
Doktor Faustus 74–5
 address modes 180, 194–6
 competition 34
 declined 34
 disparities 6, 36
 drafting 63–4
 financial factors 3
 fragmentation 80
 limitations 77, 78, 79
 metaphor and symbolism 56
 scope 194
 titles 138–9
Dostoevsky, F. 70
drafting 63
 invisibility and 63
 revision and 63–4

Elender, Ein 122–3, 129–30
engagement 60, 76
Erwählte, Der
 fragmentation 80
 titles 133–4, 140–1, 146

Faber, M. 50–1
Fehlauer-Lenz, I. 112

Felix Krull
  address modes 196–7
  competition 40
  disparities 42
  editorial control and 35
  titles 142
  financial factors 2–3, 28–9, 49, 79, 220–1
  contemporariness and 42–3, 45
  rights and 42
Frank, A. P. 16
Freeman, The 28
French terms 153, 189, 190–1, 197
  contention 104
  disparities 103–4, 189–90, 198
  italics and 104
  uncertainty 190
Freudenberg, R. 9

Garnett, C. 70–1
Gefallen 183
Geist und Kunst 122–3, 136
Genette, G. 124, 125, 127
Gerächt 182–3
Gesetz, Das 39–40
  disparities 42, 145
  limitations 40
  schism 33
  scope 50–1
  titles 144–5, 146
Gleam, A (Ein Glück) 131–2, 146
Gledhill, J. 8
Glück, Ein 131–2, 146
Goethe, J. W. von
  contention 215
  titles 138–9, 142
Gömöri, J. T. 77
Göttingen model 12–13, 15–16
Greenberg, M. 10
Grieve, J. 71
Guess, J. C. 6

Hatfield, H. 9–10
Hayes, J. 6

Heim, M. 48
Heller, E. 222
Heller, J. 63–4
Henderson, C. 79–80
Hermans, T. 7, 19
  contemporariness and 69
Herr und Hund 28, 29
  rights and 29
Hesse, H.
  censure 73, 74
  syntax 73–4
Hewson, L. 18, 121
Hoek, L. H. 123–4
Hoffmeister, W. 164
Holmes, J. 15
Holy Sinner, The (Der Erwählte)
  fragmentation 80
  titles 133–4, 140–1, 146
Hoover, J. E. 38
Horrocks, D. 73
Horton, D., 39, 42, 144, 153, 176, 179, 201
humour 157
  disparities 117–18, 162–4, 221
Hungernden, Die
  address modes 183
  titles 133

indirect speech *see* speech
individualism, universalism and 56, 66, 131
invisibility 58, 70
  drafting and 63
irony 138, 217, 221
  contemporariness and 115–16
  disparities 111, 112
  limitations 112–16, 121, 222
  scope 111–12, 148
  italics 104

Joseph der Ernährer 80
Joseph in Ägypten
  compounding 66
  disparities 67

individualism and 66
limitations 68
metaphor and symbolism 66
scope 64–7
simplification 68
syntax
 challenges 66
 disparities 67–8
Joseph novels 192–3
journals 27–8 *see also individual names*

Kafka, F.
 censure 72
 contemporariness and 72
 fidelity and 72–3
 syntax 73
Kelly, C. 71
Kelly, L. 61
Kinkel, E. 6
Kleists Amphitryon 76
Knopf, A. A. 25, 26, 30–1, 37–9, 41, 220, 221
 anthology control and 35–6
 B. Knopf and 35
  editorial control and 34
 C. and R. Winston and 41
 control and 25, 33, 34, 35
 Das Gesetz 33
 Der Erwählte 140
 Der Zauberberg 32
 design 31, 32
 editorial control and 34–5
 Felix Krull 142
 financial factors 42
 Herr und Hund 29
 Königliche Hoheit 27
 Lindley and, *Felix Krull* 40
 Lotte in Weimar 143–4, 146
 Lowe-Porter and *see* Lowe-Porter, H. T., A. A. Knopf and
 marketing 31–2, 49
 Meyer and, *Doktor Faustus* 34
 Pawling and 30

public activities control and 36, 37
Scheffauer and 29
 Der Zauberberg 33–4
stresses 33
titles 36, 141–2
Trask and, *Die Betrogene* 40
Woods and 42
 financial factors 42–3
Knopf, B.
 A. A. Knopf and 35
  editorial control and 34
 Lindley and, *Felix Krull* 35
 Lowe-Porter and, *Der Zauberberg* 79–80
Koch-Emmery, E. 5
 simplification 5
 syntax 5, 201
Koelb, C. 45–6, 47
Koepke, W. 49–50
Königliche Hoheit
 address modes 184–5
 disparities 27
 uncertainty 26–7
 underrated 1
 wordplay 137
Kontje, T. 220
Kopetzki, A. 17–18

Law, The see Gesetz, Das
Leech, G. 18–19
Lefevere, A. 20–1
 syntax 199
legal action and rights 33
Lehmann, S. 50–1
leitmotifs 106, 107, 108, 109
 address modes 185–6, 187–8, 189–92, 197
 challenges 110
 disparities 106, 107–9, 110–11
 primacy 106–7, 109, 185
Levin, H. 61
Levy, J.
 syntax 199, 200
 titles 126

Lewisohn, L. 28
Lichtenberg, G. C. 186–7
Lindley, D.
  A. A. Knopf and, *Felix Krull* 40
  B. Knopf and, *Felix Krull* 35
  Felix Krull 42, 196–7
Lotte in Weimar
  challenges 142
  disparities 6
  limitations 78
  titles 142–4, 146
Lowe, E. A. 53–4
Lowe-Porter, H. T. 1–2, 3, 20, 24, 29–30, 35, 37, 39, 53–5, 56–8, 59–60, 63, 78, 139, 221, 222
  A. A. Knopf and 21, 25, 30, 31, 41–2, 54, 57, 62–3
    address modes 176, 177
    Buddenbrooks 30, 161–2
    Das Gesetz 145
    Der Erwählte 80, 141
    Der Tod in Venedig 209
    Der Zauberberg 33–4
    Doktor Faustus 34, 36, 80
    Felix Krull 40
    fidelity and 61
    legal action and 33
    Lotte in Weimar 143
    metaphor and symbolism 60
  address modes 198
  B. Knopf and, *Der Zauberberg* 79–80
  Betrachtungen eines Unpolitischen 37
  biography 54
  Buddenbrooks 30, 52, 152, 153, 155–6, 157, 158, 159, 160, 161, 162–4, 165, 168–71, 172–5, 181–2
  censure 6–8, 61, 68, 200
  challenges 53, 58, 62
  compensation 59
  competition 27
  constraint 5, 8, 27, 221
  contemporariness and 43, 63, 68–9, 72
  Das Gesetz 42
  Der Bajazzo 137
  Der Erwählte 134, 140
  Der Tod in Venedig 6, 8, 46, 200–1, 209–12, 214, 216, 217, 218, 219
  Der Zauberberg 1, 5, 29, 56, 83, 85, 87–98, 99–106, 107, 108, 109, 110–11, 112–16, 117–21, 185, 186, 187–8, 189, 190–4
  Die Betrogene 40
  Die Hungernden 133
  Die vertauschten Köpfe 139–40
  disparities 4, 5–6, 9–10, 21–2, 35, 43, 55, 81–2, 220, 221, 223
  Doktor Faustus 56, 63–4, 78, 79, 195–6
  drafting 63–4
  Ein Elender 130
  Ein Glück 131–2
  engagement 60
  Felix Krull 40, 42
  fidelity and 60–1, 82
  financial factors 79, 220–1
  individualism and 56
  invisibility 58
  irony and 222
  Joseph der Ernährer 80
  Joseph in Ägypten 64–5, 67–8
  Joseph novels 192–3
  limitations 52, 53, 55–6, 81
  Lotte in Weimar 78, 142, 144
  Mario und der Zauberer 184
  metaphor and symbolism 56
  meticulousness 63
  prestidigitation 58–9
  primacy 19–20, 50, 220
  self-doubt 62
  simplification 5
  stresses 221

syntax 58
  censure 5
  contemporariness and 73
  disparities 201
  limitations 201
  simplification 201
  titles 127
  Tonio Kröger 8
  transatlantic translation 57
  Von deutscher Republik 79
Lubich, F. 87
Luke, D. 6–7, 8, 46
  Der Bajazzo 137
  Der Tod in Venedig 46, 212–16, 217, 218–19
  disparities 8, 9–10
  Ein Elender 130
  syntax 201
  titles 137
Lyons, J. 187

Magic Mountain, The see *Zauberberg, Der*
Man and His Dog, A (*Herr und Hund*) 28, 29
  rights and 29
manipulation school 11–12
  contention 12
Mann, H. 74
Mann, T. 1, 21, 177
  biography 41
  challenges 79
  compounding 86
  constraint 223
  correspondence 54, 77, 78, 177
  disempowerment 80–1
  disparities 50, 52–3, 75–6, 78
  exile 2
  experimentation 86
  FBI file 38
  limitations 52, 53, 78–9
  novellas and stories 44
  oeuvre 127–8
  primacy 49, 222–3
  reputation 2, 3, 4, 32, 49–50, 220, 222
  censure 221
  disparities 222
  humour and 221
  irony and 221
  retranslation 3, 24, 223
  rights and 3
  stability and 86–7
  stresses 53
  syntax
    complexity 86, 87
    disparities 87
  see also individual terms
Marek, G. 39, 40, 42, 145
Mario und der Zauberer 183–4
marketing 31–2, 49, 141–2, 144, 146
  constraint 143–4
  contention 32
  primacy 141
Mathews, A. 72
Maude, A. 71
Maude, L. 71
McNab, C. 184–5
metaphor and symbolism 56, 60, 66, 105, 128, 131, 133, 138, 139, 207–8
  complexity 210
  disparities 136, 185–6, 191–2
  fragmentation and 148
  limitations 76–7
  primacy 189, 197
  see also leitmotifs
Meyer, A. E.
  A. A. Knopf and, *Doktor Faustus* 34
  Der Erwählte 140–1
  Doktor Faustus 34, 77, 139
  Lotte in Weimar 143
Mitchell, B. 73
Moncrieff, S. 71 Morgan, B. Q. 25–6, 74
  Tonio Kröger 25, 26
Muir, E.

censure 72
contemporariness and 72
syntax 73
Muir, W.
  censure 72
  contemporariness and 72
  syntax 73
Munday, J. 34

names, personal 183
  challenges 139
  constraint 214–15, 216
  determiners and 137–8
  disparities 127, 128, 186, 188, 191, 193, 195–6, 198
  fragmentation 217
  irony and 138, 217
  metaphor and symbolism 138
  primacy 214, 215, 216, 217
  scope 138–9, 178, 179–80, 181–2, 184, 215, 217
  uncertainty 184
Nation, The 28
Neider, C. 49
Neugroschel, J.
  Der Tod in Venedig 46, 47
  titles 133
Newmark, P.
  Der Zauberberg 83
  syntax 73–4
Nobel Prize 1–2, 31
Nord, C. 124–6
notes 45
  limitations 185
  uniqueness 184–5
Oliver, K. 77
Oram, R. W. 79–80
Ormsby, E. 72–3

Pawling, S. 30
Peitsch, H. 74
periodicals 27–8 *see also individual names*
Poet Lore 53

politics
  anti-fascism 2, 37–8, 39
  communism 38–9
  contention 39
  control and 39
  disparities 37
  distancing from 37, 38, 39
  financial factors and 2–3
  limitations 37
  primacy 36–7
  public activities and 37
  see also individual names
Porter, C. E. 53
Pound, E. W. L. 55
  fidelity and 61
Prescott, O. 4
prestidigitation 58–9
Princeton University 54
Proust, M. 71
publishing industry 20–1

qualitative and quantitative analysis 84 *see also individual terms*
quote marks
  disparities 172–3
  scope 170–1
  uncertainty 167, 170
Qvale, P. 68

Reed, T. J.
  Der Tod in Venedig 219
  Geist und Kunst 136
regional languages *see* dialects
Reichart, W. A. 4
Reisiger, H. 74–5
retranslation hypothesis 44
Riley, A. 74
Robinson, A. 144
Rothe, A. 124–5
Royal Highness see *Königliche Hoheit*

Savill, M. 74
Scheffauer, H. G. 29

A. A. Knopf and 29
   Der Zauberberg 33–4
   competition 27
   Der Zauberberg 29
   Herr und Hund 29
Shookman, E. 9
Short, M. 18–19
Simon, E. 9, 99
sociocultural factors 43, 177
   underrated 20
   see also individual terms
speech 149
   address modes *see* address modes
   challenges 150
   contemporariness and 118, 153
   dialects 153, 155, 157–64, 174
   disparities 118–19, 150–1, 152, 153, 174
   French terms 153
   humour and 117–18
   idiosyncrasies 155–6
   layout 87–8
   limitations 91–2, 153, 174
   primacy 150, 174
   quote marks and 167, 170, 172–3
   realism and 151, 152–3
   scope 116–17, 149–50, 151–2, 155, 174
   syntax 151
   uncertainty 151
subtitles
   limitations 127
   marketing 142, 144
   outcome and 127
   personal names and 139
   scope 127
Swales, M. 165
symbolism *see* metaphor and symbolism

Thirlwall, J. C. 54, 58, 62–3
   compensation 59
   engagement 60
   metaphor and symbolism 60
   prestidigitation 58–9
Thompson, D. 58
Thou Shalt Have No Other Gods Before Me see Gesetz, Das
thought and narrative form 148–50, 151–2, 165–8, 170, 171–2, 173–4, 206–7
   alienation and 164–5
   challenges 150
   contemporariness and 169–70
   disparities 96, 150–1, 162–4, 168–70, 173, 174
   humour and 162–4
   limitations 171, 173, 174–5
   metaphor and symbolism 207–8
   primacy 150, 174, 218
   punctuation and 173
      quote marks 170–1, 172–3
   scope 164
   syntax 151
   uncertainty 151
Times Literary Supplement, The 4, 7
titles
   anthological coherence and 144–5
   challenges 123, 124, 127, 128–9, 133
   contention 142, 143, 146
   control and 36
   determiners and 133, 137
   disparities 122–3, 125, 133–6, 142, 143, 144, 145–6
   limitations 125–6, 144
   marketing 141–2, 143–4, 146
   metaphor and symbolism 133, 136
   oeuvre and 127–8
   personal names and 127, 137–9
   primacy 125
   scope 122, 123–5, 126–7, 128, 129, 133, 134, 135, 136–7, 139, 140, 141, 145
   subtitles *see* subtitles

syntax
  challenges 123, 129–30
  determiners and 130–2
  disparities 130
  individualism and 131
  limitations 128
  metaphor and symbolism 128, 131
  personal names and 128
  scope 128, 130, 145
  uncertainty 139–41, 142–3
Tobias Mindernickel 138
Tod, Der 130–1
Tod in Venedig, Der 202, 209, 212–13
  academic editions 45
    paratextual material 45–6, 47
    uncertainty 45
  censure 8, 46, 200–1
  complexity 207, 213
  contemporariness and 46, 47
  contention 208, 215
  disparities 6, 47, 209–10, 211–12, 213–14, 216–17, 218
  limitations 217–18
  personal names and 217
  primacy 45
  realism and 205
  reinterpretation and 48
  scope 10–11, 46–7, 202–3, 204–6, 207, 208–9, 218
  syntax
    complexity 200, 203–4, 205, 206, 207, 210, 211, 214
    contention 208
    disparities 208, 210–11, 212, 213, 214, 215, 216, 217, 218–19
    fragmentation 211, 212, 214, 215–16
    limitations 211, 212
    metaphor and symbolism 207, 210
    personal names and 214–15, 216
  scope 202, 203, 204, 208
  semicolon and 213
  thought and narrative form 206–8, 218
  titles 122, 129, 131
  uncertainty 47
Tolstoy, L. 71
Tonio Kröger 25
  censure 8, 26
  challenges 26
  disparities 42
  scope 26
Toury, G. 120
translation
  academic grounding 44
  autonomy 220
  challenges 14–15, 18–19, 61–2, 75
  complexity 13–14
  contemporariness and 43–4, 48–9, 69, 70, 71–2, 223
  defined 17–18
  disparities 4, 5, 8–10, 35, 44
  fidelity and 71
  limitations 3–5, 9, 75, 77–8, 81
  paratextual material 44–5
  proactivity and 46
  randomness 25
  reinterpretation and 48
  scope 11, 13, 14, 15, 16–17, 18, 19, 20, 21, 22–3, 24–5, 40–1, 69
  syntax
    disparities 199, 200
    primacy 199–200
    underrated 199
  unexpurgated 47
  see also individual terms
Transposed Heads, The (*Die vertauschten Köpfe*) 139–40
Trask, W. R. 40, 70
  A. A. Knopf and, *Die Betrogene* 40
  Die Betrogene 135
Turner, C. 31

United States 2, 4, 24
  contemporariness and 49
  financial factors 3
  journals 27–8
  print runs 3
  stresses 32–3
  see also individual names
universalism, individualism and 56, 66, 131

van Doren, I. 221
Venuti, L. 7, 8, 43
  invisibility 70
vertauschten Köpfe, Die 139–40
Vogt, J. 148–9
Von deutscher Republik 79
von Wiese, B. 131

Wagener, H. 36–7
Wagner, W. R. 138
Wälsungenblut 138
Winston, C. 41
Winston, R. 41
Woods, J. E. 43, 50
  A. A. Knopf and 42
    financial factors 42–3
  Buddenbrooks 152, 153, 155–7, 158, 159, 160, 161, 165, 168–9, 171–5, 181–2
  contemporariness and 43
  Der Zauberberg 50, 83, 85, 87–9, 90–1, 93–8, 99–101, 102–6, 107, 108, 109, 110–11, 112–13, 114–15, 116, 117–19, 120, 121, 185, 187, 188, 189–90, 191, 192, 193–4, 198
  disparities 10, 43
  Doktor Faustus 195, 196
  Joseph novels 193
wordplay 110, 137

Zauberberg, Der 83, 85, 119
  address modes 180, 186, 187, 188–9, 191, 192–4, 198
  censure 98
  challenges 88
  clarification 103
  competition 29, 33
  complexity 98–9
  compounding 102–3
  contemporariness and 85, 89–90, 102, 105, 119
  contention 33–4
  disparities 5, 83, 88–9, 96–7, 98, 99–100, 102, 103–5, 119–20, 120, 121
  fragmentation 79–80
  French terms 104
  headings 89
  irony and 111–16, 121
  leitmotifs 106–11, 185–6, 187–8, 189–92
  limitations 88, 97–8, 100–1, 120–1
  marketing 32
  metaphor and symbolism 56, 105
  scope 1, 50, 84–6, 87, 88, 97, 98, 99, 102, 103
  speech 88, 116–19
  syntax 88
    calquing and 101–2, 105–6, 120
    clarification 93
    complexity 94–5
    connectives and 94
    disparities 90–1, 95–6, 120
    limitations 91–2
    punctuation and 92, 93–4
    simplification 92–3, 94, 120
    speech 91–2
  thought and narrative form 96
  uncertainty 83
  unexpurgated 88
  wordplay 110
Zerner, M. 26
Zybatow, L. 68